Memorial Book of the Community of Turka on the Stryj and Vicinity (Turka, Ukraine)

Translation of *Sefer zikaron le-kehilat Turka al nehar Stryj ve-ha-seviva*

Original Yizkor Book:

Edited by: Yitzhak Siegelman and Association of Former Residents of Turka (Stryj) in Israel

Published in Israel, 1966, (Hebrew and Yiddish)

Published by JewishGen

An Affiliate of the Museum of Jewish Heritage - A Living Memorial to the Holocaust
New York

Memorial Book of the Community of Turka on the Stryj and Vicinity (Turka, Ukraine)

Translation of *Sefer Zikaron le-Kehilat Turka al nehar Stryj ve-ha-Seviva*

First Printing: December 2014, Kislev 5775
Second Printing: March 2019, Adar II 5779
Translation Project Coordinator: Mary Violette Seeman Editor of the original book: Yitzhak Siegelman Translator: Jerrold Landau
Layout: Joel Alpert
Image Editor: Jan R. Fine and Martin Burg Cover Design: Jan R. Fine
Publicity: Sandra Hirschhorn
Yiddish and Hebrew Consultant: Josef Rosin
Indexing: Irit Rosin

Published by JewishGen, Inc.
An Affiliate of the Museum of Jewish Heritage A Living Memorial to the Holocaust
36 Battery Place, New York, NY 10280

"JewishGen, Inc. is not responsible for inaccuracies or omissions in the original work and makes no representations regarding the accuracy of this translation. Digital images of the original book's contents can be seen online at the New York Public Library Web site."

The mission of the JewishGen organization is to produce a translation of the original work and we cannot verify the accuracy of statements or alter facts cited.

Printed in the United States of America by Lightning Source, Inc.

Library of Congress Control Number (LCCN): 2014957340

ISBN: 978-1-939561-26-8 (hard cover: 484 pages, alk. paper)

Cover photograph from the cover of the original Yizkor Book Back cover image from the interior of the original Yizkor Book

JewishGen and the Yizkor-Books-in-Print Project

This book has been published by the **Yizkor-Books-in-Print Project,** as part of the **Yizkor Book Project** of **JewishGen, Inc**.

JewishGen, Inc. is a non-profit organization founded in 1987 as a resource for Jewish genealogy. Its website [www.jewishgen.org] serves as an international clearinghouse and resource center to assist individuals who are researching the history of their Jewish families and the places where they lived. JewishGen provides databases, facilitates discussion groups, and coordinates projects relating to Jewish genealogy and the history of the Jewish people. In 2003, JewishGen became an affiliate of the **Museum of Jewish Heritage - A Living Memorial to the Holocaust** in New York.

The **JewishGen Yizkor Book Project** was organized to make more widely known the existence of Yizkor (Memorial) Books written by survivors and former residents of various Jewish communities throughout the world. Later, volunteers connected to the different destroyed communities began cooperating to have these books translated from the original language—usually Hebrew or Yiddish—into English, thus enabling a wider audience to have access to the valuable information contained within them. As each chapter of these books was translated, it was posted on the JewishGen website and made available to the general public.

The **Yizkor-Books-in-Print Project** began in 2011 as an initiative to print and publish Yizkor Books that had been fully translated, so that hard copies would be available for purchase by the descendants of these communities and also by scholars, universities, synagogues, libraries, and museums.

These Yizkor books have been produced almost entirely through the volunteer effort of researchers from around the world, assisted by donations from private individuals. The books are printed and sold at near cost, so as to make them as affordable as possible. Our goal is to make this important genre of Jewish literature and history available in English in book form, so that people can have the personal histories of their ancestral towns on their bookshelves for themselves and for their children and grandchildren.

A list of all published translated Yizkor Books can be found at:
http://www.jewishgen.org/Yizkor/ybip.html

Lance Ackerfeld, Yizkor Book Project Manager

Joel Alpert, Yizkor-Book-in-Print Project Coordinator

JewishGen
Yizkor Book Project

This book is presented by the
Yizkor Books in Print Project
Project Coordinator: Joel Alpert

Part of the
Yizkor Books Project of JewishGen, Inc.
Project Manager: Lance Ackerfeld

These books have been produced solely through volunteer effort of individuals from around the world. The books are printed and sold at near cost, so as to make them as affordable as possible.

Our goal is to make this history and important genre of Jewish literature available in English in book form so that people can have the near-personal histories of their ancestral towns on their book-shelves for themselves and for their children and grandchildren.

Any donations to the Yizkor Books Project are appreciated.

Please send donations to:
Yizkor Book Project
JewishGen
36 Battery Place
New York, NY 10280

JewishGen, Inc. is an affiliate of the
Museum of Jewish Heritage
A Living Memorial to the Holocaust

From the Original Yizkor Book

Dedication

The translation of this book into English, thanks to all the contributors, is dedicated to the memory of the children of Turka who perished in the Shoah.

By remembering, we prolong their lives.

Acknowledgements for the Translation and Publication of this Memorial Book

We would like to thank the following individuals who have made the translation of the Turka Yizkor Book possible:

Boaz Ben-Pelech for commissioning and funding most of the translation in memory of Turka family members who perished in the Holocaust. Jerrold Landau for undertaking the translation of the entire book. Haim Sidor for translating, alphabetizing, and cross-referencing the 'Memorial to the Martyrs of the Holocaust' section. Aytan Ben-Pelech for his expert proofreading of the translations prior to publication. Martin Burg for scanning the images from the original book.

WHO ARE WE, BUT MEMORY
IN THE MIND OF THOSE
WILLING TO REMEMBER US

Boaz Ben-Pelech

Special thanks to the National Yiddish Book Center in Amherst, Massachusetts and the New York Public Library for supplying the high resolution images used in this book.

Map of Ukraine with Turka to the West Near Poland

Geopolitical Information:

Turka, Ukraine is located at: 49°09' North Latitude and 23°02' East Longitude

Jewish Population	2,368 (in 1880), 4,887 (in 1910)
Notes:	Ukrainian: Турка. Yiddish: טורקא Hebrew: טורקה. On the Stryy River, 64 miles SW of L'viv (Lvov), 45 miles SSE of Przemyśl, 25 miles WSW of Drogobych.

Alternate names for the town are: Turka [Polish, Ukrainian], Turka al nehar Stry [Hebrew], Turka nad Stryjem

	Town	District	Province	Country
Before WWI (c. 1900):	Turka	Turka	Galicia	Austrian Empire
Between the wars (c. 1930):	Turka	Turka	Stanisławów	Poland
After WWII (c. 1950):	Turka			Soviet Union
Today (c. 2000):	Turka			Ukraine

Nearby Jewish Communities:
Melnychne 2 miles S
Nyzhnya Yablun'ka 4 miles SW
Borynya 6 miles SSW
Sokoliki, Poland 8 miles WSW
Yabluniv 8 miles SSE
Sianky 11 miles SSW
Dźwiniacz Górny, Poland 11 miles W
Tarnawa Niżna, Poland 11 miles W
Limna 11 miles NW
Strelki 13 miles N
Bitlya 13 miles SSW
Uzhok 14 miles SSW
Dovhe 14 miles E
Volosyanka 15 miles SW
Skhidnitsya 15 miles ENE
Podbuzh 16 miles NE
Lutowiska, Poland 17 miles WNW
Tykhyy 18 miles SSW
Smozhe 19 miles SSE
Stavnoye 19 miles WSW
Boryslav 20 miles ENE
Staryy Sambor 20 miles N
Bukovets 20 miles SSW
Lyuta 21 miles SW
Orov 23 miles E
Truskavets 23 miles ENE
Stara Sil' 23 miles N
Skole 23 miles ESE
Verkhneye Sinevidnoye 25 miles E
Drohobych 25 miles ENE
Stebnik 26 miles ENE
Sambir 26 miles NNE
Skelevka 27 miles N
Nyzhni Vorota 27 miles S
Sil' 27 miles WSW
Krościenko, Poland 27 miles NW
Lavochnoye 28 miles SSE
Khyriv 28 miles NNW
Verkhni Vorota 28 miles S
Chornoholova 28 miles SW
Ustrzyki Dolne, Poland 28 miles NW
Uličské Krivé, Slovakia 29 miles WSW
Ulič, Slovakia 30 miles WSW
Husne Wyzne 7 miles SSW
Husne Nizne 7 miles SSW

History of Turka

Turka is a Ukrainian town situated on the left bank of the river Stryi. It's name originates from the Ukrainian word for the wild cattle that populated the area in ancient times. The original Ukrainian speakers of Turka were governed in the middle ages by Polish noblemen until 1772 when the large region surrounding Turka, called Galicia, became part of the Austrian empire. Turka was the main city of a district that, by the twentieth century, included almost 300 small villages. Jews began arriving in Turka before the middle of the 18th century when a Polish nobleman granted all new residents low rent housing and the freedom to start new businesses. The first synagogue and an old age residence for Jewish elderly were built in 1730. The Jewish cemetery was also built at that time.

In 1903, Turka began to flourish when a railway line connected the city with Lwow and with Budapest. That same year, the Austrian government authorized the founding of an official Jewish community, with elected representation. Business expanded, especially the lumber business, which provided a means of livelihood for many Jews of Turka. Jews owned the sawmills and many Jews were employed in the sawmills. Some Jews had licenses to sell liquor. Others worked at various trades - tailoring, shoemaking, barbering, clock making, and lock smithing. All the tailors and all the builders in Turka were Jews. Many of the physicians and lawyers in Turka were Jews. Yiddish theatre came to Turka and interest was sparked in cultural events, sports events, and political events. Like elsewhere, some Jews in Turka were Zionists, some were Hassids, some were socialists, some were assimilationists. After the Great War, Galicia reverted to Poland, but nothing was the same. The city had been plundered by the Russian army; many Jews had left, and all Jewish property had been destroyed. There were Ukrainian revolts and Jewish pogroms. Nevertheless, after the War, there were approximately 6,000 inhabitants in Turka, 41% of whom were Jewish. Another 7,000 Jews lived in the surrounding villages. The Jewish population managed to rebuild. Just prior to World War II, 10,000 people lived in Turka; half were Jewish. Their troubles did not start in 1939 when the Germans invaded Poland. They remained relatively safe under the Russians. The catastrophe began when the Germans turned against the Soviet Union in June 1941 and Turka was captured by the Wehrmacht. The Jews of Turka were massacred, or starved to death, or sent to the Sambir ghetto and, hence, to the crematoria.

There are no Jews left in Turka today.

Notes to the Reader:

Within the text the reader will note "{34}" standing ahead of a paragraph. This indicates that the material translated below was on page 34 of the original book. However, when a paragraph was split between two pages in the original book, the marker is placed in this book after the end of the paragraph for ease of reading.

Also please note that all references to page numbers within the text of the book, refer to the page numbers of the original Yizkor Book, not the page numbers of this translation.

> The original book can be seen online at the NY Public Library site:
> http://www.jewishgen.org/Yizkor/turka/turka.html

Family Notes

Table of Contents

[H] denotes a Hebrew article and [Y] a Yiddish article.
A notation is omitted for those articles where the language could not be determined from the table of contents.

Table of Contents of the <u>Original Yizkor Book</u>

[H] denotes a Hebrew article and [Y] a Yiddish article.
A notation is omitted for those articles where the language could not be determined from the table of contents.

Turka – The Surrounding Villages

Destruction and Annihilation

The Holocaust in the Surrounding Villages

[Pages 7 & 8]

A Monument to the Town

The Editors

Polish Jewry has been destroyed, and its fate has been sealed; with it, the fate of our dear ones of our town of Turka on the Stryj River has also been sealed. More than two decades have passed since that bitter time, the time when destruction overtook our native town. Nevertheless, the voice of our brothers' blood cries to us from the vale of murder.

It commands us, the few survivors, to erect a monument to the town and its martyrs so that their memory will never end. This will be done in the form of the memorial book that is before us.

With trembling and awe, we approached the holy task of publishing the book. In our hearts we feared that we may be lacking in language, and might not have the ability to express in a comprehensive manner the wonderful section of life of our town before the Holocaust, and especially the destruction itself that fell upon that life. However, if we have succeeded in covering and transmitting even a small portion of the story of Turka -- it is good that we did not neglect the duty.

The chapters of this book will tell about vibrant and flowing life, from the time when the faithful city, the community of Turka and its villages, was still standing on its foundations. It will tell about wholesome, G-d fearing, upright, generous Jews; about rare Jews, pleasant and strong in body, like the trees and plants of the field around them; indeed, the beauty of the scenery and charm of nature gazed upon them.

It will tell about the youth who aspired for freedom and the repair of the nation and the world, who acted with enthusiasm; about dreams and desires that were woven and formed -- and also melted...

It will tell about the destruction and the Holocaust that overtook the town, just as it overtook the entire house of Israel, a complete community was cut off from the book of life! It will tell about the cries of babes who were tossed alive into the grave; about the "Shema Yisrael" that the Jews shouted out at the mouth of the pit. Indeed, the paths of tribulations that our dear ones suffered as they marched upon their final path will be reawakened.

[Pages 8-10]

The chapters of tribulations of the Jewish cities and of our town will blend together into a large scroll of fire that is etched into the raw flesh of the destroyers of our nation, as a mark of Cain -- for eternal shame and disgrace!

As long as they were walking among us, we did not appreciate them sufficiently. We only learned their true value after we lost them... Therefore, these pages shall serve as a monument and an eternal flame to the personalities who were uprooted from among us, and will be the source of influence, pride and splendor for us, and our children after us. We will read them and turn them over alone and together. May the holy souls shine like the splendor of the firmament -- and may their ashes rest in peace.

The Editors

[Page 11]

I Will Never Forget You

by Michael Heisler

I would have long wanted to forget the place of my birth...
However, where Jewish blood flowed freely in the streets,
And where I lost everything of mine --
Can I now ever forget it.
Years have passed, they fly by quickly --And everything remains in the memory.It seems that I can hear voices now, I see you again, as in years gone by...
At times I see you happy, radiating with joy.With you in your joy -- we walk together;And at times something stiffens my glaze --I already see everything engulfed in flames...
In the aroma of the fields. By the light already --I see you already choked in gas.The sound of your weeping overtakes me --I see you buried alive in the earth...
In my memory, I climb over hills and valleysTo at least find a sign of your remains;I found you in he hearts of IsraelIn our own home, already in our own place...

[Page 12]

A Portrait from the Landscape of my Childhood

by Tzvia Nagler-Tzamri of Kibbutz Merchavia

My native town of Turka comes up before my eyes; the memories as they were woven and etched into me during the years of my childhood. Their splendor has not been darkened in my heart with the passage of years. The images extend to the stories of the Holocaust and its atrocities.

I have not seen Turka since I made *aliya* to the Land in 1926. Indeed, even before that, my residency there was interrupted during the years of exile as refugees during the era of the First World War, and later during my studies in a different city. However, the unforgettable images and events are guarded with me, and they are a part of my essence.

Tzvia Nagler-Tzamri.

The Town

Here is the center of the town and its main street "Di Alica" with its stores, work areas, and many taverns, bustling with large numbers of Jewish residents. The din increased during the market day sand the fairs, when male and female farmers stream in from its 72 dependent villages with their multicolored garments. They arrive by vehicle or on foot, laded with sacks of produce for sale or barter. The street fills up with the bustle of people and the sounds of various animals that are being brought to the central market. On these days, the shopkeepers and tradesman have a full quota of work, with the "bounty" coming to them in abundance. By evening, one could see the farmers half-drunk -- or even more than that -- returning to their villages, laden with their bartered merchandise. The shopkeepers were content about the successful day.

*

My early childhood years are interwoven with the mountain landscape of "Upper Turka" (Gorna Turka), a mixed neighborhood of half-farmer Jews and Ukrainian farmers. The neighborhood was later called Legionow Street, perhaps in honor of the Polish officials who lived in pleasant villas, surrounded by well-tended gardens. As it continues, the scene moves on to farmers' cottages whose yards were fenced in, shaded with trees, and had a well in the center.

[Page 13]

Roads led from behind the cottages and farm buildings to the green gardens and fields. The Jewish homes, which were generally similar to those of their neighbors, were close to the highway. Here and there, a grocery store or haberdashery could be seen.

The relationships between the residents were proper, and at times even very good and friendly. The members of the two nations knew the realities of the members of the "other religion" from up close. The gentiles knew the Jewish customs, holidays and festivals very well, and never denigrated their traditional foods or sensibilities. There were those who were even able to speak Yiddish.

The town square on the market day (Wednesday).

Jewish farmers lived on the routes from the city toward the villages. Some of them worked the land, and grew fruit, sheep and horses for their own needs. These were wholesome, calm Jews. In the morning, one would see them walking toward the city with jars of milk for their regular customers. The horse merchants who lived in this neighborhood and owned plots of land stood out. They were daring and fearless, with a dynastic business that passed from father to son. The “Konieres” (horse merchants) were well-known. During the fairs, these horse merchants engaged in noisy activities. If their private farms did not provide sufficient food for their horses, at night they would cross the boundaries of their private fields to ensure that their animals are satiated... They were hot tempered, and did not shy away from daring adventures.

[Page 14]

In this neighborhood, where the city and village were intermixed, there was something that attracted the heart, with the ties to the land, to the white cottages among the green, and the charm and Jewish culture that blended well with those houses and imprinted their stamp of stability and of a native place. Their livelihood was not always abundant, but they learned how to be happy with their lot.

The Rivers

The Romantic Bridge. The Litmierz Bridge as it flows into the Jablonka.

The town was located on the banks of the Litmierz and the Jablonka, which both flowed into the Stryj River. The multicolored landscape was reflected in them. Life was reflected on both banks. In the village-like, agricultural area, strips of flax grew, which the farmers watered with wooden pitchers constructed for that purpose, so that they would whiten well in the sun's rays. Sounds of rhythmical beating could be heard from afar -- these were the washerwoman who were beating the laundry over a stone, as they washed it in the stream of water. Groups of ducks floated through the marshes, and barefoot children ran about, playing their games. The streams of the long Stryj riverbed differed from each other. There were sections with calm waters, hidden and shaded with ancient willows. In another place, there was a bathing beach for the burning summer. There were sections with willow shrubs that provided bristles for the brooms of the farmers, or willows that merited to be used for holy purposes by the Jews, who made small bundles of them for *Hoshana Rabba* to expiate sins. The Jews of Turka would gather on the banks of such rivers for *Tashlich*, as they cast off all of their sins from the year. On the other hand, the gentiles immersed the statue of Jesus in the overflow of the river.

[Page 15]

In the center of the city, where the water was calm and the beach was smooth, women and young girls went out to wash the dishes, especially on the eves of Sabbaths and festivals. There was more such activity at the time of the koshering of dishes for Passover and the expunging of *chometz* from the dough troughs and dough boards. The scraping and scrubbing was accompanied by lively conversation and joyous humming. The children played by throwing smooth stones and fishing for small fish and other water creatures. Here and there, there were male and female students who left their noisy, crowded houses in order to find a quiet corner to review their studies before an exam.

As the winter came, the river changed its form and role, and turned into a silver strip. A shiny, hard path was formed over its frozen waters. Winter sleds laden with wood from the surrounding forests traveled along the easy, smooth, clear path. The youth found in it a great arena for winter sports. The bridges over the river represented all types of passages that were invented with the development of culture -- starting from a large tree trunk that would span its width, connecting both sides of the river, ranging all the way to a bridge with poles, sockets, and a parapet.

Abundant Beauty -- and a Slithering Snake

As the riverbed approaches the city, beautifully built brides appear that would also serve for vehicular traffic. The pinnacle was the tall viaduct rising above arches of stone that formed the continuation of the railway track on its way to the tunnel in the mountains. Beneath it was a large, wide bridge, known as "The Bridge." Children never tired of raising their eyes to stare at the noisy train passing by, as they waved their hands with feeling toward the travelers at the heights above the city.

However, the peace and quiet was disturbed in the wake of the First World War. Serious anti-Semitism became exposed. The incited Ukrainians poured out their pent up wrath when the Cossacks penetrated the city. They pillaged the property of the Jews, and destroyed the city without letting up. After the retreat of the enemy, all of the booty was tossed into the riverbanks and the clear water of the river, out of fear of punishment from the authorities. Silver and gold objects, candlesticks, textiles and various types of merchandise rolled along the ground abandoned.

With the second conquest of the city, all of the Jews fled, ran off to various areas of Austria in the hinterland, and lived as refugees in camps. Life in the strange place increased the longing for the destroyed home, for the fields and gardens, for the Jewish existence. After the war, we did not find our house again, and we moved to live nearby. However, the vistas of nature did not change even then, and they received us with their good smile that welcomed back the wanderers. Life returned to its path.

[Page 16]

Turka and its beautiful area, with its forests filled with secrets and everything good, with its cool rivers and springs flowing abundantly, with its flowers that I awaited with the melting of the snow -- these were part of my birthplace. When I joined the Hashomer Hatzair chapter, the splendid body extended outside the boundary. With the excursions of the groups and the chapter, we also went to the farthest-off villages where the summer camp of the movement took place in beautiful surroundings. It is no wonder that when I made *aliya* to the Land, it was difficult for me to get used to the arid environment. I longed for my original birthplace despite the charm of the "nights of Canaan." I hoped to visit my family on occasion, to feast my eyes and my heart once again on the landscape of my childhood. However, I was not aware that a poisonous snake was slithering through that bountiful beauty. The seeds of hatred began to be expressed, and deepened their roots in the gentile population. How insignificant was the lot of those whose conscience bothered them, and whose hearts trembled at the sight of the persecutions -- the atrocities of the Second World War, of the human beasts, of the loss of all human feeling, of the destruction of the beauty and the desecration of all that was precious, holy and sublime to us, eclipsed the pure memories.

Indeed, our birthplace turned into a cruel cemetery for our dear ones. The murderers became menacing heirs to the Jewish property that had been amassed by the sweat of the brow of generations.

The youth Abba Schneller grew up in the background of the Carpathian Mountains, in a Jewish Galician town full of the grace and charm of nature. At the end of the First World War, when the Jewish refugees from the town who were scattered throughout all the corners of the Austrian-Hungarian Empire returned to their destroyed home -- the young man began to stand out, and became the leader of the Jewish youth. He established the Hashomer Hatzair pioneering-scouting movement, and he made aliya already in 1920, taking the first group of pioneers from Turka with him to the Land. Additional groups came after him. His name became Abba Hushi, one of the leaders of the Workers' Movement in the Land of Israel, and the mayor of the city of Haifa from 1950.

Abba Schneller

[Page 17]

There Was a Shtetl Turka

by Menachem Langenauer of New York

Uncaptioned. Menachem Langenauer

Our town of Turka was founded by a Polish landowner already in the 15th century (in a very old responsa, it is written "Ungvar near Turka"). After a few hundred years, the village of Turka became a small town, a Jewish town. At the beginning of the 20th century, Turka was old fashioned, pious and fanatic. All information from the wide world (Lemberg, Przemysl...) came through the wagon drivers who used to transport merchandise. Therefore, it was indeed said about our town that "the sky is plugged up with rags." The town was situated in a valley through which several rivers flowed -- the Stryj and the Dniester. The latter, which flows through a section of Galicia and empties into the Black Sea, had its source in the Turka region. The lovely villages that surrounded the town were well-known in Galicia. People came to them from the big cities in order to enjoy fresh air.

When the train first began to course through the town through viaducts, a new period of improved livelihood began, including the export of wood and other articles to the outside world. The town was almost 100% Jewish. The gentiles lived outside the city or in the dozens of surrounding villages. Jews only came into contact with the Ukrainian gentiles on market days or fair days. There were boorish Ukrainian farmers and a few Polish officials. The Jew, steeped in Torah and antiquity, held himself above the gentile population, despite the fact that worldly affairs were strange to him.

[Page 18]

General Vista

The Jews conducted their regular life in accordance with the Code of Jewish Law (*Shulchan Aruch*). They would go to the rabbi for Torah adjudications. For personal problems such as livelihood, serious illness, seeking a marriage partner, and the like, they would go to the Hassidic Rebbe. Their garb was specifically Jewish. On the Sabbath, they wore their silk *bekishe* (long robe) and *streimel*. The largest portion of the Jews were indeed scholars, simply occupying themselves with Torah and *Talmud* day and night. The sound of Torah could be heard from all of the *kloizes*. However, many other people were common folk -- brokers, forestry merchants, furriers, locksmiths, and wagon drivers. All of them were honest, G-d fearing people.

The rabbi of the town from before the First World War until the Holocaust was Rabbi Eliezer Segal Miszel. He was a genius, a student of the Lemberger rabbi, and the author of the "Mishnat Eliezer" responsa book. Aside from his scholarship, the rabbi was an expert in world literature, and sympathetic to the *Haskalah* and Zionism. In a certain sermon, he even compared Herzl to Moses. The Hassidim reproved him for this, but his great scholarship stood by him.

[Page 19]

There were many synagogues and *kloizes* for a small town such as Turka. Every Hassidic group had its own *kloiz* -- there was a Belzer Kloiz, a Sadagora, and a Czortkower. Aside from worshipping, young and old people would sit and learn in the *kloizes*. From time to time, youths with curled *peyos* would snatch a glance at a little Hebrew book under the *Gemara*. The *Beis Midrash* was a house of worship for the common folk; whereas the city synagogue, which was called a miniature temple, and where, according to the law, one did not even have to affix a *mezuza* -- was used primarily for government celebrations -- first for the birthday observance of Kaiser Franz Josef, and later by the Poles for the observances of the Third of May.

The economic situation was not joyous. The wealthy and the middle class lived well, but the poor shopkeepers, tradesmen and brokers had a hard struggle, and earned their livelihood with difficulty. The Jewish community maintained the clergy: a rabbi, two judges. They also controlled the regulations of the cemetery.

*

At the outbreak of the First World War, a change in life took place. Most of the Jews fled the town to escape the Russians, some to Bohemia, and others to Vienna and other places. In 1919, when the war ended and the Turka refugees returned home to Galicia, a new epoch in the life of Galician Jews began, especially for the youth. Having spent the war years in Western Europe, they were strongly influenced by the western German culture.

First, the youth cut their beards and *peyos*. The girls were also influenced by the German styles and romanticism.

[Page 20]

There was literally a revolution in the spiritual arena. The youth were devoted to German and Polish Literature. Instead of studying *Gemara, Yoreh Deah* and worshipping, they became interested in Schiller and Heine. In the town, there could be seen the first sprouting of modern Hebrew Literature, the rays of redemption of Zionism, and the hope for the actualization of the recently issued Balfour Declaration.

Hebrew was greatly loved by the Jews, and everyone studied and read Hebrew. It is appropriate to mention the Hebrew teacher Yisrael Moshe Shreiber, who had the greatest influence upon the youth of Turka.

Turka also had a fine library where one could find Hebrew, Yiddish, German and Polish Literature under one roof. As has already been stated, many of the youths lived under the influence of German Literature. As far as I can recall, Motia Szein of blessed memory and many others such as my brother Yosef of blessed memory became expert in German philosophy. My brother even memorized Heine's poems in Hebrew and Yiddish.

In General, Turka had great scholars. The young people were involved with their Zionist education, but unfortunately, they received very little academic education on account of the fanaticism of their primarily Hassidic parents. This was the same situation in almost all of the small towns of Galicia.

However, the call to Zion, to literally go as pioneers to lay the groundwork for the upcoming State, was very strong. Two young, enthusiastic youths come to my mind: Abba Schneller-Hushi and my brother Moshe Yisraeli. My brother stemmed from a Hassidic atmosphere, literally from the *kloiz* bench and the *Gemara*. Abba Hushi, on the other hand, was an excellent student who stemmed from a common, working family. Hushi was enthused with the Zionist ideal. He organized the first pioneering group and set out for the Land of Israel. The influence of that deed was indescribable. A band with music accompanied the pioneers, with Hushi, to the station. Later, that group, headed by Moshe Yisraeli, had a great influence upon the youth that came later. They, the young boys and girls, paved the way to the Jewish State with their sweat and might.

[Page 21]

In the year 1930, I left our dear, beloved town of Turka, with its beautiful mountains and landscapes. Unfortunately, I never saw our native town again.

Nevertheless, I found consolation when I visited Israel a few years ago. I then became convinced that "Israel is not a widower," and "The eternity of Israel does not lie." -- when I saw what Jewish genius constructed in our Land.

When I saw everything, I blurted out the traditional blessing: "May this never be spoiled," and that the great deeds in Israel should be a memorial for our pure martyrs from Turka.

[Page 21

You are my Witnesses...

by Penina Bamushi-Sternbach of Haifa

Carpathian Mountains, you tall ones
Are Witnesses to the atrocities of those days;
The mountains trembled...
Szymunka, Zawadiwka, Kicra, Borynia
Were overtaken by nightmares, exhaustion, and pain --
They walked the steps...
Carpathian Mountains, only you knowHow a settlement and its people were destroyed and annihilatedIn Turka on the Stryj;How the upright creative life bustledAnd then turned into a dirge and lament.

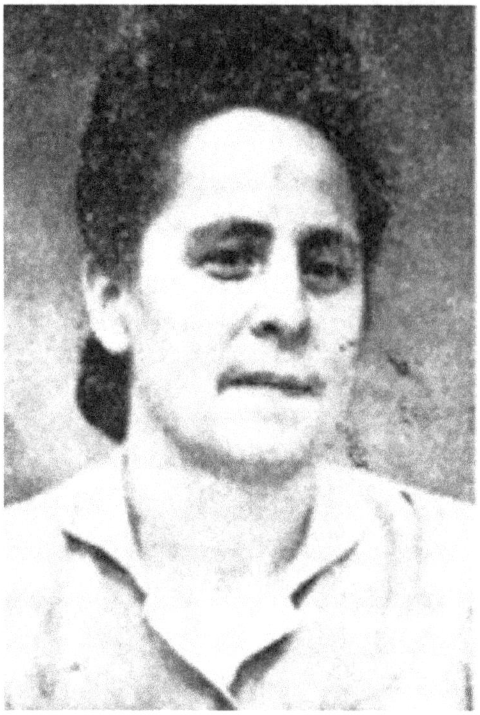

Penina Bamushi Sternbach

[Page 22]

In the treetops
Of the groves of the Carpathians
An echo still resonates --
The sound of the cries of the dead.
And the young babies
Crying from afar --
The waves of the river will no longer
Silence the agony.
The peaks of the Carpathians gaze Toward the city of trampled gravesOnly you are the witnesses for eternityFor a life that once was -- and is destroyed...

[Page 23]

Previous Generations

[Page 25]

History and Demography

A. Ancient Turka

Until the middle of the 15th century, Turka and its surroundings was a desolate place, covered with endless forests. No human foot ever trod there, except perhaps for cases when a person was forced to find refuge from the attacks of the Tatars. However, when the enemy garrisons passed, people returned to their place. It is surmised that this wild area was an ancient crossing area, traces of which remain. This was apparently a narrow and uncomfortable pathway, passing some distance from the banks of the Stryj River. This path connected the lands of Czervinski with Hungary.

We can surmise this pathway was difficult and tiring. It is told that King Ludwig of Hungary lost more than 40 horses, who died of hunger and exhaustion as he attempted to shorten his route to Hungary via this path. He and the people accompanying him only reached their destination after four years. Apparently, this was referring to the path that goes forth from Klimets near the Stryj. This was the first time that Turka was mentioned in history, and shows that the path that runs between the forests of Turka was uncharted, difficult, and unused. People did not frequent the wild areas surrounding the desolate mountains of Turka.

Ownership of the Town

There was no further mention at all of Turka for almost 100 years after Turka was first mentioned in history

In 1431, King Wladyslaw Jagiello bequeathed Turka and the surrounding estates, through the rights granted to him in Medukha, to one of his warriors of the Wallachian families and their dynasty, who excelled in their faithful service to the kingdom. The bequeathment included the rights of inheritance.

However, the borders of the inheritance were not explicitly defined. The Stryj River, along whose banks the estate was situated, was mentioned in the documents. It mentions the trees, called "Ayl" on the fields of Isa, Sursur, and Brod, as the border point between separating between the lands of the Wallachian fighter and the royal lands. For this reason, King Zygmunt I was forced to appoint a special commission in order to precisely establish the borders of the Lords of the Turcki family and the royal estates.

[Page 26]

Szymon Turcki

From a certain document from 1494, which states that Szymon Turcki gave over a portion of his lands to his four sons, we learn that the landsof the Turcki family -- after whose name the Turka family was called -- include Vyaory and Jasinicka aside from Turka. According to the most reasonable estimation, the highest mountain peak of the mountains surrounding Turka was called Szymunka after Lord Szymon Turcki.

In 1444, Wanko of Turka, one of the confidantes of King Wladyslaw, who was called Waranczyk after his death, received, due to his many rights, a plot of three square miles located between the Bukowiec River (that flows into the San) until the borders of the village of Zurawno. This right was given in Wardein, Hungary. In addition, he received a permit that applies to his former rights, that is to the bequeathment of Turka to his father by King Wladyslaw Jagiello. Their sons and grandchildren, who received Turka and its environs from the kings as a gift, called themselves Turcki. Those who belonged in Jawor called their name Jaworski, and those who settled in the Ilnyk area called themselves Ilnycki.

History

From that time on, there were many mentions of Turka in history. We will summarize the important ones in brief.

Queen Buna commanded that the road from Sambor to Turka be paved, so that all sorts of good things could be transported to her native land. She visited the area frequently in order to hunt in the forests of Turka. In the 16th century, there were already many Wallachians there who fled there to escape Hungarian oppression. They brought their customs and laws with them, which became accepted and customary there. Indeed, the settlement in all of the villages in the region of Turka was conducted primarily by the law of the Wallachians. The rights of these locales were frequently emphasized.

The Tatars, who prior to this never came between the mountains out of fear of the difficult passage and of ambush, were forced to escape in 1594 through the mountains of the region of Turka and Skola, when the Polish army headed by commander Jan Zamojski pursued them. The Tatars left a trail of ruin and destruction in the wake of their escape.

[Page 27]

Historical information about the local disputes and battles of the "Szlachta" (Polish nobility) remain with us to this day, including the attack of Szlochtong on the court of Jaworski Prakowicz near Turka, the attack of Wysocnaski on Rozmir, and of Pamientowski from Rozluch on the Dwornickes of Bobarka, and finally -- the dispute between the Szlachta of Wysock and Komornik with the people of Skoli.

Turka was destroyed by Hungarian pillagers in 1697. After the victory over the border guard Stefan Turcki, they pillaged the entire area and set it on fire.

In 1729, Turka, along with its suburb of Zawiznice, transferred from its previous owners, who lost their means due to the previous attack, to the hands of Jan Antoni Kalinowski.

(Based on Zarys monograficzny powiatu, Turczanskiego Lwow, 1939).
Translated from Polish by Ch. D.

B. Jewish Turka

It is difficult to establish exactly when the first Jews arrived to Turka and its area. However, it is clear that Jewish settlement in great numbers was connected to the name of the Magnate Jan Antoni Kalinowski. In 1729, Kalinowski purchased the town of Turka. One year later, with the authorization of the king, this town was raised to the status of a city in order to turn it into a commercial center, on account of its proximity to the Polish-Hungarian border. In order to attract new residents to the city, especially businessmen and tradesmen, Kalinowski sent his assistants throughout the area to promise in his name that all new residents will be granted freedom of action in business and trade. Therefore, the first 25 Jewish residents of Turka arrived: Avraham Szymonowicz Ratuszni who was the first rabbi of Turka, Shimon Berkowicz, Baruch Arendtur, Zalman Joselowicz, Abish Herszkowicz, Yaakov Roth, Hersh Arendtur, Shua-Hertz Zelmanowicz, Baruch Natalowicz, Yehuda Mendlowicz, Moshe Aharonow, Shmuel Nachumowicz, Daniel Marodowicz, Yosef Kanahowicz, Shlomo Szpinkowicz, Nachman Aharonowicz, Yaakov Matatowicz, Yosef Judkowicz, Shlomo Jakub, Yitzchak Brodek, and Berl Cymbalista.

The Building of the Market

Still in that year (1730), Kalinowski built four rows of houses in the form of a square (the market) on a gigantic field near his palace. Kalinowski rented those houses to the new residents at an particularly low price, even relative to that time period. Similarly he concerned himself with their religious and social needs. That year, he built the first synagogue in Turka with his own money, costing 30,000 Polish zloty at that time. He also donated through his own initiative a Jewish old age residence. He gave the Jews a suitable plot for a Jewish cemetery from his private land. All the local Jews were permitted to take the necessary amount of wood from his forests for building their residential homes and for heating. Kalinowski even set up a Jewish printing press, which published various prayer books and study books. One copy of this ancient prayer book was kept in the archives of the community of Turka until the Holocaust. The following text is written on the front page of the prayer book in both Polish and Hebrew.

[Page 28]

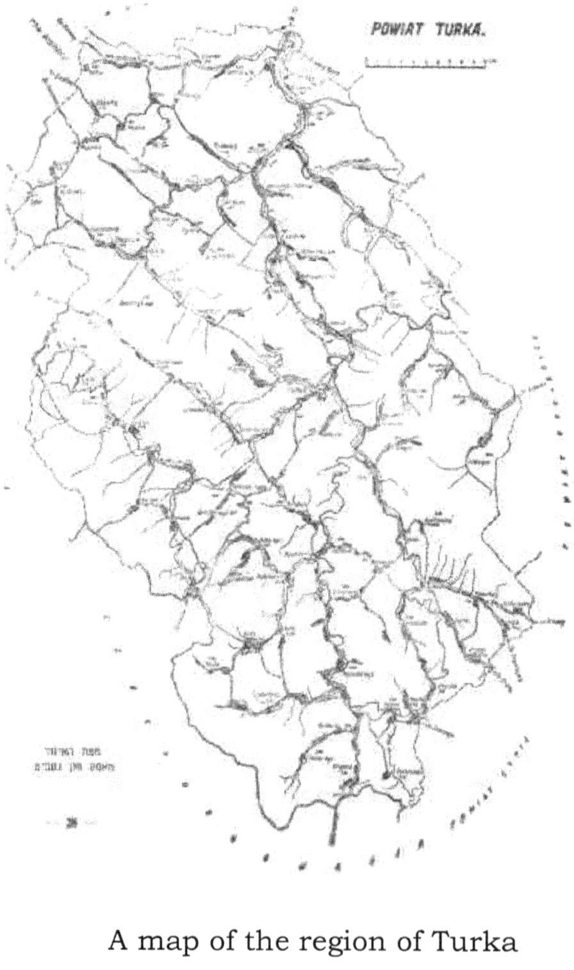

A map of the region of Turka

[Page 29]

"W Turce. Dziedzicznym miescie I. W. Imci Pana Antoniego, Pana Na Wielkich Kamionkach Turce, Beniowycz X. Kalinowskiego, Podkomorzego Inflantskiego Wojsk Jego Krolewskiej Mosci y Rze. Pos. Pulkownika Pana y Dobrodziedz."

Front page of the *Siddur* that was published in the Turka publishing house in the middle of the 18th century

Note: this is a *machzor* -- a festival prayer book. A rough English translation of the above Polish inscription is as follows. Som of the titles could not be translated literally: In Turka. To ... Sir Antoni Kalinowski, landlord of Turka, Kamionki Wielkie, Beniowce (?) and ... and colonel of HM the king and the Republic.}

United City Council

Until 1867, there were three separate communities in Turka: a) The community of the Christian residents; b) the community of the Polish nobility; and c) the Jewish community. Each community had its own official seal. The inscription on the Jewish seal was "Turka ver Yuden -- Gemeinde -- Siegel".

[Page 30]

After the declaration of the constitution and the change of citizenship rights in the lands under Austrian rule, the three aforementioned communities merged into on civic community for all citizens. After the merge, Mrs. Moshe Shechter was elected to the city council as a representative of the Jews.

Throughout that entire era, until the year 1903, no official Jewish community with a charter for autonomy and general elections existed in Turka. The people who headed the community were given the title of Regirer. These were delegates of the Jews who were elected from time to time at meetings in the synagogues. However, these people did not maintain any office, did not collect any taxes at all, and did not set up committees to administer to the needs of the community. The *shochtim* (ritual slaughterers) earned their livelihood from the income of *shechita,* and also designated specific percentages for the rabbi of the community or his delegate. Communal affairs were decided upon in meetings that were convened with sufficient frequency in the synagogues. These meetings were conducted by influential Jews, and the decisions that were taken obligated the entire community.

The Railway and the Beginning of Modern Life

A fundamental change took place in Turka starting in 1903. At that time, a railway line was built though Turka, which strengthened its economic and social life in a significant manner. Many new people with energy and initiative from the Jewish intelligentsia and commercial strata settled there then. That year (1903), the government authorized the founding of an official Jewish community, based on the Austrian law of Jewish communities, for the first time in the history of Turka. The following people then became members of the communal council: Moshe Shechter, Zalman Margolis, Avraham Zuswajn, Yisrael-Tzvi Hirsch, Chaim Hirsch, and Dr. Turnheim. The latter served as the chairman of the community. A new period of this communal organization began after the communal elections in 1908. The following were elected: Dr. Lowinger -- chairman, Daniel Ortel - vice chairman; and Peretz Klein, Abish Berman, Gedalia Mendel, Leibush Konka, Yosef Brandelstein, and Avraham Zuswain as members. The period of tenure of this communal council continued until the outbreak of the First World War in 1914.

No election to the Jewish communal council took place during the time of the First World Wår, since the residents left en masse due to the approach of the Russian Army. Indeed, the Russian army mercilessly plundered and destroyed all of the Jewish property in the city.

[Page 31]

After the First World War

The members of the communal council returned in the autumn of 1918 and began to renew the work of the communal council. However, after some time, the work was again interrupted due to the Ukrainian Revolution, and the authority of the communal council transferred to the Jewish National Council. This council only existed in Turka for a period of six months, after which authority was again transferred to the Jewish community that came to life again after the end of Ukrainian rule. The same members who had been elected a long time before the First World War continued to serve on that communal council.

The next elections for the communal council in Turka took place only in 1925. Once again, Dr. Lowinger was elected as chairman and Daniel Ortel as the vice chairman. The members were Hirsch-Leib Shreiber, Mendel Keller, Dr. Glik, Moshe Hirt, Sh"N. Majner, and Avraham Langenauer.

Elections to the communal council took place once again in 1928, on the basis of the new charter of communities of the Polish Republic. The members of the new committee were: Dr. Lowinger as chairman, Dr. Glik as vice chairman; and six members that including the rabbi of the city Rabbi Eliezer Mishel as vigilist. There were twelve council members, headed by Mr. Adolf Bernstein.

Left: Member of the communal council Dr. P. Rajntal

Right: Chairman of the communal council Dr. M. Bruch

Due to disarray in the community, the government disbanded the council and the committee, and, in the year 1935, appointed the Turka lawyer Dr. Maurycy Bruch as the government trustee. Alongside him, the advisory council consisted of Yisrael Intrator as vice trustee, Dr. P. Reinntal, Yaakov Tzvi Konka, Avraham Langenauer, Uziel Ortel, Yitzchak Engelmeir, and Shlomo Shliser.

[Page 32]

The population of Turka prior to the Second World War was 6,000, of which 41% were Jewish. The number of Jewish residents in the surrounding villages was 7,000.

(From Almanach gmin Zydowskich w polsce)
Translated from Polish by Ida Z.

C. Demographic Notes and Other Things

Administrative Divisions

The primary factor in the settlement and building up of Turka and its dependencies was undoubtedly the rivers and the abundance from the mountains. The primary administrative division was in essence the town itself: Turka on the Stryj River, which was the "capital" of the district, and which contained all of the district government offices. 273 villages and settlements were dependent on it.

Demography

1. There were 114,457 (according to the 1931 census) living on the area of 1,829 square kilometers, as follows:

2.	3. **Turka**	4. **District**
5. **Roman Catholics**	6. 1,706	7. 4,595
8. **Greek Catholics**	9. 4,211	10. 92,353
11. **Jews**	12. 4,117 (!)	13. 6,510
14. **Others**	15. 33	16. 800
17.		
18. **Polish Speakers**	19. 3,997	20. 22,106
21. **Ukrainian Speakers**	22. 1,446	23. 49,122
24. **Russian Speakers (Not Russians!)**	25. 1,571	26. 28,344
27. **Yiddish speakers**	28. 3,056	29. 4,496 (!)
30. **Speakers of other languages**	31. 25	32. 130

33.

34.

35. 10,627 Jews lived in the district of Turka. They formed 40.8% of the population of the town, and 6.2% of the population of the villages (!!) This was 141.3% larger than the number of Poles who lived in Turka itself. However, along with this, we can see that almost one third of the Jewish population of the district of Turka (3,065 out of 10,627) specified Polish as their vernacular. This raised the number of people who declared Polish as their mother tongue by 2,411 people.

[Page 33]

1. The standard of living in the district was very low. Living conditions were unbearable. 56.4% lived in one-room dwellings. 29.7% lived in two-room dwellings, and only 7.5% lived in three-room dwellings. There were only 9 physicians in the entire district, 7 of them in Turka.
2. There were 15 average sized sawmills in the district and three small ones. Four of these sawmills were located in Turka itself. Except for three, the largest of the sawmills were owned by Jews, who developed the lumber industry in the district, which was in general an agricultural region.
3. The "intelligentsia element" in the broad sense of the term, including officials in the district government offices, medics, teachers, clergy, police, and pensioners with their families -- numbered 3,229 people, forming 2.9% of the population.

(From Zarys monograficzny powiatu Turczanskiego Lwow 1930)

Railway tracks approaching Turka

[Page 34]

The Ledgers of Turka Until the Second World War

By Chaim Pelech of Kiryat Chaim

(Memories and Episodes)

Chaim Pelech

In olden times Jews of Turka lived in the same primitive conditions as the local Ukrainian population. They ate potatoes and oatmeal bread all week, and for the Sabbath, they went to the mill, milled a bit of wheat, and baked narrow wheat challos. There was no great difference between rich and poor. Even the clothing was very poor. Young people wore long shirts of thick flax and in the summer they went barefoot without shoes... For the wedding, they made the young people trestle boots, two pairs of cloth pants and bekishes (Hassidic cloaks), and shirt of thick gentile flax. They did not make much more for the girls...

Deep Religiosity

All of the Jewish children in Turka and in the surrounding villages studied in cheders. At that time, they did not know of schools, although the wealthy Jews gradually began to bring teachers from the larger cities for their children, so that they would learn to write German and Polish. For the poor and middle class Jews, the cheder was the highest level of study and education. First and foremost, one learned how to pray there, and even more. Later, various strata of the Jewish community sent their sons to the Rabbinical Yeshivas of other cities in Galicia. Therefore, many students came to Turka, who would sit day and night in the kloizes and study.

Railroad and Changes

Young men of Turka at the banks of the Jablonka

As the very old Jews used to relate, a great change came in life in Turka when they began to build the railway line. Turka continued to live with the old order as long as there was no railway line. The economic and employment situation changed completely. Together with that, the cultural and social situation changed. In truth, people relate, that even before the time of the railway, there were already a few great students n Turka, who had already secretly become Zionists and occupied themselves with Zionist literature – but this was all strictly undercover.

When the railway was built, a certain Jewish railway engineer came to Turka, and founded a Zionist organization called Mizrachi in Turka – the first organization of the new times in Turka. At the beginning, the organization was very small, for the youth were afraid to join it due to the great persecutions that they had to withstand, both from their parents and from others. They would not let the youth worship in the kloizes. On occasion such a young man would receive a slap and be thrown out of the Belzer Kloiz. This was considered to be an illness for them... they were called 'treifenicks' 1.

However, time did not stand still.. Slowly, the Zionist organization expanded and grew. Elections to the Austrian parliament took place in 1907. There were two Jewish candidates in the regions (the nationalist Jew Dr. Gershon Zipper and the assimilationist Dr. Nathan Levenstein – “A Pole of the Mosaic faith”). By then, the Zionist organization of Turka conducted a large scale activity and great agitation.

The economic changes were mainly evidenced by the building of many sawmills, for when the railway was built, they began to cut down the forests and transport the wood by train. This provided livelihood to may Jews of Turka. Jews were clerks, contractors, employees, etc. at all of the lumber enterprises. Life changed significantly, and Jews no longer had to mill flour for the Sabbath...

One profession in Turka was a victim of the railway – the wagon drivers. They, whose entire livelihood consisted of bringing in and sending out of merchandise with their horse drawn wagons, begged G-d that He should make a miracle and the axle of the train should break... However, no miracle took place, and the trains continued to ride...

Indeed, business greatly expanded, and Jews conducted commerce. But not all... the greatest number of Jews still remained poor. They worked at various trades, and were tailors, shoemakers, and others. Above everything, tailors worked with their hands, for there were no new machines in Turka. When one could obtain a new machine, there was no money to purchase it. One tailor, who had some means, purchased a new machine at that time. This was Baruch Yosef Frankel. Indeed, other tailors would come to him and pay him to make their stitches. Later, the Singer firm from America arrived. It was represented by Alter Montag, who was the gabbai (trustee) of the Tailor's Synagogue. Reb Alter gave machines to all of the tailors, which were to be paid for in installments. The terms were for a year or two, but it often dragged on to six or eight years. Alter Montag would always lengthen the terms.

In short, it was a bit better for tailors and shoemakers. However, when Thursday came, and one needed 4-5 Crowns for the Sabbath, one had to sweat hard until it came.

Societal Life

At that time, the entire societal life in Turka took place in the Beis Midrashes and kloizes. There was a Belzer Kloiz in Turka, in which Jews sat day and night and studied; There was a Sadigora Kloiz, a Chortkower Kloiz, a Beis Midrash, and also a large synagogue – where more enlightened Jews worshipped with a cantor and a choir. The Tailor's Synagogue 2 and the "Businessmen's" Synagogue were located near the large synagogue. Aside from there, there was a large Kloiz of Rabbi Langerman, and also shtibels that held services in accordance with their style. There was also a Zionist shtibel, an hand-worker's shtibel, and still others.

Young people slowly began to read the "Jewish Tagblatt" that was published in Lemberg 3. They also took interest in Yiddish theater. Troupes came from Lemberg, and various Jewish songs began to be sung in Turka.

However, not everything went smoothly. Youth still went "to sing and to recite" with their observant parents and other observant families. The older generation did not surrender so quickly, and they waged a battle with the treifeniks.

It was fortuitous that the older generation did not always have a great deal of time, and they were occupied with their own problems and difficulties. As well, G-d sent them a difficult problem when they had to choose a new rabbi after the old rabbi died. This was in 1909 or 1910. A large proportion wanted the grandson of the Rebbe of Sambor. However, the communal council and other Jews wanted only Rabbi Mishel, who was not very popular, but was very good at learning. Samborer Hassidim stormed the communal offices. There were fights in the streets, and also at tables and on chairs...

Rabbi Mishel and the Jewish community council were victorious. With them were wealthy Jews, the owners of the Profinacia (Liquor monopoly), who purchased it from the heirs of Count Kolinowski. Those heirs owned all of their lands in the Turka region, and Jews purchased these lands. All of the wealthy Jews were adherents of the assimilationist Dr. Levenstein against the nationalist activist Dr. Zipper. The Pole of the Mosaic faith once again was victorious in the elections of 1911. Great battles broke out in Turka over those elections. Moshe Shein and his Socialist group came to the assistance of the Zionist side, which was incidentally quite strong. The assimilationist group won, for it was helped by the police.

When the famous Beiles Trial took place in Kiev prior to the first World War, a large protest meeting against the Czarist authorities took place in Turka. Leibel Taubes from Lemberg spoke at that gathering, which took place in the large synagogue and was packed.

A time of cultural and political activity began in Turka at that time. Theatrical troupes began to come from Lemberg and Krakow. Then, a dramatic circle was founded as part of the Zionist organization at that time. The Turka population attended all of the performances en masse.

At that time, a table maker by the name of Hersh Fett came to Turka and settled there. Fett founded a handworker's organization called Yad Charutzim, which developed with fine activities. It was a union that included shoemakers, tailors, clockmakers, locksmiths, table makers and other professions.

The aforementioned Moshe Shein founded the first Jewish socialist organization called Zh. P. S., which was a branch of the Polish P. P. S. (Polska Partja Socialistyczna). That Socialist organization did not have a great success, for people were somewhat ashamed to belong to that organization...

Small social-religious organizations were active at the time. These included the Chevra Kadisha (which was as old as the town of Turka itself...), Psalm reciters, and others. Their members were extremely disciplined, and any command from a trustee was immediately acted upon. They stood at a very high moral level. They had respect for old people, and never battled against them. Jews were honorable and deeply religious. They eschewed tale bearing and accepted lovingly all manners of life that were thrown their way.

One Relates...

Various stories were told in Turka during those good times.

In 1912, a young man (He was a son of the Koncikers Rebbe name Oestreich) got married in Turka. He wished to open a clothing factory in town. The tailors found out about this and gave him a difficult time. The young man soon regretted this and clarified that he would not wish to take livelihood away from the poor tailors.

Rabbi Eli Kapel, a judge and great scholar, ordered two suits for his two children. The tailor delivered the work, and Reb Eli did not have enough money to pay. Reb Eli sent back the clothing, for it was strongly forbidden to wear things for which the workers the workers were not paid.

There was also an organization for giving of assistance in secret. The city knew that Chaim Hirsch would send two cranes to Mattel the scribe and to other poor Jews every Thursday for the Sabbath.

A poor Jew called Yankel Kugel used to travel around with a horse and buggy. He would conclude his work at noon on Friday. Two hours before candle lighting, he already went to worship at the Kloiz, dressed in a silk bekishe (Hassidic robe), streimel, loafers and white socks. Yankel used to always conduct services. He would worship in the Kloiz of Rabbi Langerman on Rosh Hashanah and Yom Kippur. They used to say that his praying would instill fear in the youth. His voice thundered up to heaven.

Berl Chaluk was a poor, honorable Jew. He had the custom of bringing cold water into the synagogue when Jews used to sit there on the Sabbath and recite Psalms. The Psalms reciters would refresh their heart with the water. One day, Berl met a young man who said to him, "Berl, you have taken water to the synagogue for such a long time. Perhaps you should give this over to someone younger than you?" Berl answered, "My young man, this water porting to the synagogue is my mitzvah and my custom, and I have no intention of giving it over to anybody... When I die, it should be transferred to my son Shimon..."

Translator's Footnotes:

1. From the work 'treif', which colloquially means 'non-kosher'. Treifenicks would mean 'non-kosher people'.
2. Literally, "little synagogue".
3. Otherwise known as Lvov, Lwow, or modern day Lviv.

[Page 41]

Turka

by Eizik Kurtz of Haifa

Eizik Kurtz

A. A Jewish Town

The town of Turka belonged to Austria until the breakup of the Austro-Hungarian Empire at the end of the First World War. Then it transferred to Poland. It fell under Russian rule at the end of the Second World War.

Turka is situated in the Carpathians, approximately 30 kilometers from the Beskid Peaks. The population of the city was more than 50% Jewish. There were also many Jews among the population of the large number of villages surrounding Turka. Some of them literally worked the land. Poles and Ukrainians formed the rest of the population of the city. The Polish residents were the intelligentsia of the city for the most part, including teachers, government officials, and the like. However, there was a certain degree of intelligentsia, primarily teachers, among the Ukrainian population.

There were very few Jewish officials of the general government. On the other hand, I recall two Jewish mayors. One Jewish mayor was Shechter, who was the wealthy man of the city, and the second was Dr. Landis. A Pole was appointed as mayor only in 1916 or 1917. He was the school principal. It is especially appropriate to note Dr. Landis here, for he did a great deal for the benefit of the city. Indeed, at times, the thought has come to my mind that this Dr. Landis served as a good example for our Abba Hushi...

Turka, like all of the cities of Galicia, was somnolent from generation to generation... until the *Haskalah* began to knock on the gates of the Jewish settlements -- some sooner and some later. In any case, the *Haskalah* came to us in Turka very late... Only certain special Jews were involved in it at the end of the 19th or the beginning of the 20th century, but they were not so daring as to make this fact public.

[Page 42]

B. Composition of the Jewish Population

As in most of the cities of Galicia, the Jews of Turka worked primarily in small-scale commerce and trades. For example, all of the tailors were Jews, and they also sewed for the gentile population of the villages. The builders were also 95% Jewish. There was perhaps one gentile among all of the shoemakers... This was also the case with the Jewish harness-makers, barbers, etc. Even the members of the free intelligentsia such as the lawyers, physicians, etc., were all Jews, with the exception of two physicians -- one of whom was the director of the hospital and the second of whom was the supervisor of the office of health. It is no wonder, therefore, that all of the main streets of the town were occupied by Jews until the end of the century... Gentiles only began to penetrate into the Jewish center in the years 1909-1910. Someone named Schipka, who had formerly been a servant of the aforementioned Shechter, opened up a restaurant. Someone named Kucira opened a second restaurant.

Limierz River at the time of the melting of the snow

With the passage of time, gentile grocery stores began to open up, especially a Ukrainian cooperative. There were not yet any other sources of commerce, for everything was in the hands of the Jews. A change for the worse took place during the 1930s, as many gentile shops opened up.

[Page 43]

C. Zionism in the Town

Zionism as a movement appeared in the town two to three years after the First Zionist Congress.

It was like this. The railway line between Lwow and Budapest via the Carpathians began to be completed at the beginning of the century. This railway line passed through Turka. This led to an improvement in the economic situation of Turka, and the town began to arise from its poverty. At that time, there were thousands of workers in the town and the area, primarily Italians, and there was hope. Something else helped with this: Along with the workers, a Jew named Rozenblat, who was attracted to Zionism, came to town. This engineer was the one who brought a new spirit to numerous youths of the *kloizes*. Thus, the first breach was created... Among these first ones, we should mention Baruch Maj (his daughter lives in Israel), Nechemia Shteiger, Yosef Kopel, Y. M. Shreiber, and Berish Lorberbaum. With the passage of time, other youths were added to these daring ones, and the founded a Zionist organization named "Mizracha". By the years 1907-1910, their influence on the Jewish Street was already quite recognizable. When time came for the elections to the Austrian government, and the assimilationist Dr. Levinstein who was supported by the government as well as the Zionist Dr. Ziper submitted their candidacies, a commotion broke out in the city, and there was also a Zionist demonstration.

The first beginnings of the Hebrew school also took place at that time. However, this activity was very restricted, and was not met with recognizable success.

The situation changed in its entirety during the period of the First World War. The Jews left when the Russians entered the town, and only returned when the town was reconquered by the Austrian Army in 1915. From then, things began as new. Everything was in the hands of the youth, for the older people were drafted to the army. One youth appeared at this point, who today is the mayor of the city of Haifa, and gathered a group of youths into his house, who were the sons of proper people with curly *peyos* (the writer of these lines among them), and began to speak about the founding of Young Zion, the study of Hebrew, preparations for *aliya* to the Land of Israel, etc. Indeed, we began to study Hebrew, using the book of Moshe Roth.

[Page 44]

When the refugees of the war began to return to the town, many members began to join Young Zion. The group disbanded with the passage of time. One group, along with Abba Hushi, transferred to Hashomer Hatzair, and the second group remained with Young Zion until the appearance of Hitachdut. These two groups conducted many cultural activities in the city. A library affiliated with Young Zion was opened in the city, containing books in Yiddish, Hebrew, Polish and German. At Hashomer Hatzair, we attempted to prepare for *aliya* to the Land. At that time, we obtained a plot of Land to work. We also chopped trees for the householders of the city. In those days, such activities were very revolutionary...

These activities were primarily centered in the large community hall that was built by the local Zionist organization. Already before the First World War, a Jew named Dr. Turnheim donated the land for this building.

*

The first group, headed by Abba Hushi, made *aliya* to the Land in 1920. (I did not make *aliya* with that group due to a family tragedy.) After some time, the second group, of Young Zion, made *aliya*, headed by Moshe Yisraeli.

At that time the Hechalutz movement began. Its members came from various organizations. A Gordonia chapter was also founded at that time by Manis Branes of blessed memory. I recall that Pinchas Lubianker visited the town for a leadership inspection at the time of the founding of that chapter. Activists in Hitachdut included Shlomo Pellach, Shlomo Feiler, Moshe Krabes, and others.

I especially wish to note the activities of Y. M. Shreiber, who was a Hebrew teacher as well as the delegate of the Keren Kayemet (Jewish National Fund) throughout all of his days. Absolutely everybody received their inspiration from him. In 1939, I received a letter from him containing greetings for our members in the Land.

D. Miscellaneous

It was 1918. The Hashomer Hatzair movement in Galicia was then in its full blossom. The entire movement was based on "scouting", and their uniforms made of Paulist cloth were quite recognizable.

Then the headquarters of the movement decided to hold a national convention. At that point, Abba Hushi already was able to influence the headquarters to hold the convention in the village of Torna near Turka. There was a Jewish landowner there named Tzvi Rand (a Holocaust survivor, whom I greeted here when he came to the Land), who placed his barn and some of his buildings at the disposal of the convention. The participants included Elizer Berger of blessed memory, Dolek Horowitz, Meir Yaari, Spiegel, Sarah Meirsdorf, and Abba Hushi. I recall the strong impression that the convention delegates had on the people of Turka. Their arrival by train, dressed in uniforms that resembled army fatigues, etc. -- all of this excited our imaginations, for we saw them as a Jewish army who would go up and conquer the Land of Israel...

[Page 45]

Turka During the First World War

By Chaim Pelech of Kiryat Chaim

The war during the years 1914-1918 brought great tribulations to the Jews of Turka, and a great destruction to the town. This began on the second day of Rosh Hashanah. At 2:00, a Russian cavalry patrol tore into Turka. Not two minutes passed when the whistle of a locomotive was heard. It became known in town that the train station was empty. Nobody from the town was there, for everyone fled. We soon understood that something was about to happen. Indeed, shooting was heard shortly. It became known that an Austrian patrol arrived with the locomotive and shot at the Russians. The Russian patrol fled, and the city was left empty – not Austrian and not Russian...

The Night of Horror

The Jewish community of Turka then went through a difficult night, for news spread that the Ukrainians were gathering together at night to ambush the city and pillage the Jewish population. People closed themselves up in their homes and prepared hatchets to defend themselves against the robbers. The night was completely peaceful. In the morning, the first day after Rosh Hashanah, a large portion of the Jewish population began to flee to the surrounding villages. The Russian army began to march in at exactly 12:00 noon. Large army battalions came in and immediately began their "work". They set fire to a large portion of the city between the Rynek (Market) Place and the alleyways, where the synagogue and Kloizes were located. And where the crowded Jewish population lived.

A great panic ensued. People ran from the burning houses as they were, leaving behind all of their belongings, the product of the labor of the course of over a hundred years. As stated, the fire engulfed the entire Rynek from both sides, and burnt all of the alleyways around the synagogue and the Kloizes. The synagogue, the Belzer Kloiz and the Beis Midrash all burnt. The panic was indescribable. Jews ran to save the Torah scrolls. They tore into the burning Kloizes and dragged out the holy scrolls. The Cossacks were standing not far from those Jewish alleyways, beating the Jews who were carrying the holy books with Cossack style whips.

Pillage

Many Jews fled to the "Olica"[1]. There, 6-8 families were stuffed into one room. At that time, many Christians from the villages came to city and pillaged the burning houses. Strong young people stood around some of the houses, and did not permit them to be pillaged. In such cases, the Christians brought Russian soldiers to help. Then the strong people had to flee and hide – and the Christians freely pillaged the Jewish belongings. Jews dared to ask a Russian officer why they were pillaging and burning the Jewish property. He answered that the Jews telephoned the Austrian army, telling them that they should shoot at the Russian patrol that entered the town the day before. Therefore, Jews were punished. Of course, this was the eternal libel against Jews, which was thought up in order to justify pillaging Jewish belongings.

Thus did Turka burn until the second day. The Christians pillaged until late in the night. Then, things began to be quiet... However, late at night, a new terror and panic began among the Jews who remained in the city. Russian officers broke into the Jewish houses with revolvers in their hands, and searched for Jewish girls and women... The shrieks of those girls and women were terrible. It seemed as if they would kill all of the Jews. From one house, the cry of the entire Jewish population who lived there could be heard. This continued until 2:00 a.m. Afterward, it became silent again until the morning.

The result of that night was one Jew dead and one Jew wounded. This occurred because they did not allow their wives to be violated. In the morning, all Jews left the city and fled to the villages around Turka. The Turka Jews lived there for a difficult 21 days, for there was nothing to eat. Many people died from the typhus and cholera that quickly spread among the Jewish people. The weather was also uncooperative. On the eve of Yom Kippur, there was a large snowfall. Winter lay like a heavy stone upon the hungry Jewish population, who slept in the attics of the stables of the village Jews. The rooms were filled with young children. Among other things, there was no place to lay one's head.

Thus were they tormented for the entire three weeks until the Austrian army retook Turka, and the Russians fled to Stary-Sambor. Then the Jews of Turka returned to their city, and once again crowded themselves into the Olica, 4-8 families in a room. The poverty was very great. They had no shirt on their bodies, and no money with which to purchase a piece of bread. People ran around the Christians to retrieve their pillaged items. A few indeed succeeded in retrieving something, however the great majority could not get anything.

Leaving Home

As has already been stated, there was no livelihood. The news from the front was also bad. The Jews began to prepare to flee to Hungary. The torment went on for a few more weeks – and when the Austrian army retreated to Hungary, the few Jews from Turka joined them. Only two Jews remained in the town – Yisrael Mendel Binder and Aharon Mordechai Filinger. Their end was tragic. Yisrael Mendel was dragged into Russia, and Aharon Mordechai was shot by the Russians on the spot.

The Turka Jews were homeless refugees. They were tossed into the Austria-Hungary Empire, and they spent the entire war there. The Austrian regime even gave them a significant amount of support, that enabled the homeless Jews to withstand the tribulations and permitted them to return to their former homes. In 1916, when the Russians began to retreat from Galicia, the Jews of Turka began to return home.

Returning Home

When we arrived in Turka in 1918, we already found a living town, with a new youth, with new ideas – nothing of what once was... We found a new, strong Hashomer Hatzair organization. The youth were going around with books under their arms... We read a lot we conducted discussions, there was Socialism and Zionism – it was lively in the town... We went to readings. There was a great cultural ascent among the youth, who did not yet need to seek their livelihood... Indeed, with regard to livelihood, the struggle in the town was still very difficult. The war continued on the fronts, and the elder generation sweated greatly when Thursday came and there was no food for the Sabbath.

Time passed and the war finally ended. The Jews soldiers began to return home from the fronts. There were new tones: everyone was a thorough revolutionary.

In the meantime, the Ukrainians took over the political authority, and it was hard on the heart... They granted so-called political freedom, but there was no food and no livelihood. The Ukrainians and Poles formed a common front – and the struggle became more difficult. The Ukrainians began to see where they were, and it was very cramped. Typhus began to spread again, and slowly engulfed the entire Jewish population. Many Jews died of the epidemic. The struggle became progressively worse.

Nevertheless, the youth organized themselves into various groups that sprouted up. The youth felt that a new time was coming. The Ukrainians would not be able to maintain their authority, and we would become Polish citizens.

Indeed, that is what happened. Within a short period of time, the Poles overtook the Ukrainians, and we became Polish citizens, albeit with new tribulations and new worries...

[Page 50]

Episodes from Life in Turka from Before the First World War

by Elka Moshenberg of Haifa

Elka Moshenberg

Yisrael Moshe Shreiber

Yisrael Moshe Shreiber, who served as the first Hebrew teacher in Turka and was a *maskil* and Zionist with heart and soul, was my cousin from my father's side. I will tell here about his first steps as an educator. It was approximately 57 years ago. His mother had died, and he lived with his father in our house. His father was elderly and sickly, and was always coughing. His son Yisrael Moshe took care of them with the help of my mother.

He excelled in his studies in *cheder*, and became an assistant to the teacher. His father's hope was that he would end up as a teacher to the older students.

Once, I climbed up to the attic for some reason, and, to my surprise, found a complete "treasury" in the form of a closed trunk. This was a type of "*kopertal*" in the vernacular. I opened it and found books, booklets, and other types of papers. With joy, I told my mother Rivka about this find. However, she had certainly known about this, and she forbade me from approaching the trunk. It was clear that this trunk housed Yisrael Moshe's study materials, which he used to study secular subjects in secret.

He would study every night, with his head resting on his elbow, supporting himself on the table. He would not utter any sound, but only study the holy books. However, when his father went to sleep, he would get up, take out the hidden secular books, and study them.

My later father would get up in the middle of the night to recite the *Tikkun Chatzot* service[2]. Once, he passed by him, and saw him with the "non-kosher material" in his hands. He told my mother, but my mother softened Father's stance, "The *cheder* studies are not sufficient to sustain him..."

[Page 51]

As I have stated, he later became known in the city. Everyone studied Hebrew with him. He married and had a child – but no memory of them remains.

Regarding the *Chevra Kadisha* (Burial Society)

The *Chevra Kadisha* of our city also served the Jews who lived in the surrounding villages. The concentration of Jews in those villages varied by size and circumstance. There were villages in which a *minyan* of Jews could barely be found, whereas others maintained small Jewish communities with cultural vibrancy and strong Jewish tradition. The people would earn their livelihood from grocery stores in the village, inns, and also from working the land.

These Jews would generally conduct themselves according to the principles of "tending to guests," participating in communal matters, etc. However, there were also some who acted in a miserly fashion, and did not tend to guests. The *Chevra Kadisha* knew how to repay such miserly Jews. When they would bring their dead to be buried, they would be asked to pay more than double. The incoming money was, of course designated to the upkeep of the cemetery, the costs of burial of poor people, etc.

*

There was a custom with the *Chevra Kadisha* of Turka that if they were unable to bury the dead on the day of his death, two of the members would be asked to sit with the deceased for the entire night next to burning candles.

Once, on a winter night, my father was asked to stand guard over the deceased along with another man. Indeed, my father had the opportunity to fulfill this commandment often enough, since our house was located in close proximity to the cemetery. Already before midnight, the guardians realized that the candles would not last the entire night. Therefore, the second man was asked to go to the store of Yosef Meir Bik, located nearby, to purchase candles. First, the man drank a glass of liquor, and then he sat down to rest on some bench, and fell asleep for the entire night...

My father remained with the deceased in darkness. In accordance with the custom, he had to remain with the deceased until daylight.

*

How did the Chevra Kadisha get new members? How did these members pass the first "trial by fire"?

[Page 52]

They brought the candidate to the *tahara* room[3], and left him there. If he endured this, he would be accepted as a member...

The *Raftom*[4] Week

When the mandatory draft was decreed, which at first only included bachelors, 40 weddings were arranged in one week in Turka. Therefore, this week was called – Shabbat *Raftom*...

"A Grown Up Child"

And it took place during the time of Cossacks –

Gutscha, a girl of about 15 years old, was the daughter of my uncle Neituch. She dressed up as a boy, so that the Cossacks would not set their eyes upon her. She tied a kerchief to her belt, as if she was suffering from a toothache, and a large hat that covered her forehead. She put on an old man's suit and boots – and thus did she go around among the men in the shadow of her father.

Once, a Russian soldier came to us and wanted to say *Kaddish* in memory of his father. When he wanted to include the "lad" in the *minyan*, he was told that he had not yet reached the age of Bar Mitzvah. He answered, “Without inviting the evil eye, -- a grown up looking child...”

We Became Refugees

At the beginning of the First World War in 1914, the Austrian Army decided to step over the front in Galicia. After a few attempts to take hold, all of the Jews of Turka, including the Jews of the adjacent villages, became refugees.

Our route led in the direction of the Hungarian border. There were no trains, so some set out by wagon, and others by foot, throughout all the paths and routes – the main thing was to leave the place. Even the Austrian Army retreated across the Hungarian border. Thus, our route was determined by the movements of the army. When the captains saw my two younger sisters and younger brother, they had mercy on them and seated them in an army wagon. My older brother was told to walk behind the wagon. Our aim was to go to our uncle in Berezina. My mother and I walked on a separate path. In the middle of the night, the captain who was transporting our family received an order to return to Turka. The children had to get off the wagon and wander by foot on unknown paths in the darkness of the night. Along with other refugees, we reached the Shanka border crossing. A transport train arrived there, which gathered all the refugees, and crowded them in like sardines. We could not meet up with our young family members, but it was clear that we would meet up at our uncle's in Berezina. However, when the train arrived in Berezina, the Hungarian police arrived and did not let anyone get off the trains. My mother and I succeeded in sneaking off the train and hiding beneath it, but the children did not do this, and therefore continued on the train to the city of Gaya in Moravia. Many refugees from Turka had also come to that city. My parents and I later left Berezina to go to Gaya, but this time, we were sent to Czechia[5] instead of Moravia. We arrived in the city of Klatovy, not far from Pilsen. The family was separated, and was only reunited after a long time.

[Page 53]

The Czechs were good, upright people. They had not yet felt the taste of the war, even though their children were already serving in the army. These Czechs were surprised and asked, “Why are there only Jews among the refugees?

*

The situation in Klatovy was very difficult at first. The refugees lived in large warehouses and slept on straw. There was a central kitchen which cooked substandard food, and whose kashruth reliability was questionable. Therefore, many Orthodox Jews subsisted on tea and bread. The young children contracted various childhood illnesses that spread like an epidemic. These diseases cut them down – 40 children died within one month.

The wealthier of the refugees, who had sums of money with them, were permitted to live in the city. However, these were very few. Some other refugees went on strike and refused to accept the portions of cooked food. As a result of the strike, the Austrian government built new bunks. A large kitchen was built which was available to the families for private cooking. The families received sustenance grants in accordance with the number of family members. There were also factories in which one could work and earn a salary.

For a long time, the children of the refugees did not have a school. Finally, a teacher from Poland was found who gathered four grades together and taught them. The students mainly studied German; however, it should be noted that these studies did not have great value.

*

Grandfather once went to the funeral of a refugee in the cemetery. He noticed that the deceased, who was lying in a crate, was lowered deep into the grave with chains. He said, “Me, they won't lower with chains.” He left Czechia in haste and arrived in Turka. He found his home in ruins. He wandered around for a week, and then went to his son in Berezina. He died there after about a week, at the age of 83.

[Page 54]

The town, with mountains surrounding it

Translator's Footnotes:

1. Olica is the Polish word for Street, but here I believe it refers to a specific place.
2. The room in which the deceased is ritually prepared, washed, and dressed for burial.
3. A non-obligatory, private prayer service that is recited at midnight and bemoans the destruction of the Temple.
4. It is unclear what this word means exactly, but the root 'Rft" means "to wear out."

Bohemia.

[Page 55]

Life and Youth

[Page 57]

Turka My Town

by David Yisraeli-Langnauer of Zera
Translated by Jerrold Landau
Donated by Boaz Ben-Pelech

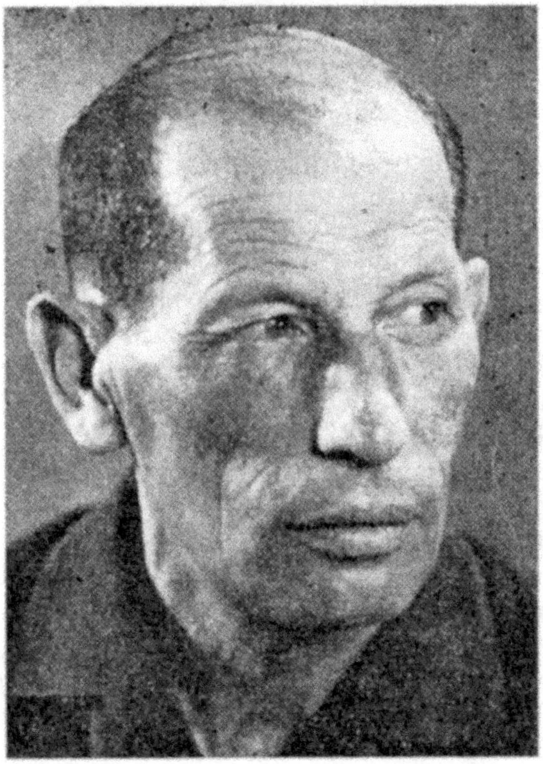

David Yisraeli-Langnauer

For my father, my brother Yosef, his family

And all of my family who are so very dear to me.

The years pass, and in their stream, a person removes his thoughts from the near past, and certainly from the distant pass – thus, slowly but surely, my town of Turka, my birthplace, and the place where my large, wide-branched family lived among very many other Jewish families, is being forgotten. My small town, where I saw light, was raised, studied, came of age, and was drawn from you many decades ago to my land – the Land of Israel. Today I bring to mind: how could it be, how did it happen that time erases many experiences of my youth from the tablet of my heart? The youthful period disappeared; the strongest impressions that were imprinted upon me were forgotten. However... is it possible to forget those days, filled with aspirations, dreams, and a desire for action? Is it possible to erase the experiences that took place within the confines of the *Beis Midrash* and the life of the movements? Is it possible through this forgetting to push aside splendid, deep images of young children, which for me were literally monumental? Is it possible to forget the various personalities whom I met each day, the friends from my childhood and youth; encounters with Jews every day of the year, whether for the bad or for the good? I knew them well, lived with them, and loved them as they were, during the entire period of my life there in the town – as mischievous kids, as students in the *cheder*, in the *kloiz* during services... during regular discussions of worldly matters, there behind the oven... in the street, in the store, at work, and in every place...

I have strong longings for my family, my friends, and the Jews of the town who perished during the terrible extermination perpetrated by the impure ones. In my imagination, I wander from picture to picture, join them line by line, image to image – and before me is the town in its wholeness. This town that had been cut off from the world and is no longer... and I am trying to revive it – is it possible? I wish now to capture the slope of the mountains, as we would climb them as children, with our yarmulkes, and our *peyos* blowing in the wind... We will relive the wonderful activities that were carried out in the Hashomer Hatzair chapter and in the other wonderful youth movements of our town... We will meet various characters, some more important, and some less interesting... We will recall many of its Jews, even if I cannot recall the name of every one, but we will recall all of the souls, for they are all holy in our eyes... We will whisper to them in any human form. We will even mock them and joke about their flaws... I will attempt to clarify in my imagination the hiding places of the distant past, but for various reasons, I will suffice myself with mentioning a few personalities, some who stood out in the life of the town and others whom I feel an important need to describe here due to their uniqueness.

[Page 58]

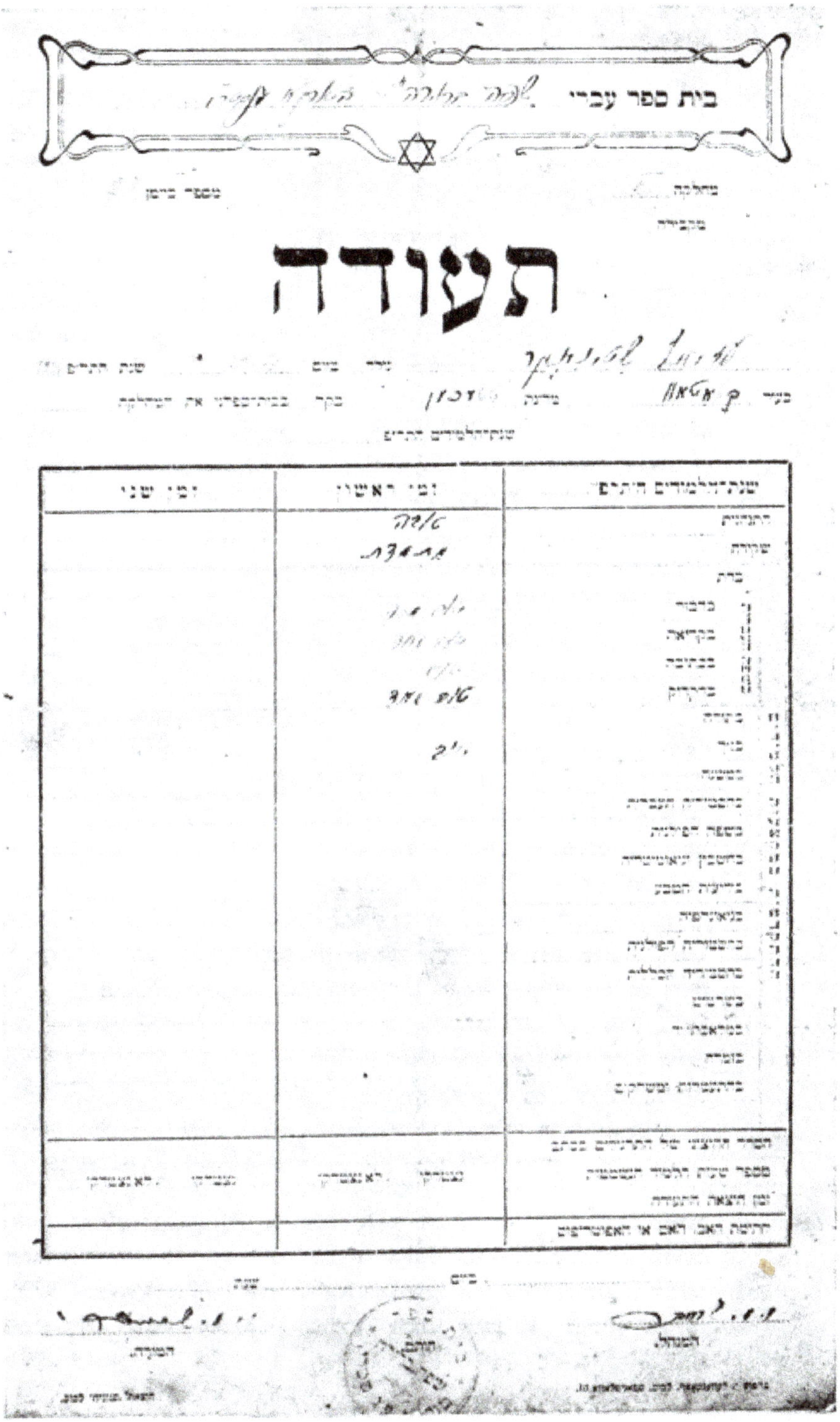
בית ספר עברי

תעודה

זמן ראשון

זמן שני

A report card. Translator's note: of the Safa Berura Hebrew School

[Page 59]

*

The first Hebrew teacher was Moshe Shreiber. This is not a derogatory name, Heaven forbid, but they called him "Shreiber Der Hoiker" ("Shreiber the Hunchback"). He was well loved even though he was an odd personality. He was short, with fascinating, refined lines on his face. He never gave in to his suffering or his physical handicap. He was saturated with Torah and wisdom, and was knowledgeable in both Hebrew and general subjects. His expertise in the old and new literature was wonderful, and he attempted to disseminate this expertise to the masses. He was one of the first to disseminate "Safa Berura" (The clear language) in town. At the end of the First World War, he returned to the town with the other refugees who had left. He founded the first Hebrew school, called "Safa Berura." At that time, this school was a thorn in the side of the Orthodox of the town, but the stream of lovers of Hebrew grew despite their anger and wrath. Children and youths studied the language, and organized clubs and groups of friends. These first ones were the founders of the Hashomer Hatzair and Hechalutz chapters. They studied Hebrew literature and Zionist history with the help of Moshe Shreiber. In this manner, the Zionist idea penetrated the masses.

Everyone who knew Shreiber related to him with love and admiration. He was the "Ben Yehuda"[1] of our town, for he spoke Hebrew to his son in his home, and everyone who came to his house spoke the Holy Tongue. His students included the members of the leadership of the chapter and the heads of Hechalutz at that time: the Schnellers (today Chushai), Weisman, Tz. Shein, Nagler, Rusler, M. Langnauer, and others. They were the ones who disseminated and literally lived the language on the street and in the various social activities. Shreiber was a dedicated Zionist. Everyone who met him was affected by his Zionist devotion, which was his practical way of day to day life. On account of his private library, many people came to read books of great importance. At his place, I secretly read Ranak[2], Ahad Haam, and Shakespeare, everything mixed up... With his agreement, I also succeeded in smuggling these books into the *kloiz*, where I studied these impure books with my friends... Indeed, in his house, the Zionist circle sprouted and flourished. It later became seriously active, bringing to life and strengthening the Zionistic pioneering philosophy that united the organizational framework of the youths and the pioneers in the town. The development and attractiveness of these splendid movements can be significantly attributed to the merit of Shreiber. To my sorrow and our sorrow, he did not merit actualizing his life's dream of settling in the land – among all of us who knew him from up close. May his memory be blessed with us forever...

[Page 60]

*

Let us now unite ourselves with an interesting personality in the arena of Jewish humor and performing arts in our town, our acquaintance Melech Brauer. Whenever I met him, he had a good joke or sharp statement fitting to the times on his lips... He had a true Jewish sense of humor. I do not know from where or from what "academy" of arts he learned his acting skills; however his readings of Sholom Aleicheim, Mendele, Der Tunkler, Moshe Nadir and others at the parties and celebrations of the movement were an experience for all those present. Who does not recall his stage performances? Brauer was the one who, in his time, dared to arrange famous plays such as those of Hirshbein, Gordon, Goldfaden, and others. He found many of his actors in our chapter. With his sharp eye, he found "acting" skills literally on the street. The rehearsals for the plays were an experience for all participants. Needless to say, everything was done under very primitive conditions... He coordinated the music himself, and the music was performed by Schwartz and the Ofermans.

I have described him with only a few lines; however I have written them with tears... and this time, not with "tears of joy"...

*

Meilech (Melech) the doctor (April) – it was with this name that both young and old, Jews and gentiles knew him. He stemmed from an Orthodox, Hassidic family. Melech came to town from Lvov or its vicinity many years earlier, and began to work as a medic and assistant of the chief doctor of the city hospital that was located at the edge of "Oyben Dorf." It was there that he obtained his great experience in the field. (How it worked out that he became the assistant to a Polish doctor – we will not know...) Many of the townsfolk would not take their sick to the real doctor before Meilech-Doctor gave his "diagnosis" and expressed his opinion about the state of the sick person... Is it possible to forget how Meilech read out the prescriptions out loud? The Latin Language took on a unique form with him, and was understood only by him... And was there in the world a more delicate and refined hand that that of this Doctor Meilech as he would examine the body of a sick person?

[Page 61]

When he would enter the house of the sick with his loving, broad smile, with his sweet and spicy Yiddish expressions, he would change the atmosphere immediately and remove "sixty measures" of the sick person's suffering. When he was first summoned, at any hour of the day or night, he hastened to offer his assistance to both the houses of the poor as well as the wealthy. How interesting it was to see him driving on a carriage to visit the sick, as he waved his hand right and left with an exuberant "*Dzień Dobry*," and smiled heartily at anyone passing through the street. He administered first aid on the second story of his home, where various instruments for different purposes were scattered on his table. "Operating" on a finger, repairing a break, and other such treatments were carried out by his special, expert hands. He never used his special talents for his own needs. If someone was unable to pay the fees, Melech would sneak out of his house in a way that even a thank you could not be extended to him... Some people said that he even used his own money to purchase the medicines that he prescribed... Indeed, he was a fine, interesting personality in our community of Turka. Who can forget him?

*

For many years, Naftali Kraus, a Jew dedicated to Zionism with heart and soul, was the patron of the Hashomer Hatzair chapter of out town. He experienced ups and downs in his economic and business life. He endured many changes in a very short time. Despite this, he never held back even one iota with his special dedication to the Hashomer Hatzair movement and other Zionist movements. It was his character to be dedicated and to concern himself with the public. Whenever a problem affected any of the movements, he did everything he could to solve it through his connections with the local authorities. He was very active during election times for the Sejm, the town council or the community. Alongside this relationship to the community, he was also a source of support in any matter for any individual. He was prepared to help in matters of work, *aliya*, preparation of papers for the district office, and other such needs. Everything that he did was done with a sense of love for his fellow Jew. Along with his children who are living here in the Land, we will remember him forever.

*

Now we will discuss a completely different type of personality – Moshe Shein. The concept of "popular orator" was exemplified in this man. From the time we knew him, he belonged the Social Democratic Party and served as it spokesman in the town. Whether it was before elections, before the First of May, or before any other communal event – Shein always stood at the head of the activity. His speeches were delivered with pathos. He would stand atop a barrel in the center of the city and speak – primarily in Polish. With his strange gestures, he would enthuse his audience, which consisted of people of all ages and types, without difference between race and religion. Most of the time, he closed his eyes and spoke everything that was in his heart... He would often move from the topic of elections to a different topic in the middle of his speech, whether to a matter connected to municipal issues or even to a debate on a religious topic... He was involved in the communal activities of the city; he was a mediator, and someone who pursued justice. Masses of people would consult with him regarding their private matters, and he would serve as a proper intercessor. He was an impressive personality in our landscape. M. Shein was of the same large, wide-branched family in the town whose children and descendents were active in the various youth-Zionist-pioneering movements in particular and often stood at the help of these movements. Indeed, they conducted all of their work with talent and great dedication. Some of them are continuing their activities in our Land. We will recall their family with reverence and love.

[Page 62]

*

I will describe a dear personality, someone I will always recall with appreciation and affection, for the man was close to my heart. He was a friend of my father of blessed memory, and a friend of my family, Reb Aharon Spiegler of blessed memory. There were not many like him in the town. He did not stand out in communal activity, nor did he elbow his way into an important position in the kloiz or any other place, for he found his honor in any place where he was found... I knew him and his family, for I would spend a lot of time in their house, just as my friend Shmuel was like one of our family. Reb Aharon earned his livelihood through the toil of his hands. He was a tailor, and two of sons worked with him. He exemplified the concept of a man who occupies himself with Torah and labor. He was an educated man. Torah never departed from his lips. Even though he was part of the Hassidic, Torah studying community from a social perspective, on the inside he was a progressive man. He was patient with his fellowman. He educated and raised his sons in the same spirit. Spiegler was knowledgeable in philosophical concepts from various schools of thought, and he was familiar with the various streams of enlightened Hebrew literature. He tried to acquaint himself with Modern Hebrew literature. He knew how to quote from classical works in their original or in translation during his family and social conversations. Debates with him on world philosophies were interesting. During the free time on Sabbaths and festivals, I would always see him simultaneously looking into holy books and secular books... He had the image of a *maskil* with fine, generous traits. It was pleasant for us young people to enter his domain and listen to his conversations.

*

Rabbi Eliezer Mishel, who was nicknamed "The Golgower Rabbi" (on account of the city in which he served before he was appointed rabbi of Turka), was a man with a Jewish heart and spirit. In the town, he was known as a "neutral" rabbi, meaning that he was not a Hassid, but was also not a *misnaged*. He was graced with sublime character traits. In addition to his greatness in Torah, he would greet every person with whom he came into contact in a pleasant manner. He was pleasant to all those who came to his rabbinical court for adjudication or to ask questions of kashruth and matters of ritual purity. He found a common language with everyone, and his influence was not small. The rabbi was an expert scholar both in the revealed Torah and in the hidden Torah [*kabbalah*]. He had a sharp mind and the gift of expression to explain various subjects in Jewish law before those who came to be judged by him. When he was in exile in Budapest during the First World War, the rabbi authored a book of response and sermons, and he also published footnotes to the *Tosafot*[3]. As a youth, I used to accompany my father of holy blessed memory to visit him and worship in his home. My father was one of those who frequented his home, and one of his friends and admirers. The rabbi's entire family was friends of our family. My father of holy blessed memory served as the prayer leader on the High Holidays in the rabbi's *shtibel* for many years. I recall his public lectures on *Shabbat Shuva* and *Shabbat Hagadol*[4], and the great event of the Balfour Declaration is etched in my memory. I recall the mass gathering that took place in the Sadagora Kloiz at that time. (Incidentally, the Sadagora Kloiz was the sole remnant after the destruction of the city during the First World War.) The leaders of the Zionist movements spoke with emotion, giving expression to this great event. The sermon of the rabbi of the city, Rabbi Mishel, was literally top notch. We felt that this was a liberation from all of the "impediments" which were restricted on account of communal relations and maintaining communal peace – both from the side of the assimilationists as well as from the side of the Hassidim[5]. His words were literally in the spirit of a Zionist manifesto, and were it not for his greatness and wisdom, the foolish Hassidim in the city would certainly not have forgiven this "sin" of his...

[Page 63]

Rabbi Mishel was a wonderful and noble personality to everyone in the city. His facial appearance befitted him. His silvery beard that flowed over his robes, exuded honor, and added the charm of his appearance. Aside from his expertise in Torah, he was expert in the ways of the world, and knew several languages. Most of the Jews found it interesting to hear his opinion on important world matters, and especially on matters of the Jewish world. To us, the Zionist, pioneering youth, to the General Zionists and Mizrachi, it was clear that the rabbi was a Zionist from the depths of his heart. It was sufficient to hear how he blessed and took leave of those of us, myself included, who were making *aliya* to the Land, and had come to receive his blessing. The manner of his farewell and his blessing was an expression of a love of Zion. It is worthwhile to note that aside from his virtues, he was also known for his simplicity. He did not set up a barrier between himself and the community, and many people were his friends with heart and soul. He was not only the city rabbi and rabbinical judge, but also a friend, a scholar, and a lover of his fellow man. There is no doubt that his personality forged the character of the

Jewish community during the period of his tenure. His honor was the honor of the Jews of the city, of all strata.

*

[Page 64]

It is difficult for me to conclude my article without mentioning with a large breath of reverence the families, big and small, who forged the character of the town, who took control of all the areas in which they set their variegated efforts – good and upright tradesman, merchants, shopkeepers, *shamashim* [beadles] and other clergy – together formed a large community.

However you should know: I do have to do this, but I do not have the power to present to you the families, with their names and personalities, one by one. How can we skip over the Jewish proletariat there, "on the Stryj," without presenting a faithful impression and picture? Indeed, these were the proletariat in the active sense, and not of a single variety. We knew them well and appreciated them at the time, when our friends worked together with them in the sawmill. This was a relatively short time before this group made *aliya* to the Land. Of course, we must turn northwest toward the "Cyglania," and then turn eastward "to the Petrik" – in every corner and every hill, we set foot on a mountain and a valley, the proud feet of the Jewish youth; we will remember all of them forever, and we will perpetuate them eternally in our hearts.

In conclusion, I will remember our father Reb Yisrael of holy blessed memory, our brother Yosef and their families, who did not merit being with us here. Can we tell about them? Can we film the experiences of our life as one family? An article will not express our love, reverence, pain and sorrow over those who were so very dear to us. Those, who were taken away from our bosom – is there a day, holiday, or festival when we do not recall you?

Let these few lines serve as a monument to my town Turka, and a recitation of *Kaddish.*

Translator's Footnotes:

36. Eliezer Ben Yehuda, one of the founders of the Modern Hebrew language.
37. Rabbi Nachman Krochmal.
38. The Tosafot is one of the major commentaries on the Talmud.
39. *Shabbat Shuva* is the Sabbath between Rosh Hashanah and Yom Kippur. *Shabbat Hagadol* is the Sabbath before Passover. It is customary for the rabbi to deliver a major sermon on both of those Sabbaths.
40. Both groups, for different reasons, opposed Zionism.

[Page 65]

As it was Back Then in the Old Home

Shmuel Spigler of Tel Aviv

Shmuel Spigler

My annihilated father and mother, Aharon and Feiga Spigler of blessed memory;My sister Pesha with her delightful child, who were killed;My murdered brothers Yehuda and MosheIn memory.

Once again I can see the small, wooden houses with the shingle roofs, the large houses and the various businesses, the market place, the Ulica, the Targowica, the upper town, the *Beis Midrashes*, synagogues, *cheders* and Talmud Torahs; as well as various organizations, including Hitachdut, Hechalutz, and Hashomer Hatzair. The people of the town, its scholars, teachers, *shochtim* (ritual slaughterers), musicians, toilers, shoemakers, tailors and water carriers. The wise men and orators – a treasury of personalities who lived and breathed, created and worked in our small town of Turka.

I again see it during the six days of the week, during its secular times as well as during its Sabbaths and festivals; in its times of agony and sadness as well as in its ebullient joy, hoping and believing. I again breathe the sweet pleasantness of the forests, the flowing of its hidden streams, and the green meadows in which we all used to sit together, dreaming and believing in a finer and better world.

Friday in *Cheder*

It was wintertime in the town. White snow covered the entire town like a large, white sheet. It was neat and clean. All of the roofs of the large and small houses were covered with deep snow. The windows were frozen, and covered with various forms of ice flowers. It was the eve of the Sabbath. We came from the upper town, and went around the mountain on sleds, until we came to the wide, wooden bridge. The river was frozen over, and children were skating over the wide river. The old, gentile water carrier would stand by the edge, filling up pails of water, loading them onto the wagons and carrying them to the Jewish houses in honor of the Sabbath.

[Page 66]

The frost "burnt". We walked on. The snow crunched under our feet. Suddenly, we see the bridge. We turned to the left, and went through the Czortkower, Belz and Sadagora Kloizes. There was an old, crooked, run down cottage not far from there. We would stand there and peer through the small, frost-covered windows – yes, this is him, our schoolteacher Yisrael-Leibele Kilowocz, as he was called in the town. We go through the wide, low door, and dressed in our *kitzmes*[1] fur coats and boots, and sit down on the wooden bench around the table. The Rebbe with his bamboo stick, begins. We open up our *Chumashes* and review the weekly Torah portion for the last time before the test.

The Rebbe begins: "Repeat, children, once again: "*vaani – un ich...*"[2]. We all began to recite out loud, with voices clanging like bells filling up the small, cold room: "*Vaani – un ich.*" Although I am troubling you with my burial, I was not able to do so for your mother Rachel, for. "*Bevoi*" -- as I was coming from Padan Aram, "*Meita – is geshtorben*", "*alay – oif mir*", 'Rachel – your mother Rachel..." Thus did we repeat the entire Torah Portion of *Vayechi* verse by verse. After that, we reviewed the Torah portion with the cantillation. We finished quickly, got dressed, went out the door, and went out side with a tumult. Then we played in the snow and ice.

With the Rabbi

It was as if by magic that the small house, the rabbi, the cane, the long, wooden table and the benches disappeared – and we, hand in hand, went further on... And then we were standing before a house not far from the Sadagora Kloiz, where the rabbi of the city, the Gologower Rabbi, Rabbi Eliezer Mishel, lived upstairs. He was a great scholar, sharp and expert also in secular subjects, and known throughout Galicia.

[Page 67]

We went inside. There were two Jewish women with hens in their hands in the anteroom, about to ask a Halachic question. The rabbi was very lenient, only very rarely declaring something non-kosher. We entered the large room. The rabbi had a splendid countenance. He was dressed in a long frock with a warm Spencer atop, sitting on a leather stool around a long, oak table, covered with a tablecloth. There were four large, silver candlesticks on the table. His two wise, dark eyes were peering into an open book before him. His high forehead wrinkled and pondered. His long white beard flowed over the Spencer. There was a large, silk yarmulke over his grey, hoary head. On one side there was a closet going up to the ceiling, packed with books. The entire room smelled like yellow parchment, holiness and erudition. A calm pervaded.

Both of his sons, great scholars themselves, sat in the second room. The oldest – as people whispered about town – even went out to a bad crowd and looked into the "books". Along with Talmud and Halachic decisions, he studied mathematics and philosophy, and would get together with youths who would discuss and debate what is above and what is below, attempting to clarify matters...

I recall as if today how our fathers used to partake of the Purim feast or spend Simchat Torah with the rabbi, as we absorbed his scholarly general conversation, filled with wisdom of life, depth and sharpness. The *rebbetzin* would look into the room from time to time, enter the room, with love and respect place a piping hot glass of tea in front of the rabbi, and exit.

In the Bathhouse

The frost was biting. We remain downstairs, breathe in again in the house and the "dwelling", and walk on further... Then we find ourselves not far from the bathhouse. Jews of the town, old and young, with bags of underwear and towels under their arms, run to bathe and take a steam bath in honor of the Sabbath. They would cast off the toil of the entire week, cast off the yoke of livelihood, the trials of childrearing and other tribulation, at least for one day.

[Page 68]

Sabbath eve at the bathhouse

We enter. It is warm and stuffy inside. There is a warm mist in the air and it smells sour. It was stuffed with people. The bathhouse was the only place where the entire town was equal... there is no eastern wall... there is no sixth *aliya* or *maftir*... there is no rich and poor. Everyone is under the same vapor, which they loved, and which was refreshing... The well-off householders sit on the upper bench along with the shoemakers and tailors – everyone whom G-d had created. They sat there with the pails of cold water in their hands, flaming red faces, and sweat dripping down. Chazkele stands as always next to the wood stove. He was an elderly Jew who loved to tipple. Whether at a wedding or a *yahrzeit* observance, he would be chief among the drinkers. He stands there, pouring the pails of water onto the oven. He then smacks the hot mist, which sprays all the way to the upper benches. Everyone calls out, "Ah, ah ah, hu, hu hu! Chazkel, another one!" Chazkel does so, for Chazkel does not economize... The heat increased from minute to minute. People would run into the *mikva* with stony steps and immerse themselves in accordance with custom. It was indeed a kosher *mikva*, and it was a mitzvah to immerse oneself therein.

[Page 69]

It was starting to get late. People left the bathhouse individually or in groups. They got dressed at home and prepared themselves for services.

In the Kloiz

It is getting dark, and night is falling. The holy Sabbath candles, kindled by our G-d fearing mothers as they wept and wished good health and livelihood for the entire family, flicker through the frozen windows. We all don our Sabbath clothes and walk with our fathers to the *kloiz* to welcome the Sabbath.

Dudi Kardish stands by the prayer leader's lectern in the Sadagora Kloiz to welcome the Sabbath, "*Lechu neranena Lashem, naria letzur yisheinu... Lechu dodi likras kala, pnei Shabbat nekabela.*"[3] We recite the Friday night service and set out for home.

Everyone is dressed in their heavy fur coats and *streimels*. The wealthy people wear expensive *karekolen* furs[4] and the regular people with fur coats that were shedding. Everyone goes home, some with a guest and some without a guest, to welcome the Sabbath in their homes.

[Page 70]

At the Covered Table

Inside the houses, everything is clean and tidy. Every corner smelled. The table is covered with a white tablecloth. The silver candelabra, the wine and the covered challas were prepared. The mother, dressed in her Sabbath clothes, with a kerchief on her head and a white apron, sits and enjoyed the surroundings. She enjoys satisfaction because G-d had helped her with everything until this point, and would likely continue to help her – does she have a choice?

The father recites "*Shalom Aleichem malachei hasharet,*" and then, the heartfelt "*Eshet chail mi yimtza*" He then fills up the cup and recites the Sabbath *Kiddush*. Everyone sits around the table. Mother serves the fish and meat, and then everyone begins to hum the Sabbath hymns with joy and faith, praising His beloved Name. "*Kol mekadhesh Shevii karaui lo," and "Ka ribbon alam vealmaya.*" The mother glows: it is a pleasure to look at her and her entire house.

The sons and daughters have already long ago left the house. They left their parents at home by the flickering candles, as they were looking into *Tzena Urena* or a book[5]. The younger generation went out to seek a new way and life, a new content. It began to be constricting in the four ells of the house and the *Beis Midrash*. New winds began to blow in the streets of the town. The era of seeking and longing for other forms of life began. The G-d of Abraham, Isaac and Jacob, *Chumash* and *Rashi*, *Choshen Mishpat* and *Yoreh Deah*[6] no longer brought joy. New gods and new ideals began to appear that attracted and carried away the youth.

Thus did Father and Mother remain by the flickering candles, with their old faith in the G-d of Abraham – as their daughters went out from the nest to seek new food, new spiritual food to calm the thirsty souls.

New Ways...

We walk on further... We already realize that aside from the Turka of satin and silk, women's head coverings and strands of pearls, Talmud and Halachic decisors, *Tzena Urena* and *Ein Yaakov*, there was another Turka -- a Turka of vibrant, creative youth, of groups of *maskilim* vehemently seeking new ways, who began to band together to attack the way of life of the elder generation. A word went around that the Turka skies were covered with rags from which new guests descended during those times, which with the passage of time became old residents and began to be the new trendsetters, penetrating the minds of the youth, bringing new notions and problems of G-d and man, man and the world, Schaffenhauer and Nietzsche, Hegel and Kant, Freud and Wininger from one side; Iveson-Strindberg, Roman Rolon-Barbis, Tolsoy-Dolstoyevsky-Gorki; and with them, the entire precious *haskala* literature in Hebrew and Yiddish: Mapu, Smolenskin, Feuerberg, Mendele, Shalom Aleichem, Asch and Bergelson – from the second side. They, the new guests, formed a new way of living and a new form of man. These were all factors in the creation of a national-worldly way of life for the youth of the town.

[Page 71]

The return to Zion, the Land of Israel, the Western Wall – which were once so far, were no longer a dream. They began to take on flesh and bones. Zionism was no longer a hollow notion, but rather became a subject around which the youth began to form various groups, the strongest and most influential of which at that time was, without doubt, Hashomer Hatzair. Already a that time, it played a significant role in Jewish life throughout all of Poland, and especially in Galicia. Throughout the large cities of Congress Poland and Galicia, Hashomer Hatzair was composed for the most part of academic youth whose mother tongue was Polish both at home and on the street. They brought that atmosphere into the movement, and the entire scouting and cultural work was conducted in the Polish language, and only partly in Hebrew. However, the development of the youth of the small towns in Poland, especially in Galicia, was entirely different.

[Page 72]

The youth of the small towns in Galicia who filled up the Hashomer Hatzair organization and bound their way of life and weltanschauung to that movement, stemmed primarily from the petite bourgeois classes of society, small-scale merchants, tradesmen, observant houses, where Yiddish was the mother tongue both in the home and on the street.

Those small-town youth brought elements into Hashomer Hatzair that were strange and lacking in the larger cities. Those elements included Yiddish Literature, Hassidic enthusiasm and devotion, and the popular melody and song. Those youth revealed the "hidden light" of the *Beis Midrash* and the Jewish home to the movement. They further branched out from the historicity of Judaism, from old content to new forms. In that sense, Turka stood out among Hashomer Hatzair throughout Galicia. With time, the "way of Turka" broke out of its borders, and moved beyond.

In Hashomer Hatzair

... It is a warm, summer night. We are strolling through the town and are now close to the Hashomer Hatzair meeting place – and a calm, heartfelt melody reaches us. A tune – long, stretched out, full of longing. It is full of longing and the agony of the world. We enter, and unite ourselves with the others. It is a small, dark room. Avraham Monaster, Leibush Mandel, and David Langenauer, all *Beis Midrash* students who found their path into Hashomer Hatzair, are sitting there. They are all sitting, crowded together, and singing with their hearts and souls, as if one was observing the third Sabbath meal on the Sabbath afternoon. Hassidic melodies filled with devotion and enthusiasm, as well folk songs filled with joy and faith fill that little rom.

On another occasion in the meeting place –

In a large room, they are preparing for a performance which will shortly take place. Melech Brauer, the play director of the town, was a broad shouldered, chubby man; but inside him was housed an artistic soul. He is standing in the middle of the room, reviewing the roles of Peretz Hirshbein's "Grine Felder" with zest and enthusiasm. Yetke Reifler, Dudi Wolf, Izik Zolinger and the writer of these lines performed in it.

[Page 74]

And further: In a third room, the counselors sit and hold a discussion with small groups regarding the Land of Israel, Kibbutz, *Hachshara*, and other day to day questions of the organization.

Suddenly, it became bright and light in the entire premises, as a fervent hora began. The circle grew from minute to minute. Young and "old" entered the circle; the singing grew stronger and wilder, and could be heard outside.

*

In this manner life went on, year in and year out, from one generation to the next, in our beloved, small town.

This all once was – and today?...

Mother and father, brothers and sisters, relatives and friends whom we loved so very much are no longer there.

Therefore, let all of us survivors of Turka, here in the old-new homeland as well as in the entire world, continue to give a backward glance to our town, which is no more...

[Page 73]

A group of older members of Hashomer Hatzair during the visit to Turka of Yitzchak Sheiz of blessed memory of Kibbutz Merchavia in 1934

[Page 75]

The Sabbath in our Town

by Zeev Steininger of Netanya

Zeev Steininger

We felt the festive atmosphere not only on the Sabbath rest day, the day on which the city rested from all work, when all the stores were closed, when the streets were quiet without movement. Despite the fact that Turka was a mixed city of Poles, Ukrainians and Jews, the Sabbath was felt very clearly, for the center of the city, from the bridge leading to the village until the beginning of the upper area, was settled by Jews, and all of the shops were in Jewish hands. We also felt this atmosphere during Friday afternoon, as the preparations to greet the Sabbath Queen were in progress.

Hastening to the Bathhouse...

The shops were closed, and most of the Jewish population hastened to the bathhouse (steam-bath) in order to bathe and immerse in the *mikva*, to remove their weekday clothes and change them for their Sabbath clothes – and to prepare themselves to greet the Sabbath.

The bathhouse was housed in a building on the banks of the river that was not overly modern. It operated on Friday with "full steam." It was in service during the middle of the week as well, but on that day, it serviced the masses. When you entered the dark hall of the bathhouse, you would immediately meet a tall, strong, mustached gentile who was in charge of the oven, which was made of smooth stones. He had a pail of water in his hands. From time to time, he would pour the water on the red hot stones, and the mist would rise upward, upwards... The bathers would be sitting on the broad, wooden steps, beating their bodies with brooms made of leaves. Suddenly, you would hear the call "Iwan, *Dowoj*" – telling the gentile to pour another pail upon the red hot stones. When the mist rose, you would hear sounds of satisfaction. It seemed like a struggle to overtake the growing heat... Apparently, these sounds housed the secrets of the bath, which, along with the preparation of the additional soul for the advent of the Sabbath, was also instrumental in preserving the cleanliness and health of the people. (Indeed, the thought would come from time to time that the strong desire of our people to maintain themselves throughout the long exile was related to the set of customs, apparently connected to religion, but also connected to elementary needs that are vital for the physical existence of man.) At the end of the steam bath, they would descend into the *mikva* of cold water. When you left the *mikva*, you would drink a cup of "*most*", which is a juice made from dried apples – the monopoly of family of Filinger and his sons.

[Page 76]

On the Sabbath Next to the Post Office...

When the Sabbath descended, everyone was dressed in their finery, with *bekishes* and *streimels*. Everyone hastened to the synagogue for the Sabbath prayers. After the prayers, they walked home calmly for *Kiddush* and the Sabbath eve meal. Then, most of the youth would gather together in their organizations to spend time in song, dance and discussions.

On the Sabbath – Reb Hersh Filinger on his way to the synagogue

[Page 77]

It was the Sabbath morning. The streets were quiet, and Jews were walking along the streets toward the synagogue, slowly and calmly, garbed in their *tallises*. They went in groups, each group to its own synagogue. A unique experience, as if it was part of the Sabbath, took place in another section of the city, where the post office was located. Next to the parapet along the street, the masses, dressed in their Sabbath clothes, waited for the post office workers to exit the post office. When the two postal workers left, one turned to the long hallway of the next building, and the other turned to the other corner. The waiting masses were standing around. The postal workers quietly removed letters and newspapers from their large sack, and distributed to each person what was coming to them. In general, the newspapers, political weeklies or monthlies according to their respective parties, would arrive on the Sabbath. After a time you would see how each person retreated to his corner, with a newspaper or booklet in his hands, and immerse himself in reading. You would also see groups discussing the issues of the day. These people were from the various Zionist groups, and generally young, progressive people. The Orthodox people and the adults were already at the synagogue at that time.

Synagogues and Houses of Worship

Most of the synagogues of the town were concentrated in one area, not far from the main street that leads upward to the Szymunka Mountain. If you turned to the left, you would find the Belzer Kloiz, which incidentally contained within its walls a large Torah library. On Sabbath afternoons, you cold always meet people there sitting next to the long table, studying and deliberating over a chapter of *Mishna*. Opposite was the Czortkower Kloiz. As you crossed the narrow street, there would also be the central synagogue of the city – a large, spacious, fine building, built during the 1930s. Again to the right, on a small hill, was the largest synagogue – the Sadagora Kloiz. It was a very spacious building. The Tailor's Synagogue (Das Shneider Shulchel) was located next to the central city synagogue.

Of course, all of the synagogues were full of worshippers on Sabbaths. Each Hassid went to his own synagogue. Each synagogue had its own eastern wall, and against the eastern wall, each synagogue had its own honorable members. During the High Holidays, another house of worship was added – the "Ochoronka" (Orphanage) – in which, for the most part, progressive folk and Zionists worshipped.

The Rabbi of the City

If you would take a few more steps from the Sadagora Kloiz, you would end up at a large, spacious building.

[Page 78]

At least half of it was in ruins, and after you ascended the steps which were literally affixed to the air, you would enter a long hallway. If you turned left, you would enter a small room, and find three or for *minyanim* of Jewish worshipping. This was the seat of the rabbi of the city. During weekdays, the long hallway served as the waiting room for those coming to ask questions or to clarify a matter of law.

The rabbi sat in the interior room, upon an upholstered armchair with a rubber pillow. He had white hair, his beard was well-groomed, and he was dressed appropriately. He was always hunched over a *Gemara*, and he looked into it even during the times of prayer.

At times, we would see the rabbi riding in a carriage on weekdays, dressed in a black *kapote*. He was apparently on his way to some reception or mission to the local authorities. We, especially the Jewish students in the schools, would also meet him on official national holidays. On such days, all of the students would gather in the Sadagora Kloiz for a festive gathering of school students. The students, accompanied by their teachers, would enter the synagogue in rows. Government figures would also be present, occupying places at the eastern wall. Kardish, a Jew who had the established claim for doing so at such events, would then ascend the podium and offer a prayer of thanks for the government and the head of state. Following him, the rabbi would ascend, and deliver words of blessing appropriate for the holiday in a weak and quiet voice. It was hard to hear his words exactly. He would only raise his voice at the end, and conclude his words with a call of "*Hoch, hoch, hoch.*" The Great Synagogue not only served as a gathering place for masses of Jews on Sabbaths and festivals, but also served as a gathering place for special occasions.

[Page 79]

The Eve of Yom Kippur

by Shmuel Spigler of Tel Aviv

(a section)

... The shops were closed early enough, and the streets were almost empty of people. In every place and every corner, I felt as if something great and sublime was approaching.

Some of the residents of the town went to supplicate at the graves of their dear ones, asking them to be righteous intercessors before the Heavenly court, so that they would be granted a good year, a year of good livelihood, a year of peace and contentment.

Those who were stringent and exacting throughout the entire year about both light and heavy matters, and who would be even more so approaching the great and awesome day, went to the *mikva* to immerse their bodies and purify themselves for the Day of Judgment, so that they would be spotless when they went to approach the Creator of the World with a serious spirit and broken soul.

The Beis Midrash located in the center of the town was still empty, aside from a few Jews who stood by their lecterns immersed in prayer from the time they arose in the morning. Among them was Reb Berl the *shochet* (ritual slaughterer).

Reb Berl the *shochet* was an upright, G-d fearing Jew. He walked with G-d all of his days. Throughout the year, he would earn his livelihood from *shechita*, and on festivals, especially on Rosh Hashanah and Yom Kippur, he would serve as the prayer leader without expectation of payment. He did not make his prayers into a spade with which to dig[7]. Reb Berl would supplicate with a sweet voice, and it was certain that his sweet prayers emanated from his heart, steering their course among the thousands of prayers that stream heavenward on the night of Yom Kippur, bringing a good year and a positive conclusion of judgment upon the congregation of worshippers.

Just as he knew how to take caution in the laws of *shechita*, and would sharpen his knife with fear and trepidation every morning before services, lest it have a knick that would cause pain to a living being; he would spend the days and nights between Rosh Hashanah and Yom Kippur in the *Beis Midrash* with afflictions and prayers, in order to prepare himself for the great and holy night – the night of Yom Kippur.

[Page 80]

During the afternoon, one would find the Jews of the town hastening to recite *Mincha* (the afternoon service), and then returning home immediately after the conclusion of the services. Slowly the streets of the town would empty out, and no living soul would be seen outside. Everyone was at home, around the table, partaking of the concluding meal, the final meal before the great day. Father and Mother would kiss their children with tears in their eyes and stifled sobs, as they would wish them a good year and a positive sealing of judgment, a year of blessing and not a curse, plenty and not scarcity, a year without illness and evil afflictions. Father donned his white *kittel*, and put on the leatherless shoes. Mother was resplendent, dressed in a new dress, with a silk kerchief on her head and a festival prayer book under her shoulder – prepared to leave momentarily together with us children to go to the House of Prayer.

The sun was already giving off its last rays, with a reddish hue behind the town. Evening was descending, and the Jews of the town, elders and fine young men, dressed in their white *kittels*, socks and slippers, their *tallises* and festival prayer books under their shoulders, and set out for the synagogue along with the women and children.

בשם השם יתברך!

קערת ערב יום כפור

לטובת

ישיבת דגל התורה

בטורקא על נהר סטרי

עשה למען תנוקות של בית רבן!
הרם דגל התורה ותתרומם!
עורו והתעוררו למען ישובו בנים לגבולם!

In the name of the Blessed G-d!
The plate of the Eve of Yom Kippur
For the benefit of
The Degel Torah Yeshiva
In Turka on the Stryj River
Act on behalf of the students of the house of study!
Raise up the flag of Torah and be elevated!
Arise and arouse yourselves for restoring the children to their bounds.}

[Page 81]

The Beis Midrash of the Belz Hassidim continued to fill up moment by moment. Inside, there was great light from the chandeliers and lit candles, placed in jars, pots and various other vessels. The rabbinical judge Rabbi Yehuda was already standing next to the Holy Ark, enwrapped in his *tallis*, with its heavy adornment sparkling from afar. Honorable householders, 'fine Jews" were sitting at the eastern wall. Behind them were the shopkeepers, tradesman, teachers, and other clergy. The horse merchants, wagon drivers, water carriers, and tree hewers sat near the rear (in the "*polish*") , all enwrapped in their tallies, with their prayer books before them.

Reb Berl the *shochet* was already standing at the prayer lectern, as he had already had the rights of serving as the prayer leader for *Kol Nidrei* and *Musaf* of Yom Kippur for many years. Silence fell upon everyone. Stifled weeping and sighing could be heard only from the women's section. The Holy Ark was opened, and Reb Berl the *shochet* began with a loud, ringing voice, in awe and trepidation:

"Light is sown for the righteous, and joy for the upright of heart." The entire congregation along with the rabbi, as one unit, repeated this verse seven times after him with devotion and great love. The melody continued on, breaking through the walls of the **Beis Midrash** and filling the atmosphere of the town with the splendor of holiness. "With the consent of the Almighty and the consent of the congregation... *Kol Nidrei...* And the entire house of Israel shall be forgiven along with the stranger in their midst... May our supplication ascend from evening, and may our prayers come to you in the morning..." One prayer chases another, and the entire service with its unique melodies penetrated the recesses of the body. I stood affixed to the side of my father, in awe and trepidation from the great and holy sight that was revealed before my eyes...

[Page 82]

From the Hassidic Religious Life in our City

by Rabbi Alter Weinberger of New York

Rabbi Alter Weinberger

Hassidism is not the monopoly of Torah scholars, of dignified Jews, and of so-called well-pedigreed Jews. Hassidism does not know of such things. The essence of Hassidism equalizes and elevates every Jew, discovers the quintessence of everyone and brings it out to the open, as we say: "He examines and investigates the hidden storehouses"[8] – the Blessed G-d seeks out the good that is hidden in a Jew, even if he is coarse and weekday-like, very weekday-like. However, there is a treasury of good within every Jew, and the Blessed G-d seeks it and draws it out.

This is what I want to say about this: to write about Hassidic life in our city does not only mean to write about specific Hassidim – from the Sadagora Kloiz, Czortkow Kloiz, Belzer Kloiz, Zidichower Hassidim, Komoriner Hassidim, or Blazower Hassidim – and our town was indeed rich with them. The main thing is to write about the influence, the indirect influence that Hassidism had in general on the local synagogue Jew, village Jew, and tradesmen, such as shoemakers, tailors and the like.

As an example, I wish to write here about what took place in our town in 1939. When the Hungarians took over Carpatho-Rus from the Czechs "with the permission of the entire community," young Jewish people from Carptho-Rus and Hungary began to escape. They fled to seek out better things. They fled and found. For the most part, they fled over the border at Uzhok, Sianki, Volovech, and other such places. The fearsome, well-known Polish police fortified the border guard, and of course captured people and beat them with cruel, deathly blows. Then they came out with a new decree –

[Page 83]

in any Jewish house in which they would find "such merchandise", they would deal with the entire house, and it would not be honey that they would lick.

Thus it was: At that time, I and all my children, may G-d avenge their deaths, were sick with typhus, may G-d protect us. My following friends happened to be sitting with us at the time: Reb Shimshon Hirsch may peace be upon him, Reb Shmuel Yeger may peace be upon him, Reb Shlomo Heler, Reb Tzvi Filinger may G-d avenge their deaths. Suddenly, my friends Reb Melech Brauer and Reb Matis Maus, may G-d avenge their deaths, entered with great brotherliness, and they shouted: That night, they deported the Krupka family of Jablonka to Sambor. The family included the elderly father Reb Shlomo Yitzchak and his two sons Menashe and Yechiel. Their crime was that they found two young refugees from Hungary in their house the day before. They were undertaking great efforts to arrange to free them. The tragedy was even greater, because the two children Menashe and his brother Yechiel were literally supposed to leave to America on the last ship! Therefore, they begged me to write to Rabbi Dr. Mizes, may G-d avenge his blood (who was my friend) that he should intercede on their behalf. I told them, "How can I help, I am lying here with 42 degree fever?"

I asked Reb Shmuel Yeger of blessed memory to write to Rabbi Dr. Mizes in my name. Thus it was. Three days later, Reb Melech Brauer and Reb Matis Maus were again here. They said that it was working out well, but we must immediately provide 300 zloty. Then, they would be released, and would be able to travel to America. However, from where could one obtain the money?! I gave them advice. They went and came – the time was indeed very awkward. It was evening, but we were literally talking about the redemption of captives. What could then do?! And here I was tied to my bed, Heaven protect us. I then told my friends Melech and Matis: "Please forgive me, call my uncle Reb David Weinberger, may G-d avenge his blood, and we will talk together about the burning problem." I then used my good influence on my dear uncle to ask him to procure the money. He went and did so – he sold 300 meters of Kraszniak linen, and gave them they money. Thus they were able to free the prominent Krupka family from prison in Sambor. Menashe and Yechiel, may they be well, set out for America in peace on the last ship.

The Ukrainians assisted the Polish police to capture our Jewish children – and our fellow Jews, all in unison, helped and saved them with great dedication. May their memories be blessed.

[Page 84]

Hassidic Personalities

I now want to characterize certain personalities from the Hassidic community of our city:

From the Belzer Kloiz:

Reb Yisrael Langenauer – A Jew who earned his livelihood from the toil of his hands in a bakery. He was a scholar, pious in his ways. To look at such a Jew, with his comportment and his pure manner of speech, one would be filled with respect for a Hassidic Jew. May G-d avenge his blood.

Reb Abish Shreiber – A Hassidic Jew from Vilna. Full of charm. Of blessed memory.

Reb David Weinberger – A joyous Hassid. He would bring joy to troubled people, and extend a hand to help everyone with purity, brotherliness, and respect. He was a wonderful host of guests. He led the society that tends to needy brides (*Hachnasat Kalla*) on Saturday evenings. On the Sabbath before someone's wedding, the society would go out on Saturday night with a drum to play a round of *Mazel Tov,* and make a celebration. They would accept money from a wealthy groom, and give money to a poor groom. May G-d avenge his blood.

My brother-in-law, the young man Reb Yosef Weinberger, may G-d avenge his blood – would give lessons, guard and serve on the leadership committee[9] – all without recompense.

Reb Eliezer Karpiol Was a Modern-Hassidic Jew with a great deal of refinement and sharpness. May G-d avenge his blood.

Similar to them were: Reb Avraham Hirsch, Reb Chaim Hirsch, Reb Hirsch-Leib Schreiber the son of Shmuel, and Reb Shaul Keller.

Sadagora Kloiz:

Reb Gedalia Mandel was a great scholar, a Jew who loved Torah. He served on the *Yeshiva* committee and used to take great interest in the *Yeshiva* students.

[Page 85]

Reb David, who was called Dudia Kardish, was a beloved Hassidic Jew, and a fine prayer leader. May G-d avenge his death.

Among them were also: Reb Berish Shochet, Reb Shmuel Rozen.

Czortkower Kloiz:

Reb Shimon Hirsch who was known as Reb Shimon Sanis, was an exquisite, refined personality, who spoke little. May G-d avenge his blood.

Reb Shlomo Heller, a dignified Jew, was very knowledgeable in Hassidism. He was one of the directors of the *Yeshiva*, without receiving recompense. May G-d avenge his blood.

Reb Shmuel Yeger, was a remarkable Hassid, and a great doer of good.

Reb Avraham Langenauer was a scholarly Hassid, and a refined person. May G-d avenge his blood.

Reb Chaim Aharon Treiber as a fine Jew.

I must say that such a Jew as Reb Leizer Monaster was a fine thing and a jewel for the city. He was full of good, and a sincere prayer leader. May G-d avenge his blood.

*

On a Sabbath or festival in our city, all Jews were like one family.

One a winter night in the Belzer Kloiz, everyone, young and old, would occupy a place with a candle, and sit and learn for hours.

If a Rebbe was in the town, it was like a holiday for all the Jews for the entire eight days.

The Talmud Torah

The Talmud Torah was admirable, with the discipline, fine behavior and great success in study of its students. We set up the Talmud Torah literally without money. The basis was 25 dollars each month from the Turka Society in America.

We had 170 children distributed among 12 teachers. Half the number of teachers would have also been sufficient. However we did not want to encroach on the livelihood of the teachers. It was literally difficult for them. They were not paid with cash, but rather with coupons for the grain businesses, for which we all paid.

[Page 86]

Rev Wolftshe the teacher was the supervisor. He would visit the teachers every day. Each term, he would set a major test, with gifts of food for every child in accordance with his knowledge. This was very practical...

A Beis Yaakov (Girls' School)

There was a Beis Yaakov in Turka with girls from the area as well. The teachers were from Tarnopol, the sisters of the editor Dr. Hillel Zeidman, Malka and Rachel. The righteous woman Mrs. Chaitshe Dinstag, the wife of Reb Moshe from Sokolika, may G-d avenge his blood, should also be remembered positively. She was the living spirit of the Beis Yaakov and also of the *Yeshiva.*

The Yeshiva

The Degel Torah Yeshiva was fine – the pride of the city and region., Approximately 120 students studied there, 80% from Turka, and 20% from the region – from further afield places such as Przemysl, Kozowa, Ostrog, and others. The Yeshiva made a good name for itself. A great deal was written about it from visitors from "Tag" and "Heint".

[Page 87]

The studies were exceptionally good. We sent students to the Yeshiva of Chachmei Lublin knowing the three *Bavas* (*Bava Kama, Bava Metzia,* and *Bava Batra*) by heart[10]. We also sent students to the Keser Torah Yeshiva in Sosnowiec, as well as the Yeshiva of Belz. We primarily sent children from poor homes. We had a special fund for expenses – we sent five zloty per month for each student.

The Degel Torah Yeshiva in Turka

The directors of the *Yeshiva*:

Rabbi Alter Y.A. Weinberger was the founder, the president and *Rosh Yeshiva*, may he live long. Today he is the rabbi and *Rosh Yeshiva* in Kew Gardens, New York.

Rabbi Hershele Nagler, the son of Rabbi Yechiel Nagler, was the vice spiritual director and lesson giver. May G-d avenge his blood.

Reb Shlomo Heller was a great help, working 4-5 hours each day, without pay. May G-d avenge his blood.

Reb Shimon Hirsch was the *Yeshiva* father to every child, with love and affection. His son Moshe ran a special restaurant for the *Yeshiva* students.

The community, headed by Shua Nachman Meiner, paid a salary of 150 zloty per month to the *Rosh Yeshiva*, Rabbi Weinberger.

It is interesting to write about a large examination, one of the largest by-heart examinations of the three *Bavas*, of the highest class, and also of all the classes according to their ability. The holy Gaon Rabbi Pinchas Twersky, a Stoller rabbi and son-in-law of the Admor of Belz of holy blessed memory, may G-d avenge his blood, came to the festivities of the exam. He had previously lived in Sambor. He examined each student, and was full of amazement. The aforementioned rabbi and Tzadik said, "Bring cake, drinks and wine to the celebratory meal, I will pay for it!" The celebration lasted for the entire night.

[Page 88]

The Turka musicians also came and requested to participate. They played the entire night. It was an honor for the town, as well as for the strangers, to have such a guest.

The voice of Torah was heard day and night throughout the entire city.

A major examination in the *Yeshiva*. From right to left: The Admor of Sadagora of holy blessed memory, the Admor of Wonowice of holy blessed memory, and the Rosh Yeshiva Rabbi Alter Weinberger.

A Debate

There was a debate with the Zionist groups of Turka, headed by Reb Shua Erdman, may G-d avenge his blood. With time we emptied things out, bringing nearly all the children out from the organizations. Of course, this was not so desirous for the aforementioned groups. When I saw that things began to take on sharp forms I requested a meeting. We got together and talked in a very brotherly fashion. Thank G-d, I won them over with the truth. I told them that the children would like to learn with us today, and the next day they would be prepared to be good Zionists. However, if they go to the organizations today, they will not belong to you tomorrow, but rather to the left, the extreme left – which is sufficient to understand. They understood well – and there was peace upon Israel.

[Page 89]

Famous Performers of *Mitzvot*:

It is appropriate to mention Reb Moshe Hirt and his righteous wife Malka the daughter of Reb Shlomo Erdman of Jasienca, may they live. They helped greatly in providing daily fare on a rotational basis[11] for the *Yeshiva* and *Talmud Torah* students from outside the city. Reb Nachman Brenis as well as Intrator-Horovich helped the *Yeshiva* with wood. May G-d avenge their blood.

Avraham Pelech, the tailor, helped by taking children from the *Yeshiva* who were not enjoying success in learning the holy Torah and teaching them tailoring. May his memory be a blessing.

Reb Leizer Monaster, a proper Hassid, pious and upright, was a sincere prayer leader, filled with fear of Heaven.

Reb Leizer Bart, was a synagogue Jew, a sweet Jew filled with charitable deeds. He was a good friend of the *Yeshiva*, and helped greatly.

Reb Tzvi Filinger was a dear man on the *Yeshiva* committee, who helped greatly. May G-d avenge his blood.

There were two Moshe Rosens. The large Moshe was an important, dear man, and a friend of everybody. The small Moshe, the son-in-law of Reb Tzvi Rotenberg the *shochet*, was an important, dear man, good to his fellow.

The Rabbinate in our City

(From what I know, and from what I have seen in the cemetery.)

The holy Gaon Rabbi Shlomo Seredir, the brother-in-law of the holy Gaon of Rozin, may his merit protect us.

[Page 90]

The "Kitfot Haeifod," the holy Gaon Rabbi Pinchas Aryeh of holy blessed memory. All the males born in the year of his death were named after him.

His son, Reb Yankele the Holy One, was dedicated to the wellbeing of the city during the time of the epidemic, may we be protected. It is said that he took it upon himself to redeem the city, and he died that very day. May his merit protect us.

The Gaon Rabbi Meir Leibish Langerman, was a man of wonders, a Gaon in both the revealed and the hidden Torah[12], may his holy memory be a blessing.

His son Rabbi Nachum Langerman, of holy blessed memory, was a great prayer leader and singer. His took his father's place.

The rabbinical judge Rabbi Mendele Motkiver, was a great scholar and sage. He once said, "I am not angry about a fool because he is a fool, but I am angry: you fool, if G-d created you as a fool, why do you want to be a sage?!"

The rabbinical teacher, the Rabbi and Gaon Isserlis, the holy man, the grandson of the Rema'h of blessed memory[13].

The Gaon Rabbi Eliezer Mishel, the author of the book "Mishnat Eliezer." He was sick for ten years and lay in bed. I helped him throughout the entire time. He died around the end of 1939. He was eulogized by the *Rosh Yeshiva* Rabbi Weinberger, and, to differentiate between the dead and the living, Rabbi Yitzchak Rubin, the rabbi of Sztilka. They made a canopy for him in the new cemetery. May his holy memory be a blessing.

The rabbinical judge, the wise and erudite man, Rabbi Yudele Roizenheg, the son-in-law of the rabbinical teacher Rabbi Isserlis.

The rabbinical judge, the upright and pure man, Rabbi Aharon Wolf Weisblum, the grandson of Rabbi Elimelech, may his merit protect us, and the son-in-law of the granddaughter of Rabbi Mendele Motkiver, may G-d avenge his blood.

The Admorim in Turka

The rabbi and tzadik, great in Torah, the revealed and the hidden, the Vonovitsher Rebbe, Rabbi Yeshaya Shalom Rokach, may G-d avenge his blood, and the Admor of Sambor, Rabbi Avraham Yaakov Jolles, may G-d avenge his blood.

The rabbi and Tzadik, Rabbi Micheli Brandwein of holy blessed memory lived in Turka for several years, and then went to America. He was a famous worker of wonders.

The rabbi and Tzadik, the holy man, Rabbi Alter Sopron of Stryj-Sambor. Every year, winter and summer, he would come to Turka and remain of an extended period. He was dear in the eyes of all the Jews and all who saw him. He was righteous and pure. Of holy blessed memory, may G-d avenge his blood.

Translator's Footnotes:

41. I am not sure of the exact meaning of this word, but it is evidently an article of winter clothing.
42. This means 'And I'. The word '*vaani*' would be the Hebrew version in the Torah, and '*un ich*' would be the Yiddish translation. From the context of the following sentence, this is from Genesis 48:7.
43. Phrases from the Friday night service.
44. Obviously, a type of expensive fur.
45. *Tzena Urena* is a Yiddish commentary on the Torah designed especially for women.
46. *Choshen Mishpat* and *Yoreh Deah* are two of the four sections of the Code of Jewish Law (*Shulchan Aruch*).
47. I.e. a means for earning livelihood.
48. From the High Holy Day liturgy.
49. This sentence is very vague, and seems to be missing some detail.
50. These are three major, complex Talmudic tractates dealing with civil law.
51. A traditional way of supporting *Yeshiva* students from outside the city – with householders hosting them for meals on a rotational basis.
52. The hidden Torah refers to Kabbalah.

The Rema'h was Rabbi Moshe Isserlis of Krakow, the author of the Ashkenazic glosses on the Code of Jewish Law.

[Page 91]

The Hashomer Hatzair Movement in Turka During its First Years

by Yitzchak Rand of Merchavia

At the end of the First World War, our family found itself in Czechia, where we were refugees for four years. We returned home with the other refugees at the time of the declaration of independence of the Czechoslovak Republic. We made our journey on a transport train, and reached our destination of Turka after eight days. When the train reached the village of Jawora, the locomotive rebelled against its conductors and refused to continue... The reason for the rebellion – the fuel ran out. When the passengers found out, they spread through the adjacent forest to collect wood to fuel the locomotive. They returned with bundles of wood on their backs. The locomotive had sufficient fuel, and continued to bring us home.

Yitzchak Rand

I was a 12 year old boy when I returned to Turka. Fragments of pictures are preserved in my memory, some clear and some blurry, from the realities of the town at that time. Around the time we returned, we found ourselves caught up in the war between the Poles and the Ukrainians. The Ukrainians were fighting for their independence in Eastern Galicia, whose population was, as is known, primarily Ukrainian. I understood the justice of the Ukrainian cause only in my adulthood, when I found it hard to understand how the Polish nation, which had just been freed from its own oppression, learned so quickly how to suppress another nation. However, when I had already returned to Turka, I felt the injustice of the oppression of another people in a very tangible sense: for the Ukrainians, themselves oppressed, oppressed and afflicted another nation that dwelt in their midst -- the Jews. This was not only political oppression, but rather straightforward maltreatment. I recall how Ukrainian soldiers snatched Jews on the street for various types of work, and how they stole their property.

It was not only the war between the nationalities that imposed fear upon the Jewish residents of Turka. During the war as well as after it, Europe suffered from an illness that afflicted the population without discrimination based on race and religion – "Hispanka"[1] – which did not pass over Turka. Dozens of people became ill daily (in our seven person family, only one person evaded it), and the number who died was significant enough.

[Page 92]

Vibrant Life Amongst the Ruins

The town was destroyed. Many houses were not yet renovated after the destruction that had been perpetrated by the soldiers of the Czar. Amidst all this, we can be surprised as to how a vibrant national and cultural life flourished through these disasters. Various parties and circles were formed, which appeared on the election lists. A local drama troupe was founded (I will never forget the strong experience that I had when, as a 12-year-old child, I attended the performance of The Jewish King Lear). Enthusiasm for Zionism was felt due to the influence of the Balfour Declaration. The enthusiasm also affected circles which were far from Zionism, and even opposed it. The study of the Hebrew Language served as an expression of the nationalist-Zionist spirit. One could hear people delving into the depths of Hebrew grammar, and debating whether the word "*shulchan*" (table) is feminine or masculine – for the word "*shulchan*" in the singular seems to be masculine, whereas the plural "*shulchanot*" has the markings of a feminine word. The debate between the supporters of the masculine version and the feminine version continued until they asked a man of authority, the Hebrew teacher Schreiber, who gave his verdict.

Not only did they study Hebrew. The desire to know, to understand and to study was felt. Since the gymnasium had not yet been founded, they all studied "general subjects", which included German language and literature. The names of the German poets and philosophers were known by everybody and served as a topic for debates on the street and in meetings that were convened. It was a common sight: people wandering through the streets of the city with heavy books under their shoulders – a sign of erudition and intelligence.

The Hashomer Hatzair Chapter

The Hashomer Hatzair movement had a special place in communal life. When I returned with my family to Turka at the end of 1918, a Hashomer Hatzair chapter already existed, one of the first chapters of this movement in Galicia. It had two sections: for boys – headed by Philip Weissman, the son of a half-assimilated family; and for girls – headed by Abba Chushai – already at that time an active youth, encouraging others to activism as well. When these two sections united after some time, Abba Chushai became the head of the entire chapter.

[Page 93]

During those days, the young man Anshel Treiber often visited our house with a bundle of books under his arm. He had been our neighbor before the war, and today is a member of Beit Alfa. He is the one who told us about the Shomer organization (*"farein"*), in which he was a member. Due to the influence of his stories, my sister decided to "register" me in the organization. Thus, at age 12, did I enter the Hashomer Hatzair movement, which was simply called *"farein,"* to differentiate it from the other organizations, which were called *"Tzionister farein," "Mizrachi farein"* etc. The *"farein"*, with the definitive article, as the *"Hashomer farein"*, without any additional adjectives.

It was known that all of the Shomrim were *"treifniks"*, *"apikorsim"* [heretics], and Sabbath violators. Because of this, many parents objected to their children joining the movement. The children gave in to the parents or continued to attend Hashomer Farein secretly, without their knowledge. The situation was not thus with my parents: not only were they followers of tradition, but I myself was a very Orthodox youth, with *peyos*, studying in *cheder*, worshipping every day and even reciting all the additions to the prayers. Their Orthodoxy and my Orthodoxy did not prevent me from belonging to the *Farein*. It should be known: I was the only Orthodox child in the chapter. My Orthodoxy also did not keep me from basing myself within the spirit of national and social revolution that was pervading the city at that time. I felt the refreshing atmosphere that was penetrating Turka from the outside world, as a result of the "storm and the breach" that had passed over Europe at the end of the First World War. Our first group head was Aharon Rozler, who took it upon himself to educate us to be "proud Jews and good people". How does one become a proud Jew? -- by studying Hebrew and fostering the aspiration to make *aliya* to the Land. How does one become a good person? – through fostering humanitarian values. We had to learn the ten commandments of Hashomer by heart. Group activities took place every day of the week, and on the Sabbath, we would go on a hike in the Shomer Forest, accompanied by dozens of youths who were not members of the *Farein*.

Manual Labor

As has been stated, there was no gymnasium in the city, and aside from a few exceptions, the members of the chapter were lacking in higher education. The chapter wished to impart general knowledge along with the Hebrew and general educational theory. It became known that the group heads, despite coming from well-to-do families, were lacking higher education. This had its effect on the education within the groups. I recall how one of the heads of the groups read to us 12-13 year old boys some inferior novel of Lateiner (this was during the time of the Ukrainian retreat and the conquest of the city by the Poles). Most of the education was indeed related to the Land of Israel, to the "building of the Land and the nation." A great deal was said about the normal composition of the Jewish nation with most of its members working as middlemen, and about the need to exchange the ethereal livelihoods for building and creativity, mainly through the work of the land. As a first step toward realizing this sublime goal, the chapter leased a plot of land on the other side of the city, and developed a splendid vegetable enterprise. It was not only to agriculture that one had to return, but to labor in general. Every work, even the most black and "degrading" was holy. The vegetables had to be shipped to the city. What did the older members of the chapter, headed by Abba Chushai, do? They took a wagon, loaded the vegetables on it, and, instead of horses, harnessed themselves to the wagon and dragged it through the streets of the city, as an example to the masses that they do not reject any labor. Some residents of the city disparaged these "horses," whereas others were enthused with this idealism and personal example.

[Page 94]

We were not educated only for fitness for work. No less value was placed on education to the love of the Land of Israel and the people of Israel. We studied "Palestina-Graphia" and the history of the nation, and we enthusiastically sang the songs of the Land. However, we gained the bulk of our Zionist faith and enthusiasm from the "Hashomer" book, which includes chapters of life and might from the era of Hashomer (from whose name was the movement called Hashomer – later Hashomer Hatzair). I recall my great emotion upon reading the braved deeds of the Shomrim, including Marika Chazanovich who fell on the fields of Merchavia. I did not know that the fate of my life would be tied with that place...

The First Group Makes Aliya to the Land!

Our eyes looked forward to *aliya* to the Land as the realization of a distant vision. This vision began to unfold before our eyes with the preparation for *aliya* of the first group of Shomrim in 1920. The Shomrim from Turka were among the first ones of the Third Aliya. Not all of those who made *aliya* were members of the movement. From among those who joined the group a few months before their *aliya*, one lives to this day in the Kibbutz of Ramat Yochanan – Elazar Weiss. The preparations for the *aliya* of the first group inspired great emotion among the Jews of the city – some were enthusiastic, others cursed, and even chased their children out of the house. The chapter turned into a sewing workshop in which the women of the city sewed clothes for the first pioneers on a voluntary basis from textiles that were donated in part by the residents of the city.

The great, awaited day arrived, the day of actualization of the sublime vision, the day of *aliya* to the Land. The previous night was a night of watching. We, all the members of the chapter, waited in the hall of the chapter, nervously awaiting the great moment when the entire group would bid farewell to our beloved head of our chapter – Abba Chushai.

[Page 95]

Hashomer Hatzair in Turka.

At 3:00 a.m., there was a roll call of the chapter, and the farewell words of Abba streamed forth and penetrated the recesses of the hearts... At the end of the farewell speech, the entire chapter organized itself by groups. With coordinated steps and measured paces, to the light of the clear moon, they accompanied the first group of pioneers passing through the roads of the city on the way to the train. The entire way, the marchers marched to the sounds of the city band, which brought many people out of their houses.

The chapter went through a great deal of development from its founding during the war years until the *aliya* of the first group. The kids turned into goats -- to group heads and new counselors. The work in the chapter took on a more serious character and even we 15 year olds began to prepare for *aliya*.

Once again: the gymnasium had not yet been renovated, and anyone who wished to finish high school – and there were such people amongst us – did this as an externist (the exam was in Sambor). Then a call came from Abba Chushai from the Land: "All of you should study trades. In contrast to the 'life of the air' of the Jews, the Land requires trades." Indeed, all of the members of the older group began to study trades such as locksmithing, woodcutting, etc. I chose carpentry. The matter was not easy for me. My parents, my mother in particular, objected to this. I still studied in *cheder*, and my mother, in accordance with the advice of my rebbe, desired that I continue in *Yeshiva*. I presented my parents with a *fait accompli*. I began to work with Mendel Feiler the carpenter without asking permission of my parents. Having no choice, they accepted the situation.

[Page 96]

Our entire interest was then directed toward *aliya* and actualization in the kibbutz. This actualization became an obligatory principle in the movement. We founded a fund for the group that would assist the members of restricted means when the awaited time for *aliya* arrived.

What were the sources of income of the fund? First of all – chopping trees. We had strong competitors for this work – the gentile woodcutters, who were experienced veterans in this trade, and earned their livelihood from it. And we were only 14 or 15 year old children... If you reduce the fees for this work (I am recalling our faults here), and factor in the sympathy of several Jews for this, we succeeded in taking on this "coarse" work – the work of the lower class gentiles. How great was our pride in that we succeeded at this holy work! We did this work primarily in the late afternoon hours during the winter. One day, as I was among the wood choppers and evening had already fallen, we still had a few trees to chop. It was not worthwhile to put off the completion of the tree chopping for another day, and therefore, we decided to finish it that night to the light of a kerosene lantern. This decision caused me a great deal of perplexity and a difficult internal battle. I was still an Orthodox youth who worshipped three times a day. The time for *mincha* had arrived, and here I was – chopping trees! A difficult battle raged inside of me, what was I to do? How could I go to the synagogue while the group of workers was toiling so diligently for this holy objective?! However, if I keep my faith with my friends and the work – I would be sinning before G-d? I struggled hard with myself. Finally, I found a solution that satisfied my conscious, and certainly also G-d. I worshipped as I was chopping trees. Only two people heard my prayers: G-d and me.

Another source of income for the fund was the distribution of wedding invitations, porting, and other such jobs. We would also dress up on the evening of Purim, visit the homes of the wealthy people, and sing the songs of the Land. The head of the house would donate his part through signing his name on a sheet of paper. We did not reject any work, even the most coarse and difficult. On the contrary, the more coarse or difficult the work was, the great our pride in it.

The *Aliya* of the Second Group

A short time after the *aliya* of the first group of Shomrim in 1920, the second group made *aliya*. This group consisted of "Stam Chalutzim" [General Pioneers] (a movement which was under the influence of Hashomer Hatzair). After them the rest of the veterans of the chapter went. In the interim (it was the year 1922-23), signs of disappointment set in to the movement due to the realities of the Land of Israel that afflicted the members of the Third Aliya. News came from the Land about the disbanding of Zionist projects. Many left the kibbutzim and the Land, some to seek their personal fortune, and others to build Socialism in Russia. (The latter, as is known, built Socialism in Stalin's prison and never returned from there.)

[Page 97]

The influence of the situation in the Land on the movement in the Diaspora was destructive, and the Turka chapter, one of the finest and strongest in Galicia, was also affected. One example: at this point, the chapter was housed in a four-by-four room which barely had room for a table with two benches – and even that tiny room was large enough to accommodate the members of the chapter in the city, who numbered at most 6 or 7 boys and girls of ages 16-17. These youths made *aliya* in 1926, and were among the founders of Kibbutz Aliya Aleph of Hashomer Hatzair of Galicia, which was the kibbutz that later settled in Merchavia.

How serious was the situation of the chapter during that time: the disappointment and despair regarding the situation in the land affected everything. The Zionist movement was at a nadir. All *aliya* to the Land ceased.

We, the 6 or 7 youths of the movement, guarded the flame so that it would not go out. Despite the uncertainty about what awaits us in the future, we did not give up on our faith in our Zionist mission. We knew that the Zionist eternity and the upbuilding of the Land would not prove false. Indeed, there was reward for our activities.

When the end of the crisis came with the beginning of the Fourth Aliya in 1924, we succeeded in rebuilding atop the ruins of the chapter. We rented a large dwelling. We broadened our literary framework, we added new groups, we reestablished Hechalutz, and our members engaged in intensive activities. One of the great successes of the chapter during that timeframe was the fact that a large number of *Beis Midrash* students joined Hashomer Hatzair – the Bilu Group. It was one of the signs of the times that a portion of them rejected Zionism after their *aliya*. They left the Land or were expelled from it, and like the previous deserters, experienced Stalin's prison. Through intensive activity in the Hashomer chapter, we, the older group, made preparations for achieving our goal of making *aliya* to the Land. We were prepared for such already in 1924, at the beginning of the Fourth Aliya, but the issuance of passports was delayed by the Polish authorities, and our *aliya* only took place two years later, in 1926. We set out on our way with the knowledge and faith that we left behind a strong, vibrant chapter that would continue to prepare its members for actualization. Indeed, we were not disappointed. Even though a chapter of Gordonia was set up in Turka as well as a Communist movement also began to organize the youth of the city; Hashomer Hatzair saw success in its actions, and the Shomrim and Shomrim Chalutzim made *aliya* to the various kibbutzim. Members of Hashomer Hatzair and Hechalutz from Turka are found in many Kibbutzim – Beit Alfa, Mishmar Haemek, Merchavia, Mizra, Sarid, Tel Amal, Gat, Hamaapil, Kfar Masaryk, and Ramat Yochanan.

[Page 98]

We cannot forget the help of the friends of the movement who formed the Supervisory Committee (*Opajka*). First and foremost, we recall the activities of Naftali Kraus, who never withheld his assistance from the chapter. Naftali Kraus was able to appreciate the great power realized by his movement, a movement that not only preaches appropriately, but also actualizes what they preach. We found him to be a help and support for us in any way needed during times of decline as well as times of pride.

The Influence of the Chapter on General Social Life

The influence of the Hashomer Hatzair chapter in Turka on the Jewish community and the youth in the city far exceeded its numbers. Their role in the Zionist activity in the city was great, and they did a great deal toward the revolution of Hebrew as a spoken language. It was true that many people outside of Hashomer Hatzair learned Hebrew, but the acquisition of the language by the Shomrim was identified with personal realization as well as *aliya* to the Land. At all celebrations and other cultural events organized by the chapter, Abba Chushai began his speeches in Yiddish and then switched to Hebrew. Our movement was the only one that put on performances in Hebrew. Hebrew was the language of the educational activities in the groups of members as well as the spoken language of the graduates of the chapter. The study of the Hebrew Language and its use as a day-to-day language set the Turka chapter apart from the other chapters in Galicia, which conducted themselves in the Polish Language.

Hashomer Hatzair in Turka.

The chapter of Turka differed from the other chapters of the movement in other areas as well! When she participated in a debate at a certain national convention of the movement, one of the graduates of the chapter, Tzipora Chushai, characterized the Turka chapter as "simplicity within greatness." We absorbed our simplicity from the populist atmosphere of the town and its realistic approach to life. Unlike other chapters, which were raised on the lap of Polish Literature, we were diligent in the appreciation of the value of Hebrew and Yiddish Literature. We suffered along with Morris Rosenfeld, the poet of the Jewish "shop" in America – who portrayed in his Yiddish poems the suffering and tribulations of the Jewish proletariat. Along with Bialik, we expressed pride through "Al Hatzipor" about the warm, beautiful Land. From Mendele Mocher Seforim, we learned about the forlorn Jewish towns in the Russian Pale of Settlement. Deep in our souls, we lived the experiences of Amnon and Tamar in Mapu's Ahavat Tzion, and we joined Feuerberg in his tragic question "Where?" We laughed heartily along with Shalom Aleichem, whose books we dramatized and performed (we used horsehairs for makeup, and stuck them to faces with hot carpenters' glue!...)

[Page 99]

We were anchored in Yiddish and Hebrew literature, but this did not restrict our horizon. The German Language opened a window to the wide world for us, for it had large inroads in Galicia, which had formerly been part of the Austro-Hungarian Empire. Through that language, we became familiar with the creations of the great German poets and writers, as well as the creations of Ivson the Norwegian and especially the Russian classicists.

Due to the lack of a gymnasium, anyone who wished to learn studied with a private teacher. A gymnasium student would have free time for additional study. On the other hand, we were studying trades, which meant that we had a difficult ten hour workday over and above the hours we spent at the activities of the chapter. We were not left with much time for studies. Nevertheless, we studied and read a great deal, making use of every free moment. Our work prevented us from taking hikes in the nature as well as engaging in scouting activities, which were cultivated in other chapters. The scenery of Turka was known for its beauty and charm, exciting the eyes of all beholders, and strangers came from afar to enjoy the shade of the forests and clear air. The movement in Galicia desired the pleasant environment of the Carpathians, which surrounded our city, for its summer encampments and annual conventions.

[Page 100]

Starting from 1918 until 1926, the year of our *aliya*, Hashomer summer encampments took place in Tarnowa Wizna (twice), Strzy³ki, Ilnik, and Jablonka. We would go out on a hike one day a year – on *Tisha Beav*. We did not work that day, so we enjoyed a full day in the bosom of nature.

Another point of praise for the Turka chapter was the material assistance given to the needy Shomrim. One of the rooms of the chapter headquarters had potatoes, and anyone in need could take some home. I recall one Purim when one of the older members (Hela Reifler) took measurements of our heads for hats. This was strange to me for I did not need such. A few days later I saw a poor lad wearing a new hat – given to him as a Purim gift. I then understood the reason for the collective measurement.

*

The Hashomer Hatzair chapter in Turka was a branch of a thik tree that sent forth deep roots in the reality of the Jewish nation. The tree was the Hashomer Hatzair movement, whose goals were the freedom of man, the nation, and the working class. The members of the chapter who today are found in kibbutzim, are fulfilling the "historical prescription of the movement and its line of upward development! When fathers, sons and grandchildren march together under the same flag..." they "draw from deep sources the suffering of the Jewish nation and the vision of its redemption; from deep sources of the suffering of man and of the dream of liberation."

I am convinced that many natives of the city who were educated in Hashomer Hatzair during their youth, whether they are found today in kibbutzim or outside of them, whether they continued on in this movement or found their paths in other movements, will remember forever the days of their youth as Shomrim.

Translator's Footnote:

53. The Spanish Flu pandemic of 1918.

[Page 101]

Ideas and Memories from the "Hashomer Hatzair" Group of Turka

by Yafa Gorlitzki of Tel Aviv

Yafa Gorlitzki

Normally, it is difficult for a person to write down the experiences and impressions that are hidden away deep in her life. It is similarly very difficult to forge a bridge between the present and the past, and to bring forth memories of the family, sociological and geographical environment that etched deep impressions in the personality of a person.

And behold, it was a wonder. At the moment that I sat down to bring forth memories of my distant past from decades ago, the wellsprings of impressions of my town magically opened up, and I find myself in a sense of alertness and strong emotion, as if this happened just yesterday...

I see my beautiful town surrounding by high mountains, valleys, expansive forests and green meadows that spread out to the endless distance – everything hints to song... You would feel that every place is a part of your personality and soul. That beauty and natural splendor that you absorbed within yourself will never be erased. Similarly, the experiences of life in the Hashomer Hatzair movement are so strong and unforgettable.

As is known, this was a historic era; the birth of new events and processes of development that imparted a sense of yearning for a new world and way of life in opposition to the existing order. The First World War, bringing destruction and ruin in its wake, educated the person to understand the sociological factors that are connected to war. After the war, the downtrodden person found a way of life in scientific literature.

Notions of national liberation, social justice, and proper, guaranteed human rights -- Hashomer Hatzair began its existence within this historical climate. I entered the movement after the *aliya* of the first group to the Land of Israel. Our chapter was not large; however it encompassed the best of the academic, enlightened youth who streamed to it from all segments of the population. Certain members from the extreme religious stratum also joined the chapter. The chapter included several groups, headed by a group of counselors whose job it was to impart concepts of Zionism and Socialism to their charges and to prepare them for a life of actualization. A very serious spirit pervaded the chapter. The members thirsted for knowledge and the counselors had to take upon themselves the difficult task of educating the younger generation that was filled with progressive aspirations. This was a stormy period, fraught with ideological dilemmas. Would the mountains, gardens, and meadows in which stormy discussions and debates took place had the ability to whisper – they would reveal a great deal of the epos of the lives of our young people in the chapter. The process of personal and intellectual maturation took place early. With the urgent pressure of the objective conditions, our youth in the chapter broke forth from the realm of normal youthful life that finds its expression in personal objectives and narrowly focused matters. The vital energy of our youth turned toward the constructive vista of pioneering actualization.

[Page 102]

Hashomer Hatzair in Turka

Our chapter forged a serious type of youth, hungry for knowledge, with a healthy psychology and optimism. Our lives as youths could provide a great deal of didactic material for professional education in the aim of raising the energy level of young people toward a sublime level of constructive cultural life. Indeed, our lives were full of content, and variegated. Our chapter was among the finest of the chapters of Hashomer Hatzair.

[Page 103]

There are those who tend to refer to a period of life such as ours in the chapter as a romantic era -- one that passes in a usual manner with age and with time, never to return. However, that was not the way it was. Different logic indeed applied at different times; but, on the other hand, an eternal truth existed, and no small portion of the seeds of this eternal truth was hidden within our weltanschauung during the era under discussion. One should not think that the pioneering spirit became outmoded with the passage of time. This was a pioneering ideology that imparted a healthy approach to life, on account of the pioneering education. Many of the members of the chapter remained in kibbutzim, and some are even involved in the development of communal life in the Land. This is true even though there is no shortage of people who remained outside the realm to some degree, for the spark of new life in our Land did not enchant them fully.

During that era, the nature of strong youths was forged in such a manner that the era of technology and automation did not have the power to cut off the truth of their lives, lead them off of their way of life, and remove them from their world of sublime values.

Turka was a superbly ordered town. Would it be that I had the ability to describe the picture in its entirety, as the parents returned from the synagogue on the Sabbath imbued with a spirit of holiness, while the youths swarmed on the streets discussion fine literature and sciences. Apparently, most of the parents were graced with a healthy educational instinct, and their relatively calm reaction flowed from their understanding of the danger of fighting against the nature, aspirations and interests of the younger generations. Therefore, most of the members did not stumble upon serious opposition from their parents.

Endless enthusiasm pervaded on the Sabbath. The youth would stroll through the streets of the city on their way to excursions, singing songs of enthusiasm and pride. The youth in the chapter would hike in the nearby area as well as farther off places, travel to summer camps, to work places, and to pioneering *hachshara* – all without serious conflict. This was a sort of agreement between two worlds that lived under one roof, as they toiled incessantly to preserve peace and to ensure that one side does not vex the other. The parents saw that their children were abandoning their way of life in accordance with the spirit of the times.

As is known, our city was blessed with a spirit of splendor and glory. The geographical environment imbued with the muse of the arts. The railroad entrance to the city went through a tunnel. It is told that people worked for years until they bore a hole through the tall mountain, and the tunnel was one of the largest in Poland. When the train exited the tunnel, it would "fly" through the air on the bridge that spanned the river. Indeed the hand of the Creator granted our city an abundance of mountains, valleys, plains and rivers. The power of expression is insufficient to describe the experiences that made their imprint on the character of the person. It is said that the members of our chapter were sentimental. Indeed, the splendid nature wove very thin strands in the spiritual realities, and a person could sense the secret of the world and the language of the inanimate...

[Page 104]

During that era, we loved the books of Meterling and Tagore. We did not only read the books, but we lived them. The concepts described therein were not merely abstractions. We were sated with happiness and joy in the bosom of nature: whether on group hikes or alone, far away from the bustle of the city, seeking, "a quiet corner to dream..." Indeed, our lives in the Hashomer Hatzair movement were filled with meaning. This was a romanticism that was not ephemeral. Rather, it forged the person to understand and love his fellow.

These are only a minute portion of impressions from our beautiful city that was destroyed by the Nazi soldiers. Everything that took place there is hidden in all of our hearts until our final day.

Turka at the foot of the Kychera

[Page 105]

From Within the Walls of the *Beis Midrash* to the Hashomer Hatzair Chapter

by David Y.

The Hashomer chapter in the town of Turka on the Stryj River in the Carpathian Mountains was one of the earliest of our movement. The influence of the chapter was great in the Jewish street, especially among the youth of the academic, bourgeoisie and poorer classes.

It was first founded within the general background of the times, the economic anomaly, the cultural detachment, the severed community, the destruction of the Jewish town in the wake of the First World War, the lack of public schools and modern *cheders* – all of this strengthened the blessed work of the Hashomer chapter among the youth of the town.

The *cheders* of the city waged a holy war against it. They regarded the movement as the troubler of Israel and apostates among the nation. Despite all this, the chapter and its organizers found the proper path with which to arouse the hearts of the youths. It is clear that the revolutionary changes of the era that shook the general world as well as the Jewish world (the Balfour Declaration) laid the groundwork for fruitful Zionist activity and instilled faith in a national revival.

The influence of the conventions and summer camps that took place in our region, the region of the enchanting Carpathians, upon the activities of the chapter was great. The scouts who spread through the streets of the city instilled Jewish pride and reverence for the Shomer, for our special uniform, and for our independence. Indeed, the life of the chapter attracted many people from all strata of the youth.

The Jewish youth in the town felt himself boxed in by his way of life, his family, his school, and the *cheder*. He was living in the area of mountains, forests, an enchanting landscape, and a wide open world – and he was not able to enjoy the beauty of nature at all! With the influence of the movement, they were attracted toward the vibrant life of the Shomrim in the chapter and in the cap. The singing and bonfires at the peaks of the mountains hinted to and lit up the dark corners of the lives of the youths, and summoned them to come up!...

I will not write about the entire story of my life – but I will relate a bit about it: We were a group of friends who studied together in the *cheder* and in the public school, and remained together for some period within the walls of the *Beis Midrash*. Over and above the page of *Gemara*, we would read and philosophize about the values of Judaism and the influence of the revolutions and changes in the world in general, and the Jewish world in particular. We secretly delved into new doctrines that awakened the thoughts. We read the "invalid books." We read and were affected. From this stemmed our own great "revolution."

[Page 106]

A few of us (some of them are presently in various kibbutzim) "rebelled" and entered the chapter immediately. This deed caused a very serious debate and self-reflection. We felt that that the ice within us had melted. Something trembled in the strands of our hearts. We became "others"[1]. The leadership of the chapter took advantage of the situation, and we forged a connection with them. They provided us with literature on the values of the movement and the worker's movement, all mixed together: the books of A. D. Gordon, Lenin, Kropotkin, Tolstoy, etc...

Of course, an internal debate took place within each of us. Everybody struggled fiercely... This was an issue of abandoning the tradition of the generations... The toil was difficult, and what wonder is in that? It was not easy to cut oneself off from the past, from the petite bourgeoisie social class, from the family, etc. However, the opposition grew day by day. The internal revolt against the way of life of the home and the street increased. Some among us fell off, for their ideas were immature. The remainder forged their way along path that led to a lovely, bustling life – to the chapter and the Shomer movement.

We came to the chapter when we were old enough (the average age was 15-16). We appointed a group head for us. We took upon ourselves the principles of the movement, its realities and its banner. In its arena, we saw the path toward a new life and self actualization: to a life of work, and an aspiration for *aliya* to the Land.

A group of members on a hike near the Turka tunnel

[Page 107]

Sections on the Akiva Youth Movement in Turka

by Shimon Keller of Tel Aviv

Shimon Keller

It is difficult to write solely from memory; therefore it is possible that this article will be lacking some substance. Indeed, it is only possible to draw from the past those episodes which remain etched in the memory.

An exemplary youth movement in our town from the perspective of its organization and cultural and educational activities existed in our town at that time. From it came the first graduates who made *aliya* all together along with Abba Chushai – today the mayor of Haifa. Its educational influence spread far beyond the bounds of the chapter in the city. It was known by all of the thinking and studying youth who were not numbered among its members – and who from among the youth of Turka did not study? Its Zionism, its education toward scouting, its songs, and the like were recognized by all the residents of the city. Nevertheless, many of the youths remained outside the walls of the movement.

Hela Shreiber, a charming girl with great energy and ideological inclinations, appeared on the scene during the 1930s. She was a native of the town and was educated in the city of Krakow, where she lived for the duration of her studies. Several youths, male and female, whose hearts were touched by the serious issues of Jewish youth, began to congregate around her. Nevertheless, they did not find their way into the existing movement. Those few began to gather the youths into groups, and a new movement arose...

The new movement was quite similar to the existing movement in its external form, for it was also oriented toward scouting. However, its educational content was completely different than the existing form. The Socialist doctrine continued to develop. The educational foundations were based upon traditional Jewish values in the progressive spirit. Ahad Haam[2] was the personality according to whose doctrine they wished to educate the younger generation. That group that regarded the problems of the Jewish world from a different vantage point than the doctrine of Hashomer Hatzair understood that it must concern itself with the cadre of the youth who would actualize the aspirations of the movement. It began to enlist 15-16 year old youths as educators of the new doctrine whose task would be to concern themselves with the youths who were younger than themselves.

[Page 108]

Day to Day Activity

Members of Akiva on the occasion of the *aliya* of Aharon Shefer

In accordance with the protocols of the Akiva Zionist scouting youth movement of Krakow, they gathered youths from among the public school students, and organized them into groups and brigades. Most activities took place on the Sabbath. In the summer they would go to the natural meadows and groves that surrounded the town. The march toward those places, to commands issues in the Hebrew Language, was an experience in its own right, which educated a new generation of proud, disciplined Zionist Jews. The games that took place in the groves also served a similar role, as did, of course, the discussions and songs that filled the time in the grove or the meadow.

All members of the movement took part in such activities, even though they were primarily directed toward the younger members. Throughout the entire week, evening meetings of the older members took place. The locale of such meetings became a financial problem, for one had to pay to rent a premises. To solve the problem, the group of those responsible had to impose fees, set up organizational institutions, and do other such things. Thereby, they attained an exemplary organizational situation. They obtained premises for meetings in accordance with their means and the size of the movement (based on the number of members), starting with a small, rickety room in the depths of the city, lacking electricity and minimal sanitary conditions; and ending with a premises of several rooms. The older group, full of energy and dynamic spirit, conducted their meetings in the first, small room. They would remain until midnight, and at times even later, reading articles about the leaders of the generation and conducting lively discussions and debates on any topic related to Jewish life in the Land and the Diaspora. I recall an evening of stormy debate when we read the article of Z. Jabotinsky, "Ya Brechen." The meeting almost broke up in anger on account of the differences of opinion, and people stopped speaking to each other... However, after a few days, they again sat together for the purpose of actualizing their common sublime goal of disseminating the general Zionist idea among the youth, and calling them toward *hachshara* and *aliya* to the Land. That same group of youths struggled to maintain the existence of this youth chapter. They wandered from place to place, from one end of the city to the other, in accordance with their financial means and the number of members, until they reached tens, and more than 100.

[Page 109]

*

Between each wandering, meetings took place in temporary locations. There was a time where there was no place for the 11-13 year old members to meet, so they held their meetings outside. They would march together to one of the groves or meadows outside the city, and conduct their discussions and games under the open sky. I wish to note here one interesting episode about the temporary meeting places that will shed light on the period.

This was one room out of two, that was placed at our disposal for out meetings two to three times per week by the older Zionists (I think it was Achva). During that period, the state government decided to work against the Communists, whose movement had flourished greatly despite it being illegal. Several secret policemen were brought to this activity. I was a high school student at the time.

One day in the middle of class, I was summoned to the principal's office for questioning. They examined my handwriting, and asked me all types of strange questions. They finally informed me that they suspect me of belonging to the Communist movement, since the secret police saw me at times at the place known as the "Old Courthouse" – where the Communist meetings would take place. To my good fortune, I lived in that house, and it was therefore easy to explain why I am often found there... One of the secret policemen who was present became distraught.

[Page 110]

In addition, I admitted that we indeed conduct meetings there, but we are Zionists and not Communists. After a long explanation of our goals to all present, including the security men, the police, and the high school principal, the situation was understood. The period of suspicion against us as Communists and the investigations against other members of our group ceased. Furthermore, even though membership in any movement was forbidden by the charter of the school, we received at that time a form of unofficial permit for our meetings, for the principal knew about them and did not object... I recall that a brief time after this incident, the principal spoke before all the students of the high school around the time of the Christmas vacation, and expressed the following, "I am jealous of the movement that is able to attract you to this degree, and I wish that the school, with its various clubs, would have the same power of attraction toward all the students as your movement has toward yourselves." Indeed, with the passage of time, it was obvious that all of the good students belonged to our movement...

*

With the wanderings of our movement in terms of a premises, I recall two places in particular in which our chapter managed to remain for a longer period. One of them was at Felder's at the foot of the mountain, from where the path led to the village of Jawora. The second was on the mountain, leading to the monastery. During that period, the chapter reached its pinnacle of development, with respect to number of members as well as organizational activities. It was at that time that a dispute broke out among the leadership, which brought the organization to the threshold of a chasm. It turned to the highest institutions in Krakow for mediation. After an investigation by a representative of the high leadership in Krakow, the dispute was settled and matters continued on as previously.

*

One event, apparently not unique, is etched in my memory. I will describe it here. It took place on the night of Purim during a celebration in the chapter.

To this time, all of the institutions of Jewish societal life existed in the fashion that has crystallized during the final generations of the Diaspora in Poland. One of them was the night of Purim, centered on the Purim feast. All honorable families would partake of a feast at a table decked with delicacies and special foods. The feast would continue until a late hour at the night, for on that evening, children in costume would visit the houses in order to receive Purim donations. Groups of people in costume also came around and performed snippets from Biblical stories or complete skits; as did groups of people who were not in costume, whose task was to collect donations for various charitable purposes. These people stayed for a little while for a snack, general conversation, or to listen to words of Torah and issues of the holiday.

[Page 111]

This was the first time that the feast in our home did not run to a late hour, as was customary. I believe that this was in 1933. The number of people in costume and the number of groups declined, and there seemed no point to sit around the table and wait... I recall the mood of my father of blessed memory – and he gave us permission to leave the house and go to the chapter.

There, we gathered together in large numbers to celebrate Purim together, without any preparations. We began to sing spontaneously a tune related to the words, “Sacrifice, sacrifice in righteousness, sacrifice for G-d.” The song was brought from Krakow. It was a “circular” Hassidic melody that had no end... We all then joined together in a dance, in Hassidic fashion, with both hands on the shoulders of the person in front of us, and we all, without exception, danced. Hand on shoulder, we circled the rooms, mounted the tables, went out to the yard, and then returned to the rooms... This continued for a long time, and the enthusiasm brimmed over. As the singing continued, the dancing turned into a drawn out singing parade that filled the space. There was a mystical devotion that was not connected to the words that were sung. All the participants felt a full sense of happiness, joy and mirth.

To me, this evening symbolized the past era stamped with the Diaspora Jewish lifestyle merging with a group with a different lifestyle. The singing, dancing procession was the beginning of the march toward these new paradigms...

The Akiva group in Turka at a Purim celebration. 5695 (1935)

[Page 112]

The "Akiva" Hebrew Youth Group in Turka

by Hela Kaspi-Schreiber of Jerusalem

The city, located between mountains and valleys, with a splendid natural environment, was destroyed and burnt completely during the First World War. Its Jews scattered as refugees in the neighboring countries in order to save themselves. When they returned to Turka at the conclusion of the war, they found their houses burnt and the city desolate. Failed farmers of that area would not be able to restore themselves. They were illiterate and completely destitute. The Polish government did not pay much attention to that district. The Ukrainians did not excel in their appreciation of the national aspirations of the Polish government. Their leaning was toward a free Ukraine. Therefore, the city may not have been resurrected at all were it not for its diligent Jews, full of initiative and Jewish culture. Indeed, the Jews of Turka were not only erudite scholars and enthusiastic Hassidim, but also carpenters, tailors, builders, shoemakers, and experts in all other trades needed to reconstruct life in the city. Of course, there was also no shortage of businessmen with initiative – and the city had been rebuilt with their own hands and money within a few years after the war. It bustled with life.

Hela Kaspi-Schreiber

Despite the hatred of the Jews and the "*numrus clausus*" (quotas) in the universities of Poland, the Jews of Turka, as in other cities, aspired to raise their children on the social ladder. There were many Jewish children in the city high school.

Angst in the Midst of the Youth

Prior to the Second World War, the youth of the city tended toward various directions. There were some who turned their ears toward the disseminators of Communism and Socialism. As in the entire world in that era, the Jewish youth in particular felt the pain of the oppressed, the failed, and the unemployed whose numbers were very high in Poland at that time. The youth asked themselves whether the solution to the human problems would also bring redemption for themselves as Jews. For the most part, these were Jews who were immersed in Jewish culture.

[Page 113]

A small portion of the youth even aspired to shake themselves free of Jewish culture, "to hide their Jewish essence," and to assimilate and lay down roots within Polish culture.

A New Movement Arose…

A group of members of the Akiva group of Turka

It was 1931. A group of high school students of the city began to articulate new ideas and founded a chapter of the Akiva Hebrew youth movement, which was headquartered in Krakow. To their dismay and the dismay of their parents, they interrupted their studies, and did not agree to become the succeeding generation of the Diaspora. In this manner, they smashed their parents' dreams and aroused their anger. The group indentified with the ideals that were promoted by the Akiva movement, and with great enthusiasm "stalked and ambushed" every male and female young person who was not yet a member of an organization. They were particularly enthused with the Zionist idea of personal actualization as well as with the kibbutz idea. To them, this was not an objective in of itself, as with the leftist movements, but rather a means for building up the Land and setting "the state on its path." The uniqueness of that movement in those days was that the Akiva Movement already awakened the aspiration to restore Jewish consciousness. At that time, its leaders already sensed the empty vacuum in which the Jewish youth was immersed. They were enthusiastic for a "change of values" with respect to the ancient storehouse – without knowing with what to replace it. Therefore, the members of Akiva began to delve into the articles of Ahad Haam. They studied Hebrew not only to master the language, but also to be able to understand chapters of the Bible. They also delved deeply into Jewish history. They set up special courses for counselors dedicated to mastery of the aforementioned subjects. Large gatherings were organized, dedicated to words of warning about the enemy that was lurking at the gates of Poland. All the members of the chapter were honorable, and enthusiastic toward actualization of their dreams. Many were also alert to the problems of justice and equity in the world, and also wished to actualize the ideas of Socialism in the work life in the land and in the kibbutzim. Even though they did not affiliate with the leftist faction, they stood for the ideas of A. D. Gordon and studied his writings.

[Page 114]

All the members of the Turka chapter knocked on the doors of the leaders of the movement, and pleaded to be sent to *hachshara* and to be granted permits for *aliya*. However, only a small number received what they wanted. The remainder waited impatiently and often bitterly. Great disappointment and despair was their lot, for who knew better than them what was impending?... We will appreciate their honorableness and faithfulness toward the national idea if we recall that the parents were very much shaken by the aspirations of their children, and they opposed and fought against them. A Zionist son or daughter in the family was considered to be a greater tragedy than a child who became attached to Communism. Indeed, the Jewish father knew that the youths would be "cured" of Communism when they got older, but Zionism was a "snare" for their children. It robbed them from their house and bore them to a far-off place from where there is no return. Even at that time, on the eve of the Holocaust, the Jews deluded themselves with false ideas, for they were afraid of the reality, and immersed in concerns regarding livelihood, some in comfort and some in poverty.

The Delusions of the Generation

The delusion regarding the following generation, of their financial and cultural heirs, to them was like craziness in the face of despair. In 1937, I received a gift from home – a travel ticket to Poland. This was after two years of living in the Land as a member of the Beer Yaakov group. These were years of struggle for Hebrew work in the orchards, years of want, austerity and other difficulties. The group stood up to the challenge and believed that it would attain its goal. When I arrived home to Turka, the entire family gathered together for a festive meal in honor of the guest. I felt that the hope fluttered in their hearts that I may have "smartened up" and may even wish to remain with them. Apparently, the fear that was embedded in the hearts of everyone constantly aroused debates between those present at the feast. With the enthusiasm of the conversation and faith in the correctness of my words, I forgot that I was standing before my own family members, and I portrayed the cruel enemy that would come to Poland, steal their property and even attempt to take their lives, as he had promised in his book[3]. My words were not novel, but everyone was afraid and shaken. They lectured me – how can a daughter state such curses before her parents. With contrite and apologetic language, I attempted to sweeten my words, for in those days, I myself was afraid of them...

[Page 115]

The "Akiva" Movement – the Dream and Realization

by Moshe Zauerbron of Beit Yehoshua

Moshe Zauerbron

I merited being among the first in March 1939, when I received a permit for *aliya* to the Land after several years of *hachshara*. This was approximately a year prior to the outbreak of the Second World War. During that timeframe, the expectations for Aliya Bet[4] began to awaken in our town as a result of the severe restrictions on legal *aliya* by the Mandate government. Already then, people began to feel some sort of internal insecurity and insecurity; and fear of what was to come increased, especially in Eastern Europe.

I well recall the days before I left Polish soil (Turka) . My feelings of joy were tempered by sadness. I parted from my family with a heavy heart, as they grasped my hands and expressed their feelings of jealousy. They did not understand exactly the meeting of the thing, but everyone sensed instinctively that something was about to happen (even though nobody would have imagined such a terrible Holocaust!) The atmosphere where we were was already oppressive and poisoned from the perspective of the Polish population on one side and the Ukrainian population on the other side.

My parting from my eldest brother Naftali was a particularly moving scene. His strong desires and aspirations for *aliya* formed a part of his life after many years of Zionist activity in the Hechalutz organization. However, due to family responsibilities, he filled a holy duty: After the death of our dear parents, he was the sole livelihood earner who cared for his two younger brothers.

*

We lived for many years in a single story house with Alter and Etti Montag. (He died in the Land and she died in Turka several years before the war). We lived downstairs and they lived upstairs. Their private residence served as a house of worship on Sabbaths and festivals until the completion of the building of the "Shul" (there were many *kloizes*). Alter himself and his close friend Ben-Zion Ferbel exerted themselves greatly in gathering donations and collecting names for contracts for completing the building. They did not stop until they completed their work.

[Page 116]

When the month of Elul and the days of *Selichot* [5] approached, Chezkele Chomitz would pass through at 2:00 a.m. with a kerosene lantern, knock a the windows and chant the customary melody for awakening people for *Selichot*. If someone did not arise upon hearing his strong voice, he would be forced to wake up. Avrahamche Bruner served as the usual prayer leader during the High Holidays. He conducted the services with emotion and good taste. He was already about 70 years old, and I am still amazed to this day as to how a man of that age would be able to stand at the prayer podium constantly from *Kol Nidre* until *Neila*, including *Shacharit* and *Musaf*! Apparently, physical power was not the sole explanation. One requires strong faith and a warm heart.

Activities in the Chapter

Despite the fact that I belonged to a different movement than my brother Naftali, and despite the internal debates and differences of opinion between us, our family relations were not impacted by the disputes that we had witnessed in other homes. I belonged to the Akiva chapter (of the General

Zionist stream) that was founded in Turka in 1930 by Chaya (Hela) Schreiber (who lives in the Land today), and was centered in Krakow. She studied in this city for many years, imbued the city with the ideology of the movement and later imprinted her stamp upon the local chapter. At first it seemed that this meeting place was designated solely for students and well-placed people. However, the error was quickly clarified: within a brief period, this became a populist framework that encompassed the best of the local youth from all strata of society. During those years, specific parents, especially the Orthodox, objected to their sons and daughters belonging to such movement (as they called in "Farein") out of fear of demoralization and leading them off of the straight path. However, they expressed their agreement once Akiva entered the scene. They felt that this was not like the other organizations where people cut themselves off and freed themselves from the past immediately upon joining. Here, the situation was exactly the opposite: Tradition and the Jewish reality were nurtured; the connection between Judaism and nationalism was strengthened; the Sabbath was observed or at least not violated publicly; there was respect and proper regard for other sacred values, etc.

The celebration of the Sabbath during the twilight hours was a natural way of doing things within the Akiva movement. We would gather and sing together. A pleasant social atmosphere of love for one's fellow was forged. We would organize clubs for Bible study. A group of people would get up at 5:00 a.m. every morning during the summer holidays to go to the mountain atop the tunnel. They would study and delve into the explanations of Gordon[6] until the train rushed through the tunnel at 7:15 and passed through the entire city over the viaducts, with a plume of smoke ascending, as if hinting to us, "Sirs, the time has come to eat breakfast!" We would close our Bibles and prepare to descend from the mountain.

[Page 117]

A member joined us whose calm, quiet demeanor stands before my eyes to this day, and whom I will never forget: Aryeh (Leib) Kraus, a refined soul, intelligent, and a symbol of conscience. We always compared his facial appearance to the Idek (Yehuda Ornstein, one of the leaders of the movement) of the Turka chapter. Here, I have fulfilled one of the three adages of Yehoshua ben Perachia[7]: "acquire for yourself a friend." Indeed, he was my close friend. I placed great faith in him, and he never disappointed me. We always had a topic for conversation that was never completed... When we returned home from the chapter late at night, I would always accompany him for half the way – he lived in "Oiben Dorf". We conducted discussions in Hebrew, despite the mistakes that we made. There was always a struggle for a morsel of bread in Turka, as with all Jews. Livelihood was not plentiful in his family as well. He earned his tuition fees by giving lessons to students, on the advice of his teachers who held him in great esteem.

The Ideological Connection with the Movement in the Land

At that time, life in the chapter was vibrant. This was the bright era. There was wonderful internal sense of fulfillment and full understanding and cooperation between the group heads and their charges. The youth heeded everything stated by the group head. At one of the meetings, the chapter leadership had a serious discussion about the need to prepare the youth while they were young for *aliya* to the Land of Israel, by having them learn a trade. We preached morning and night that the Land and the kibbutz had a need for tradesmen. Within a brief period, we were witnesses to positive results in this activity. We began to study carpentry, locksmithing, blacksmithing, etc. We must feel great sorrow for the wonderful youths who did not complete the task and actualize their dreams and aspirations.

In 1933, the fist members of the local chapter made *aliya* to Kibbutz Akiva in Petach Tikva. We were always eager to find out what was taken place, and the happiness was very great when we received letters from the Land in general, and from the Kibbutz in particular. To our sorrow, the news about what was transpiring at the Kibbutz was not always encouraging. Frequent crises affected life therein, as well as internal debates and disputes regarding the way of life and characters. The human content was also variegated. There were differences of outlook and opinion regarding Jewish life and the relation to Jewish tradition. All of these of course affected the communal life.

[Page 118]

After difficult and unsuccessful attempts, a new idea was floated – to create *hachshara* units while still in the Diaspora, so that the members will affiliate with a specific group from the outset. The older members from Turka belonged to a group that was called "Retzon Haam" (The Will of the People), and their *hachshara* location was in Krakow. Its goal was to establish an independent settlement somewhere in the land. In the interim, the Petach Tikva Kibbutz split up. One group established a new settlement called Neve Eitan in the Beit Shean Valley. Several Turka natives live there to this day. Another group, including the leadership of the movement, established the Beit Yehoshua settlement in the Sharon, named after the prominent Zionist leader who has served as the head of the Jewish faction in the Sejm (Polish parliament) and strongly protected Jewish rights – Rabbi Dr. Yehoshua Tahon of blessed memory.

Changes and Actualization

After a decade of existence, the Beit Yehoshua Kibbutz was forced to disband and turn into a settlement of workers. Among other reasons, there was the issue of the loss of the human resources of the movement in the Diaspora due to the complete Nazi annihilation. Even according to our kibbutz-oriented understanding based on the ideological foundations of the movement, this was a case of ideological actualization – for the Kibbutz was only supposed to serve as a means toward the ultimate aim of establishing a Jewish State, and not a way of life in of itself. It is worthwhile to note here that the Kibbutz turned into a workers' settlement immediately at the conclusion of the War of Independence, as if this was a prophetic actualization... Today, the village has more than 70 families and is located in the heart of the country. Four Turka families who have been there since 1940 have bound their fate to that place eternally. The traditional character that existed at that time was carefully preserved to this day thanks to our spiritual leader and friend Yoel Driblatt of blessed memory, who was sensitive and concerned about that spirit, and instilled the love of Jewish tradition within us. The fact that the next generation was educated in this spirit brings us joy.

Last year, we built a splendid synagogue in the name of Yoel of blessed memory, which beautifies the landscape of the entire village, and not solely from an external vantage point... It infused an internal light: Every Sabbath, one can find youth and children in therein, forming close to three *minyanim* [30 people]. The synagogue is a vibrant center of cultural and social life. No form of cultural activity or entertainment can replace the traditional Jewish reality.

The terrible Holocaust that affected this generation has provided us, as reparations, with a sovereign state to ingather the survivors. Despite the fact that it is surrounded by enemies, we believe that they will not have the upper hand, and the longed-for peace will come. Indeed, through the establishment of Israel we will be comforted from the loss of the dear life in the Holocaust.

Translator's Footnotes:

4. There may be a play on words here with the word "*acher*" (other). This is term used in the Talmud for the sage Elisha ben Avuya, who abandoned his belief in Torah.
5. See http://en.wikipedia.org/wiki/Ahad_Ha%27am
6. Presumably Mein Kampf.
7. See http://en.wikipedia.org/wiki/Aliyah_Bet
8. Penitential prayers recited early in the morning during the period prior to Rosh Hashanah, and between Rosh Hashanah and Yom Kippur.
9. See http://en.wikipedia.org/wiki/A._D._Gordon.
10. A Mishnaic sage. The quotation is from *Pirke Avot*..

[Page 118]

The Gordonia Movement in Turka

by Pnina Vamushi-Sternbuch

Youth Without Prospects

The strongest and largest youth movement in Turka was Hashomer Hatzair, to which the majority of the youth belonged. However, not everyone joined Hashomer Hatzir, and for various reasons, a large portion of the youth remained outside of any organizational framework, and had not yet found its way. It was clear to everyone that great danger awaited the Jewish youth in all the cities of Galicia, and the youth themselves knew that they had no prospects for the future in Turka. The question "to where"" gave them no rest and always boring through their brains.

It is no surprise, therefore, that this youth always welcomed with blessing and enthusiasm every new idea in which they hoped to find a solution for their lives. The Youth of Turka was alert to everything that took place in the Jewish world. One day, a law student appeared in Turka. He was a tall, think youth full of energy. He gathered together a group of studying youth, and delivered an enthusiastic and convincing speech on the subject of A. D. Gordon. This student was Pinchas Lubianiker, today Pinchas Lavon[1].

Since the youth in Turka lived in the bosom of nature, in the region of fields, groves and forests, it wsa easy for them to understand the doctrine of Gordon. One of the most active people who joined the movement and was taken by the ideas and doctrine of Grodon wsa Manis Branis of blessed memory. He was the first to immediately begin to organize Gordonia, to which he dedicated most of his time and energy.

New Motto: "Actualize!"

The Gordonia motto, "Actualize!" was particularly enchanting. In the streets of Turka, in which to this point only the blessing of "Be strong and of good courage" had been heard, a new motto was heard – "Actualize". This enchanting word brought a stream of members into Gordonia. Many debates began on the means of actualization, with the labor doctrine of A. D. Gordon being at the center of the aspirations. This included the love of the land of the Land of Israel and agricultural work, "To participate in life and creativity," etc.

In excursions in the vicinity of Turka with the beautiful landscape in the background, we saw before us the fields of the Land of Israel. Instead of the coniferous trees that grew in abundance in that vicinity, we imagined the mountains of the Land of Israel forested with palms, olive trees, and citrus trees... In our imagination

[Page 120]

We not only strolled in the fields and groves of Turka, but also in the fields of our Land... To the joy of the first members of Gordonia in Turka, many joined the movement, and there were already approximately 200 members of the movement in the first month. The movement continued to grow from day to day. Apparently, this was also due to the fact that many conventions of the national movement took place in Turka, on account of the wonderful scenery that nature bestowed upon the area.

I recall the convention that took place on the peak of Zawizonicz. Indeed, this was an unforgettable experience!

Translator's Footnote:

4. See http://en.wikipedia.org/wiki/Pinhas_Lavon.

[Page 121]

The "Poale Zion" Organization and Around it

by Chaim Pelech

Members of the Poale Zion organization in Turka taking leave of their member Dr. Manes Brenes just before he made aliya to the Land

At the beginning of 1919, Shlomo Pelech founded and organized the Poale Zion Zionist workers' party in Turka. Moshe Shein, the former Zh. P. S. member, joined it. Since at the time there were no other workers' organizations in Turka, Poale Zion encompassed all of the workers in the city, and even many small-scale businessmen from our city. It conducted wide branched cultural and societal work among the poor Jewish population.

Work Committees

The work was organized into work committees. Each committee made several improvisations. The cultural committee arranged readings on various themes. Those readings attracted workers and young people due to their interesting repertoire. Yosel Brenes undertook the dramatic work. His task was to organize a dramatic club, and he did this successfully. He assembled a dramatic group that played the best literary pieces. Melech Meiner worked in that group. There was a story that Melech Meiner had it in his head to perform "The Robber" of Schiller and Yossel Brenes was against it: "For you cannot do such a thing with amateurs!", he said. Melech Meiner continued to persist, and said that he would take the entire task and responsibility upon himself. Thus it was. Melech Meiner toiled and led that undertaking – and Turka had what to laugh about for two years... The performance went from 8:00 p.m. until 4:00 a.m. You can imagine what took place after that in the town...

Uncaptioned – a photo of a group gathering

However Melech Meiner, who was influenced by German literature, was not behind the times... He then had the idea of holding a debate about "Virtue and Addiction – a Philosophical Contract". Yossel Brenes and Mordechai Pikholtz complained: "Melech, this is not for your sake; you cannot hold such a debate..." Melech Meiner did not obey (Shlomo Pelech supported him)... On fine Sabbath, Melech Meiner held his philosophical debate... Do not ask what went on... The audience confused him, and they laughed a great deal. Such a topsy-turvy piece of work had not been seen in Turka for a long time.

The Poale Zion party was very popular in town. They had a large premises in Yaakov Liber's house. In that premises, they performed Yiddish theater, made balls, and conduced widespread activity.

Poale Zion worked in all the institutions that existed in Turka at that time. Their representatives were included among the assistance committee of the Joint, they were volunteers of the Jewish orphanage, and they worked on the Jewish national committee. And conducted a struggle against the bourgeois Zionists.

Rifts

Things went on as normal until... discussions took place in the party regarding the right and the left. Melech Meiner, Chaim Chiel, Chaim Pelech, Yosef Ortel and Ziel Zawel were among the left group. The discussions were dogged. Shlomo Pelech warned that they should not break up the party, and if such is not possible, the dictatorship must be from the proletariat, so it will be good for us...

One fine Friday, a delegate came to use from Lemberg. He was a Hebrew teacher by the name of Barkowski, and completed the rift. Both sides remained in the same location, and conducted joint activities on occasion. The youth group, consisting of 48 people, went over to the Left Poale Zion. After some time, the Right Poale Zion united with the Hitachdut Party and became very active, particularly in various election campaigns, in the city council and in the cultural organization, they had their representatives in the orphanage, in the Gemilut Chasadim (Benevolent) Bank, in the certificate committee, in the Keren Kayemet committee, and in Keren HaYesod.

The party conducted cultural activities. I remember the literary judgement regarding Stringdberg's [1] wife, which went on for four Friday evenings, and arose great interest among the Turka public.

The Hechalutz organization in Turka, 1933

Translator's Footnotes:

11. August Strindberg was a Swedish dramatist, 1849-1912.

[Page 125]

Zionist Activity in Turka in the Years 1930-1935

by Zev Steininger

In memory of my dear parents, my brothers and sisters, relatives and friends who did not merit witnessing the birth of Israel.

Even though our city was located far from the large Jewish centers, Zionist life bustled there with full strength. The many Zionist youth groups as well as the pioneering *aliya* that streamed to the Land of Israel starting from the beginning of the 1920s testify to this. The *aliya* continued throughout the entire time -- whether through certificate or through illegal *aliya*.

The majority of the youth were organized into the Labor Zionist camp. This was natural, since the majority of the Jewish population of Turka and its environs were of the working class, tradesmen or middle class.

*

The merit of being first belongs to the Hashomer Hatzair youth movement. It was the only one in our town for several years. Only with the increase of Zionist activity in Poland did its echoes begin to reach us too. Representatives of all the movements began to influence and organize the youth.

The Hebrew Akiva youth movement, which had the goal of organizing the studying youth, began its activities at that time among the others. The activity was successful, and the majority of the youth who studied in the gymnasium gathered around that movement. The movement drew the youth toward Zionist actualization by studying the Hebrew language in its many clubs, by sending its pioneering members to *hachshara*, and by activities on behalf of the Jewish National Fund.

The Akiva movement was the only one in our town to organize a mass gathering when the Nazis, may their names be blotted out, ascended to government. It sounded an alarm regarding the great danger that was hovering and approaching us. The gathering took place in the large Proszbyta Hall, and the young, talented lawyer Yosef Szprung delivered a fiery speech.

[Page 126]

Aside from the youth movements, there were also organization of the older people. It is appropriate to note here the Achva movement of the general Zionists. There was also Hapoel Hamizrachi, which served the religious wing of Zionism in our city.

The crowning achievement of Zionist activity was the Sabbath afternoon meetings. All of the youth gathered in their headquarters and arranged roll calls, and then set out in their groups and brigades toward the open fields outside the city, where they conducted discussions on issues of the day. It is interesting that the place at which all the groups met was called "Das Shomer Veldl" (The Shomer Grove) by the people.

All of the youth movements of our city joined together in another important field of endeavor. A local convention took place with representation of delegates from all the factions and youth movements. This was a successful activity because, in addition to the meetings of the delegates, large scale educational activities took place amongst all the various Jewish strata.

The Achva Zionist youth in Turka

[Page 127]

One of the foundations of the Zionist education delivered by the youth movements was education toward a Jewish personality who had pride in his Judaism and who would also know how to defend himself in the event of tribulations.

*

Then, the evil decrees began for Polish Judaism: The decrees of Mrs. Prystor[1] and the ban of Jewish *shechita* (ritual slaughter), the pogroms of Przytyk, and the anti-Semitic incitement in every city and town. Of course, the tribulations did not skip over our city. The gentile stores, barber shops and bakeries began to add the notation “Christian” to their signs...

The anti-Semitic incitement increased especially among the Ukrainian population who lived on the edges of the city. They often attacked Jewish passers by, especially the Jews of Upper Turka, who had to pass through their neighborhood. The Jews would often defend themselves and return the beating. Such an incident took place on one Sabbath eve when the Jews returned home after the service to Welcome the Sabbath. In the fracas that broke out, the Ukrainians received severe blows from the brave Jews, like the descendents of “Noach Pandre”[2]

The Achva Zionist youth in Turka

[Page 128]

The organized youth reacted to what was taking place to them in those days by clarifying the situation at internal meetings and preparing for self defense. Rumors spread that the surrounding population was planning to perpetrate an attack to plunder the Jewish stores on the market day that took place every Wednesday. The situation would have come to actual violence were it not for the strong reaction of the Jews toward the local authorities. As a result, the authorities took restraining action, and the plans of the hooligans were thwarted.

*

The economic situation worsened day by day. The youth began to leave the city and search for other places to live. Many made *aliya* to the Land through various means.

The parents remained, and many hoped for the opportunity to reunite with their children, many of whom had arrived in the Land. Alas, all contact was lost at the outbreak of the war, and all hope was lost.

Members of the editorial committeeof "Iton-Chai" (Living Newspaper)
Standing: Yitzckak Karafiol (living in Haifa)
Sitting from the right: Naftali Zauerbron of blessed memory, Abish Artel of blessed memory, Moshe Press (living in Haifa), Yaakov Weiss of blessed memory

Translator's Footnotes:

54. Mrs. Janina Prystor, a deputy of the Polish Sejm and wife of former Polish Prime Minister Aleksander Prystor. In 1936, she introduced a government bill that would ban *shechita*.
55. A character from one of the books by the author Zalman Shneur.

[Page 129]

Zionist Activists

By Chaim Pelech
Translated by Jerrold Landau
Donated by Boaz Ben-Pelech

Yosef Koppel

In the Zionist organization of Turka, the oldest organization in the city, there were many people that excelled with their activity as general activists. Yosef Koppel was one of them. Koppel excelled as an honest and honorable activist and as a nationalist Jew. He was the director of the Gemilat Chassadim Bank. That institution developed greatly under his directorship. The bank functioned very well and efficiently, and administered assistance to hundreds of small-scale merchants and craftsmen. He led the bank for more than twenty years – always with responsibility and without subterfuge.

I recall the following fact: Once I went to him to purchase something. I chanced upon his wife (she was involved in the business) weeping strongly. I asked her, "Mrs. Koppel, why are you weeping?" She answered me, "Why should I not weep – I have a husband who is a bank director, and my husband, the director protested about my five promissory notes that were not paid... He protests about his own promissory notes!..."

I had long known Koppel as an honorable Jew, a son of the judge Elia Koppel. However that fact left a strong impression upon me as something unbelievable.

He was also a very educated man. Under his leadership, the Zionist organization in Turka displayed a great deal of activity in many realms of political and societal life. Still later, when the organization was already led by Dr. Winter or later by Dr. Glick, his influence was still strong. He was numbered among the oldest and first Zionists in the city.

He also took part in the electoral activities for the Austrian parliament on behalf of the Zionists. He campaigned in the city for the candidates – for Dr. Zipper against the assimilationist Dr. Levenstein.

The Hechalutz Organization of Turka, September 15, 1934

The Brothers Baruch and Nissan Maj

Baruch Maj was also numbered among the first Zionists in Turka. He was an intelligent and honorable man. He worked for the party for his entire life, and stood in its first ranks in the darkest of times. Already in the years 1907 and 1911, he was involved in the great struggle for the nationalist candidate Dr. Zipper. At that time, it was still difficult to be a Zionist in Turka. However, Baruch Maj was not from among the cowards. His idealism and dedication to nationalistic matters overcame all difficulties.

His brother Nissan Maj was also a dedicated activist in Turka. In 1919, Nissan Maj was the secretary and council member of the Jewish national council. He demonstrated that he was very capable in political affairs. The opposition did not know what to do about him. Still, everyone had the greatest of respect for him because of his capabilities.

In 1920, Nissan left for Pressburg, and from there for Israel. He died in Israel in 1963. His older aforementioned brother Baruch died in Turka when he was very young.

Uncaptioned. A group photo

Matis Operman

He was a representative in the cultural organization. He excelled in his willingness to work for the Zionist organization. As a great liberal, he acted for the entire Jewish population of Turka. He was probably murdered by the German murderers.

[Page 133]

Yiddish Theater in Turka

by Eli Montag of New York

Eli Montag

To the holy memory of my dear wife Peshi and my son Moshele.

I recall that after the First World War, the spiritual and cultural baggage of our town was especially rich. Various groups and organizations of all persuasions constantly sprouted up like mushrooms following a rainfall. Lectures, speeches, and literary evenings of all types were a weekly occurrence.

Prior to the First World War

The theater played a very important role in the cultural and social life of our town. It is also worthwhile to mention that from speaking to people older than me, it is clear to me that theater troupes from the former Lemberg and the former "Singer Brothers" used to come to town often and perform Yiddish theater with great success. Already at that time, years before the First World War, Turka had a good drama club with a very active director. His name was Melech Brauer. Under his directorship, they performed plays of Jacob Gordin[1], Avraham Goldfaden, Latiner[2] and others on countless occasions, and the audience literally licked their fingers. It is especially worthwhile to mention two actors from that time. The first is Henia Zuswajn. Incidentally, she stemmed from a well placed family. Her father was the honorable Jew, Avraham Zuswein. People who knew her told me how she played Mirele in Gordin's "Mirele Efros"[3]. They said that her playing of that role and her performance on stage can be compared with the best actresses who played that character on the Yiddish stage. The second, Pinchas Rotenberg, who was actually called "Pinchasl" played comical roles. His performance of "Leizer Badchan" in Gordin's "God, Man and Devil" was something special.

[Page 134]

After the War

Immediately after the First World War, when Jews began to return to the town and the majority of the houses had been destroyed during the war, including the only theater house with a stage; there were some people who found a house that had a large hall, rented it, set up a *galiarke* as they called it, constructed a stage. Yiddish theater groups from the former Galicia began to come, and theater was once again performed! Truth be told, neither the repertoire nor the performance of the actors was the best. However, the audiences came en masse; first of all because people hungered for Yiddish theater during the war years, and second, because viewing Yiddish theater, hearing and learning to sing a Yiddish song was something that flowed in their blood.

Theater Troupes Visit Turka

The rise of better Yiddish theater in Poland also came through our town. In the coffeehouses and the conversation groups, people began to talk about the "Vilna Troupe" and all of the other fine Jewish theater groups that began to appear in Poland at that time. People who had been in a large city and had seen the "Dybbuk" or "Night in the Old Market" there would express their amazement and talk grandly about what they had seen. In fact, Turka was the last point on the map of Eastern Galicia, far off in the mountains near the Czechoslovak-Hungarian border. Nevertheless, the Jewish theater contractors knew that Turka was a town where people craved the best Yiddish words, Yiddish songs, and Yiddish melodies. The finest Yiddish theater ensembles in Poland began to visit Turka. Even American theater groups that came to Poland and only visited the largest cities would come to perform also in Turka. In truth, it must be mentioned that at times they bypassed larger cities on their way to Turka and did not perform there. It is not boasting, but rather a description of the cultural level, to list some of the theater troupes and actors that performed in the town from 1928 to 1939. The list is as fallows: The "Azazel" Kleinkunst (cabaret) theater of Warsaw; the "Ararat" Kleinkunst theater of Lodz; Ida Kaminska and her troupe; Jonas and Zygmunt Turkow with their troupe; Boris Tomashevsky from America with his group; Pesachke Bornstein from America with his troupe; Rachel Holtzer, Yosef Kamen, and many, many others. They did not come once in a jubilee, but rather quite often, both in summer and winter. They always performed before a packed theater. The better the performance, the more enthusiastic was the audience, and the bravos deafened the theater hall. We knew that the name of the town of Turka must be well known by every Jewish theatrical contractor, and had an important place.

[Page 135]

Local Drama Circles

I always took great interest in theater in general and certainly for Yiddish theater. Between 1928 and 1940, I worked as a director and at time an actor in several drama circles in our town. With modest means, I always succeeded in creating the best that was possible. Under my direction, we performed Shalom Aleichem's "The Grand Prize," "It is Hard to be a Jew," "People" ; Peretz Hirshbein's "Green Fields"; David Bergelson's "The Deaf Man" and others, which were rehearsed countless times.

I remember the following about the preparations and performance of one of them: At around the end of 1930 or perhaps later, the Y. L. Peretz Jewish Culture League set up a dramatic club and I was asked to prepare a performance. I told them that I was prepared to help only on the condition that they forget about light theater and quick performances, but rather work on a long performance that would bring out the best that is possible. Everyone agreed, and even boasted of the idea of preparing a spectacle of a high artistic level. I suggested that we take on "The Deaf Man" by David Bergelson.

[Page 136]

After the first reading, at which strong interest was expressed, we discussed the assignment of roles. We abandoned the customary form of "one role for one person." Two people were selected for each role so that there could be a choice. The tryouts lasted for several months. The participants, young lads and charming girls, created the best character types. A great deal of work took place on the technical side. A special set was constructed, under the supervision of an overseer who made constant demands. The set reflected to a theatrical time and place. In short – we invested a great deal of work in the performance.

It would be improper to neglect to note here the name of Levi Hamerman, under whose supervision every technical detail was prepared with exactitude. At the end, the performance was performed in the town at a very high artistic level. It was considered among the best that had been performed in our town. The performance resonated very strongly within the theatrical world.

Finally, I wish to recall all of the fine young men and women who gave so much of their free time with goodwill toward this fine work; as well the theatrical world, on whose behalf the entire work was conducted, theater goers who themselves for a part of the Jewish way of life., and who took the Jewish word to their hearts and soul. It is a shame that they are not here any more...

[Page 137]

Klezmers Come to the Shtetl

by Chaim Pelech

Musicians in Turka
1. Chaim Pelech – Musicians Arrived to Town

One a fine morning at the beginning of 1870, a horse and covered wagon entered the Turka market square, driven by a Jew with a not bad looking beard. Turka Jews soon began to gather around the wagon, thinking that they were wayfarers. The non-local Jew realized this and then said, "Good morning, Jews. I have come to you because I have heard that you have no Jewish musician in town who would play genuine Jewish music at Jewish weddings."

The non-local Jew continued on, "I present myself before you. I have come to you from Bessarabia. I am the bandleader. This is my wife, and this is my band. I want to play for you at Jewish weddings in such a manner that you have never heard before..."

A wife and five not yet grown up children sat in the wagon. Together, they formed the musical family. The father was named Fridl Operman, and his sons were Shmuel, Moshe-Avraham, David-Itzik, Berl, and Yossel.

The Jews of Turka received him well, simply because they needed them very badly...

The bandleader did not let the Turka Jews down. They were first class wedding musicians. This was despite the fact that they could not play from notes, but only by ear. They specialized in genuine Jewish wedding music, and the Jews of Turka and its environs were very happy and took great pride in them...

Their name began to spread throughout Galicia as well as into Hungary... Rebbes and wealthy Hassidic Jews from Munkacz, Sighet, Beregszasz and other cities in Hungary hired them to entertain the guests at their weddings. They were "torn" in that sometimes Turka Jews would have to postpone weddings because the band was taken over by the world...

[Page 138]

The Operman band

The musician brothers grew up and led a very interesting Jewish life in Turka. Three of them had beard and *peyos*, whereas two of them shaved. The oldest brother Shmuel led the band, and Moshe-Avraham was his second-in-command. The band owned all the instruments needed to play at Jewish weddings.

In those days, weddings were very joyous. Young people used to shout out, "Moshe-Avraham, a Kozokl, Moshe-Avraham, a Brogzl![4]" Then the youths dressed in *streimels* and silk *bekishes* went to invite the women to dance with a kerchief in the hand[5]... They came to the women, and quietly laid down the kerchief. The women would take the kerchief and go to dance. At first, they would lower their heads a bit and blush – and the youths with *streimels* danced enthusiastically. When the musicians stopped playing, they would shout out, "Moshe-Avraham, continue, continue, more, more – we will work out the accounts later!" The musicians played, and things got steamy! Who can imagine and comprehend today the great joy that overtook the crowd during those weddings. The Turka band cooperated wonderfully.

[Page 139]

The Orchestra in the New Times

by Moshe Frum

With time, the primitive musicians modernized and became accustomed to the new times. The sons of Moshe-Avraham and Shmuel Operman learned how to play from notes and formed themselves into an organized orchestra that not only played at Jewish weddings, but also gave concerts and played in theatrical performances and dance evenings that were often organized by the modern Turka youth.

The orchestra developed especially after the First World War. The Opermans studied music when they were refugees in Vienna. When they returned to Turka after the war, they once again took up their former livelihood.

A movie theater with talking films was started in the city. They would accompany the show with music. Often, the audience would derive more pleasure from their accompaniment than from the film... When various theatrical troupes from all places in Poland would often visit the town, they would engage the orchestra as accompaniment. The Ukrainians and Poles would also engage the Jewish orchestra for their performances that took place in the Sokul and Prasawyta cultural centers.

Thus, the orchestra was loved by the entire population of the city. Its good name also spread far beyond the bounders of Turka. When the Munkaczer Rebbe of holy blessed memory married off his daughter, he specifically hired the Turka musicians for the wedding. Even though Muncacz was situated within the borders of of Czechoslovakia at that time, the Rebbe obtained a special permit for them to travel across the border. The orchestra remained there for a month and entertained the guests in the rebbe's court. The Turka musicians would not forget that wedding for a long time... Aside from the fact that they ate and drank the finest and best of the rebbe's table, they returned home laden with money. The payment was sufficient for wood and potatoes throughout the entire winter, and there was enough left over for shoes and outfits for the children.

[Page 140]

The unfortunate thing was that such wealthy weddings took place one in a blue moon... In general, our musicians were paupers who struggled hard for their existence. They would often have to perform more tricks to provide for the Sabbath than to perform music... Therefore, each of them had to have a secondary source of livelihood, otherwise they would have been unable to sustain themselves.

*

The Operman family remained the primary kernel of the orchestra. Their name was synonymous with musical activity in Turka. As has already been mentioned, some of them studies music in the Vienna Conservatory when they were there as refugees in Austria. One member of the family even became a great virtuoso, but he remained in Vienna and did not return to Turka... The chief leader of the orchestra was Itche Operman, who was known as "Itche Grotsz" (Itche the Hot Headed). He took care of all the administrative details, however he did not play the first violin in the orchestra itself. He was a householder. He had his own small house on the Railway Street and a house full of children... He earned his livelihood with difficulty from the bow, and he broke the musical tradition of the family – he permitted his children to learn other trades...

His brother Leibish Operman was a good violin player. Aside from playing in the orchestra, he also gave music lessons, thereby earning his livelihood for his large family.

[Page 141]

The greatest musician in the family was Matis Operman. He was the only one for whom music was lifetime employment. His primary livelihood was from a colonial business for musical instruments located on the Railroad Street. He only took part in the orchestra for serious endeavors such as concerts or musical theater accompaniment when a Jewish or Ukrainian theater troupe would visit the city. He would seldom play at weddings. If a local wealthy person would marry off a child and specially request that Matis Operman play at the wedding, it would be much more expensive. Not everyone could permit themselves such excessive luxuries.

In truth, it was a special experience to hear Matis play first violin. He would stand earnestly before the entire orchestra and majestically move the bow up and down, bringing out hearty notes from his fine instrument. One did not have to be a special connoisseur of music to realize that a talented musician was standing there.

Things were so good for him that he did not play his music for the purpose of livelihood. He perhaps occupied himself with his music more for his spiritual world. The other orchestra members played more confidently when he was playing with them... They would then all play more seriously, with some sort of special responsibility. They would not rush, and they made sure that they got through it properly. People used to say, "When one has a good wagon, it is also easier to go by foot..."

Pinchas Schwartz was also a good musician. He played many instruments: the violin, trumpet, double bass, and others. He could also sing from notes, and he indeed organized the choirs of the youth organizations and directed their performances.

Pinchas Schwartz came to Turka as a young child already before the First World War. He worked with the city cantor Isser Maj, and sang with him as a singer in the synagogue. With time, he got married and became a resident of the town. He did not make a great fortune. He worked a great deal: playing at night and giving lessons during the day. Even from all that, he did not have enough for the Sabbath... In order to support his wife and four children, he also had to work as a night watchman in a lumber warehouse...

[Page 142]

Leibish Artel played the clarinet, flute, alto, and also the violin. However with all this: with all the instruments and the meager livelihood – he also worked as a hairdresser.

Hershele Poyker (the Drummer) also belonged to this group. He was a small Jew, who worked as a bricklayer as his main source of livelihood. He played the drum in his free time. That is why he had the nickname "Poyker."

*

An amateur orchestra in Turka under the direction of Pinchas Schwartz

Indeed, our musicians did not earn an easy livelihood. As has been said, they always struggled hard for their existence. However, they lived respectable lives as householders and raised their children well. It is worthwhile to emphasize an interesting phenomenon that characterizes their decency. In contrast to them was the merchant class, whose members always fiercely competed with each other, and often came to disputes and even to blows, frequently ending with a Torah based judgment or a court case. On the contrary, peace always pervaded between our musicians. They lived literally like a single family, and never came to any battles. They worked hard for their hard-earned groszy. They were indeed loved greatly by the local population, both Jewish and Christian.

[Page 143]

Berish Miriam's engaged in a conversation about current events on the street

Translator's Footnotes:

56. See http://en.wikipedia.org/wiki/Jacob_Mikhailovich_Gordin
57. See http://en.wikipedia.org/wiki/Joseph_Lateiner
58. See http://en.wikipedia.org/wiki/Mirele_Efros
59. Names of dances.
60. So that there would be no physical contact between the sexes.

[Page 144]

Moshe Shein

By Chaim Pelech
Translated by Jerrold Landau
Donated by Boaz Ben-Pelech

Moshe Shein was an interesting and special personality. He was the first Socialist in town; he founded the Z. P. S. (Zydowska Partja Socialisticzna) Jewish Socialist organization, which was, on a nationalist scale, a division of the P. P. S. Polish Socialist organization.

This took place still in 1911. Moshe Shein rented a room in the attic of Mordechai Klein's house. There, he assembled the “proletariat” of Turka: a few young tailors, a few young shoemakers, and a couple of young carpenters. There were no women there, for they were ashamed...

Shein was connected with the small P. P. S. group that was in Turka; He was liked by them as well, for he appeared on stage at their meetings, where he spoke with enthusiasm, gesticulating greatly with his hands... On May 1st, 1911, he organized, together with the P. P. S., a workers' demonstration. This was the first time something of this nature took place in Turka. Jews indeed claimed that this was the end of the world: Such smart Alecs going in the streets of Turka with red flags, and together with the Christians!

However, Moshe Shein did not listen to them. He was very active. Still in the same year, during the election campaign between the assimilationist Dr. Levenstein and the Zionist Dr. Zipper, he worked on behalf of Dr. Zipper. He organized election meetings and demonstrations against Dr. Levenstein day and night. He was not afraid of anyone...

Aside from this, he had some sort of a “speech job” in Turka. In a certain house on the Rynek, he had a table with a bench – and he delivered Socialist speeches to Jews and gentiles. He had a Ukrainian friend named Kopushtak, and both disseminated Socialist propaganda. When Moshe was speaking, Kopushtak sat on the stool and acted as chairman... He loved it when Moshe spoke. He was dressed with a bright red bow. He stood at the table and delivered fiery propaganda regarding a Socialist order...

Shein was never lacking a topic for a speech. His topics included the matters of the profinancia 1 that suddenly took hold; the Starosta 2 Lokamski with whom Moshe Shein had spent the years; and other topics. Above all, he was a very honorable person and a nationalist Jew.

After the First World War, Moshe Shein changed somewhat. The world concerned him less, and he began to take interest in Jewish problems. He then joined the Poale Zion party, which had been founded in Turka by Shlomo Pelech. He served as chairman of the party for a long time, and was also a representative on the Turka city council, having been elected by Poale Zion. His popularity was very great among both the Jewish and Christian populations. Everyone trusted and had faith in him.

Later, in 1933, when Hitler took control of Germany, he said that Jews must flee from Poland. He used to say that Hitler is not only in Berlin, but he would soon be in Turka too...

He indeed set out on his way. He sold his small house in 1935, and left for the Land of Israel. Unfortunately, he did not live long there.

Translator's Footnotes:

5. The liquor monopoly.
6. Starosta is a mayor or regional head.

[Page 146]

Personalities of Turka

by Shmuel Kraus of Haifa

Heshio (Tzvi) Buchman

He still stands before my eyes in full stature, despite the decades that passed, as a student in the local gymnasium. He was quiet, polite, with the outline of *peyos* on his cheeks. He was well-known for his talents and knowledge. He inherited the scholarly quiet from his father. His father was modest, and a great scholar. According to Reb Hershel Rand of Tarnowa, he was a religious Zionist with consciousness – the first in our town.

He stood out in the gymnasium on account of his diligence and quick grasp. In addition to his secular studies and his *Gemara* studies with his father, he studied typesetting and printing in Grossman's printing house. Aside from playing the mandolin, he composed actual lyrics appropriate for the realistic situation in the school for all the "hit songs." He translated poems, drew caricature illustrations, wrote articles for the school newspaper, and helped those who were struggling without exception.

He studied oriental studies in university. I recall that when I met him before I made *aliya* to the land, and he told me that the famous Polish orientalist Smogozynski visited Saudi Arabia at the end of the 1920s and received an ancient Arabic manuscript as a gift from King Ibn Saud. After he translated it, he felt the need to publish his research with the source. On account of his fluency in Arabic script and knowledge of printing, Heshel[1] arranged, printed and published the first book in Arabic writing in Poland.

Buchman was also involved in the translation of the poems of Bialik, Tshernikovsky and others into Polish, a long time before Shlomo Dikman of blessed memory. He published his translations in the daily newspapers of Poland.

Abish (Abba) Artel

He was a scholar with pleasant mannerism, and a friend. Political differences of opinion did not cloud our friendship. He was among the founders of Gordonia in the city. He was active and urged others to be active in our cultural life, especially amongst the youth.

[Page 147]

He began to study medicine in Prague, but he interrupted his studies for reasons that are unknown to me. When he returned, he dedicated himself with heart and soul to Hechalutz, and was also a member of its headquarters. After I left Turka, echoes of his successful work along with his friend Ruchia Zulinger reached me. In the Land, I dreamed that we would be together, and I awaited the moment of his arrival. He was killed along with Ruchia in the forest a short time before the liberation.

An entire family was cut off in this manner, for his brother Tovia, a member of Nir-David and a soldier in the brigade was murdered by the British on the "Black Sabbath"[2] on his way to fortified Ein Harod.

The Priest Kolkowski

We could often see him as he descended from the Polna with his black robes. He had a protruding stomach, an ugly face filled with youthful blemishes despite his advanced age[3], a thick, red nose and bleary eyes.

He reached the rank of prelate in the hierarchy of the Catholic Church. He preached tolerance. I heard this when I remained in the classroom by chance during the religion classes at the gymnasium.

When Turka was captured by the Nazis, the Ukrainians demanded a "free hand" to wreak judgments upon the Jews. He, the priest, presented himself before the German command and demanded that by virtue of his authority that this be prevented. Using polished German, he succeeded in his objective on that occasion, even though this did not help during the time of organized mass murder.

It is fitting to recall him in a positive light for this deed.

The Circle of the Intelligentsia

During the First World War, the same thing happened to the Jewish youth as happened to the youth from various countries who arrived in the Land during the period of the ingathering of the exiles. The older youth, who were forced to wander from Turka into the bounds of Austria or Bohemia with their families in the wake of the Russian advance during the First World War, stood face to face with the secular, western culture, especially with German culture. Of course, this had its influence and left its mark on all areas of the life of these youths. When they returned to their towns before the end of the war, they were recognized by their dress, mode of conversation, occupations and comportment.

[Page 148]

I recall the small group of that type. Motty Shein, Elisha Reichter, Yosef Baranka, and Eigler belonged to it. They would sit until late at night and discuss the meanings of the concepts of "subject" and "object," and the difference between Hegel and Nietzsche. They would recite "Hapaamon" (The Bell) by heart, and delve into the meaning of Faust with breadth and sharpness. They also occupied themselves with the "modern" subjects of that time, such as telepathy, hypnosis, spiritualism, and the like. They were also additional groups of this genre. Their intellectual consciousness and serious relationship to matters of the spirit are etched deeply in my memory and have not left to this day...

The Poale Zion group in Turka

[Page 149]

Memories from my Parental Home

by M. and Ch.

Reb Avraham Alter Montag

Father was a tailor by profession, but tailoring was a minor component of his life. Her primary activity was social and communal activism.

First of all, there was the Chevra Kadisha (burial society) which he headed. Incidentally, there was a tradition amongst the tailors to be involved in that organization. The cemetery, which was located on the mountain and covered completely with trees and greenery, was close to the home of Reb Avraham Alter. On Sundays during the harsh Carpathian winter, when the wagons from the villages around Turka, which were home to many Jews, began to bring the reapings of the Angel of Death from the latter days of the week – there was no need to inform Reb Avraham Alter, the head of the Chevra Kadisha. He came himself. He saw those wagons from the window of his house and ran “upward” to take care of things. He fulfilled this task with exceptional devotion, for he regarded this as a true act of kindness. He regarded this type of activity as the purpose of his life, which provided some sort of mystical connection with the world of truth... The entire household was affected by this spirit. For example, Reb Avraham Alter's mother prepared exceptionally fine shrouds for herself during her lifetime.

His communal activities generally took up his entire mornings. Only afterwards did he sit down to work in his trade... His house was a meeting place for activists, and served as the gathering place for the “prayer quorum” not only on Sabbaths but also on weekdays. His wife was also affected by this spirit and agreed to host the prayer quorum, whether willingly or whether because she had no choice. She also served as the head of the prayer quorum for women on Sabbaths and festivals. She was a righteous woman who loved to give and assist.

*

Reb Avraham Alter's home was built in that place in the latter part of the 19th century after the “Great Fire.” In general, that fire served as a reference point for marking time: a certain event took place so and so number of years before the fire; and another, so and so years after it... With the passage of time, when the Great Fire was forgotten, the large and small floods took its place: so and so number of years after the Great Flood... Thus, for example, Reb Avraham Alter's mother, who was a beloved midwife and who took pride in that over “half of the children of Turka” were hers, that is to say, that they came to the world through her midwifery – she herself counted the years with reference to the floods: so and so many years before the a certain flood, and so and so many years after another one... Indeed, everyone knew that she was already an octogenarian...

[Page 150]

Indeed: Reb Avraham Alter's home was built immediately after the Great Fire of the town, along with other houses, in the well-known “Ilyca.” At that time, there was a feverish building effort in the city, and the bricks were brought to the building site straight from the over in the kiln. The builders stood by and waited for their materials...

Turka Arranges an Exile

Near the house lived a Ukrainian blacksmith who was an avowed anti-Semite, despite the fact that many Jews lived near his workshop. He always plotted to do something against his neighbors. He eventually found a propitious moment: when the Jews of Turka arranged an exile; when they escaped the wrath of the "Puni" brigades at the outbreak of the First World War, this anti-Semitic blacksmith was the first one to break into the homes of his Jewish neighbors, first and foremost the home of Reb Avraham Alter, in order to pillage everything that remained.

Reb Avraham Alter set out in haste at the head of the Jews of our town in order to go into exile, as has been said, to foreign parts of the Austro-Hungarian Empire, until the wrath would past. Everyone went out bereft of everything – taking only such things as could be carried by hand. However, Reb Avraham Alter did not think of his personal effects. He took in his hands the Torah scroll that was in his house. Thus, they reached the village of Sianki. There, the found out that one of the Jews remained in the town, and that the hooligans were not letting him leave... Reb Avraham Alter left behind his family and the wandering refugees at a certain point, and decided to return himself to the town to redeem the Jews. He took with him a unique means of persuasion: a bottle of liquor...

The Refugees Return Home

After the war, the Jews of Turka, including Reb Avraham Alter, returned to their ruined houses. The Ukrainian blacksmith once again took advantage of the chaos that pervaded during the change of regime, and plotted murderous deeds. In the darkness of night, he sent soldiers to the home of Reb Avraham Alter to plunder and murder. There were several non-family members as well as family members, including his brother, in his narrow house at that time.

When the hooligans broke into the house, they started to deal with Reb Avraham Alter and were about to murder him. The children raised an outcry, but none of the neighbors were brazen enough to come and save them... The situation was very bad. However, salvation came from the uncle who was sleeping in a hidden corner. When he realized that the hooligans were beating Reb Alter, he burst forth suddenly, extinguished in the darkness the candles that were in the hands of the hooligans, and began to take away their guns in the darkness. The hooligans felt that a large Jewish resistance was being mounted, and they fled from the house.

[Page 151]

Attacks were perpetrated also in other places in the city. The Jews saw that their blood was forfeit, and mounted a "self defense." At that time, the young Abba Chushai began to operate in the town.

*

Reb Avraham Alter succeeded in making *aliya* to the Land in 1937, and died at an old age in Haifa in 1952.

Reb Avraham Alter Montag

Translator's Footnotes:

61. Heshel is another nickname for Heshio.
62. See http://www.jewishvirtuallibrary.org/jsource/History/Black_Sabbath.html

I suspect that this is a reference to pimples.

[Page 152]

The Activist from Turka Shlomo Pelech

by Moshe Kershner of Haifa

Uncaptioned. Shlomo Pelech

Shlomo Pelech was the head of the Zionist-Socialist organization, the so-called "Right leaning Poale Zion"[1] for twenty years. He was also active in various professional institutions. He helped tens and perhaps hundreds of Jewish youths to find their way in life. There is only one thing he neglected: his own work, his tailor shop...

Meetings during the day, gatherings in the evening, he ran to and fro intervening with the authorities for those who had need of him.

One must state: In the political struggle for his convictions, in his principled stance and in his societal life, he was consistent and not quick to give in... On the other hand, his political lectures during the weekly Friday night gatherings of the “Hitachdut Poale Zion Union” were rich in content and dealt with the perplexing Jewish problems of the entire world. Nevertheless, Pelech was a Jew with a deep national consciousness, and he therefore exhibited a deep love for his people.

I now recall a fact that indeed characterizes Pelech. Once, the Polish minister Maruszewski came to Turka and convened a gathering. No Turka Jew dared to say a word. One did indeed say something – Shlomo Pelech. He indeed attacked the minister for his stance toward the Jewish question. The minister was insulted, responded with anger, and rebuked him strongly.

[Page 153]

He struggled in the city hall on behalf of the impoverished Jewish population, as well as for the village Jews... He also made sure that the philanthropic organizations would distribute their monies in an equitable fashion.

The Turka orphanage

It is no surprise that he was a member of the committee of the Turka orphanage for twenty years without interruption.

In brief, he was a wellspring of toil, energy and might that was evident not only in Turka. The Orthodox, religious circles in Turka also appreciated him due to his good manner with people.

May his soul be bound in the bonds of life.

[Page 154]

The Final *Hoshana Rabba*[2]

by Eli Montag

One cannot find any organization that existed in any Jewish city or town that did not exist in Turka. We can note them – the Bikur Cholim (visiting the sick), Chevra Kadisha (burial society), Chevra Mishnayos (*Mishna* study organization), Chevra Tehillim (organization of Psalms reciters), and many more. Each organization had its trustee and its separate little room. Each one fulfilled its obligations honorably, and held their own *kiddushes* several times a year. One would drink liquor at those *kiddushes*[3], but not to the point of drunkenness, Heaven forbid, but rather to get happy, to wish each other "*Lechayim*," to forget the concerns of livelihood for a while, and to talk with longing about former times when one could purchase liquor from large casks, called *pesser*, and nobody knew of any monopoly yet...

Among the organizations in our town, there was an organization called "Chevra Sheimos". Whereas some of the groups consisted of important householders, the Chevra Sheimos consisted of course Jews, tailors, shoemakers, bricklayers, peddlers, and regular common folk. Aside from holding their regular *kiddushes*, and *Melava Malkas*[4], their activity consisted of collecting the *Sheimos*[5] from all the *Beis Midrashes*, and taking them to the cemetery on *Hoshana Rabba* with a large parade to bury them.

I do not know of such a group, or such a custom in other Galician towns. In Turka, this took on a colorful form that was well noted. The interesting thing is that everyone in town, without exception, derived great enjoyment from this. Of course, this was understandable for the members of the organization itself. This was their own joyous occasion, for which they waited an entire year. They prepared the large boxes in which the *Shemos* were laid. They themselves arranged the horse and wagon which was to carry the boxes, and arranged that the orchestra would come to play on a voluntary basis. They rode before the crowd. In short, it was their celebration, their parade. However, as has been mentioned, the large crowd of simple Jews, young and old, *cheder* children, and ordinary white comrades[6], all who had waited a long time for such a noisy opportunity, derived enjoyment from this.

[Page 155]

The custom was as follows. In the large synagogue and *Beis Midrash*, and in all the smaller *Beis Midrashes*, a large carton lay in a corner of the anteroom. Tattered *siddurim* (prayer books), *machzorim* (festival prayer books), and individual pages, worn and faded, that were lying around – were all placed in the carton by ready hands so that they would not lie around and be desecrated. There were also people who would not hesitate to pick up *Sheimos* from the street, and would bring them to the designated place. The cartons would get fuller and fuller throughout the year. Then the day of *Hoshana Rabba* arrived, when the *Sheimos* from all the *Beis Midrashim* would be gathered together and brought to the synagogue, in order to carry them to the cemetery.

Then came *Hoshana Rabba* of 5699 (1938). Jews from the Chevra Sheimos worshipped earlier than everyone else, and came home quicker than usual in order to eat quickly. The weather was sunny and warm. Groups of Jews from all areas of town hastened to the synagogue. The horse and wagon upon which the crate of Shemos would be transported was already standing ready in front of the synagogue. In the anteroom, people were busy emptying the cartons of *sheimos*. Outside, the crowd grew from minute to minute. The Jews forgot about their livelihood concerns as well as the black clouds that had already gathered in the Polish skies. Everyone was in a jovial mood. People spoke witticisms to each other, joked, and mocked the entire world. In the midst of the small talk, the crowd forgot about the preparations which were taking place in the anteroom, and the reason why they had all gathered together.

Suddenly, a deep voice was heard, "We are setting out!" All eyes turned to the exit of the synagogue, from which four people carried out a large crate covered with a *tallis*. Many others pushed forward because they wanted to be one of he carriers. The crate was slowly laid on the wagon. The coach driver gave a pull on the reins, and the entire crowd set out on their way. In truth, this did not seem like a religious parade, with everyone arranged in rows of four, or the children holding hands in pairs. No, it had the image more of a Jewish wedding during the *chuppa* ceremony, with everyone pushing forward. Old and young Jews pushed from both sides, from behind and from below. The procession went from the synagogue gate through Doctor-Lande's Street, over the bridge, out onto "Lokacz" and then along Sambor Way. The journey passed through hills with fields on both sides, from which one could clearly see the entire town in the valley.

[Page 156]

Melech the peddler rode in front with his reddish yellow horse[7]. The mains of the horses were tied into pony-tails, decorated with colored ribbons. Melech himself was a husky person with wide shoulders, a reddish blond beard, and a jovial face. He was dressed up in a Purim fashion, with a light colored crown on his head – appearing almost like a real king. When the band started playing their instruments and the horse started stomping its hooves in beat, he strongly took the bridle in his hands. The crowd enjoyed this greatly.

Immediately after that, the band arranged itself in a wide row. It was one of the finest and most well-known Jewish bands in old Galicia. Throughout the entire journey, they never tired of playing their musical instruments. The air was full of heartwarming, joyous Jewish melodies. All kinds of young boys and girls stood along the root. Some of them whistled, played pranks, and laughed out loud.

The crowd grew as they got along. There was no shortage of *cheder* children, young and old. Joy and gladness poured forth from their charming, childlike faces. Here, they had to walk in pairs and hold hands, in the manner of school on the Third of May. Here they were going – and what does it mean to be going! – Literally wobbling along with the adults, with the musical instruments, and looking out at Hershele Poyker (the Drummer) carrying his drum, which he wore in front of him. If they wanted, they could have touched the belt in which the drum rested, and even the drum itself! With one jump, one would be right beside the horse and wagon. Soon they would find themselves around Melech the peddler, who was the top attraction for the crowd.

[Page 157]

Slowly, the entire crowd began to approach the "Holy Ground." Old Jews would check their belts. The Chevra Sheimos closely surrounded the wagon. Then, the entire crowd halted. A silence overtook everyone. Slowly, and with awe, the Jews took down the crate of Sheimos and carried it through the main gate of the Jawarer Way for burial. The crowd stood in silence for another while, but soon they got back to their usual selves.

Everyone in his own manner looked for a short route back to town, which was spread out over the valley. Some went by the foot path right next to the fence of the cemetery, and some went up the hill over the tunnel. Others simply enjoyed G-d's fine world in the late summer, and slowly paced through the straight path. Young people, however, remained until late in the evening, strolling over the broad fields. The surroundings were full of laughter and song, which echoed long through the surrounding hills.

This was the final *Hoshana Rabba* in Turka, which no longer exists.

Translator's Footnotes:

63. Poale Zion divided into right and left factions around 1920. The right faction was mainstream Socialist, whereas the left faction tended toward Marxism. See http://en.wikipedia.org/wiki/Poale_Zion
64. *Hoshana Rabba* is the name of the seventh day of Sukkot.
65. *Kiddush* is the prayer that introduces the evening and noontime meal on Sabbaths and festivals. Here, it refers to a mini-celebration accompanied by refreshments and the recitation of the noontime *Kiddush*. It often celebrates or marks an occasion.
66. A *Melave Malka* is a meal had at the conclusion of the Sabbath.
67. Literally "names." Refers to worn our holy books containing the Divine Name that are not to be discarded in the regular fashion, but rather buried.
68. I am not sure of the exact implication of this obviously colloquial expression.

The word here is '*bolan*'. I am not sure of the exact meaning.

[Page 158]

Ordinary Dear Jews in Turka

By Chaim Pelech

Translated by Jerrold Landau

Donated by Boaz Ben-Pelech

The Turka Orphanage

“Don't cast me away at the time of old age…”

There were many dear and nice Jews in Turka. They were called up to answer to every need that a portion of the Turka Jews required.

Avraham Yaakov Sprung was a highly upstanding Jew and person. He had a flour processing plant. Every Thursday, he gave flour to many Jews for the Sabbath and said, "You will pay me next week." He did this in a manner that nobody would know, without publicity. This was the giving of charity discretely.

Nachman Brenes was a dear Jew. He gave large donations of much more for various benevolent institutions. He was a popular man with a good character.

Malka Hirt gave the greatest contributions in the entire city to all the benevolent institutions. She had an open hand and a good heart, which was a rarity. There were no poor people in town who did not receive a stipend from Malka Hirt. Weddings of the poor, circumcisions of the poor, sick Jews, sick children – Malka gave to them all. There was no equal to her in goodness. May she live long.

Pinchas Gotlieb at the marketplace

Chaya Dinstag lived in Sokolik and was a very pious woman. She came to town every week, and gave weekly stipend to her poor women. She gave especially to religious causes.

Mordechai Warzoger was a dear, upright Jews. He was a veteran Zionist. He went to the Land of Israel, returned, and was murdered in Lemberg.

Leizer Bort was a good Jew, who gave charity with an open hand.

The Rynek

The optician Feldman was a fine person and a good Jew. When a new synagogue was built in Turka, it cost a great deal of money. He gave charity with an open hand to all philanthropic institutions. He was chairman of Yad Charutzim for many years. During the Ukrainian period, he ran to the Ukrainian lieutenant in the city, and with self-sacrifice, he chased the Ukrainian soldiers from town, holding the revolution in hand. May he live long.

The director Bernstein from the large sawmill in Stryj was the chairman of the Jewish orphanage. He built the house and maintained in during difficult times.

Avraham Weiss, Asza Weiss' son, was the administrator of the orphanage. He dedicated his entire life to the orphans.

Dr. Rozenberg, himself a sick man, always went by foot to poor sick people. Often, he would take no more. Dr. Rintel and Dr. Freundlich were involved in the same business.

Melech Brauer was a veteran Zionist activist. Baruch Koppel, Naftali Kraus were veteran Zionist activists. Berish Laberbaum, Matis Maus, Mendel Filinger, Shlomo Feiler (the son of Izak), Moshe Krebs, Moshe Rozen (the son of Shlomo), Yossel Brenes (the son of Yaakov), Shlomo Ceckis – all of them constantly worked for various Jewish nationalist and philanthropic organizations.

[Page 162]

Chalvikes

by Moshe From of Haifa

Paupers, destitute people, and ordinary poor people existed in every Jewish town. In Turka as well we had no shortage of them. However, our poor people cannot be compared with the beggars of other Jewish cities and towns. For example, you can search throughout all of Poland – where would you find poor people living like one family in a single house, with a tradition of several generations?...

No. It seems that this type of peculiarity can be found only in our town...

On the main street of the Ulica, between the houses of honorable householders, there was a house; not just a small house, but rather a communal house with a second story, a balcony in the front, and a workshop that housed a large tailoring business. From the outside, this house looked no different from all the neighboring houses. However, all the people of Turka, from young to old, knew that the city paupers lived there. They were called "Chalivkes."

From where does that name originate and what does it mean – nobody could explain. It seems that even the Chalivkes themselves did not know... There were various versions of the explanation, but nobody could ascertain the truth.

All of the Chalivkes lived together and formed one large family and community of men, women, and children. Nobody knew their kinship, and it seemed that even the Chalivkes themselves barely discussed this... Despite the fact that they lived alone in cramped conditions, they fulfilled the commandment of hosting guests. Their house was a type of guesthouse for all types of poor people who would come here from all over Poland... There, they could spend the night, eat something, and set out on their way. The Chalivkes never lost their openness to guests. The wealthy householders would often permit themselves to refuse a guest, but they would not. Their home was always open for those in need... This is how they always conducted themselves, and all of the itinerant paupers knew this and used the opportunity well. They would come from all over Galicia, and even from cities and towns in Congress Poland.

[Page 163]

Indescribable poverty and loneliness pervaded in the rooms of the Chalivkes. The furniture consisted only of beds and plank beds (*pritsches*), upon which there was old bedding with uncovered pillows. Flies buzzed about from the floor to the ceiling. The broken windowpanes were plugged up with red cushions, half inside and half outside, imparting a melancholy atmosphere...

Small, dirty children wandered around in that mucky place with noisy feet. Only their charming eyes peered out from their pale faces. They rarely ventured out to the street to play, for unfortunately they could not go down upon the broken, wooden steps which were missing many boards... With the passage of time, when they got older and were able to go with their own power, they would enrich the town with several other beggars...

*

Berl Chalvik was the oldest of the Chalvikes. He was a tall Jew with a black, unkempt beard, which had apparently never experienced a comb... He was always dressed in a black *bekishe* [Hassidic frock], a *gartel* [Hassidic belt], and a black hat on his head, definitely reminiscent of the times of Count Kalinowski...

[Page 164]

Berl belonged to the *Chevra Kadisha* [burial society] and the society of funeral attendants. When he would appear on the street, one would know that a misfortune had occurred somewhere, and that a funeral would be taking place shortly... He went around with a large, tin charity box and collected charity. He would stop every few steps, pluck at his beard, and shout out with a wail: "Charity saves from death"... A pall would then fall over the householders... People were more afraid of him than of the Angel of Death himself... People would indeed very quickly toss a coin into the charity box, and be free of him as quickly as possible...

A fact: When the lawyer Dr. Lowinger died, he stated in his will that the *Chevra Kadisha* should send another member rather than Berl Chvalik to the funeral... The community made sure to fulfill his request, and "Charity saves from death" was shouted out in a hoarse voice by Mordechai Zindel the beadle.

*

Berl had a brother named Leib. He was more formally referred to as Leon Chvalik. He had a dark, embittered face, upon which a smile was never seen. He would make the rounds to the houses seeking donations like a trustee after a payment that was owned... One could not free oneself from him with a piece of bread or a small coin. He would stand at the open door for a long time, staring with his piercing eyes until he received what was coming to him...

A specialist, their sister Rivka Chvalik, would collect pieces of bread, old outfits, and remnants from the tables of the wealthy. She was a small, short woman with a disheveled head of hair. She could barely drag herself along on her sick feet. That is how she went about all day to the homes of the affluent people to get a pot of cooked food, a bit of milk for the children, pieces of bread, old, worn-out outfits – everything that the merciful householders would give her.

[Page 165]

*

An especially unique character in the family of Chavilkes was Zalman Chvalik. He was a tall, broad-shouldered Jew. He was a porter on call. He always had a thick rope tied up in the front, with a sack for an apron. The merchants used to engage him to carry various items of merchandise, and the wagon drivers used to hire him to load and unload heavy sacks of flour, rice, and sugar, barrels of herring and other merchandise. For him, it was no big deal to carry a sack of flour on his shoulder from Sprung's flour warehouse in the Rynek to Hinda-Moshe-Hentche's shop at the end of Ulica. When Zalman took the sack down from his shoulders, placed it in its place, and received his payment, he would straighten out his bones and yawn so loudly that he could be heard from one town to the next... That is how he would notify his employers that he, Zalman, was prepared for his next mission.

As long as Zalman maintained his strength and earned his own morsel of bread, he did not go around soliciting donations. He would visit the homes of the affluent people only three times a year: before Passover for *Maos Chittin*[1], on Purim for the feast, and on Chanukah for a Chanukah gift.

*

Aside from Zalman, there was another productive element among the Chalvikes, living from their work and earning their livelihood in an honorable fashion: shoemakers who used to fix shoes that no other tradesman would take into their hands... there were also tinsmiths, painters and other tradesmen who would toil hard. However, to rent a dwelling and tear themselves away from the Chalvikes was not something that they were able to do.

[Page 166]

*

In the year 1939, when the Soviets entered Turka, everybody thought that the new Social order would finally bring a salvation for the poor Chalvikes. However, the reality was otherwise: their situation worsened. Private enterprises were liquidated and there was nobody willing to give donations... There was a shortage of bread, and the tables of the middle class became leaner. No leftovers remained... The situation declined further during the difficult winter of that year. The temperature went down to 30 degrees, and there was no wood. Therefore, our Chalvikes suffered from hunger, cold, loneliness and need.

When the German murderers liquidated the Jewish settlement of Turka, they did not pass over the Chalvikes. On that occasion, they treated them exactly like everybody else... Along with the affluent and important householders in town, they went along their final way to the extermination camps.

However, nobody was referred to as a "*Meit Mitzvah*"[2] on that occasion. Neither Berl Chalvik nor Mordechai Zindel the beadle clanged their charity box and shouted "Charity saves from Death!"...

Translator's Footnotes:

69. Literally "Money for wheat." Donations given to the poor prior to Passover for the purchase of the needs of the holiday, such as matzos.

A "*Meit Mitzva*" is a dead person whom has nobody to tend to him. It is considered a very important commandment. "*Mitzva*" to occupy oneself with the funeral arrangements of such a body.

[Page 167]

Stories from Turka

By Chaim Pelech
Translated by Jerrold Landau
Donated by Boaz Ben-Pelech

A. Reb Hirsch and the Get [1]

There was a Jew with us in Turka called Reb Hirsch. He used to enjoy drinking a little. One evening, he came home and said to his wife, "Gittel, dress up in your Sabbath clothes with your head kerchief. We are going to the rabbi to get divorced. Get dressed quickly!" Gittel saw that her Hirsch was drunk. She said to him, "Go lie down to sleep, for you are not completely with us today. And secondly, why all of a sudden do you want to get divorced from me? We already have grandchildren – in your old age did you decide that I am not suitable for you?" Hirsch said to his wife, "Gittel, you know Hirsch very well. If Hirsch says we must get divorced, then you must go to get divorced. Fifty-five years was enough to be plagued with you..."

Gittel realized that she cannot do anything with him. She dressed up in her Sabbath clothes with her head kerchief. Reb Hirsch took Gittel under his arm and they set out to the rabbi. The door opened and he said, "Good evening, Rabbi". The rabbi answered, "Good evening, Reb Hirsch. Oh, what type of a guest do I have? Sit down Reb Hirsch." After Reb Hirsch sat down, the rabbi asked, "Reb Hirsch, to what do I owe the honor that I have a guest now?" Hirsch answered, "Rabbi, I came to you to get divorced from my Gittel. Rabbi, I beg of you, do not ask me why and what. I am going to get divorced from my dear wife, and nothing will come from your questions. If Hirsch says to write a Get – you indeed know Hirsch well – nothing will help."

The rabbi saw that Hirsch was as drunk as Lot, and that it was impossible to reason with him. He searched for a pretext against him. Hirsch was a poor man, he had no money. He would request a large sum of money for the Get, and certainly nothing would come of it. He told Hirsch, "Good. If you, Reb Hirsch, want a Get, I will write you a Get. What can I do with you? ... I will make it cheap for you – the entire Get, including the writing, will cost you 30 Crowns. (In those days, a Get costs 6-10 Crowns)..."

When he heard this, Reb Hirsch jumped up from the bench and told the rabbi, "Rabbi, G-d is holy and the Torah is holy, but you, rabbi, are a sheketz of skotzim [2] and a devil of your father's father until Abraham our patriarch... You want 30 Crowns from me for a Get. Gittele, go home and cook supper... Good night, Rabbi!..."

B. Roizele's Wedding

Many years ago, there was a girl called Roizele in Turka. She was a little "odd" but not crazy... She loved to dress up nicely, but more often than once she went around "spiffed up" in torn dresses. She used to go into many rich homes, talk a great deal and tell various stories. She was gladly received in all of these places, and everyone in the city became her acquaintance.

One year in the early summer, a Jewish worker from the wide world came to Turka. He was probably a bit like her, and he fell in love with Roizele. Roizele went around boasting that they would soon be getting married. When the town found out about this, some Jews, especially women, went around to collect money for a wedding of a poor girl. Everyone gave money for Roizele's wedding! The wedding was indeed planned with great pomp, and all of the women of means came from all sides to help Roizele.

A few days before the wedding, Roizele went around from house to house to invite everybody. Roizele said, "My wedding will be a wedding the likes of which Turka has never seen since its founding... the ceremony (chupa) will take place in the middle of the Rynek. Many relatives will come to me, and everyone will see how beautiful a bride I will be!..." People made sure that the wedding dress would indeed be decorated with various sparkling stones and pieces of metal, and the chupa was indeed planned for the middle of the Rynek.

The wedding took place on a Sunday at 3:00 p.m. Two boys – one of them was Anshel Reis – ascended the roof of the city hall, one on one side of the roof and the other on the second side. At exactly 3:00, they began to blow trumpets. They thereby alerted the entire city that Roizele's wedding was commencing.

As soon as everyone heard the blowing of the trumpets, all of the Jews, including women and children, set out for Roizele's wedding. Jewish homes were emptied and locked, and everyone went to the Rynek, along the route from Moshe Shechter's place until the bridge that led to the small alley where Roizele lived with her poor mother. Then the entire band of the large Operman family, with all of their assistants, drummers and flutists, began to play. The musicians were divided into two groups. One group played in the alley near the bridge where Roizele lived, and the second group played in the Rynek itself. The trumpeters on the roof also blew incessantly. In the meantime, hundreds of Christians ran out from the city. They thought that the Jews had taken leave of their minds...

Finally, they went to the chupa. One group of musicians accompanied Roizele to the chupa, and the second went opposite her. But then something happened: so many people were passing by that it was impossible to lead Roizele through. The route from the bridge to Moshe Shechter's house was one solid mass of people. People shouted and begged: "Let the bride and relatives proceed to the chupa". However, it was impossible... They could not pass. Everyone wanted to see Roizele the bride, and people were afraid that the young couple would proceed on...

At that time, there were a few Jewish bricklayers in Turka. They were healthy, communally-conscious people with strong muscles. They saw the fear, and they began to push through and make order. With great effort, after two hours, they succeeded in getting the couple to the chupa. After the chupa, the real celebration began.

Afterward, another curiosity arose: loafers arranged a different spectacle. They arranged a makeshift room for the bride and groom so that they could have some privacy after the chupa. When the couple was already inside, someone from this group pulled at a string, and boards of the room separated...

Don't ask about what took place...

C. A Scandal in the Tailor's Synagogue

On Sukkot of 1922, a large scandal took place in the Tailor's Synagogue of Turka. Some pregnant young woman, who wished to have a son, bit off the pitam of the only etrog in the synagogue – such ill fortune! [3]

It happened like this: The Tailor's Synagogue purchased an etrog for use during the services, and for it members to recite a blessing over in their homes. To that end, the gabbai (trustee) of the synagogue, Reb Avraham, asked someone, Shlomo the Geregerins [4], to go around to the houses each morning so that the families of the tailors could recite the blessing over the etrog. As the gabbai was an experienced and practical man, he told Shlomo that as he goes from house to house, "You should not give the etrog to anyone n the hand. You should be especially careful in a house where there is a young wife – for such people are always interested in biting the pitam..." Shlomo answered him, "Don't worry, Reb Avraham. Don't be concerned about the etrog. You can leave it to Shlomo..."

And indeed. Shlomo was a relatively tall Jew with a fine beard – and one could trust him...

Shlomo went out and was supposed to return with the etrog before the services began. He could not be found... It was already 8:00, 8:30. The gabbai was supposed to go to the synagogue with the etrog, and Shlomo was not there... The gabbai began to think that something happened with the etrog – and there are no other etrogim that can be obtained in the city! Without having an option, the gabbai went to the synagogue without the etrog. As he neared the place, two Jews ran up to him and explained that Shlomo had brought the etrog to the synagogue. As they drew nearer, two people ran to him to inform him of the misfortune. They opened the little box and saw – the pitam had been bitten off!

Do not ask about the end of the story. When the congregation recovered from the great misfortune, they ran to the surrounding synagogues... for one cannot worship without an etrog! The rabbi indeed issued an edict that if the congregation has no etrog, it can conduct the services without an etrog – but this did not help!

The synagogue was empty for the entire holiday, and the gabbai had to beg a few young people to come to minyan (the quorum required for services)! He himself was ashamed to seek out a strange place to worship...

D. Feiga Malia the Woman of Incantations

Feiga Malia the Anshprecherin (Incantation recitor) was a very interesting woman from the older generation. When a woman or a child became ill, they called Feiga Malia. She extinguished the coals – for this was a means against the evil eye. Her other remedies included: incantations over various metallic coins, or simply direct incantations over the sick person that they should become well. If someone had been frightened by a goat or a dog – she had to resort to more technical means: She hoarded lead, which showed whose child was frightened... With an incantation directed to the lead, the child was helped. At least, that is what Feiga Malia said...

Aside from this, Feiga Malia was the leader of the woman's Chevra Kadisha (burial society), which sewed shrouds and washed the deceased women. She was also the official "beggar of pardon" of the deceased women [5]. Nobody knew how Feiga Malia had learned her trade. She had a special incantation with a special tune for every occasion. Nobody could even imitate her. The manner of her begging of forgiveness was not so simple - she did it so masterfully. Aside from this, she had a different incantation for each deceased person.

She also knew where everyone lay in the cemetery. When the month of Elul arrived, when all of the women went to visit the graves of their parents - she was the person whom everyone approached, for the women from the city and surrounding villages did not know where their dead lay, and they were afraid to wander around the cemetery. Feiga Malia saved everyone...

If a woman came to her, Feiga Malia would speak curtly and almost officially, "Who are you, what are you called, and from where are you?". As soon as she said her name, Feiga Malia knew everything. She led the woman to the grave of her mother or father, and shouted out, "Lay down, Rachele, on the grave of your holy mother, the great pious Gittel the daughter of Yente, and request from her that she should run to the Heavenly Bezn (Beis Din) [6] and beg that your husband and your children should all be well, and that no illness should come through the threshold of your house. Your husband should have a livelihood, and his livelihood should be with riches and honor. G-d should send your eldest daughter her appropriate match, so you will be able to make a wedding for her with an upright and observant young man, and you may have contentment from your daughter as with all good Jews..."

The woman finished hearing Feiga Malia's statement. Then she threw herself onto the grave and wept and shouted with all her energy. Some women became so engrossed in weeping that they no longer knew where they were in the world...

However, Feiga Malia kept her accounts. When she concluded her first statement, she knocked the gravestone with her cane and shouted out, "Gittel the daughter of Yenta, your pious daughter Rachel lies over your grave. Arise and run to the Heavenly Bezn (Beis Din), beg and tear through worlds for your honorable and pious daughter, that she her husband and children should be healthy, that they should have livelihood and all good things; that no evil eye should harm them. Go, run and beg for your granddaughter, Rachel's eldest daughter, that G-d should bless her with her appropriate match. Go and beg for all of your children, and for all of the Jews, that they should be helped, and our enemies should not have joy, until the Messiah comes, Amen!"

When Feiga Malia finished that second statement, she leaned on her cane, and shouted out for a third time: “Enough Rachel, you have done what you can for your holy mother...” The woman quickly arose from the grave, paid Feiga Malia her fee. Feiga Malia then went over to another woman who was waiting for her...

Feiga Malia worked hard for her entire life. She never had any time to rest. During every spare moment, she would concern herself with her ill and poor women and children. She would go around to the houses of the poor to inquire and see what is going on in the house. If she found that the woman was ill, Feiga Malia would say, 'Sara, you are ill again... Has Melech the Doctor visited you already?”. When the ill woman answered, “No”, Feiga Malia would then summon Melech the Doctor that he should quickly come. Feiga Malia had the greatest of respect for him. After such a visit, Feiga Malia would take out a cloth from her pocket, and go around to collect money for the ill person.

Above all, she would collect money for poor people for the Sabbath every Wednesday and Thursday. On Friday, she would go around an entire day with a bag to collect rolls, challas, and candles for the Sabbath – everything for poor Jews. She never rested. Day after day, she had someone to worry about.

When Feiga Malia went off to the other world, there was nobody to intercede. There was no second Feiga Malia in town. Women remembered and siged, especially the women from the surrounding villages...

Translator's Footnotes:

5. A Get is a Jewish divorce document.
6. A sheketz (plural shkotzim) is a derogatory term for a gentile.
7. An etrog (citron) is one of the four species that are used as part of the Sukkot ceremony, as prescribed by the Torah. The pitam is the woody stamen of the etrog. If the pitam is removed from the etrog, the etrog is no longer valid for the commandment. It is considered by some that biting off the pitam of an etrog (of course after the holiday is over) is a fortuitous omen for the birth of a male child.
8. Shlomo the Gregerins means Shlomo the son of the mother who was known as the noisemaker.
9. The Chevra Kadisha conducts a formal ritual washing ceremony (called a tahara – purification) on a dead body. Women perform this rite for women, and men for men, for obvious reasons. After the tahara, a representative of the Chevra Kadisha begs forgiveness of the deceased person for any impropriety that took place during the ceremony.

Court of Law – referring here to the Heavenly court. The text makes a point of showing how she mispronounced the word.

[Page 174]

There Were Jews Who Lived Very Well...

by Mirialm Taller (daughter of Yosef-Meir Bank) of New York

An episode

Miriam Taller

Jews lived very well in Turka, especially in former times. They felt at home in Turka and did not strongly feel the exile...

A story is told of Shlomo Rozen who lived on Ring-Plaz. It took place on a certain *Shavuot*. Rozen dressed up in a festive manner and went out to the street. A certain Christian named Pajowicz met him and told him:

"Mr. Rozen, when will it be already? I Pajowicz will be in exile and eat *kreplach* [crepes], and you, Mr. Rozen, will chop stones for a highway... Indeed, how woud you like that, Mr. Rozen?..."

[Page 177]

Turka - The Surrounding Villages

Jews in the Villages Around Turka

by Aharon Shafer of Haifa

Aharon Shafer

The Turka district contained approximately 91 villages, which had a larger Jewish population than Turka itself. They lived from agricultural work. They had their own fields and businesses. Jews worked in the lumber business in the surrounding forests and sawmills.

The relationship with the gentiles, who were mainly Ukrainians with a lesser number of Poles, was different in every village. In general, Jews were not victims of anti-Semitism there, and they lived in friendship with the gentiles. However, the situation was different in those villages where the priest was an anti-Semite...

Upon entering a village, one could immediately recognize which houses belonged to Jews. They were larger and covered with shingles or tin. On the other hand, the gentile houses were covered with straw, and the cow and horse lived under one roof with the gentile... The Jew, on the other hand, had a separate stall for animals and for the stable. Inside the Jew's house, there would be a bit of furniture, fine bedding, a table with chairs, etc. There would be a brick oven in the kitchen with a smokestack coming out of it. The gentile houses were very poor. The bed would have been hacked together from coarse boards. There would be an inferior table with long benches, and the oven in the kitchen would be built of bricks, with a hole in the roof for smoke... The walls were indeed always black from smoke, and when the oven was lit, the smoke would go through the straw

[Page 178]

roof, and the entire hut would be smoking... In the deep chill of the winter, the gentile would also bring the cow into his house, so it would be warmer. This would obviously also take place when the cow was calving. Then the calf would be kept in the house for eight days.

On the way to Rozluch

Food was also different between the gentiles and the Jews. Jews baked bread every week from their own corn meal, and for the Sabbath from wheat flour. Sometimes, they would purchase white flour. The gentiles, on the other hand, used to make do with oat pretzels. Potatoes were the chief food both for the Jews and the gentiles.

The clothing of the Jews was made of fabric. Young Jews were at times permitted to even make an outfit from pure English fabric. They wore shoes in the summer and boots in the winter. On the other hand, the gentiles wore homemade clothing. They planted seeds, from which they grew flax and oakum. They spun the threads with a hand spinner and made linen. The linen was then spread out in the sun to bleach and whiten. Then, it was made into trousers and shirts. The gentiles had no concerns about shoes. They went barefoot in the summer, and wore clogs made out of pieces of leather in the winter. They would make a Cossack or a fur hat from sheepskin. The Jew in the village enjoyed a higher standard of living than the gentile. His needs were greater.

[Page 179]

There was a public school with four to seven classes in every village. All the children of the village went to that school, where they learned to read and write Polish and Ukrainian. Most of the older generation of gentiles were illiterate. In the afternoon, the Jewish children went to *cheder,* which lasted until late in the night in the winter. The teacher came from the city, or from somewhere far off. He was hired for a term or for an entire year. The children studied *Chumash* with *Rashi,* and the older children studied a bit of *Gemara* with *Tosafot.* There was a custom on the Sabbath to examine the *cheder* children on *Chumash* with *Rashi.*

On Sabbath mornings, everyone came to the *shtibel* to worship. Nobody was absent. If someone did not come, people knew that he was sick, so people went to visit him. During the services, people also talked about all of the events of the entire week. There, they also heard the gossip from the week. There, Jews would forget about the weekday tribulations and worries. People came dressed in their finest clothing. The adults wore silk *bekishes,* with a *streimel* on the head. The young wore black or grey outfits.

Weather was never an obstacle to attending services. It might have been snowing or raining – and everyone would still come. When there was a joyous occasion in the village, such as a wedding or circumcision, Jews would come from the surrounding villages by horse and wagon or sleigh, and would dance and revel until the end of the day...

[Page 180]

Jews in the Villages

by Chaim Pelech

The Jews in the villages around Turka were no better off than those in the city. There were indeed many Jewish people who owned much land, and were numbered among the wealthy. However, in truth, they were not quite as one says: The earth in the Carpathians was very bad, and they did not make great profits. In many villages, the well-placed Jewish people sold plots of land to the farmers – and from this they earned their living. The others lived only from the good graces of the well placed people, and were in debt over their heads...

The Jews in villages who also had businesses did not live badly. The businesses and the plots of land which they worked gave them a very fine livelihood. Their livestock that they held – a cow, a little calf – also provided them with livelihood.

However, a large portion of the village Jews were small landowners, and lived from their own agricultural work. The Jewish farmers in the villages around Turka, such as Ilnik, Losinets, Melnicna, Prislip, Shimnats, Yavlenka and others, carried milk and dairy products into Turka every day to sell – and this is how they earned their livelihood. Indeed, Jewish farmers who possessed the same type of land and performed the same work in villages that were farther from the city were in a worse situation. They did not have anyone to whom to sell their milk.

There were also village Jews who did not own any land at all. They toiled for their entire life. Their poverty was very great. Their children, still in their early youth, were sent to the world to work. They served as maids in Turka and other cities.

Indeed, many Jews lived in the villages around Turka. Their standard of living was low – but there was a great deal of variance. Jews, many Jews, earned their living from agriculture.

[Page 181]

Jewish Agriculture Around Turka

by Michael Heisler of Sde Yitzchak

Michael Heisler

In a Corner of the Carpathians

What was the reason that Jews settled in particularly that poor corner of the Carpathians, disconnected from a larger Jewish community? Second, in what era did the migration take place? Third, who were the first three Jewish pioneers who developed such a large Jewish settlement in that corner of the Carpathians?

Of course, it is difficult to find an answer for all of these questions. No details regarding this were transmitted from generation to generation, and we must suffice ourselves with a minimal answer – the wandering staff of the exile led them here. One thing is clear, however: the first Jewish pioneers who arrived brought with them a great deal of the Jewish cultural baggage of that era, Jewish national traditions, and a strong belief in the Creator of the World and the redemption of Israel. They indeed built their existence exclusively according to the verse: on Torah and on Divine service.

Relations between the Jews and their neighbors were good. Anti-Semitism was still foreign to the population at that time, and both sides were graced with mutual trust. On account of that trust, the Jews lived as if "at home" without fear of any opposition to them.

[Page 182]

Jewish Agriculture

The primary source of livelihood was agriculture, and they were not at all behind their gentile neighbors. In truth, the Carpathian landscape was very lovely, with high mountains and valleys, and healthy fresh air. However, the terrain was inferior, not fertile, and very hilly. The terrain was originally given over to an owner after being purchased from the estate owner. It was then passed down from father to son as an inheritance.

Despite the particularly difficult Carpathian conditions, and despite their minority status among the local population, the Jews succeeded in upholding their national origins, culture, traditions, and language. Furthermore, they received moral and spiritual help from their Jewish brethren from the town of Turka, with whom they were closely connected. There were no cases of apostasy or intermarriage. Jews would marry Jews from neighboring or far off villages, as well as from the town of Turka. In this manner, the entire Jewish region along with the town formed a large family, bound and connected with a common communal council, rabbi, *Chevra Kadisha* (burial society), as well as a common cemetery...

City and Village

In order to observe Judaism and Jewish traditions, the city-town *supplied* the villagers with Torah scrolls, *tefillin* (phylacteries), *tallises* (prayer shawls), *tzitzis* (fringed garments), *mezuzas*, and a large supply of various holy books so they could study Torah. The city also provided Passover flour for matzos, and *maos chitin* (Passover charity) for the poor. They brought in *esrogs* and *lulavs*[1].

The city also did not neglect to send in living merchandise, such as teachers who would study with the children, religious judges, jesters[2], matchmakers, and musicians to play at weddings. Weddings were indeed celebrated in the village in full Jewish style, in accordance with the traditions of Moses and Israel. Even chefs to cook for weddings came from the city. Wedding dresses, outfits, wedding rings – all of these could only be obtained in the city.

[Page 183]

Even though the city was only as large as a yawn, it had everything in abundance: the right and the left, Zionists and Marxists, tailors, shoemakers, locksmiths, furriers, and other tradesman; wood merchants, cattle dealers, storekeepers, ordinary workers, and unemployed people. There were also Jews in the city who studied Torah day and night in the *Beis Midrash*, which was open for everyone.

The city was able to exist because of the large province with many villages around. All of the produce of the city was brought in by the farmers for sale. The farmers would utilize the opportunity to make purchases for personal or economic needs. The daily noise of the farmers' wagons, the swarm of people, the buying and selling – gave the impression of a large bazaar. People would say, "It is boiling in town like a kettle." In truth, for the gentile holidays or, to differentiate, the Jewish festivals, the town did boil like a kettle. The stores did a brisk business, and there was what to put on the table and in the bank...

Village People in the Cemetery

Things were especially stirred up in town on the *Selichot*[3] days, when the village Jews would come to the city to visit the cemetery. City Jews would also go to the cemetery, but they did not wait specifically for the *Selichot* days. For them, the cemetery was accessible the entire year. It was located above the city, on the mountain. It was so close that from the center of the city one could read the inscriptions on the white monuments that were peering down from above.

The situation of the villagers was different. The city was far away. The route was difficult, with hills and mud. People could not always undertake such a difficult journey, especially the older folk who desired to do such. People waited an entire year for the *Selichot* days to make the pilgrimage to their parental graves, and simultaneously to make their purchases for the holidays.

[Page 184]

The route from the city to the cemetery was surrounded on both sides by poor people soliciting donations from the visitors to the cemetery. As soon as one entered, one encountered Itzik Aharon the Shamash. To him, the entire cemetery was like his own shop, and he was the shopkeeper. Without him, nobody would know where the dead person was lying... He would guide everyone to the grave that they were looking for, recite the "*Kel Maleh Rachamim*"[4], and remind them of the date of the *yahrzeit* if they did not know exactly. The voices and weeping reached the Seventh Heaven. It was no small matter to come from so far, loaded with so many requests for health, livelihood and a cure for illness; one person had a daughter to marry off; over there stands a woman weeping rivers of tears – for unfortunately she is unable to bear children. Everyone has their own bundle of tribulations – and where can one cry out and weep a bit if not here, in the cemetery?

Jewish Life

Village life was a great deal calmer than city life. Furthermore, the worries about livelihood were not as great as in the city. If the village Jew had two or three cows in the barn, a bit of home grown wheat, some potatoes, and other home grown products, the concerns were not great. A fair took place every week in the region. Various merchants would come from the city – one could obtain a few groszy from the broker, or simply sell and buy. Aside from their own farming economy, others had a small store or an inn. Everyone lived a modest life. Everyone exuded the charm of a person satisfied with his lot, and almost everyone was content with living from his own land.

As soon as one entered a village, one could figure out where a Jew lived and where not. The Jewish houses were built differently from the gentile cottages. They were whitewashed on the outside, and the yards were tidy. True Jewish charm sparkled from them. A *mezuzah* was fixed to every door.

[Page 185]

Inside there was modest furniture, a large bookshelf, and a picture of Moses holding the tablets or Abraham our Forefather taking Isaac to the altar on the eastern wall, a wall clock, and other Judaic objects. One Friday nights there were the candlesticks with the lights of the Holy Sabbath. On the Sabbath itself, there was the taste of the Garden of Eden... Even the poorest Jew of the village felt a bit of that spirit.

The Holy Sabbath was strictly observed in the village. Not even a straw would be torn on the Sabbath. The High Holy Days and other holidays brought with them the true feeling of "You have chosen us"[5]. Who does not remember *Simchat Torah* in the village, with the rejoicing of the Torah and kissing it – the joy was boundless. All Jewish customs were meticulously observed. For example, Chanukah with *latkes* (potato pancakes) and *dreidels* (tops), Purim with the costumes – oh, how did everyone get dressed up! On the other hand, there was *Tisha BeAv*, upon one could witness the destruction from all corners over the gentiles' heads. The members of the household were depressed and pale from fasting – in short, it was a veritable destruction!

A Jewish Wedding in the Village

A Jewish wedding in the village was no simple matter... There was a style to arranging a wedding. The in-laws would stumble across various complications such as paying the dowry or that the pedigree was not considered appropriate – so they would put off the wedding for a time. Sometimes, there would be a misunderstanding between the bride and the groom – and one of them would delay the wedding or even abandon the match. The wedding turned into a *kapores* hen[6] over every minor issue... Of course, matches were arranged in those days, and the bride and groom barely got to know each other... This all led to great trouble and toil until the time that the young pair appeared under the wedding canopy. People prepared feverishly for the wedding for entire months – not only the bride and groom, but also the entire circle of Turka... There were indeed villagers who were connected and linked to the entire region. – if not from the groom's side, then from the bride's side. There must have been some sort of hook. How can one not go to such a wedding?!

[Page 186]

The wedding itself was very lovely, especially during the wintertime. The guests would begin to arrive already in the afternoon of the day of the wedding. They would come by sled, as there was no other means of transportation. The horses were beautifully decorated with red, white and blue ribbons and noisy bells, and were accompanied by the singing of Hassidic songs.

A unique wedding custom took place in the village. Since the wedding would take place in the village where the bride's parents lived, the bride would send a "special delegation" of young lands to fetch the groom, who was to come in from a different village. The task of that delegation was to bring the groom at any price. To that end, the delegation brought cake, liquor and a roast turkey with them in order to purchase the groom. The groom, resembling a king, did not ravel alone. A group of guardians from among the young chaps also wanted to bring the groom to the wedding. Thus, a fierce battle broke out, for live and death, between both delegations... They did not, Heaven forbid, fight like the gentiles, but they struggled a bit over the groom, dragging him here and there, covered each other with snow, overturned the sleds, and perpetrated other such acts of mischief. Finally, both sides reached an agreement, began to travel, drank a toast, and snacked on a piece of turkey – and brought the groom to the wedding with song.

Translator's Footnotes:

70. The citron and palm frond used for the *Sukkot* service.
71. To provide entertainment during weddings.
72. *Selichot* are the penitential prayers recited from prior to Rosh Hashanah until Yom Kippur. The first *Selichot* service takes place on the Saturday night prior to Rosh Hashanah, unless Rosh Hashanah falls early in the week, in which case it takes place two Saturday nights prior to Rosh Hashanah.
73. "G-d full of mercy..." the opening words of the Jewish prayer for the dead.
74. The opening paragraph of the main festival prayer "*Amida*" begins "You have chosen us from all nations."
75. A colorful expression, referring to the *kapores* ceremony on the eve of Yom Kippur, where a hen, rooster or chicken is used as a symbolic surrogate form of atonement. Here, it refers to a major effort or difficulty.

[Page 187]

Jewish Life in the Village of Vysotsko Vyzhne

by Meir Hirt of London

The village of Vysotsko Vyzhne was located 30 kilometers from Turka. To get there, one had to travel through the villages of Melnitsa, Borinya, Vysotsko Nyzny, and Kasaring. There were Jewish settlements, big or small, in all the aforementioned villages. However, as soon as one arrived in Vysotsko, one would immediately see large-scale Jewish life. Almost the first house was Jewish, with a *mezuzah* on the door. One was not ashamed.

A Jewish Town

Indeed, this town was brimming with Jewish life. It was quite large, 10 kilometers long. Just as the first house had a *mezuza*, so did the last house. Between the two houses, for a distance of nine kilometers, lived a Jewish settlement that was seething with Jewish life. Indeed, there was no rabbi in the city, but there was a *mikva* [ritual bath], a *shochet* [ritual slaughterer], and other Jewish necessities.

The *shochet* David Hersch was a scholarly, charitable Jew with a large family. He was a Boyaner Hassid. He also responded to *halachic* questions and served as the *shochet* for many other villages. He would slaughter in the areas where the mountain Jews lived – for every Jewish home needed meat for the Sabbath. In the event that such was lacking in the house – one must ensure that there would be...

Other scholars in the town included David Frenkel and David Kraus. They were the chief experts of the village. David Kraus was also the teacher of the village for many years. The village had over 50 Jewish families, as far as I can calculate. On the Sabbath, services took place in five private homes. There was no synagogue. The *minyanim* [prayer quorums] took place in the homes of Yosef Bart, Yosef Hirt, Yisrael Hirt, Shlomo Kraus, and Yoelche Goldreich.

[Page 188]

Most of the Jews lived in the center of the village. In the middle of the week, a *minyan* took place only when there was a *yahrzeit*, when someone had to recite *kaddish*, or on occasions when a rebbe visited the village. The latter was a very frequent occurrence, especially in the summer time. The rebbes would visit for the fresh air, and would thereby impart some Judaism to the village Jews.

Organizations and Hassidism

There were Zionist organizations in the village: the General Zionist Achva, and Hechalutz. There was a feud between the two organizations, but this was more personal than ideological... The youth of the village also took interest in literature. Achva had a fine, well-organized library. There were books by Shalom Aleichem, Peretz, Mendele Mocher Seforim, as well as Karl Marx, Nordau, and others. People also subscribed to Baderech – the prime readers being Ziel Rosenberg, Leizer Singer, Mendel Weiss and my brother Zelig Hirt. All of them have now passed away.

The majority of the population was Hassidic, primarily of the Boyaner sect. Not all of them were fond of the work of the Zionist groups, but the main thing was that they reached an understanding and lived in peace...

Everyone earned a living. People conducted business and carried on their lives. There were also Jewish agricultural enterprises, shoemakers, tailors, textile shops and merchants of cattle and wood. Market day took place very second Tuesday, and Jews earned well. Jews from Turka and the surrounding villages would come on market day – bringing some bounty to the Jewish residents.

Most of the Jews were not wealthy. They worked hard for a living. There were indeed a few families who could be considered wealthy, such as Shlomo Kraus, Abish Rosenberg, Anshel Lew, Yosef Hirt and Yosef Bart.

[Page 189]

Yosef Bart was a Hassidic Jew. In his younger years, he was considered to be an erudite Jew with an enlightened outlook. He loved to read a Yiddish newspaper, and at times also a Hebrew one. His house was similar to that of Abraham our forefather. If a Jew were to come for the market day, or just for an ordinary day of the year, he would find there a place to sleep, eat and drink. If anyone required a charitable contribution he would obtain such from Yosef Bart or from his two sons Yossi and Yoel. The three of them would always seek opportunities to do good deeds to other Jews, setting them on their way and giving charity.

Chaim Goldreich and Moshe Bronstein also loved to do good deeds. Shlomo Kraus' house was almost destroyed in a great tragedy only a few months prior to the war. The village of Vysotsko was also the cradle of the well-known, dear Goldreich family. The children were well educated in Judaism and general knowledge. The writer of these lines was a frequent visitor of the family.

*

As I have already mentioned, the second Zionist organization, which also maintained a Jewish National Fund committee, was also involved in Zionist activities: the distribution of *shekalim* [tokens of membership in the Zionist organization], and the emptying of the Keren Kayemet charity boxes. The work was often conducted in conjunction with other villages and settlements in the area.

With the help of Ziel Rosenberg from Lyubsha, an amateur Yiddish theater would be conducted from time to time. The income went to the Keren Kayemet. The youth would often come together for readings and discussions. This took place primarily in private homes, but during the latter period, also in a rented premises. The General Zionists also had the Singer family as members. This was "Herzl-Singer." The family consisted of three sons: Yosef, Leizer and Shmuel (Yosef is in America), and two daughters.

[Page 190]

They all played the fiddle. Of course, dance evenings were often arranged, and the "brothers" would often play so that the audience would be entertained. The income went to the Keren Kayemet.

The active members of the Achva chapter included my brother Zelig, my sister Dvora Hirt, Ziel Rosenberg from Lyubsha, Leizer and Shmuel Singer, the two sisters Pesel and Rosa Goldreich, Yisrael Teichman, and Abish Rosenberg. The writer of these lines participated as the treasurer of the Keren Kayemet.

Despite the fact that the village was large, all of the Jews lived together as a large family. They were also connected to each other with actual connections. The bonds extended and encompassed several villages.

*

I must state that my mother, may G-d avenge her blood, (Ita Hirt) was involved with Zionism, but my father Abish Hirt was a Hassidic Jew. When rebbes would come to the village for the Sabbath, they would often stay in our house. On such occasions, a Torah would be brought to our house, and we would celebrate Sabbaths with rebbe's table celebrations. Jews from the entire mountain area would come together. People ate where they could and slept in the barns. Indeed, the mountain Jews loved rebbes. For such a mountain Jew this was no difficult matter, so long as they could spend the Sabbath with a rebbe.

On the other hand, as has already been said, my mother was a central figure within Zionism, and my brother Moshe (who was then still a small child) used to gather the youth together and read Zionist material and literature to them. People knew to come to us from all the surrounding villages. One could obtain a couch to sleep at our house, so it would be not too crowded for the multitude of guests. At night we would cover the house with straw, spread out bedding, and everyone would sleep.

Thus did the Jewish people live, spend their time, and conduct themselves in the village of Vysotsko Vyzhne among the multitude of villages in the Carpathian Mountains.

Today, nothing is left of this.

[Page 191]

Ilnik – My Childhood Village

by Meir Gottesman of Kfar Neter

Meir Gottesman

In memory of my dear parents Chaya and Moshe

Through the length of the village of Ilnik, two miles from Turka near Stryj, flows a river of fast-flowing water – the Rika. There are cultivated fields on both sides of the village. In one direction there is a road that connects the village with Turka. The other side is connected with many other villages. There are forests and mountains behind the cultivated fields. I still remember the tall Kycyra Mountain, which was covered with snow until the middle of the summer.

A light rail traveled through the village, which carried wood from the forests to the sawmills of Turka.

Ilnik was a large village. Obviously, the majority of the population was gentile. However, approximately 40 Jewish families lived among them. They were occupied with agriculture, and some were involved in commerce. Life was difficult. One struggled for livelihood for an entire week, and concerned oneself that nothing would be lacking for the Sabbath.

On the Sabbath, one cast off the yoke, dressed up in the finest clothes that one could afford, put on the *streimel* – and went to worship. There were three *minyanim* in three separate places in Ilnik: At Reb Yosele Hans, Reb Kiva Hans, and Hersh Nachman Singer.

[Page 192]

I recall that Reb Yosele used to wear work clothes with a *streimel* on the Sabbath. His wife Malka, with her pleasant Sabbath greeting, wore a white kerchief on her head like all the other mothers... Reb Yosele was the chief doer in the village. Every person who needed some sort of favor would go to Reb Yosele Hans. His house was open to every person in need.

I was orphaned from my father at a very young age. He went away during the First World War and did not return. Mother died a few years later. May their memories be blessed. I was housed in the village with non-relatives. They were all good friends, and all remain in my memory.

Reb Mendel-Shua conducted a *cheder* in which I studied. This was for the sake of the good deed, with no tuition fees. He was a scholarly Jew, a prayer leader, a *mohel* [ritual circumcisor] – and he did this all for the sake of Heaven.

Mirche, Yosele Hans' daughter, remains strongly etched in my heart. She took me in to Skuli and treated me as her own child. I worked and lived with them. Also unforgettable are her two sons Ziga and Itche, as well as the entire Ornstein family.

*

It is the eve of Passover. Matzos were baked in the village with great cheer... The baked matzos were tasty, and were enjoyed from afar... The wooden casks were filled with water for matzo in a timely fashion. A *borscht* was fermented in a second wooden cask already after Purim. It smelled like good wine...

On festivals... the high holydays... Reb Feivel Wolf, the Torah reader, was over 90 years old, with a splendid countenance. The Unetane Tokef[1] recited by Reb Yosele Hans or Yekutiel...

And nothing remains...

*

[Page 193]

The following are the Jewish families that lived in the village:

Anshel Weis, David Yona Gleicher, Feiga Kirshner, Yosef Gerber, Wolf Gerber, Avraham Gerber, Binyamin From, Chaim Dan, Hersch Berg, Yekutiel Spilman, Avraham Spilman, Shlomo Berg, Dvora Berg, Yisrael Schwartz, Yitzchak Schwartz, Yitzchak Wolf Schwartz, Modl Loterman, Yitzchak Mendel Hans, Leibish Berg, Akiva Hans, the Schindler family, Yosef Aharon Fuchs, David Singer, Moshe Singer, Hersch Nachman Singer, Mendel Fuchs, Esther Liba Fuchs, Abish Shuster, Shimon Floshner, the Arbel family, Yosef Hans, Yisrael-Avraham Hans, Berish Fish, Akiva Wolf, Anshel Schwartz, Berish Schwartz – all of blessed memory

[Page 193]

The Village of Vysotsko Nyzny

by Avraham Tuchman

The village was destroyed during the First World War and then rebuilt. I recall that, when I was four years old, our entire family fled to Czechoslovakia. When we returned in 1947, the entire village was burnt. In the center of the city, where our barn was located, not one house remained. The houses of our Ukrainian neighbors were also burned then, but they had already rebuilt them. A few Jews, including my uncle, also returned earlier and began to reconstruct their farms.

In general, the Jews of the village were poor and earned their livelihoods with difficulty. A few conducted business with forest lumber, and others were tradesmen such as shoemakers, tailors, carpenters and millers. Life was not easy. People struggled to sustain the family. We also suffered from the Ukrainians with some frequency.

There were thirty Jewish families in the village. They conducted societal and factional life. Branches of the parties existed – the Zionists, Akiva, and others.

[Page 194]

Rozluch and Beniva

by Tzipora Zelmanovich (Katz) of Netanya

Tzipora Zelmanovich (Katz)

Rozluch

A. Rozluch

The village of Rozluch was located 14 kilometers from Turka. Nature endowed the town with a great deal of beauty. It was surrounded by beautiful mountains, which turned into fine gardens for strolling. The forests, with water falls and streams, imparted special charm to the village. Wealthy Jews from Lemberg, Sambor and the district spent a great deal of money to build lovely villas with parks, which served as summer homes. The air was fresh and wholesome.

[Page 195]

A pool was built in the modern style, in which we bathed. There was mineral water that was fit for drinking. Everyone in the district who had the means would travel to spend the summer in Rozluch. The beauty was compared to Vienna; many people would refer to it as Little Vienna. An entire street with villas was built, called Molerman Street.

The Jews in Rozluch lived happily. People made efforts to expand and beautify their dwellings – for this would bring in significant income over the summer. Not too many of the Jewish residents of the town were old timers. Most were families who had recently arrived. I now wish to write what I remember about them.

The youth of the town was organized into various Zionist organizations. Many *chalutzim* [Zionist pioneers] would come in the summer from other cities. They would visit the well of Dniester, located in the mountains of Rozluch.

[Page 196]

Many young people attempted to travel to the Land of Israel, and special *hachsharas* [preparation activities for *aliya*] were made. I spent my *hachshara* in the city of Kosice in Czechoslovakia. Thanks to this, I was saved from a great misfortune. I escaped to Hungary, and reached Israel after many adventures and wanderings.

B. Beniva

I was five years old when I left Beniva, and I pined for it for many years. I indeed used to visit it later.

The town was surrounded by forests. The train station was in Sianki or Sokoliki, four or five kilometers from the town. There was no *Beis Midrash* in Beniva. Services were conducted at the home of the family of Yaakov Apelderfer.

Jews of Beniva were involved with business and agriculture.

Translator's Footnotes:

12. A central prayer of the Rosh Hashanah and Yom Kippur services.

[Page 197]

The Jews of Husna Vyzna and Husna Nyzna

Meir Goldreich- Netanya

Translated by David Clodman

There were seventeen Jewish families in Husna Vyzna and Husna Nyzna, with approximately four hundred families in the village. The majority, as most, were Ukranian Christians. These seventeen families, in addition to their various regular activities – as farmers, shoemakers, landowners, flour millers, wagon drivers and shopkeepers - also supported themselves through business, and thus managed to supplement the remainder of their needs which they wouldn't otherwise have been able to meet.

Originally, Jewish life unfolded with tranquility and they left their signatures on this place and this I will try to depict.

Sabbath eve, candle lighting time in the Jewish homes announced to the entire village that the Sabbath Day, the day of rest, had arrived. Actually, the Sabbath and the few Jews with their Streimel hats and long black coats awakened such respect that it was as if people passed by on the tips of their toes.

During the Sabbath afternoon, when our parents went to sleep after the prayer and cholent which followed, the youth would go out to the street, where we gathered and would walk to the edge of the village. We made use of Fishel Seeman's house as a way station and from there we would walk to the houses of Fital Fiddler and Isaac Stein. The village was very wide and we traversed it as if we were the rulers over the Jewish people there...Who would disturb all this? Near the Mill we waited for Dvor, a woman who bought the mail from Visotski. Even on Fraknohan Street where most of the mail was supposed to belong to us, next to the mill the mail bag was passed to us empty...

The third meal came and then before we lit the candelabras and the lights in our house, in spite of the fact that most of the Christians had turned on their lights, the village appeared to be covered in darkness; it remained dark until the lighting of the candles and until we heard the words "Here is my Lord, my saviour".

And for the Days of Awe there was much respect felt in all parts of the village. The birds seemed to chirp in quieter voices than usual so as not to disturb the sanctity of the Festival.

The Christians who comprised 95% of the local population had criticisms and complaints against Jews. For example on Shavuot, during the time of completing the plowing and planting, the soil had a need for rain. If the holiday turned out to be a beautiful day, we the Jews were held responsible for this because our prayers prevented the rain from falling. On the Jewish New Year when the farmers needed nice weather to give them extra time to harvest their crops and it rained, apparently it was the fault of the Jews because in our many prayers we made it worse by bringing more rain. Who could have believed this? The essence of their attitudes was the intense belief in the status of Jewish prayer - an honour and a responsibility of the (Jewish) people. There existed in the power of their prayer the ability to control the falling or cessation of the rain.

And this did not just happen on holidays. Also on days of mourning there was an influence on the entire place. On the fast of Ninth Day of Av there was this absolute sadness as if not just the Jews but all non-believers were conspicuous in their fasting. Everyone conducted themselves with a slowed pace and a fatigue that is fitting for those who fast.

In this climate there also were the beginnings of Zionist activities among the few Jews of the area (in one photograph we see the girls after the Zionist Congress. It appears to me this was in 1933 at the house of B.H. Goldreich, when there was a failed attempt- 49 votes against and 49 uncertain ones that were ?sold?. There were three competing groups. The Mizrachi, Popular Zionists, and Shomer Hatzair). With the conquering of the region by the Nazis, this whole way of life - all the people who lived with us over several generations- those whose lives bent and swayed together with ours- changed their skins and became predatory animals overnight.

My friend from school and our closest neighbour whose father taught us to play the violin/fiddle and with who we lived one beside the other - it seems he had to show me his rifle when he became a Ukranian Legionaire. So with (in spite of) this type of assistance from these people, we did manage to live and to create, but they liquidated Jewish life in this place.

I hope that my comments will serve as a mitzvah to remember those people who weren't able to see the results of the work of these murderers and the founding of the State of Israel.

I hope these comments will serve, like the light that never extinguishes, as an everlasting memorial to my dear parents, Baruch Hirsh and Rivka Goldreich, to my sister Pseeya and her husband Abraham Reichman, to their children and to my brother's children, to our friends and acquaintances and to all the descendents of the village of Husna Vyzna and Husna Nyzna.

Translator's notes

There are a few lines where I guessed. ie the one about the mail, I wasn't sure what the house or place was related to where the mail was picked up. I also guessed about the line related to the count of votes re the election for Zionist leaders. Finally I wasn't sure exactly what this Ukranian neighbour did with his gun to the author- I guessed the author was being sarcastic ....

[Page 199]

Life and Death in Lomna

by Menachem Rosen and Yechiel Hirt of Haifa

Uncaptioned. Evidently the two authors, although it is unclear which is which.

Jews and Gentiles

Lomna was a village between three cities: Turka, Lutewisk and Stary_Sambor. Two rivers flowed around the town – the Dniester and the Chastsiwonia[1]. From the southwest vantage point, one could see endless forested mountains. The Jewish quarter was located in the center, along the Chastsiwonia River. Wooden balustrades served as a barrier along the river. They simultaneously provided a place for loafers or regular citizens to snatch a conversation, while reclining or moving along against them... Three roads spread out in various directions from the center: one road to Turka, the second to Lutewisk, and the third to Stary Sambor.

The houses were situated on both sides of the street – one house inward, and one house outward... The houses were built of wood and covered with shingle roofs. There was a brick house in the center, first built by the wealthy Y. M. Engelmeir. The palace later served as dwellings for the following generation. Near that house was a large *Beis Midrash* with a gallery for women. The *Beis Midrash* could accommodate the entire Jewish population. The police station was located near the *Beis Midrash.* There was a slaughterhouse near the river. A bit farther on was a steam bath with a *mikva* [ritual bath]. In summary, the Jewish settlement was more or less compact.

[Page 200]

Reb Baruch Hirt, Lomna

Prior to the First World War, the Jewish population consisted of approximately 80 families or 350 people. There were also a few Polish families, consisting of officials, schoolteachers, tradesmen and police. The majority of the population consisted of Ukrainians and Katzapes[2]. They earned their livelihood from agriculture and lived in the periphery of the town. There was a women's seminary and church in the heart of the town, protected by a fence constructed of four meter high boards. One could barely peek inside through the several cracks. Inside was a closed-in kingdom of women. The personnel consisted of nuns who were also the teachers of the seminary. The seminary conducted its own agriculture in an area of several hundred dunams. The labor was very intensive for that time.

The Development of the Town.

During the second half of the 19th century, Lomna and the entire region belonged to Duke Parma, the father of the woman who later became Empress Zita[3], the wife of the last Austrian Kaiser (Emperor) Karl. Duke Parma build a large paper factory in Lomna, which was one of the largest paper factories in Galicia at that time. The raw material came from the surrounding forests.

[Page 201]

In the winter, the duke would come to go hunting with his entire family. This would bring a bit of life to the village. Undoubtedly, the paper factory was the foundation of the development of the village. Jewish officials and merchants moved to the town. Various businesses, bakeries, and shops were set up to serve the workers of the factory. The farmers would work part time in the factory, while others would provide the wood from the forests, which served as raw material for the paper, and also would transport the finished paper to the closes train station in Strzylki.

According to legend, the count once said during a winter hunting expedition that if he would not succeed in shooting a wild animal, he would abandon the factory. Thus, one day, the factory was abandoned and, after the passage of time, was destroyed. The foundations of the large millstones that were used to grind the wood in the factory remained until the later years. Those foundations were constructed of lead. Some Jews who knew the secret indeed became wealthy from the lead, which had remained ownerless...

A large, steam-driven sawmill was built on that place in the later years. It remained in action until 1910, when the surrounding forests had been completely exploited.

The *Beis Midrash* and the Studying

The town built up an independent, Jewish community, with a rabbi, *shochet* [ritual slaughterer], *mohel* [circumcisor], steam bath, and *mikva.* It had a large synagogue and slaughterhouse, which also served the surrounding region.

In those days, Jewish cultural life revolved around the *Beis Midrash.* Almost every youth who concluded *cheder* and the public school transferred over to the *Beis Midrash.* There, he began to study a page of *Gemara* with his own efforts. If there was something he did not understand, he would always be assisted by the older scholars. With time, the diligent studiers would reach the level of scholars, and would then assist the weaker ones with a lesson in Talmud or *halacha.* Thus, the youths of the town would become known as scholars, and seek a marriage partner in the larger cities.

[Page 202]

On a winter night, when the *Beis Midrash* was well heated, all of the tables were occupied by ordinary householders and youths, learning with enthusiasm. The sweet sounds of Gemara studying reverberated through the *Beis Midrash.* The diligent ones would learn all night twice a week. In the middle of the learning on the long winter nights, they would collect money to purchase seasonal fruit and other refreshments, so that they could cheer themselves up a bit.

The rabbi of Lomna.

[Page 203]

The side room of the *Beis Midrash* served as a location for the youths to conduct their own prayer services on Sabbaths and festivals. Thus, it also served as a "seminary" for upcoming Torah readers, prayer leaders and cantors... Those who excelled with cantorial voices served as assistants to the cantor on the festivals and high holidays.

For the most part, the householders would partake of the third Sabbath meal with the rabbi, Mordechai Engelmeir, where they would listen to Torah discussions on the issues of the day. The rabbi was a great expert in Talmud, Rambam and general didactics. For the entire week, the Hassidim would tell over the novel ideas on torah that they had heard.

The youths over the age of thirteen would put a morsel of bread in their pockets, enter the *Beis Midrash,* sit around the tables and sing Sabbath hymns in the dark. At that time, the *Beis Midrash* belonged to the youth. Each of the older youths had the rights to lead a certain segment of the hymns, and nobody would encroach upon the rights of his fellow... The newly minted candidates would have to wait for one of the current youths with rights would get married and leave the town... The third Sabbath meal was one of the experiences for the youth. Each one had the opportunity to place his neck in the window, evading the wrath of the congregation.

Reb Moshe Hirt (son of Yechiel), Lomna

[Page 204]

The "Plagers"[4] Group

When the youths approached the age of military service, they formed a group that was called "The Plagers". Their aim was to go on a strange diet, fasting a few days a week, and not sleeping at night. The objective was to become underweight, appear sickly and therefore avoid military service... The cheerful-sorrowful group would come together to the *Beis Midrash* at night, and sing and dance until they were out of breath. In order to be happy, they had to make sure that there was a bit of drink and a morsel of herring. They would charge the householders a certain sum of money – and woe to the householder who would refuse to pay his portion of the "*tikun*"[5] (that was the name of the fund)... The group would perform some sort of prank upon the recalcitrant people, which would cost a certain sum of money.

In the winter ,the group of "Plagers" would bring in the heating wood for the poor people. They would take the wood from the wealthy householders at night and carry it to the homes of the needy... Indeed, the Plagers served at that time as woodchoppers and water carries, and also served as one of the locations for purchasing drinks. During that era, this group provided an opportunity for the Plagers and ordinary loafers to release their youthful energy, which would be suppressed in normal times. It became an acceptable custom that the Plagers were "permitted" everything, and they were forgiven for the various pranks that they perpetrated...

A musical band of volunteers was set up by the Plagers. The instruments included a fiddle, bass, drum and flute. Of course, during those times, the musicians did not study notes, but they fiddled for an extended period until they learned the skill on their own... The band would play in the *Beis Midrash* at night, and the Plagers would dance to their accompaniment. The band would also visit homes at various opportunities, such as on Saturday night party prior to a wedding, when they would come

[Page 205]

to help the bride or groom rejoice. They did not differentiate between poor and rich. The same thing would take place at a circumcision ceremony that took place on a weekday, as well as during the ceremony of the redemption of the firstborn [*Pidyon Haben*]. On Purim they would go from house to house, taking the young people of the town along. The income from the band was used to purchase books for the *Beis Midrash.*

The Friday Steam Bath

On Friday at noontime, one could already feel that the Sabbath was approaching. In the afternoon, the householders went to the bath with their families, with a broom and a towel in their hands. The bathhouse contained a stone steam bath with seven steps, a *mikva*, and a warm and cold bath. There were three bathtubs for the "intelligentsia". They would be filled with pails of cold water. The distinguished people would sit in the anteroom to rest. At the same time, this was the first session of the town's naked parliament... There, people talked about general politics and local events. The second session took place on Saturday morning prior to services, and after the immersion in the warm *mikva*. Then, they would discuss local news mixed with a bit of gossip. At that time, a father would be able to indirectly learn about the "good deeds" of his children. This would on occasion be the cause of a spoiled Sabbath...

On Friday after the steam bath, the wealthy householders would go to a tavern to drink a glass of beer with a plate of piping hot chickpeas. For the poor people, on the other hand, a plate of noodle juice was waiting for them at home. After that, the householders took a nap, cast off their weekday worries, and entered the Sabbath spirit with the additional soul. They felt like the Sabbath angels.

The Sabbaths and festivals were distinguished by their joyous mood. Friends and family visited each other, and talked from the heart.

[Page 206]

Livelihood

The chief form of livelihood in town was commerce. This was often a grocery store, or a general store which had a bit of everything, according to the needs of the town and the area. Other sources of livelihood included inns, bakeries and butcher shops. Some people earned their livelihood as peddlers. The visited the villages in the region. They bought, sold, or bartered merchandise with the farmers. Some were brokers for any merchandise that came to their hands. They would visit the fairs in the surrounding towns. They would be happy if they succeeded in bringing home a coin or two for the Sabbath. A small number of people were tradesmen, such as tailors, shoemakers, bricklayers, bookbinders, and wagon drivers. In general, the town was not noted for people of great wealth, but everyone was able to earn a reasonable livelihood, some more some less, in accordance with the notions of the times.

Society and Education

There were organizations for charity, visiting the sick, and providing for weddings. All the youth attended the public school, which consisted of four classes. For the most part, that concluded their secular education. In 1911, a teacher with a great deal of general education wandered into the town. The teacher conducted various courses for the youth and grown ups in the German language. The courses lasted for approximately two years. Then, just as the teacher had suddenly appeared, he suddenly disappeared, leaving no trace behind... Later, it became clear that he had been a spy, may Heaven protect us. In time, the course for the older students consisted mainly of German and general literature, with a significant dose of the theory of Karl Marx. This served as the foundation for the brand new Jewish intelligentsia of the town.

[Page 207]

Youth movements and organizations were not popular in town at that time. On the other hand, the youth enjoyed seasonal sports. People would go to the rivers in the summer, for almost everyone knew how to swim. They would go out to the surrounding mountains, hold races, catch fish in the rivers, and also go to the forests to collect raspberries, and – after the rain – mushrooms. In the winter, they would skate on the ice and go sledding on the high mountains. This was often fraught with mortal danger.

New Times

During the period of the First World War, after the first Russian invasion, the majority of the Jewish population moved to Hungary, Czechoslovakia, and Austria. Later, when Galicia was liberated by the Austrian Army, a large portion of the population of the town returned. They were disappointed with their destroyed little houses, and some of them rebuilt them anew.

The returning “worldly folk” brought with them a bit of culture and civilization. A large portion of the youth had already read classical and general world literature. Some have already started to study Hebrew, and these were the first steps of the Zionist movement in town. The *Beis Midrash* was no longer visited frequently, and free time was spent on societal activities and communal life.

The upcoming generation no longer reclined at their parents' tables. They began to do business in the villages on their own to help the family with livelihood. In that manner, they expressed their independence and became known as youths with worldly experience. This was, however, a life from one day to the next, without a future, which on occasion brought the youth to despair. Some moved to the larger cities, and others to America and Israel.

[Page 208]

The End

In 1940, the Germans, may their names be blotted out, marched into the town from the direction of Ustrzyki Dolne and Lutowisk. They put a German commandant in charge of the Lomna police station, and the police themselves consisted of Volksdeutschen (the so-called Schwabs from Wilcze) and Ukrainians. They knew that they had whom to neglect...

The first beginning was: A truck with ammunition got stuck in the Dniester River. They hauled all of the Jews from the town, and beat them with whips and sticks until the Jews dragged the truck out of the water... Then they were told to bring all of the ammunition to the police station, which was four kilometers away. The Jews fetched a horse and wagon to arrange the transport – but they, may their names be blotted out, answered that this was a pity on the horse... This was the first lesson in forced labor.

A little later, the order came regarding the Star of David insignia. They mobilized all of the men and took them to Boberka. Some worked in the sawmill, and others worked under inhuman conditions in the forests. Women and children remained in the town. The Germans pillaged the homes, as the Ukrainians sat around idly.

*

Thus did the suffering and murdering continue until 1942. Then an order came that all of the Jews, without exception, must move to the Stryjer sawmill in the Turka Ghetto. There, they were forced in to the barracks. Only 40-50 men with work cards for the sawmill remained in town. The old and sick men, as well as the women and children, were shot in ghetto. Those remaining were herded to the train station, loaded on transport wagons, and sent to Belzec, from where nobody returned...

[Page 209]

In Lutowisk

In the town of Lutowisk, where there were no workplaces, the entire Jewish population of the town was driven out in 1941 to the fields of the Rand family. There, the unfortunate Jews dug mass graves for themselves. Approximately 1,500 people were shot there.

In 1942, an ordinance was issued that all of the holders of work cards would be transported to the Sambor Ghetto. The Jews already knew what this meant, so they decided to flee into the Carpathian Mountains. They organized and sent professionals out to the Carpathians, near Gorna Istryk, to build bunkers. Then, they began to bring in stockpiles of dry provisions. Five or six men would go out at night, laden with whatever they could carry. This was a distance of 60-70 kilometers. The undertaking lasted for months. Shortly before the aktion, they succeeded in escaping to the bunkers, which had been prepared with a great deal of superhuman effort.

However, to their ill fortune, a young man from Kryvka was captured as he was bringing his family to the bunker. After great torture, he led them to the bunker… and nobody survived. The details of that liquidation were told by Yoshe Wolf of Bereszki, the sole survivor.

Translator's Footnotes:

7. I could not identify this river definitively but I believe it is the Chaszczówka.
8. A nickname for Russians.
9. See http://en.wikipedia.org/wiki/Robert_I,_Duke_of_Parma and http://en.wikipedia.org/wiki/Zita_of_Bourbon-Parma.
10. Sufferers.
11. "Tikun" literally means "repair", but is often used as a term for refreshments served in the synagogue.

[Page 210]

Krasna – Life and Destruction

by Moshe Schindler of Kiryat Tivon

Moshe Schindler

The Village

The village of Krasna was situated 30 kilometers from the town of Turka, and was dependent upon it. The area of the village was relatively large relative to its population of 1,200. The population included 15 Jewish families, numbering 70 souls. To its good fortune, the village was located next to the small town of Smozhe, in which a large weekly fair took place on Mondays. On that day, all of the farmers of the region brought in their produce, and of course, Jews came to buy and sell all types of merchandise, as well as horses and various types of animals.

The majority of the population of Smozhe was Jewish. The community was headed by a rabbi, and the most of their livelihood was derived from the fairs. This was a typical Jewish town. On Sabbaths and festivals, quiet pervaded everywhere; and on Simchat Torah, the Jews would go out to the center of the town with the Torah scrolls, singing and dancing in a Hassidic fashion and performing all types of tricks. The gentiles would stand around, some out of honor and others out of plan curiosity. There were those who look upon them with disdain, but nobody was so brazen as to open up a mouth to them.

House of Worship

Despite the fact that Krasna was divided in to three sections, and there were areas which were approximately four kilometers from the center, the Jews would gather each Sabbath at the home of my uncle Reb Izik Gissinger for a prayer service. Almost all of the attendees were capable of leading the services in the traditional Hassidic fashion. My brother Avraham and I would often come early with our father, but we never succeeded in coming early than Reb Wolf... Despite the fact that Reb Wolf was already at an advanced age, and that he lived at the other end of the village, he was always first.

[Page 211]

Reb Wolf had a character trait – he loved serving as the prayer leader very much. No cold or rain could prevent him from coming first, let he lose, Heaven forbid, the great opportunity to display his fine, melodic voice. In the home of Rabbi Izik, one would be treated with a cup of hot coffee by Aunt Chava, who was a modest woman and the daughter of the great scholar Reb Lemel Zadilisker.

We, the youth, were happy with chance to get together. In between the prayers we would loaf around a bit in secret, but we would behave respectfully in the presence of the adults. Reb David Hirt, a scholarly man, would serve as the Torah reader. During the reading, we would chat about the teachers. The teacher Teichman, who was not overly diligent in his observance of the commandments, lived in our home for many years and studied various subject with us, including Bible. He would give practical interpretations to most matters... Therefore, people did not especially respect him, and would say that there was a teacher at the home of Berish Schnitzler with regard to whom the following adage can be applied, "it is a pity on the wine that it is situated in that flask." He was literally a "Deitch" [Germanized Jew]. Nobody wanted to enter into a debate with him, since that man had well-founded answers for everything, and he had his sourced upon which to rely. Those with secular education would say that if Yisrael Teichman had obtained his erudition through the customary means, he would have been a great professor. However, he had amassed his knowledge through his own efforts. Later on, he set up the Achva Zionist group along with his brother Leib, to which most of the youth of the area belonged.

Zionist Youth

My brother and I signed up for the nearby chapter in Smozhe. Everyone was surprised – from where do we already know Hebrew songs? They had not yet succeeded in even learning these Zionist songs in Yiddish. At our house, even the gentile maid knew how to sing, for every day, she would hear how we were learning to sing. Since she worked with us for many years, she knew Yiddish and also Yiddish songs. One of them that I remember: she would sing "*Frei , Frei, Palestina Frei...*" This was the era of Zionist awakening in Poland. We were well organized, and we gathered together at meetings. Many even went on *Hachshara* [preparations for *aliya*].

On one occasion, we arranged a get-together with the Slovak Jewish youth, across the border from Poland. We walked several dozen kilometers by foot and slept over in Vysotzko. There, we were divided up into various houses to spend the night. Early the next morning, we set out toward Mount Piko. Along the way, I a girl of about 15 years old. She was blond and thin, but very charming. She mentioned that she was studying in the gymnasium in Turka. This was Ela Gissinger. We arrived at the summit of the mountain, the tallest in the Carpathians, at approximately 10:00 a.m. About 200 of us spent two days there. Of course, we deliberated over *aliya* to the Land of Israel most of the time.

[Page 212]

We also had family problems with respect to convincing our parents to permit us to make *aliya*. Of course, we went to the house of worship on the Sabbaths, where there were people who mocked us and asked, "What will you do in Palestine? There is nothing there except for sand and Arabs." Already on that Sabbath we did not go to the afternoon service, but rather to meet with the youth. There, we found out that a few older youths had decided to make *aliya* to the Land.

Festivals in the Village

Festivals were not celebrated in a mundane fashion in Krasna... Even Purim was a festival. We would read the *megilla*, dress up and make merry... Festive parties were arranged where people dressed up. However, the festival of Passover was most beloved by every Jew, poor and rich. People prepared all year for it. They prepared goose and turkey fat. Homemade wine would be made in every home. Matzos would be baked two or three weeks before the festival. Machines were brought in from Turka for that purpose. However, matzo *shmura*[1], was an entirely different matter. Everybody participated in that effort. One person would prepare the dough, and women would make the matzos. Two men would stand next to the over, and command, "Put in a matzo!" Everyone wore clean clothes and wishes each other that they should merit to bake once again the following year along with their families.

The eve of Passover was a joyous day. First of all, we would help Father filter the wine – and there was a "benefit" to this in that along with working with the wine, we would taste it. Then we would enter the kitchen, which was pervaded with the atmosphere of Passover. Everything was new, clean and polished. Mother, wearing a new apron, stood next to the stove and prepared potato pancakes with turkey fat. These pancakes were not simple pancakes, for they had a unique taste and smell, entirely different from the pancakes of the rest of the year... The Passover *seder* with the entire family did not end before midnight. After the four questions, we would read the *Haggadah* with interruptions for eating. We would sing between each course. The four cups would somehow greatly expand, and everything was happy...

War

In 1939, when the Germans attacked Poland, we were unsure who would be "coming" to us – the Russians or the Germans. When the news spread that the Germans were coming, we gathered on the mountain and prepared an escape. We went through the mountains and reached Tuchulka. There we found out that the Russians were coming... We therefore disbanded the group that had been organized in a communal fashion. We did everything in communal fashion since not all the youths had the proper financial means. Now, we each went our own ways and returned to our homes.

[Page 213]

The Russians arrived three days later. We were afraid at first, but everyone quickly got settled with work. Our cousins Yitzchak and Avraham (Shlomo did not return from the Polish Army) continued with their agricultural work in which they were strongly established, and Aunt Rachel assisted them. I worked for some time as the secretary of the village. Later, I was transferred by the authorities to Borinia, and from there to Slawsko near Skole. I was looking forward to this, for my brother Avraham worked there at that time. However, to my sorrow, the joy was not long lasting. After a month, the Russians began to vacate the area and turn over their places to the Germans. My brother was drafted into the army, and I was enlisted for work. In accordance with their command, I set out by wagon to the gathering area along with six other Jewish girls. Suddenly, the wagon broke down, we got stuck along the way, and nobody wanted to take the girls on their vehicle. I begged them to run away, and I would do so on a horse, for the Germans were already behind us. However, the girls did not wish to do so, and convinced us not to abandon them. I finally obtained a wagon and we were saved.

The Germans in Krasna

During that time, the Germans were already in the villages. The Ukrainians gathered all the Jews to the local council, which was headed by Mikahil Mochko, a well-known anti-Semite. He turned to the Jews and said, "I have a paper upon which is written that you are spies. Therefore, you must be brought to judgment on this." Of course, everyone was quite confounded and began to swear that they have no idea about the issue. Did the gentile know that none of us was interested in anything other than agricultural work? Several Ukrainian youths wandered around the council room with drawn guns, and it appeared that they were just waiting for the order... Suddenly, Baruch Aharon of Turka, a well known merchant, appeared with a German captain. Baruch Aharon was the wagon driver of the German. After several words, he asked us and we gave him gold and silver objects, which he gave over to the German. Then the German issues a command to free all of us immediately.

After this incident, we attempted with all our might to become involved with public works projects. With great difficulty, we succeeded in obtaining work preparing trees in the forest. The work was very difficult. We worked by quota. I, my brother Avraham, and Malka Hirt succeeded in meeting or exceeding the quota. However Esther Liba Schindler and several other women were unable to meet the quota under any circumstances. Therefore, we helped them discharge their obligation. When these jobs ended, everyone dispersed, for the Germans began to perpetrate aktions. Everyone hid as best they could. Mochko took me as a farm worker, meaning as a slave. I worked with all my might, but it was to no avail. After a few days later, he informed me that he could no longer employ me, since there was going to be an aktion – and who knows how it would turn out. Therefore, my brother Avraham and I decided to escape to the forests. We remained in the forests at night, and went into the village in the evening to steal potatoes.

[Page 214]

Siege

All Jewish property became open for all. We more or less knew who pillaged our property. At times we asked our former neighbors, to whom we had given over a portion of our property, to return some items. At first, we would get something, but later, when Hillel Fisch asked Mochko, to whom he had given over valuables and clothing, for a single shirt, he asked Fisch, "Why do you need it? In any case, you will not live, so why do you need a shirt?" All of those who hid their belongings with their gentile neighbors received such answers. The situation continued to deteriorate. It was completely impossible to approach any of the residents, for it was fraught with the danger of being turned in to the Germans or to those Ukrainians who made efforts to be crueler murderers than the Germans themselves.

The winter was very difficult, so we were forced to remain in the bunker in the forest without food. We were very hungry. We lost our energy and were unable to walk out at night any more. The snow also impeded us. In this difficult situation, we decided to approach one resident whose name was Roman (Hartzendeshen) of Kariw, with whom we had always had excellent relations. When we came to him, we no longer had the form of human beings. He received us well, gave us some food, and told us to come again. We indeed did so, even though we were very afraid that the man might turn us in, which he did not do. He cleared a place fro us and agreed that we can dig a pit in the barn. We sat there during the days, and at night this gentile sent us to fetch what he felt it was possible to steal for him... In this manner, we received food once a day, as well as information as to what was transpiring in the region.

Destruction

One day when the gentile returned from church on a Christian holiday, we saw that we were very nervous. He had heard from the priest Marhold Pyoter that if anyone knows of a Jew and does not turn him in – all the villages in the area would be destroyed by the government. Among other things, he said that Hirsch Mendel Wolf was found dead and frozen in the forest and that Hillel Fisch escaped to Dolzhok where he was murdered along with his wife. Yehuda Wolf had been murdered by a German near a little river in the brush, and the residents of Muchnacha immediately started pillaging and stripping his clothing... The Ukrainians brought the Germans to Yosef Wolf, who had made a bunker for himself in the Czrena forest. After wild screams, Yosef exited the bunker along with his wife and three children, who were all very beautiful. When Yosef saw that he was surrounded, he jumped upon the German with his bare hands and tried to kill him. However, at that moment, he was shot by another murderer who stood behind Yosef's back. Then they were able to perpetrate the rest of the murderers that they desired. First they killed the children, and then their mother. When they went down to the bunker, there was enough food to sustain the family for three years. At that time, the murderers also liquidated the Hirt family. First they murdered their son Yitzchak, and then shot them.

[Page 215]

Yehuda Gissinger was hiding with Mlutach Lorczio. For some reason, Wasyl Krowky, who had been the close neighbor of the family of Yisrael Yosef Gissinger, informed the authorities. From there, they brought him to Smozhe. Along the way, they tortured him and administered endless beatings. When they brought him to the Ukrainian policemen, he already requested that they kill him, for he could no longer take the tortures. He shouted and asked why he was guilty for having been born a Jew. The family of Reb Izik Gissinger, a scholarly observer of the commandments, was hiding in the latter period with Mlutach Lungin. One day, the Ukrainian murders Andrishyn Yasin and his friends came (the secretary of the Krasna council Josef Zovkovich headed this aktion), and removed them all: Izik, his wife Chava, his daughters Feiga and Ethel, and his son Moshe-Yosef. They brought them all to the Zadvorshtasha grove and started to torture them. They first amputated the breasts of the girls. Then they tortured Moshe-Yosef, their uncle Izak and aunt Chava. During the atrocity, the tortured people cried out so much that they were heard in the nearby town of Smozhe. Later they were murdered by blows on the head, since they had no weapons. They were only able to carry out this barbaric murder by using sticks. Since this took a long time, and the victims screamed and screamed, the murderer Zovkovich stood next to them and shouted, "Shut up, Jews, I am telling you to shut up..."

The next day, the Volksdeutche [ethnic German] Ginter, who had heard the screams, came to Krasna from Smozhe. He began to ask people what happened. When they told him, he went to the Gestapo, and asked them, "Why do the authorities permit murders of citizens by the Ukrainians? If the government authorities are able to give directions and ensure that things won't become wanton, the Ukrainians are liable to perpetrate the same thing against the Volksdeutchen in the region..." The Gestapo immediately sent its men, who came to the town of Krasna, took the secretary Zovkovich with them, and hung him in the city of Drohobycz. In Krasna itself the authorities hinted that if there was to be any killing, it must be with their agreement... In the meantime, Manes Steininger, who suffered hunger along with his family just like the rest of the Jews, went out and found or purchased an animal carcass. He got sick and died after he cooked and ate it. His children Monek and Avrahamele fled to the mountains, where they apparently met their deaths. His wife and young daughter were taken to the ghetto.

[Page 216]

My father Reb Berish Schindler and Aunt Rachel Schindler were apparently taken to the Skula Ghetto. His explanations in the German language, which he knew fluently, that he had served in the Austrian Army for seven years and possessed a rank, were to no avail. They were brought to the Mount Tluste, which was on the route to Skula, where they were murdered one at a time.

*

My cousins Yitzchak and Avraham continue and relate the following:

Since the gentile with whom we were hiding was going to leave the place, we left him. We heard that there was a Volksdeutsche in Smozhe, Lorenz Ginter, who assisted people to cross the Hungarian border in return for payment. When we entered that man's house, he barely recognized us despite the fact that we knew him well. We had beards, were full of lice, and were filthy. He gave us a lot of food and promised to do something for us. He gave us another half loaf of bread for the journey. At his home we found out about other Jews that were still alive: Shmuel Freilich of blessed memory and his family, Moshe Eisenstein of Tuchulka, and others. When we left the house and began to look for the way to the mountain in the direction of the forest, it was very dark, and every bird frightened us... Even though we had eaten a fair amount with Ginter, we began to pine for the half loaf of bread which was in Avraham's hands. When I asked Avraham if there was any bread left, and he answered negatively, I did not believe him and searched his pockets (I regret that to this day)... After a short period of time, we began to steal across the border along with the Freilich family. We walked at night and sat in the forests during the day. We often made a mistake, walked for hours on end, and returned to the same place from where we had set out... When we arrived at the river and had to cross it, the strong dragged along the weak. I, of course, dragged my brother Avraham. The water was very cold, and we sometimes fell together into the water. We got up wet and oppressed, but we continued on...

[Page 217]

Tarnawa Nizna

by Aharon Shefer

Tarnawa Nizna is a village in the Turka region. It is situated along the San River. It borders the village of Tarnawa Vyzna, on the east, the village of Dzvinyach Gurny on the west, mountains on the north, and the high Polonini Mountains on the south, forming the natural border with Czechoslovakia. The population was primarily Ukrainian, with Jewish and Polish minorities. All of the residents were workers of the land. In addition to agriculture, the Jews were also occupied with trade, and the Poles served in government institutions such as the police, the post office, and teaching at school.

There were a total of four grades in the school, in which all of the children of the village studies. The veteran teacher Mrs. Torowska served as principal of the school. The language of instruction was Polish, and from the second year of study, also Ukrainian. The Jewish students also studied in the *cheder*. There, they studied *Chumash* with *Rashi*, as well as Yiddish and German writing. Thus, it turned out that an eight year old Jewish child had already learned to read and write in five languages at once... However, the period of study ended at the age of 11 or 12. From that time, the children had to assist their parents in the farm and in the work at home.

The Jews were Orthodox and pious. They worshipped at home during all the days of the week, and they worshipped as a community on the Sabbath. There was no general synagogue, but rather two *minyanim* in private homes, where one room was dedicated to communal prayer. One *minyan* took place at an edge of the village at the home of Shlomo Breier. He was a good Jew, a farmer who owned land, but his main source of pride was his large, fine Torah scroll that he purchased with his own money and was used for reading in the *minyan* that was conducted at his home. Most of the Jews of the nearby area worshipped there, as well as some of the Jews of the village of Dzvinyach. His son Yosef served as the Torah reader, and Pinchas Neuman served as the *gabbai*.

The *minyan* in the home of Binyamin Breier took place in the east side of the village. He was a wealthy Jew with a splendid countenance. He served as the Torah reader. His close neighbor was Leibele Schreiber, a great scholar and fearer of Heaven. He settled in the village as the son-in-law of Yisrael-Leib Pras, and worked all his days at studying Torah and teaching Torah to the children of the village.

[Page 218]

On the High Holidays, the two *minyanim* merged and jointly hired a prayer leader from the city or the nearby region. The Jews truly celebrated on Simchat Torah. After the serves and the processions in the synagogue, they went out in song and dance from one Jewish house to the next, bringing out the *cholent*[2] and liquor. The Jews celebrated...

*

There was also a Zionist movement in the city. All of the youth belonged to Hapoel Hamizrachi. On Sabbath and festival afternoons, they gathered together to listened to a Zionist lecture by Hershel Rand, who was active in all the Zionist movements in the region, whether left leaning or right leaning. Everyone aspired to make *aliya* to the land of Israel, but only very few succeeded in reaching their objective.

Plucking Feathers

by Aharon Shefer

The feather plucking was a cause for a cheerful evening in the village. Every Jew had many geese and ducks. At the beginning of the winter, they would slaughter the geese. They would eat the meat every day, and leave the fat until Passover. However, the feathers had to be plucked. (Every child who left the home would receive two pillows and a featherbed...) This was a boring job... so what could one do?

An evening of feather plucking was organized. They hitched up a pair of horses with a large sled, and road through the length of the village in order to collect the girls for feather plucking. Nobody was absent, for everyone knew that it was going to be a joyous evening... Boys came along with the girls...

The girls sat down in a circle. The women who were in charge of the event fried latkes to treat everyone. The boys sang and told jokes. It was a joyous evening, and the feather plucking event was the cause of more than one match.

By A. Sh.

Translator's Footnotes:

10. Matzo prepared with extra stringencies for use on the *seder* nights.
A slow-cooked stew generally served on Sabbath afternoons.

[Page 221]

Destruction and Annihilation

The Russian Chapter in Turka During the Second World War

By Chaim Pelech

First Panic

When the Jews of Turka had discussions: “Yes a war”, “No war” – They awoke on September 1, 1939, and the war was a reality... Whoever had a bit of money ran to purchase various foodstuffs. One did not think about, and one could not imagine what type of a misfortune the times were bringing upon us Jews, despite the fact that there were enough pessimists who sighed and said, “God should help”.

The general mobilization took place shortly. Many Jews were enlisted into the Polish army. That same day, at 11:00 a.m. a German airplane bombarded the sawmill in Stryj, and there were two Jewish victims. Two other Jewish workers were wounded, and the first panic in the city ensued. A terror enveloped everybody. A few days later, Polish army divisions arrived and began to demonstrate what they were: they beat Jewish passers-by with rods and sticks.

Fortunately, they did not remain for long in the city. However, the nervousness of the Jewish population grew day by day, for the German airplanes flew through Turka from Slovakia every minute. The moment that an alarm signaled that they were flying – and people hid in their cellars. The news in the city spread from mouth to mouth that the situation was bad, that the Germans were nearing us with quick steps, and that the Polish army is beginning to leave Turka. Indeed, one day later, the Polish army left Turka completely along with a portion of the Polish population of official status. Turka was left without a government. It became known to us that a certain division of the Polish army murdered two Jews in the city – a Jew from Rymanow and a youth from Nizhneye Vysotskoye, a certain Feiler who attended the Yeshiva.

At that time, the Jews in Turka lived through difficult days. People did not sleep, but rather guarded their houses with axes in their hands, for they were afraid lest the Ukrainians attack the Jewish population. When they heard that the Russians were coming into Turka, they were able to relax a bit.

The Germans suddenly entered into the city on the eve of Yom Kippur, and remained in Turka for a total of 26 hours. They did nothing to the Jewish population. When they left, the Jews were very happy, and they waited impatiently for the Russians to come all the faster.

The Russians Arrive

The Russians indeed arrived a few days later, and the Jewish population relaxed a bit. The Russian commando arrived that same evening, and the next morning, several ordinances were already posted. One order is that the businesses must be opened, and that one must not charge higher prices than were charged during the Polish time. The Russian soldiers and officers indeed fell upon the stores like hungry wolves and purchased everything that was possible. Within 14 days, they completely emptied the stores at the old prices, at the time when the same articles would have cost 40-60 percent more in Russia. Thus did the Russian liberators conduct a legalized robbery of the majority of the Turka Jews, and thus was the Jewish population in Turka greatly impoverished and left without livelihood. It was no longer possible to do business in Turka, and there were no places of work such as factories in Turka.

Need and Terror

Heavy dark clouds slowly crept up over the Jewish population. Everyone worried greatly: What would be? From where will we earn our livelihood?... What should we do?... People sold household good so that they would be able to purchase a piece of bread. The most important food products were lacking: there was no sugar, there was no flour, and there was no rice and other products. Only bread could be purchased, and it was hard to come by. One had to get up and 5:00 a.m. and wait in a queue until 8:00 in order to obtain a kilo of bread.

In the meantime, there were arrests. They arrested Jews – and nobody knew the reason. People were slandered, and they came in the night to take people away. Very many Jews were arrested during the brief time that the Reds were in Turka. Turka had never seen so many Jewish criminals. Something arose again that Turka had never known about. People were afraid... everyone was afraid. People talked in the city that one must not say anything. People whispered to their acquaintances, and one began to run to the other... And this was indeed not fruitless: It was obvious that there was much investigating going on by the N.K.V. D. of each individual person, and each night, many people were dragged off for interrogation. Every detail was written in a file: how rich he is, how is he employed, to what party does he belong, and who leads the parties in the city – everything was asked and written. One can imagine what type of fear this instilled in the Jewish population. Public trials began to take place in the city, and if one watched them, it would darken the eyes.

A small number of Jews were working, but their salaries were very small, and impossible to live off of. This was mainly the handworkers, who gave up their own work rooms and went to work in the army workshops. As has already been noted, the monthly salary was sufficient for a week of living. You can certainly already imagine how the workers and handworkers lived during the time of the Red rule.

In the meantime, people lived, moaned and sighed, for one fine night, some Jews were rounded up and deported to Siberia. For what? -- Because they were "wealthy" during the Polish era. This was despite the fact that there were no wealthy Jews in Turka. Turka was one of the poorest towns in Poland. Not even one "wealthy" Jew in Turka was able to establish even the smallest factory. Nevertheless, this did not stop them from taking innocent people and deporting them to Siberia. And if this was not enough – they were talking in the city that there would be a deportation of may more Jews. Jews packed small bags and fled from Turka to wander around in larger cities. The party leaders also fled from Turka, for they would have been among the first who were searched and arrested. It was already known that in other cities, they had already arrested all of the party leaders, especially the Zionists.

All of this broke the Jewish population, and people wandered about like shadows. Everyone hoped that they would live through the night peacefully, for there was fear in Turka during the nights: the Russians arrested people at night, they interrogated at night, and they perpetrated frightful tribulations during the investigations – all at night. However, everyone thanked G-d that they were not under the hand of the Germans.

However, as the Jewish population of Turka went around "without a head", and asked "what would be later" – they could still not imagine and foresee what type of misfortune was awaiting the Jews of Turka and the Jewish population in general from the hands of the German beasts.

The war between Germany and Russia broke out in June 1941 – and the Jewish misfortune began.

[Page 225]

Stories of the Great Misfortune

by Y. M. Zeifert of Los Angeles

Y. M. Zeifert

For Jews in general, the year 1939 was already unbearable. Pestering and restricting the Jews at every step was the daily program of the officials of the regime, from the highest to the lowest. Anti-Semitism was already so widespread that it could be felt and sensed even by those not so involved in politics. For ever Jewish person, this was the prime time to leave accursed Poland in general, and Galicia with its boorish Ukrainians in particular. I myself had already made all preparations to travel to the Land of Israel. However, to my regret, a great personal tragedy overtook me - the sudden death of my wife.

The war between Poland and Germany broke out. The German airplanes flew over the town every day and sowed disorder and death. The panic was great. There were new alarms every hour. I myself was not afraid. I often thought that a bomb would provide relief from my suffering, that death does not come when one wishes for it, and that I had remained alive to endure greater tribulations and pain.

The Retreat

It was not long before the Polish Army retreated and fled; a portion of it went through our town on its way to Hungary. Of course, "our" Ukrainians did not feel any regrets over this, and they prepare covertly. Indeed, as the Poles were leaving, the Ukrainians immediately hung their national flag on the town hall. In the meantime, however, about 15 men from the Polish K.A.P. returned, ripped down the flag, and beat everyone that they came across with murderous blows. Some people died, among three foreign Jews. The last Poles left the following day, and a committee was immediately set up to ensure order, to which the hot-headed Ukrainian youth paid little heed. Jews lived through days of great fear.

[Page 226]

The first German patrol entered the town on the Eve of Yom Kippur, and a division of the Germany Army arrived a few hours later. For Jews, it was a double Yom Kippur... the weeping was doubled... People were afraid to go to Kol Nidre. The worshippers that came (I myself came, for I lived close to the synagogue) recited their prayers quickly and in fear.

The next day, Yom Kippur, the synagogue was half empty. Young people came, whereas middle aged and older people stayed back and worshipped in private *minyanim*. At the taking out[1] after *Shacharit*, people allowed themselves to go out to the street to take a look at the German soldiers who were standing not far from Ringplatz.

In the meantime, people were already telling "stories" about German soldiers. One soldier had felt it necessary to say that one year from now, there would not be one Jew here... Another went to the barber shop and found his colleague getting a haircut there. Hearing that the barber was a Jew, he refused his services, saying that he does not want a Jewish barber to touch his neck... The German who did get a haircut said that not all Germans share the same opinion... And there were many such stories.

[Page 227]

In the meantime, persistent rumors began to spread that the Germans were going to leave the place, and the Russians were going to come in their place. It was not long before one saw that the Germans were already gathering together along the way. Everyone already recited the *Neila* service in a happier frame of mind - at that time, they would already be willing to be seen outside.

Christians and Ukrainians once again undertook to keep the order. Jewish Communists again raised their heads and prepared to greet the Red Army. Since I was a graphic artist, they would come to me with red canvasses, upon which I would hastily write slogans in various languages with gold letters. "Long Live the Red Army," "Long Live the Soviet Union, the liberator, the redeemer," etc. These slogans were then posted on specially erected towers on the main streets. I cannot talk about any payment for my work - I was just a worker, and I had to actively participate in the great joy. In truth, I was indeed happy, as were all the Jews in town.

The Entry of the Red Army

The great joy with which the first vehicle with soldiers of the Red Army was greeted is indescribable! Their outward appearance was pathetic. It seems that they were trained agitators. As soon as they jumped off the vehicles, they gathered small groups around them and explained what was happening and what will be: we will simply be in a Garden of Eden. Within a few days, rallies were already taking place, and propaganda films of the new powers were shown. The town was boiling like a kettle. Many former Communists had now become militiamen with weapons that they had been apportioned. Others obtained higher leadership roles.

The shopkeepers began to take in a great deal of money. The purchasers were primarily Russian soldiers. For them, there was no such thing as bad merchandise... They also did not quibble over the price... It was not long until the shelves of the shops were empty... Our people, seeing what was going on and hearing that zlotys would be forbidden as currency, wished to exchange their money, but were too late...

[Page 228]

We began to line up in lines... Bread was lacking. A little later, the situation improved. Institutions of the civilian government such as cooperatives for basic provisions and other things were organized. People also began to obtain government positions. It was a pleasure to enter the government bank. 90% of the employees were Jewish girls, primarily from poor homes, who had previously taken such supplementary courses. The home militia was dismissed, and Russians took their place. Other people also obtained jobs according to their calling and capabilities. Those who were considered wealthy were deported to Russia and had their belongings confiscated. At that time, this seemed terrible - but later we were jealous of them. Some businesses remained, but they were mainly small, impoverished food shops. They could barely maintain themselves due to the multiple fees imposed upon them. Many fees were also imposed upon the handworkers, and they were driven to organize themselves into cooperatives[2]. Some Jews looked for business by travelling to other places and bringing back things to sell. It was not so bad for them at the beginning, but one by one, they fell into the hands of criminals.

Later, life normalized even more, and livelihood was easily attained. One could purchase everything in the cooperatives. The Soviets concerned themselves with the youth and the children. Many kindergartens were opened, where children would remain from 8:00 a.m. until 4:00 p.m. Therefore, the adults could work calmly without being disturbed by children. Adults also received "political education," but free living, every person where he wishes, was not possible. This evoked a certain dissatisfaction with the regime. Thus did things go on for more than a year and a half.

[Page 229]

The German Invasion

Suddenly, as if falling from heaven, the invasion of the German military took place in June 1941. On the first day, the Russians still boasted that they were not afraid and that they had enough power to take a stand against Germany. By the second day, they had already fled in a disorderly and hasty manner, leaving behind heavy belongings and merchandise in the civilian and military warehouses. Entire wagons with canvass, uniforms, foodstuffs and even ammunition were left behind. Many people, including several Jews, were arrested. The youth, most of whom were in military service, were quickly drafted into the army. Many of them fled along with the Russians, and the town was left empty and hollow. However, for the remaining Jews, the true hell was now beginning.

The Ukrainians Rampaged

This time, the Ukrainians did not sit back and rejoice. Seeing the haste in which the Russians had left the town, they immediately broke into the armaments warehouses and took as many weapons as they wished. They immediately formed a militia and began to rampage.

This took place on a Sabbath morning. Shots began to be fired, and Jews no longer went out to the street, but rather closed themselves into the houses. Later, it became clear that these were shots of rejoicing, and things became a bit lighter... However, were there to be an escape, and a few Jewish youth indeed escaped, we were curious to see what would happen. They later returned, and explained, with fear on their faces, that it smells like a pogrom against the Jews. While searching the cellars for Russian soldiers, the Ukrainians found a few dead bodies, and immediately spread a rumor that the militia cellars are full of dead Ukrainians who were cruelly murdered by the Jews. The heat grew from moment to moment. Jews fled to Christian acquaintances and requested that they intervene and calm down the hotheaded Ukrainians. Some intervened, but it did not help at all. A large pogrom was about to break out, until some sort of miracle intervened: Someone let out a few shots from atop a hill, and immediately a rumor spread that the Russians were returning... They immediately fled back to the surrounding villages; The pogromchiks who were already along the roads in the city turned back.

[Page 230]

The militia in the town ascended the hill with great heroism and found out that some simple shepherd who had weapons let out a few shots of great joy...

In the meantime, the dead bodies were dragged out of the cellars. There were four dead people in total: one Ukrainian, one Pole, one Jew, and one Soviet. The dead rescued the town from a terrible pogrom that hovered over everyone's head. The warehouses that the uncircumcised ones pillaged diverted the attention from the Jews. They spent an entire day pillaging and in order to prevent the Jews from appearing on the street, they let out a shot.

At night, there were a few attacks on the Jews, but everyone was overtaken with fear and shame. There were no victims.

*

Until the Germans actually arrived in the town, we encountered various patrols. Sometimes it was a Hungarian (with whom the Ukrainians were scarcely happy) patrol, and sometimes it was a German one. Their task was to seal the remaining warehouses.

In the meantime, some of the youth who were "lost" returned from the Russian military, into which they had been recruited. They did this with dedication, for it was very difficult to return home. Some came straight from the Russian border. Many who were found by the Ukrainians along the way were shot. When they arrived in town, the youth felt that they had been rescued... but later they were all bitterly disappointed.

Germans

The Germans slowly settled in Turka. The border guards in Turka paid more attention to the warehouses, and the Ukrainians to the Jews. First, they began to snatch people for work, such as sweeping streets, cleaning toilets, and other lowly and vexing jobs. They also did not withhold beatings. For the most part, they beat youth who returned from the German side, to where they had fled from the Soviets in their time. The harshest beater was a certain Sobol, a nephew of the priest of Turka who had become the district commander of the Ukrainian militia. They also arrested youth without knowing the reason or pretext.

[Page 231]

Further terrible news came from other places and familiar villages. Entire families were brutally murdered by the Ukrainians, and in some villages not one Jew was left. In Turka at that time, there was a commandant of the border guard named Fidler who saved Jews on certain occasions. As in other cities, the Ukrainians in Turka conducted a "funeral" to "bury" Stalin. The Jews were given pictures, images and books of Stalin to carry. They bound a red band on bearded Jews and prodded them to the cemetery, where they were to bury Stalin together with the rest of the people of the funeral. A great weeping broke out. Wives fainted and men recited the confession, for a similar event took place in Stary Sambor. It was only the intervention of Fidler that saved the Jews from a certain death.

At that time, my brother and his wife, who were saved from a pogrom in Boryslaw in which 500 Jews were murdered, came to me in Turka.

The Establishment of the Judenrat

The Judenrat was established a few weeks after the arrival of the Germans, Nobody elected them, heaven forbid; but rather, as if it was a communal institution, they first enlisted the communal representative Shua-Nachman Meiner. He brought in his nephew, also named Shua Nachman (Erdman), as well as Melech Wizner. These were the troika, who had to serve as the spokesmen and representatives for the few Jews of Turka. The Jews came in contact with that troika of the Judenrat for all matters, as well as with the secretary Berish Lorberbaum. They received yellow armbands with the inscription "Judenrat." Leibush Mates was co-opted as the cashier and bookkeeper.

[Page 232]

Their first task was to take whatever money was left from the people. Then they had to provide workers for the Germans and Ukrainians. Since the work was of a nature that not everybody liked, they would drag the entire town into the Judenrat, and instead of five, the number grew to 50: secretariat, court, payment office, and executive. Later the Jewish militia and officers were appointed. The higher roles were played by the first five: they were the money collectors, the dispensers, and the suppliers. In fact, they concerned themselves first and foremost with obtaining means. In truth, their task became more difficult and, they did not seize anything - but later, they became very profitable.

With the arrival of the German gendarmes to Turka, the tribulations and expenses of the Jews increased. The Judenrat was the de facto providers for all the Germans and their institutions. They would come to the Judenrat for the smallest minutia, and the Judenrat had to provide money for everything. The gendarmes themselves enlisted 20 workers-bricklayers, carpenters, tinsmiths, painters and unskilled labor. The Judenrat was supposed to pay them, but they did not do so. If anyone refused to work without pay, he would be reported and be whipped 25 times on his naked body. People would say that if the Gestapo comes to visit, they would suck money and blood from everyone. During the most severe times of hunger, they would allot two or three kilograms of bread per person per month. Sugar was not allotted for the most part, but was sold for a high price, with the excuse that the Judenrat was in need of money. Nevertheless, the end of all the Judenrat members with their belongings was no different than that of the other Jews.

[Page 233]

*

The first gendarmes came riding into Turka on Rosh Hashanah. Already the next day, they searched everyone and went through the attics and the cellars. They were indeed successful in many cases. They took various types of merchandise, clothing and provisions - for them, something kosher did not exist; everything was *treif.*

Various decrees were issued. Everything was forbidden for Jews: meat, butter, and wheat. Then, there was the decree to wear armbands made out of white canvas with blue Stars of David. The Ukrainian militia greatly excelled in upholding the decree. They would often arrest a Jew while standing at his own door, who was not wearing an armband.

The work office (*Arbeitsamt*) that was quickly formed had an outside office at the Judenrat. It concerned itself with stable work without wages for everyone. Bread became scarcer, for the Germans forbade the Christians from bringing any supplies into the city. If anyone brought anything, it was immediately confiscated. In the streets, and later also in the homes, they would search the smallest packet and take even two or three kilos of potatoes or oats, the primary sources of food in the town.

The hunger continually increased. People began to swell up and die. Well-to-do people would leave their houses, having no choice, and beg for something to eat. A bit of bran was the best type of food that a person could beg for. The people's kitchen that the Judenrat had founded provided about 200 people daily with a bit of soup - in truth, a bit of dirty water - thereby satisfying the suffering of the hungry people for a few days.

At the same time, announcements were posted in the Judenrat that the building enterprise was seeking workers who would be paid and also would receive a half a loaf of bread daily. People who felt they had the energy, or even barley felt that they had the energy, went to work at rebuilding damaged bunkers and other buildings. This came in the winter time, and most people did not have any warm clothing, for they were already long given away for a bit of oatmeal. They went out to work in light summer clothing. The work was very difficult, lasting for twelve hours a day. They received a half a loaf of bread for the first few days, but when the saw that more people signed up, they began to divide up the half loaf...

[Page 234]

People worked very hard, dragging iron wire, large rafters and sacks of cement. They exerted themselves with their last bit of strength, and they would often become weaker and weaker at the work and fall under the heavy loads. The supervisors did not believe that they had no energy and they shouted that they did not want to work... Every day, some people went home beaten. They were not able to leave the work, for the Ukrainian militia already knew how to force them to return to work. They were also threatened by the Gestapo.

There was already enough fear in town. Different angels of destruction came every day -- at times the S. S., at times the E. S., and a times regular civilian Germans who went from house to house taking everything that they wanted.

Above everything, Jews lived with the hope that the salvation would come. People talked about various types of help for our town, including that which may be offered by the Hungarians, but nothing came of it.

The Great Tumult, or the First Aktion

On January 6, 1942, the 7th of Tevet, that which we had only heard about from other cities took place here. At noontime, four Gestapo men arrived, and by 3:00 p.m., a great panic and escape took place from the Ukrainian militias, who fell upon their victims like wild beasts. At the outset, this took place from all corners of the city together. They would capture people from the streets and houses and prod them to the militia, where they were beaten and murdered.

There was no family that did not suffer from the misfortune. The capturing continued the next day.

[Page 235]

Reb Avraham, the *gabbai* of the Wanowiczer (Vanovichi) Rabbi

A few youths saved themselves at night by jumping from the first storey onto the ice of the stream that flowed near the militia building. More would have been saved, but the Judenrat misled them. Meilech Weisner arrived just at that time and assured everyone that the young people were to be left alone, and they had no reason to fear...

[Page 236]

Thus did they remain due to the promise - and died just like the others. From those who saved themselves, we found out about the murderous beatings and the difficult torments endured by the Orthodox Jews, especially the rabbi of Wanowicz. They said that during the time that the murderers were beating him fiercely, he did not contort himself, but rather continued with his recitations. They tormented him by stating that if he was a man of G-d, G-d should help him...

The next day, all of the transport wagons that were in Turka bitterly came. They took away all the unfortunate victims from the militia building to a place far behind the city, beyond the brickyard, where large graves had already been prepared a few days earlier. After they made the victims remove their clothes, they shot them with machine gun. The victims fell one atop the other, some still alive, and then they covered them over. Those whom they were not ready to handle that day were driven back to their place of arrest with vehicles, and then shot first thing Friday. I received a greeting from my mother, indicating that she was still alive on Friday. This greeting was given to us by my mother's brother's daughter-in-law Sara-Nistl, who succeeded in escaping, already undressed, not far from the grave.

A command was issued that nobody dare to approach the mass grave where the victims lay. We hoped that with this, the misfortune would end, and things would get better in the city... However, to our disappointment, this was only the beginning.

Every time the district commander [*kreizhauftman*] came to Turka, he brought with him a new decree. Even before the tumult, he honored us with a visit. The Jews, hearing that the district commander was present, already made sure not to appear on the street and awaited a new tribulation. If it did not come, it was fortunate; but his visits were so frequent - and here he comes again! Now the Jews must register again, and the decree would come a few days later - without difference between the sexes, everyone must cut their hair, beard and *peyos* very short. When people met on the streets, they could not recognize each other...

[Page 237]

Two or three months later, there was a new decree: People age 17 and over who did not have a stable, legitimate work situation were to present themselves at a committee which would inspect their health situation for work. People came, and fifty of them were sent immediately to Sinawick where they worked at building a railway bridge. Letters arrived from there in which they described the terrible situation in which they found themselves. The work was very difficult, and was supervised by murderous supervisors. The main thing was they did not receive food. Their situation was desperate, and they requested help from the Judenrat. A committee was formed to collect money and to send them bread from time to time. It later became known that only a portion of the bread was given over. Some people succeeded to escape from there with great self-sacrifice and return to Turka. Others swelled up from hunger and died there. Others were killed by the murderous overseers. An escapee from there related that an overseer tossed the carpenter Shlomo Binder off a bridge over the water. Seeing that he was struggling to the edge, the overseer went down and beat him to death.

The Sunday Aktion

On a fine summer Sunday about six months after the first tumult, a vehicle with Gestapo men arrived unexpectedly and began to snatch people from the streets and the houses - young, old and children - a total of 150 people. The only information was terrifying. Yosef Birenberg, a hairstylist, was exiting the militia office where he had been serving a few murderous Ukrainian policemen. On the doorstep, he was severely beaten on the head, and tossed dead onto a cargo truck where other victims were already lying. Almost all the victims of that *aktion* were captured in the same manner. Berish Lorberbaum the Judenrat secretary and Anshel Goldberg of the militia were also snatched in that action. For the first time, young children were also taken.

[Page 238]

I cannot describe how much pain the ban on worshipping in the *Beis Midashes* caused even for the non-religious people, and even for those who never prayed. Perhaps this was because so many Jewish children had been orphaned, and there was no place for them to recite *Kaddish*? Later, an order was issued to remove the furniture from the *Beis Midrashes*. Regarding this people would say that they had heard that in a certain city, they gathered the few Jews into the *Beis Midrashes* and burnt them down.

The district commander came again and again, each time with new decrees. Six months had elapsed between the first *aktion* and the second; but now, decree after decree was issued. People began to escape and lie around in the cellars, attics and empty places. People built shelters which were mostly covered, and thereby, some Jews were saved in the interim.

Then, placards were posted decreeing that all the Jews who live in the villages must immediately leave and transfer to the city. Then there was an influx of villagers. Wives, children and older people - the younger people who were busy with legitimate, steady work were left alone in the meantime. The influx lasted for several days. Many people besieged the work office of the Judenrat in order to obtain work legitimacy papers. However, these quickly became worthless.

The Large *Aktion*

On August 4, 1942, the snatching began early in the morning. The adults were already weak. Hearing that children were also being captured during this misfortune, we all went up, barely dressed, to the attic in a great hurry. I had prepared some sort of shelter there, and I locked us in. In a few minutes, we heard the voices of the Jewish militia, who were calling out in all the houses - all the Jews must present themselves at the train in an hour. Every person is allowed to take 25 kilograms. This was a thorough liquidation. In a few minutes, I heard the easily recognizable voice of the gendarme Shlamilch, the representative of the post command, and recognized his merciless beatings. He was shouting: All Jews must go the train within half an hour; whoever does not go will be shot immediately. There was a commotion on our lane. I looked through a crack and saw that people were going, small and large, young and old... entire families.

[Page 239]

I understand that a few neighbors remained. I heard further shouts from the Jewish militiamen as well as the Gestapo. I heard repeated shots, and the movement became greater... About three quarters of an hour passed, and then everything became quieter and quieter... I was hot in the attic, and we were sweating from the heat and fear. Hearing that everything was calm, my sister-in-law began to become afraid. She claimed that she wanted to go to the train, and does not want to be shot here. I, however, decided to die here in the attic from hunger rather than in some camp.

At about 2:00, when we were still in the attic, Judenrat members and other hired people began to transport the Jewish belongings, including furniture, bedding and clothing, and pile them up in the *Beis Midrashes* and the synagogue. At 3:00, we heard the train depart. Shortly thereafter, we heard them drive to our street, and saw them load up the meager belongings from the neighboring houses. They went from one house to another, and then stood near ours. As they slammed our door, the Jews who were helping load up already realized that we were there. I opened up at a moment when the gentile wagon drivers were not present, so they would not find out. The Jews finished with my house as quickly as possible - but nothing more happened. My brother Yehuda and I opened the door and saw, as if it were, the helpers loading up the furniture. When the opportunity presented itself, we went out from our dwelling, got dressed, and took something for the children to wear. As we were opening up the house, two *shkotzim* [gentiles] ran by and stole from us two outfits, a pair of boots, and a pair of shoes.

[Page 240]

We spent an entire day and night sitting in the hiding place. The next day, we found out that many people had been shot. Those that had legitimate papers from the quarry gendarmes were freed from the train. They told of the terrible scenes that they witnessed at the train.

About a hundred elderly people and children were shot on the way to the train. At the station, everyone had their luggage removed, and then they were beaten with murderous blows. Gestapo men and soldiers traveled in cars. The entire gendarme and the Ukrainian militia also took part in the *aktion*.

Small transports of people were also sent the next day, Wednesday, as well as on Thursday. The gendarme Jaski, who himself shot 50 people, excelled as a good murderer. As he was returning from the command office, he told Avraham Kleist, who worked regularly with the horses of the gendarmerie and knew him well, "Go home, I shot your wife and child, as well as the others who hiding with them." When he returned home, he indeed discovered that the murderer was not joking... The gendarme Shlamilch also repaid his hairstylist Wilojsz as well as the veteran hairstylist and manicurist Freida Weicher for their good service; he himself brought them to the second transport.

Two thousand people were taken away during the second *aktion*.

A few weeks later, they distributed the articles and furniture that had been collected in the *Beis Midrashes*. First, they selected the best items and gave them over to the *Reichsdeutchen*. Then, the *Volksdeutchen*[3] took their share, and finally, auctions took place. Thousands of gentiles from the city and town came and took everything that was left gratis.

[Page 241]

The Contingent

Two weeks after the large *aktion*, a new registration was ordered. Soon afterward, a decree was issued that 100 people must present themselves. This time, it was carried out solely by the Jewish militiamen. One can imagine what type of situation it was when a Jew had to turn over another Jew to the enemy for a certain death. Jewish militiamen did not refuse to participate in that work. They gathered the people and sent them to Sambor.

The contingent was delivered and the systematic extermination of the Jews did not stop. A few days later, on a Friday at 12:00 midnight, there was another knock on the door. I heard that they were talking in Yiddish. I heard a woman's voice begging for mercy, that they leave her alone. The weeping stopped and I heard that they were knocking on other neighbors... In the morning, I found out that there had been a "small" *aktion* at night - they only captured sixty something people. This time, it was perpetrated by the Polish criminal police who worked according to a list given by the Judenrat. They were assisted only by the Jewish militia. After this it was told that one Polish criminal policeman who apparently unwillingly fulfilled the function of rounding up innocent people to be shot, asked them, "Why do you Jews not kill, and why do you let yourselves be shot as sheep, without resistance?"

New decrees: We had to set up a separate quarter for Jews. Among other things, it was further stated that they were requesting from the Judenrat several hundred people without legitimate work papers to be sent to Sambor. This was primarily a decree for women and children... One decree led to the other: they were discussing the place becoming *Judenrein*.

The Sabbath Aktion

At 5:30 in the morning, my brother went out to work in the quarry, which had lately become a hell for the Jews. There was an engineer there who was a sadist, who mercilessly beat Jews with a whip at work. I was also selected to go to work, and I set out. Miriam Rand came up my steps and told me that I should not go, for just now, two Ukrainian militiamen took Bertshe Malka Beiles (Hauftman) from his house with his wife, whose house shared a wall with her. She and her children escaped from the house, leaving everything unprotected.

[Page 242]

I immediately knocked on the door. My sister-in-law and her children quickly got dressed, and went to the hiding price together with this woman. I remained in the house alone. I soon heard knocking on the doors of the neighboring houses. I looked out and saw the Ukrainian militiamen driving out people. At 2:00, the murderers were at my door. They knocked it down with axes. I heard them going up the steps, where they found the second door closed inward. Now, they knew for sure that there were still people there. I was certain that they were going to pry it open, so I shouted to them that I would undo it. When I went out, a bullet immediately flew by my ear. Then two militiamen immediately attacked. One of them hit me, making my ears ring. "Give over what you have," said the second militiaman. I felt that I could buy him off, so I gave him several hundred zloty. He took it, and then immediately began to search and overturn the house. Then a *shegetz* [gentile] whom they sent over came in. Together they took whatever they wanted. Then they asked me about my family. I answered that I was alone, for the others were at work. They began to search, and went up to the attic where the shelter was located, but did not discover it.

Four militiamen led me away. I tried to beg them and show them my work papers. They took it and put it in their pocketbook... Three of the militiamen went away from me, and I asked the last one to leave me alone. I promised him some leather. He agreed, but he wanted the leather immediately. I then realized that it had been tossed away[4], as was the money that I had given them.

[Page 243]

He led me to the militia post. The commandant entered. He recognized me, for I had worked for him on several occasions, and he was always happy. “Leave this man alone!” he told the militiaman. To me he said, “Escape home!” I ran out, and when I had already gone a distance, the same militiaman shouted to me again that I must stand still. He captured me again and took me to the station, where the transport was. I met the post commander of the gendarme by wagon. I asked him again, and he recognized me. Immediately, an order was given to the militiaman to free me. I went home.

I went off knowing that I had remained alive. I heard the departure of the train.

We had been saved for the meantime. We prepared to leave the city and find a hiding place with a farmer in a nearby village.

Translator's Footnotes:

76. I suspect that this refers to the taking out of the Torah, which does take place right after *Shacharit*.
77. Artels. See http://en.wikipedia.org/wiki/Artel
78. The *Reichsdeutchen* are the Germans from Germany and the *Volksdeutchen* are the local Germans.
79. This likely means that giving it over had proven useless.

[Page 244]

A Girl in the Storm

by Ester Roter (Shein) of Jerusalem[1]

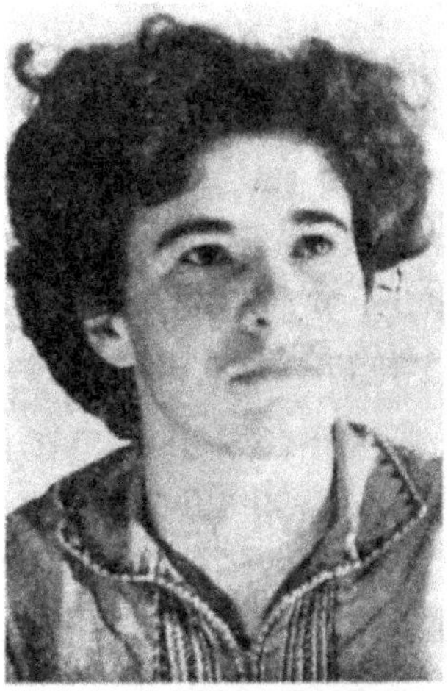

Ester Roter

Only now, at the beginning of 1947, will I try to write down the events that happened to me before I arrived in the Land. These days were difficult, and therefore they are etched so deeply in my memory. It seems to me that these things occurred only yesterday or the day before, despite the fact that about five years have passed since then. My happy days of childhood before the outbreak of the war, when I was with my parents and dear family, today seem to be as a pleasant, sweet dream that passed and is no longer. Perhaps it was never a reality... All those days seem to me as from behind a thick, unreal veil...

Prior to the Outbreak of the War

The vacation days were coming to their end, and with that, the anticipation of beginning of school. I had completed grade one in a fine fashion. In that grade, we only learned Yiddish, and we were to start learning Russian in grade two. There were already new books in Yiddish and Russian at home. They were beautiful and merry with their colored pictures. At time, I would approach them, and peer at them, as if to say: In another few days, we will start... A certain fear came over me as I was waiting for that happy, longed-for day when I would finally be able to put these books into my schoolbag and go to school with them. I cannot explain this feeling that I already felt already then, of fear that I would not succeed in this, and that fate was bringing difficult, terrible days for me.

And the War Broke Out

The war broke out on June 22, 1941. The city was bombarded at dawn. Echoes of the bombardment woke my parents. They jumped up and went outside. An astonishing site was revealed before their eyes: The Red Army was seen leaving the city in haste. It seemed that this was already the end of the retreating Red Army, and that it was already too late for my parents and others like them to leave the city along with the army. Had they known the full situation before, they might have accompanied the retreating army.

[Page 245]

I continued to sleep, and the bombardment did not awaken me. I got up, as usual, with the warm June sun rays. It was only after I got up that I found out about the bombardment of the city and the hasty retreat of the Red Army. I got dressed quickly. I tied my wild curls back and ran outside. At that time, we lived in Grandfather's home in the center of town next to the marketplace. The area was primarily Jewish. Outside, I saw many Jews gathering in small groups and discussing what was happening. My parents, like most of the Jews of the town, did not leave. They had to concern themselves with my grandfather and grandmother. Escaping with the remnants of the Russian Army seemed too dangerous. And to remain?... It seemed that it was difficult to conceive of what was about to happen.

The Germans Arrive in Town

I recall well the day that the Germans entered town. It was literally in center of town, and it was possible to see very well what was going on in the entire city from Grandfather's house. Their entry was with great splendor and fanfare. The Ukrainians greeted them with joy and flowers. The Poles appeared less merry. The Jews hid in their houses, waiting for what was to come. The streets of the town were decorated with German flags and yellow Ukrainian flags.

The Jews were not left for long in false hope about the future. The decrees were not long in coming. When the evil began, it broke out without break, and without any possibility of catching one's breath and getting a reprieve. As we were still groaning from one decree, the next one came -- harsher and crueler than the first one. First, they ordered the Jews to bring their furs in order to contribute to the wartime efforts of the Reich. After this came the ban on Jewish children from attending school. All of the children, starting from age 12, were forced to wear the Blue Star of David as a sign of their Jewishness. The Jews were forbidden from selling anything to the gentiles, and the gentiles were forbidden from providing food provisions to the Jews. Thus did the tension of the Jews increase even before the *aktions.*

At first, the Jews attempted to circumvent the decrees to the best of their ability. People continued to conduct barter transactions with the gentiles in order to obtain a bit of food, and we children continued to study. A small group of children was organized, to be taught in secret. We studied Polish and Ukrainian. The conditions of study were not simple. We had to change the place of our studies each week. During the hours of study, someone had to stand outside constantly and guard us. I was among the few children who continued to study in this organized manner, but this did not last long. The danger increased continually. Our studies ceased completely when the large *aktion* came and our teacher was caught in it.

[Page 246]

The Era of Atrocities and Fear

The summer ended. These were not easy days. Slowly, our human image and the source of faith in humanity were removed from us. Hunger tormented us. Many people went bankrupt. Here and there, one could see people swollen with hunger, but for most of us this was still a period in which it was possible to live somehow - and was a Jew not schooled in suffering and tragedy? During this period, they did not yet nullify our lives with force and suddenness, but rather in a gradual fashion... Nevertheless, this allocation did not satisfy the Nazi beast, and the period of mass murder began with the *aktions.*

The First *Aktion*

The first *aktion* took place at the beginning of winter. This was on a Wednesday afternoon. I was sitting with a neighbor when another neighbor entered and reported that she had seen Ukrainians dragging away a Jewish woman. We did not want to believe this, but we went out nevertheless to see what had happened. When we realized that this was something suspicious, and we all fled to my grandmother's residence. I was sent to call another neighbor who lived near our house. I went, but I did not reach her home. I stood for a few moments pondering what was transpiring, and I did not grasp what my eyes were seeing. Ukrainian policemen could be seen around, dragging men, women, youths and babies behind them. I stood for a moment and suddenly understood that something terrible was unfolding before my eyes. A deep fear overtook me, and, with a sudden instinctive decision, I turned back and ran to Mother. When I reached the door, I already saw her going out to look for me. Everyone was already worried about me. We all sat down in my grandmother's dwelling on the second storey of the building and waited. We sat that way all night, avoiding all light. We did not shut our eyes. My father and grandfather were not at home, and we were worried that we were already separated. Thus did we sit until 4:00 a.m. Then, we decided to go down to a small, back room on the first floor, which seemed to be safer at that time. About a half an hour after we went down to that room, we heard footsteps approaching the dwelling which we had left. We heard strong knocking on the door, and then a wild voice. Our hearts melted. We did not believe that we were indeed saved.

At 5:00 a.m., we heard light knocking on door of the room in which we were sitting. This was my grandfather. He joined us, and from his words, we found out what had happened to him. That whole time, he was in a neighboring house, when he suddenly heard footsteps and knocking on the door. All the men in the room went down to the cellar. From there they heard how all the women, who had remained in the house, were taken. The men were unable to help, so they continued to lie down in the cellar, frozen. Toward morning, my grandfather went out to go home. Along the way, he saw a flickering light that was lit for a moment and then went out in the small room in which we were. This light led him to us. He ended his story with sadness, “The truth is, I thought that I had nobody left, and therefore I decided to endanger myself and go out.” He was very perplexed, and from that time, he became very hard of hearing.

[Page 247]

This aktion ended at 10:00 a.m. on Thursday. Then my father also appeared. We found out that, at the beginning of the aktion, he escaped to a certain house and hid there.

When we returned to my grandmother's dwelling, we found that it had been broken into. The rooms were desolate, and the cold was terrible. We were hungry, thirsty and in despair. The news on what had happened arrived later, when people already dared to leave their houses. We found out that about 500 Jews were taken in the aktion. Children were not taken in that aktion, and mothers who held their children next to them were also saved. Pieces of news of the atrocity arrived in quick succession. The 500 people were murdered by the Germans close to the city, in a place called Cygalnia (the brickyard). The Jews were shot into an open common grave.

We were distressed. All possibilities had been closed off. We understood what awaited us. They had already succeeded in "domesticating" us. We had already entered into a state of dulled senses and the lack of all options of a "sit and do nothing" state.

The aktion passed, and life, as is customary, returned slowly to its "normal path." The story of our salvation seemed to be ludicrous and illogical, for people hiding in more secure places had been exposed and perished in that aktion. According to the Germans, the pretext for that aktion was the capturing of several Jews at the border with furs. Of course, it later became clear that the reason for stating pretext of this aktion was the premeditated, pernicious politics, the purpose of which was to mislead, subdue, and apparently convince the Jews that this aktion was a singular occurrence due to a one-time deed; and that there was no need to fear and suspect anything so long as they heed the commands and fulfill them with precision. Indeed, this was just a portion of the opium that was fed to the Jews in order to mislead them in a grand fashion... And this was only the beginning of 1942.

The Second *Aktion*

The second *aktion* was not long in coming. It took place on a Sunday at the beginning of the summer. It began very suddenly. My mother and I were in the city on our way to my friend, when we suddenly saw a Ukrainian policeman running. My mother fled, and I followed her. Our paths separated. Jewish men quickly took me into their home. My father and several other Jews fled to the Jewish cemetery where they hid until the end of the *aktion*. After a short time, my mother succeeded in finding me, and we remained in a hidden room at the home of a Jewish family. We returned home at night.

[Page 248]

This *aktion*, which only lasted for a relatively brief time, was very cruel. Anyone who was in the path of the murderers, including elderly people and youths, children and mothers, were taken. This time, they did not pass over the communal officials. In this *aktion* as well, the Jews were taken to a place outside the city and murdered between Rozluch and Volosyanka.

*

The *aktion* passed, and those that remained returned to their torments. The hunger grew in the city. Many people went bankrupt. Potato peels became a desired commodity. Most of the Jews had already traded their property for a morsel of bread or a few potatoes. The nice furniture was removed and replaced with old, broken furniture. Clothing was reduced to a minimum. Incidents of Germans torturing the Jews became daily occurrences.

The situation became progressively worse in our home as well. I often felt pangs of hunger, despite the fact that the four adults withheld food from their mouths in order to provide for me, their only daughter, to the extent possible. At the time I did not realize, and I only found out later, that they went to lie down at 6:00 in order to skimp on supper, which they would then give to me.

My mother and grandmother sold everything in order to purchase food. At that time, my parents decided to move to the dwelling in which we lived before the arrival of the Russians. This was in a house on the other side of the bridge, close to the Jewish cemetery. During that era, the Jews began to better understand what was awaiting them. Hiding places were prepared in every house, so that they would not be as completely helpless as they were during the first and second *aktions*. Our plan was to escape to a hiding place at my grandfather's. In the meantime, the residents of the house in which we now lived decided to prepare their own hiding place, and we joined in as well. They decided to break the floor on the first floor to create an entrance to the cellar, and to camouflage the entrance. However, the Germans did not wait until the end of the preparations... The third *aktion*, later known as the Large *Aktion*, began the day after the commencement of the work of preparing the hiding place.

[Page 249]

The Large *Aktion*

It was early in the morning. We woke up to the call of our neighbor, who awakened my mother and told her that she saw a woman knocking on the door of a neighbor. After she told us what she had to say, everyone got up and fled from the house. We got dressed quickly, and my father ran to the communal office to find find out what happened. When my father tarried, my mother sent me also to call him. I ran and returned quickly to tell them that I did not find him there. When I returned, my parents and other residents of the house, one large family, were standing and preparing the little bit of provisions that we had. The food was packed, for we were going to escape to our grandfather that day, because the hiding place that we were going to prepare in our house was not yet ready.

Suddenly, shots were heard from all sides. We stood there without any possibilities. We were trembling like captured rabbits, surrounded by hunters. Without any choice, we went down to the unfinished hiding place, which seemed like our last resort for salvation despite its obvious shortcomings. Our eight-person family, as well as my good friend of the same age, sat there together. Despite this, Father decided to try to go to Grandfather and Grandmother, come what may. He indeed succeeded in getting to their house, but he no longer found them there. Their good hiding place that they had prepared had been broken into, and was empty. He returned in despair and joined us.

We all crowded into the cellar. My mother and I took the place closest to the door. We all sat there trembling from cold and fear. After sitting there for about a quarter of an hour, we heart the shouts of the Jewish policemen announcing that all the Jews must present themselves at the train station with 15 kilograms of luggage. I loved traveling by train very much, and I wanted to go up to our home to begin to pack our belongings - but my mother displayed exemplary calm... She said that in her opinion, we would not hold up the train, for it was impossible to fit all the Jews from the city and area (the Jews of the area were also gathered for this *aktion*) onto one train. We continued to sit there, waiting for what fate would bring us.

We sat quietly. The announcements stopped. Here and there, we heard isolated shots. There was a barn nearby, and we heard the mooing of the cows from afar. The isolated shots that we heard on occasion proved to us that there were other Jews who, like us, did not go to the train. The feeling that we were not alone strengthened us, and we continued to sit in the darkness, crowded, hungry and thirsty.

[Page 250]

This *aktion* lasted for four days, and the little bit of food we possessed was used up. The thirst particularly afflicted us. We sat in quiet, when we suddenly heard the voice of a man speaking in Ukrainian to our neighbor, a Ukrainian girl. She opened up the door of her locker in the cellar. They broke into the other lockers one after another. They got closer to our hiding place, which was in the last locker in the cellar. The locker next to us had been broken into. The knocking of the Ukrainian policemen approached, and their voices grew louder. My heart stopped beating out of fear. I nestled up closely with my mother in order to quiet the chattering of my teeth and to draw from her the full quota of strength and hope that she had in her power to give me. We waited - and the moment arrived. They reached the door of the locker in which we were sitting. We heard the knocking on the door of our locker. It was clear to all of us that this was the end from which we had tried to escape. From fear, we continued to sit there, frozen and paralyzed. Suddenly... the knocking stopped. In the quiet that pervaded, we heard the voice of one of the Ukrainians: "There is nobody here, don't waste your energy."

They left the cellar... and we began to breathe. It was hard to believe that we had been saved that time as well. This was on the first day of the *aktion*. We continued to sit there as each of us tried to express our feelings and thoughts at the moment we heard the knocking on the door. We all began to believe in some strong power that was watching over us and directing our steps. We continued to sit there for a day or two (I do not know exactly for how long, for we lost track of time due to the extreme darkness) until we once again heard them entering the cellar. The locker door of the Ukrainian girl was broken into. Then, they came to the door of our cellar. This time, it was the Germans - but they satisfied themselves with several knocks on the door of our locker, and they disappeared. We were once again saved with a new miracle. It is hard to understand why they passed over this locker. There was no difference between it and the other four lockers that they had broken into previously. However, as we saw, strange events took place that cannot be explained or understood with straight logic. After the second visit, we understood that there were still Jews in hiding, and that we were among many others. Needless to say, this feeling imparted us with a certain strength.

This terrible *aktion* lasted for four days. At the end of the *aktion*, we went to our dwelling, which had not been harmed or pillaged during this *aktion.* My mother gave the Ukrainian girl many presents. The girl told us that she told the Germans that we had already gone to the train. We were not certain about her trustworthiness, but we attempted to maintain good relations with our Ukrainian neighbor.

Almost every family, including our family, lost some of their relatives in this *aktion.* This time, my maternal grandfather, my aunt and uncle were taken. (My uncle later jumped off the train - and was saved). My paternal grandmother and grandfather, whom I especially loved and with whom I had grown up and been educated, were taken. We later found out the story of how they were captured. When Grandmother heard the announcements, she hurried to pack two suitcases, one for her and one for Grandfather. After she called other neighbors, they all set out for the train. Along the way, near our house, Grandfather attempted to escape in order to find out if we too had left. He was beaten by a Ukrainian guard when he attempted to turn to us. Only then did they realize that something is amiss, but it was too late.

[Page 251]

The loss of Grandfather and Grandmother affected greatly. After that *aktion*, I sat and cried a great deal. I could not pass by the dwelling in which they had lived without bursting out crying. After some time, I got brave and went to their dwelling. I saw a terrible sight. The house in which I had grown up, ran, danced, rejoiced and played stood before me empty and ruined. Letters from my uncle in the Land of Israel were scattered on the floor. This was a terrible moment, and I have no words to describe what was transpiring in my soul. Only then did I realize that everything that had taken place around me affected me directly. Indeed, everything that had taken place happened in order to accustom me to the idea that death was lurking, and would soon catch up with me. I left the place and ran home with my remaining strength. I fell upon my bed and lay down paralyzed. My heart was about to burst from the great pain locked up within it. After some time I succeeded in bursting out crying, and the tears eased my pain...

That night, I spoke at length to my father. I told him that I was afraid of death, that I wanted to live... My father tried to calm me, or more precisely, to lead me to acceptance of what was awaiting us. He explained me that all of those killed go directly to Heaven, where things are good. There, they receive a recompense for every feeling of the pangs of death. He promised me that there I would meet my grandfather and grandmother, and that my parents would also be there. All of this calmed me. Indeed, from that time, I stopped being so afraid of death. Certainly, I did everything to guard my life, but death seemed very close. Again, there was something about it that was good and recognized. The fear that had overtaken me earlier was assuaged...

The Fourth *Aktion*

It was a Saturday, and we were all still lying in our beds. (At that time, another family, the Richter family who were friends of my parents, lived in our house). Suddenly, we heard strong knocking on the door and heard shouts from the other side of the house. We had nowhere to flee this time... Everyone instinctively searched for some sort of shelter. My mother jumped under the double bed. My mother's friend, Chancha Richter, who slept with my mother that night, jumped into the closet. I ran under the third iron bed that had no mattress, and upon which nobody slept. My father was the only one who sat quietly on his bed and began to get dressed. In the meantime, a policeman broke the door of the kitchen and even broke into our house. He approached my father directly shouting, "Where are the others?!" The policeman did not wait for my father's response. He bent down and began to beat my mother who was lying under the bed. I saw blood flowing from her leg, and no longer had the power to remain quietly in my hiding place. I came up from under the bed and pleaded with the policeman to stop beating my mother. I told him that I was already dressed, and would go. He looked at me, and with a final act of mercy stopped beating my mother before my eyes. He ordered us to get dressed quickly, and left the room in haste. All of this lasted for a few minutes. My father finished getting dressed and went out. My mother went out to the front porch in order to see what could be done, and returned immediately. On her way to the stairwell where all the residents of the house were gathering, she succeeded in telling me that I should not leave the house under any circumstances, but should go to hide under the bed. I decided to hide under the quilt. We debated for a few minutes. My mother suddenly ran out of the room, and I chose a place under the quilt, for I thought that they would certainly not look for me there.

[Page 252]

I lay down quietly without moving. A policeman entered the room to check whether we had all left, and I continued to lie quietly. It began to rain outside. I heard shots and the barking of dogs. I lay down, trembling in fear. I was especially afraid of the dogs. In the eyes of my spirit, I saw a giant dog falling upon me and tearing me apart with his teeth. I felt sorry for myself. I understood that I would not be able to mislead a dog. I recalled all the stories of the good hiding places that had been revealed with the help of the German dogs. In the meantime, everything became quiet around me. Even the barking of the dogs became more distant. I continued to lie quietly, afraid to move a hand or foot. Hours passed in this manner. I got off the bed during the afternoon and walked about the room. I suddenly realized that I remained alone... I began to weep quietly. I knew now that instead of dying next to my father, I would die alone.

Suddenly, I heard someone calling my name. The closet door opened, and my mother's friend Chancha got out. It was easier for me, for I was no longer alone as the only Jew in the city, as I had thought. I resolved in my heart that I would never leave her if she would only agree to go with me together. I asked her if she would take me now (of course, I already understood at that time that we children were often an obstacle in the path of escape of the adults). Together, we tried to leave the dwelling in order to hide in the cellar or the attic. We tried to open the door, but to our dismay, the door was locked form the outside by a hanging lock. We were in despair. Having no option, we returned to our hiding places. After a short time, we again heard a strong knocking at the door. The door was broken into with force. In the room, we heard the loud voices of the Ukrainian policemen, including that of the infamous Vlochok. (As is known, before every *aktion,* they would bring in Ukrainian policemen from Stara-Sambor to perpetrate the deed.) The door of the closet was opened, and I heard how they captured Chancha. They demanded silver and gold from her, but she told them that she had nothing to give them. They continued to search through the room for hidden people and money. I continued to lie quietly, without moving a limb. The policemen lifted the quilt of the bed next to mine, and tossed it on the bedpost. Then they approached the bed in which I was lying. They felt through the quilt, but did not lift it up as they had done on the other bed. They lifted a pillow that was resting at the edge of the bed, and threw it in the middle, right where I was lying. From under the bed, they took out boxes with various things, and put them on the bed, that is, on top of me, searching for gold and silver, as they had told Chancha. They then took her and left. I remained quietly in my place, without daring to move. Then, I put my head out a bit in order to breathe. Again, I was not taken. Again, I remained alone, having attempted to protect my eight-year-old life. Even today, as a 14-year-old girl, I am unable to understand my behavior of that time. Apparently, this was the urge to live, an instinct of self preservation, a feeling of a pursued animal that urged me to continue and seek salvation.

[Page 253]

After a short time, I again heard voices in the room - this time, quiet ones. For some reason, I let down my guard and raised my head. The lifting of my head caught the attention of two Ukrainian policemen, who approached the bed. I lay quietly, but some of my hair was apparently exposed. I heard their conversation as they approached my bed. One policeman said to the other: "Here is a young Jewess - is it worthwhile to shoot her?" I did not wait for an answer. It was clear to me that if I were to look at him directly, he would simply kill me. I jumped out of the bed and looked straight into the eyes of the policeman who asked the question. He shouted at me to lie down quietly. I heard him answer, "Leave her, there is no reason anymore." I again lifted my head and asked them to save my parents. I told them that I would give them money in return for this, but they laughed at me. I was afraid to lie down, and decided to go outside.

I put my shoes on quickly and left the house in a hurry, leaving behind the two policemen to pillage anything they wanted. I went down the stairs. After thinking briefly, I went to our Polish neighbors who lived in the next house. I entered, told them what had happened to my parents. I asked them if they knew anything about my parents, and if perhaps they would be able to let me stay with them until the end of the *aktion*. Then I would try to check who is left of my family, and figure out what to do. I knew this family well. They had a daughter of my age with whom I used to play frequently. I often visited their house. But this time, they literally chased me out, "Jewess, your presence here will endanger us all. Go, go." I stood there for another second attempting to hold back my tears. I suddenly felt how alone I was: without parents, without a protector, with a short skirt, with old, wet shoes (it was raining outside). I again lost my will to live. I went out and started to amble through the streets, looking for my parents, waiting for the moment when they would take me too, for what was awaiting me that was worse than death itself. On the street, I met the Ukrainian girl who lived in our house. In the meantime, she moved to live somewhere else, in a less Jewish neighborhood. The girl asked me to come with her to her dwelling. I realized that the danger existed that she might take me straight to the Germans. She was very friendly with the Ukrainian policemen who came to town. Despite this, she often said that she wanted to help Jews. Our relationship to her was "honor her but suspect her". I agreed to her offer. I began to walk with her, or more precisely, to walk behind her, so that we would not be seen walking together. As we approached her house, I heard a voice calling my name. This was Bruner, a friend of the family and a customer of Grandfather's store. I then thanked the girl for her willingness to bring me to her house. I explained to her that anything could happen to me at any moment, and I preferred to be together with Jews. I entered Bruner's house, told him everything that I knew, and asked him about the situation. He told me that the snatchings have now stopped. The train already left the city, but the policemen are still present, and it was not clear if this was the end or simply a brief break. Perhaps another train would arrive and the *aktion* would continue.

[Page 254]

I remained there for a brief time, and felt the stifling atmosphere of fear. I felt that I had no more energy to sit in a closed Jewish house and flee whenever I would see the face of a German or a Ukrainian policeman. I decided to continue wandering through the city. Outside, the rain had stopped, and the air was clear and pleasant. I wandered through the streets of the city, without even stopping at puddles. Before I stepped in such a puddle, I stopped for a moment and recalled the warnings of my mother not to walk in puddles. I then deliberately stepped into it, as if to say that I can do whatever I want... I no longer had a mother or father who would get angry, and I should enjoy the brief bit of freedom that I still have before they take me as well. I recall that aimless ambling through the streets, without any purpose, as I enjoyed the freedom after the stifling atmosphere of the hiding place. I walked and visited all those places that I loved, as if to bid them farewell... I was enjoying the clear air after the rain for the last time. I ignored my thoroughly wet shoes, and the incidents of people pointing to me, saying, "See, a Jewess remains!..." Here and there, I heard derogatory remarks about the little Jewess. I was already immune from these remarks. I was fully engaged with my inner world, recalling memories of my brief childhood and my dreams that would never be fulfilled.

[Page 255]

On my strange walk, I passed the house of a member of the communal leadership. Awakening from my thoughts, I decided to go up and hear if perhaps they know something about my parents and my relatives. I went to them. They listened to my story in agony, and told me that they do not know anything about my parents. They added that the situation is still unclear, and they advised me to remain with them until it would be possible to clarify anything. There, I took off my wet shoes. They gave me big, warm boots to wear until my shoes would dry out. We all sat in the kitchen, as one of them looked out of the window to see if the Germans or Ukrainians were approaching. Once, two Ukrainian policemen were seen coming in the direction of the house. They all escaped to their hiding places. They left me behind, saying that I was small and could hide behind the bed. I did this. It was not pleasant for me to remain alone again, but I had no choice. Apparently, they did not want to bring me into their hiding place and reveal it to me. It is also possible that they were not looking for another person whom they would have to feed. (They were not bad people. They were not at all worse than the others, but such was the situation. Everyone worried only about themselves and those closest to them. They concerned themselves with a hiding place and food, and were not prepared to add another concern to their concerns.)

After it became clear that the incident with the policemen was a false alarm, we returned to the room and sat together until nighttime. We all ate something. They also gave me something to eat, and told me to go to sleep in the other room. It was hard for me to fall asleep. I only fell asleep after a long cry, and I woke up on occasion with nightmares. I got up very early in the morning, and entered the kitchen where voices were calling out. I entered - and good news awaited me. They quickly told me that my father had survived! He came to them at 12 midnight, and they told him that I was there. He looked at me and did not want to wake me up. He decided that he would come the next day to take me home. I did not have the patience to wait. They covered me up in a large sheet, gave me a pair of boots several sizes too large - and I went home. It was still dark outside. Encouraged about the news of my father, I hurried home. I would have actually run, but the large boots held me back. I finally reached the gate of our house. I knocked and called out "Father." He heard my call, and came to greet me and open the gate. The gate opened, and my beloved father stood next to me, hale and whole. I fell into his arms crying, and asked about Mother. He told me that Mother had also survived. With this news, we went up to our dwelling.

[Page 256]

It was clear that they had not slept all night. A light was burning in the kitchen. Mother prepared coffee. Father's friend Elisha Richter was also in the house. I had been a witness to the snatching of his wife Chancha. I told him everything that I knew and had heard about his wife before she was taken. The family that lived next to us, who had been with us in the previous *aktion*, had also been taken. The house was almost empty. Our house had been pillaged. Only a few old things, which the robbers did not succeed in taking, remained.

We all sat together, and each of us told our story.

Father's Story

As I have already stated, my father had left the dwelling and entered the stairwell, where the policemen were gathering all the residents of the house. He went down to the yard with all of them. There were many other Jews from the nearby houses there. He took advantage of the confusion, with the shouting and weeping, and began to run. The policemen shot after him. One bullet skirted his sleeve. He continued to run and did not stop. He managed to reach a nearby house where he hid in the cellar. After things quieted, my father left the cellar, and went up to our dwelling to see what had happened. It seemed to him that the dwelling was empty, so he decided to lock the door. He then escaped to the cemetery and the fields, where he hid until night. After he heard that the *aktion* had ended and that I had survived, he returned home. When he reached home and knocked on the gate, Mother opened up. She was weeping for me. From him she heard that I had also survived.

Mother's Story

After she left me in the room, she went out to the stairwell. There she saw that the policemen were surrounded by Jews who tried to offer them everything in return for their lives. There was a great commotion. Mother decided to take advantage of the commotion to save her life. She quickly removed the patch with the Star of David from her arm, opened the door of the large porch that was common to the entire house, and went out to the porch in "security," pretending to be cleaning the fence of the porch. From below she heard the voices of the local Ukrainians and Poles pointing to her, "Here is a Jewess." Mother answered them "with self-assurance," "stop joking; you know that I am not a Jewess." She continued to clean the porch in this manner until she reached the side of the porch that was hidden from the yard in which the Ukrainians were standing. There, she thought about jumping down, but she realized that there was no chance of landing in one piece from such a height. An old, disintegrating mattress had been tossed in that corner of the porch. Mother lay down on the porch, covering herself with the old mattress. Thus did she lie quietly. In that area of the porch, there was a window that looked across to the stairwell, between one end of the stairs and the other. There, my mother heard how they were all going down the stairs. She lay down quietly. When it quieted down somewhat, she opened the window and jumped into the stairwell. She ran to the door of our dwelling where she had left me, but she found that the door had already been locked from outside. She quickly went up to the upper storey and hid there. Another neighbor was hiding there with her baby. In the evening, the neighbor's husband came to inform her of the end of the *aktion*. My mother went down to the dwelling of this neighbor, where he remained until my father arrived.

[Page 257]

*

This *aktion* took place on Saturday and lasted for about half a day. It was perpetrated with great suddenness, so most of the people were captured in their houses, without any possibility of escaping to the hiding places or the fields. This was the final *aktion* before the liquidation. There was indeed another *aktion* after this *aktion*, but it was perpetrated by Jewish policemen from Sambor, and lasted for a night and the following half day.

With No Way Out

It was the winter of 1942. It was already clear that the end was beginning. There was clear talk of liquidation, of transferring all the Jews out of the city and concentrating them in the Sambor Ghetto. Only few Jews remained in the city, and they tried to save themselves in any manner that they could. A large number tried to escape to Hungary, where the situation of the Jews was still secure. However it was not easy to reach Hungary in those days. It was the height of the winter, and crossing the border was fraught with danger, especially the danger of being followed. Some of those to be transferred collaborated with the Germans. Often, after they received a large sum of money from Jews, they would haul them directly to the hands of the Germans.

Some of the Jews of the city tried to hide with gentiles in the city or the region. Another group, the younger ones in particular, built bunkers in the surrounding forests and hid there, with light weapons that they succeeded in obtaining. However, the majority of the survivors sat and waited passively for the liquidation, which was indeed carried out in December 1942.

Another group of the Jews of the city chose to commit suicide rather than falling live into the hands of the Germans. The most common form of suicide was poisoning by coal fumes. The victims did not suffer much in this manner. I heard my father discuss this possibility with my mother. This was at night, and my parents apparently thought that I was sleeping - but I was awake and heard the entire conversation. From that time, I was very afraid of sleeping. I was also afraid of leaving my parents alone. One day I told my mother about my fear and about my concern that they were going to flee to Hungary and leave me alone in a different hiding place. My mother promised me that under no circumstances would she leave me against my will. These words of my mother calmed me a bit. At that time, my mother would frequently run from one of her Polish or Ukrainian friends to another, attempting to find a hiding place for all of us, some of us, or at least for me. Many parents tried to hide their daughters, for the most part, with the farmers of the area. My mother prepared a packet for each of us with necessities. She also sewed three small sacks, one for each of us, where we put the bit of money that we still had.

[Page 258]

*

After a great deal of searching, my mother succeeded in finding a place for me with a Ukrainian family. I was not happy to leave my parents and to remain alone again, as had happened during the *aktion*. At the same time, however, I realized that my parents had found a good place for me, and this would be the only way I would be able to survive. The survival instinct again guided me, and I agreed to the advice of my parents. My father explained to me that they would be freer without me, and that they would find some way to escape and save themselves. My father told me, "You must remain alive. You have seen and understood everything that happened. Most of our family has already been murdered. Someone must remain alive to tell the story of what happened. You, as a child, have great chances for this." They made me memorize the address of my uncles in the Land of Israel, and commanded me that if I survive, I must write to them immediately. I must tell everything to the relatives in the land, and they would take care of me. (My father had two brothers in Israel, and my mother had one brother.) Equipped with the blessings of my parents and their charge to me to continue to live in order to tell the story of what happened to our family and many other Jewish families of the city, I parted from my parents.

During the final days before leaving the house, I saw my mother standing all the time near the oven and weeping. She would look at me on occasion and weep again. The day of my departure approached. It was a cold, snowy day. My father set up a meeting with the gentile outside the city. I approached my mother to bid her farewell. She was standing, as usual, next to the oven and weeping. She hugged and kissed me, and we wished each other that we should survive and see each other again. I parted from her, trying not to think about what was going to happen in the future. Father accompanied me outside the city. Waiting there was the wagon with the gentile, who was to transfer me to another gentile with whom I would live. Father walked in front of me holding a blanket in his hands, and I walked behind him in order not to arouse attention. My father carried me up to the wagon, covered me well with the blanket, told me, "Be successful, my daughter," and left. The wagon moved quickly, sliding over the white snow. Through my tears, I saw the precious image of my father getting smaller and smaller. He continued to walk straight, without turning his head toward me. His image disappeared in the distance. That was the last time that I saw him.

[Page 259]

I went to a Ukrainian family in the village of Komarnik, and my parents went to the Sambor Ghetto along with the remnants of the Jews of the town.

With the Ukrainian Family in Komarnik

My first stop was the village of Borinya, where I stayed with a gentile acquaintance, and from where I was transferred to a Ukrainian family in the village of Komarnik. My parents did not know that family. The eldest son of that family, Pyotr, transferred me. He came the next day at 2:00 p.m. to fetch me. This Pyotr did not live with his parents, but rather in the village of Borinya. He wanted to reach his parents' home in Komarnik in the dark in order to avoid the attention of the neighbors. The journey from Borinya to Komarnik seemed endless to me. I lay down in the wagon, doubled over and frozen, constantly asking when we would arrive. We arrived at dark. I heard the barking of a dog, and Pyotr told me that it was their dog. Our journey ended.

When we arrived, the entire family came out to greet Pyotr. He descended from the wagon and called his parents aside. After a brief conversation with them, they all turned to me. They took me down from the wagon, brought me into the house, and sat me near the oven so that I could warm up a bit. They received me politely. After I warmed up, they gave me something to eat, and then we went to bed. I was a given a place in a joint bed where four other children were sleeping. I was very tired and I fell asleep quickly.

The house was a small cottage that consisted of three compartments - a medium sized dwelling area, a grain storehouse, and a barn. The room was low, made of wood. There was a bit of poured concrete on the floor. There were two small windows, such that if a person was passing outside, one would only see the middle of his body. The furnishings in the room were simple and typical of poor farmers. The oven occupied the lion's share of the room. In the room, there were two beds, a chest for dishes, and a large table with two benches on the sides. A closet was hanging on the wall, the size of a large chest. This was all the furniture in the house. The room was clean and neat. The seven-person family lived in the room. Aside from them, the following people were part of the family: Pyotr who lived in Borinya and who brought me there; another son who was taken to work in Germany, and two adult daughters who lived in Drohobycz where they were employed as household help.

[Page 260]

The First Crisis

The crisis of my soul already began the following day. I suddenly found myself in strange, unfamiliar surroundings. In my great despair, I began to cry and beg them to take me back home. It was enough, I was not looking for places to hide and save myself, I wanted Mother and Father, and anything that would happen to them would happen also to me. The gentiles were good to me, and tried to comfort me. Pyotr succeeded in convincing me by promising to go to my parents and bring my mother. This idea calmed me, and I decided to really be good so that the gentiles would agree to keep us.

At the beginning of my stay, I was able to walk around freely in the room. I only fled and hid on top of the oven, below it, or in some other place when I heard the dog bark. Sometimes, the dog did not bark, so I did not succeed in hiding quickly. Then I would run to some place, and there was already a suspicion that the person who came saw me. They were very afraid, and they told me that my stay with them would only bring disaster to them. After a short time, they decided to no longer endanger themselves, and to return me to their son Pyotr when he would return; however, Pyotr simply did not come, and I lived in constant fear. I began to suspect that the farmers might kill me themselves out of great fear. (It later became clear to me that there was no basis for this fear.) I already understood that I should not wait for the arrival of my mother. In the meantime, all the Jews of the city were transferred to the Sambor Ghetto, and the city of Turka was officially *Judenrein*.

A new era began. We heard terrible things that happened to the Jews who were captured at the border as they attempted to escape to Hungary. We also heard about Jews who were captured in the forests and were even found with gentiles. All of this news was spread on Sundays, when the farmers returned from the churches in the nearby towns. In essence, the church was the primary source of information. There, they found out everything that took place. In this manner, they later found out about the Warsaw Ghetto uprising, albeit without exact detail. I recall well that on a certain Sunday they said that there was a large-scale Jewish revolt in the Warsaw Ghetto, and that many Germans had been killed. Incidentally, the words of the priest of the church had great influence upon these farmers, who for the most part were believers. At times, when the priest delivered a sermon from which one could understand that one should help the Jews, they returned home very encouraged.

[Page 261]

In the mean time, the Germans issued a decree that demanded that all gentiles of the area turn in the Jews who were hiding with them. Whoever did not do so would be put to death. The gentiles with whom I was hiding did not know what to do; they were afraid for their lives and the lives of their children. They sent urgently for Pyotr to discuss what to do with me, but Pyotr only came after three months. He received their shouts calmly and promised that he would come very soon to take me. At that time, he also brought them a few things, such as clothing, money, etc. I even began to take out money from the pocket that my mother had given me, and I gave them a bit of money on occasion. Thus did I succeed in remaining there. In the meantime, I learned Ukrainian with great diligence. I also diligently and quickly learned their prayers. Within a brief period I spoke fluent Ukrainian and properly pronounced the letters R and L, which are pronounced in a unique manner by them. They praised me and added that nobody would ever be able to claim that I was not a Ukrainian by birth, based on the language and the prayers that were fluent on my tongue. However, my external appearance was a disadvantage. They all had blond hair and blue eyes, and I had black hair. My dark hair attracted everyone's attention. I realized that they were proud that they had turned me into a good Christian, and I did everything in order to appear such... hoping that this would protect me, for they would want to protect and save my soul for Christianity.

After a Year

The days marched on slowly, and a year passed. Christmas arrived. When my hosts returned from the church in the city, they brought me a cigarette box filled with candies, and told me that my parents are still alive in the Sambor ddddd

The Tribulations Prior to the End

It was summer. Everyone went out to work in the fields, and I remained alone in the storehouse. To my good fortune, there were Ukrainian books there, and I continued to study how to read and write Ukrainian. Throughout this time, they often changed my hiding place. I hid in a tall bean field, in haystacks, in nearby groves, in the forest near the house; as well as on top of the oven, beneath the oven, and, in the latter period, in a pit in the barn. At that time, I would also go into the hiding place that they had prepared for me in the barn. I would enter this place immediately after breakfast, and remain there until late in the evening. On day, I tarried in the house for a long time, as was unusual. This was a cloudy fall day, and I simply did not have the desire to leave my place on the oven and to go into the hiding place in the barn. I would be alone in that hiding place all day, and therefore, I did not like it much. That morning, I spent a long time eating the meal, and also spent more time remaining in the house. Plusia, the farmer's wife, urged me to finish my meal. She went out to check if the path to the barn was clear. She immediately returned, quickly and with a commotion, for she saw a German and Ukrainian a short distance away approaching the house. I was immediately sent under the oven, where I lay curled up and afraid. The German and Ukrainian went strait to the barn - my regular hiding place at that time. The only searched in the barn. When they found nothing, they returned to the village. This was a clear case of informing. After the Germans went away, the gentiles transferred me to the nearby forest, where I remained until late at night. (I will never forget the deathly fear that fell upon me when I was forced to remain alone in the grove, especially during the nighttime hours. I was afraid of wild beasts. There were many wild pigs and other such animals in the area. This fear of wild beasts and of remaining alone at night disappeared only after some years. Repeated nightmares of persecution and attacks by Germans and Ukrainians, and of wild beasts, afflicted me even during my first years in the Land of Israel...)

They brought me home at night, hungry and damp to the bones. The days continued to march on. We heard news of the advance of the Red Army, and also of revolts of the Jews in Poland. All of this encouraged me and imparted me the desire to continue to live. It would be unfortunate to be caught and put to death now in particular, when the future began to look brighter. The summer days came to and end and the winter days arrived, with the following dangers: the fear of footprints in the snow, and the difficulty of remaining in a grove or in the forest without freezing. Then a greater danger arose: One day, the Germans were seen in the city, and they were very close to the house. The possibility of bringing me to the grove was no longer in the calculations. My hosts remained without recourse, not knowing what to do with me. The farmer's wife took charge, for she had to protect the lives of her children. She grabbed a blanket, quick as lightning covered me in it, and ran me in the direction of the well near the house, where she buried me in the snow. This was the only possibility of hiding me without leaving any trace. I was indeed saved from the Germans, but there was only a hairbreadth between me and death - from freezing. After the Germans left, the gentiles quickly took me out of the snow and I slowly recovered.

[Page 264]

Then, when the possibility of hiding in the area and in the grove no longer existed, they dug a pit for me in the barn, where I had to lie quietly without moving (indeed, there was no practical possibility of such). The pit was small, narrow and musty. My bed consisted of a bit of straw with a burlap covering. This was my most terrible hiding place. Were it not for the liberation, this pit would have led to my demise. I constantly saw mice in that dark pit, and they were so active that at times, I burst out in hysterical cries of fear. The gentiles sometimes heard my screams, and they threatened me that if I do not behave properly - which might lead to their deaths - they would simply throw me out.

I did the best I could to control my frayed nerves. I had no internal energy to continue to suffer. At times, continuing to live seemed to lack any purpose. To live? -- Why do I need life?... Who needs it... I was an orphan, and possibly the only Jewess in the region. What could I do with myself... I asked myself and repeated this and other questions to myself many times. I could not do anything else in that terrible pit, so I continued to ask, and think... This was the situation to which, perhaps, one should not go: The twisting of the thoughts was apparently dangerous.

The Echoes of the Hammer of Hope…

The spring days, filled with hope, approached. After the gentiles realized that, despite all my promises, they heard talking from the barn - they hastily took me out to the grove. There, I strengthened a bit: The clear air; the beauty of the budding trees and the blooming flowers; the wild berries and mushrooms - all of these enchanted me and distanced me from my thoughts... They healed me. However, this was during the day... The day was wonderful; the forest was green; the birds returned and filled the forest with their songs; and the heart was full of pleasure... However, the night was difficult. The fear of wild beasts, and the thoughts that afflicted me returned.

[Page 265]

I remained in this grove for the final month prior to the liberation. I received sufficient food. From afar, I could hear the sounds of the cannons - these were the echoes of the hammers of hope... The Russians were approaching. It was 1944. The Russians arrived. The liberating army passed through Komarnik on its way to the Hungarian border. I remained with the gentiles, for I did not know what to do with myself and my life that I had tried so hard to save...

*

One day, the gentiles informed me that a certain family was searching for me diligently, and I should return to the city. I traveled to Borinya. There, I remained for a short time with a certain family, and then I continued on to Turka. It then became clear that the Bruner family, who had survived, searched tirelessly for me in all the villages of the area. This is what happened. My parents knew that Bruner was not going to the ghetto, but rather, to hide with a gentile. Before my father was taken to the ghetto, he asked Bruner to promise that if he survived, he would not forget me, and do everything to return me to a Jewish environment and my uncles in Israel. Bruner fulfilled this promise. He spared no effort to find me. When he found me, he and his family took me in to his bosom, as if accepting a true daughter by birth. They were good, pleasant, and dedicated to me. They raised me, educated me, and fed me. Primarily, their good heart and trustworthiness slowly restored my faith in humanity. It was only thanks to them that I succeeded in overcoming the tidings of Job with respect to the loss of my parents. It is interesting: They told me, and I realized, that my parents had been killed; however, subconsciously, I continued to wait for years - perhaps, despite all, they would appear from somewhere...

I remained with the Bruner family for a long time. They took me to Poland. There, we parted, and I went to an orphanage in Bielsko. The Bruner family took me once again, and I went to Germany with them. There, we wandered from one displaced persons camp to another. We were in Regensburg, and then in Fernwald. I remained in the latter camp until April, 1946. Then I joined a group of children, with whom I went to Israel. After a period in the Atlit Camp, I reached the bosom of my family in May 1946.

*

The dream of many years was realized. The circle was completed in April 1958, when my first born son was born on Holocaust Remembrance Day. This son bears the name of my murdered father.

Translator's Footnote:

As a follow-on to this story, Mrs. Ester Roter of Jerusalem is featured in a YouTube video describing her story, and her subsequent meeting with the family who saved her, who were designated as Righteous Gentiles by Yad Vashem in 2005. See http://www.youtube.com/watch?v=SMxnZfy3mnU

[Page 266]

From the Bundles of Testimonies[1]

Yonah... Born in the year 1928 in the city of Turka, distinct of Sambor in eastern Galicia, where he lived until the end of August 1942, tells:

... Our town Turka on the Stryj River is situation 25 kilometers from the Hungarian border. When our situation worsened to an unbearable point, the Germans shot and murdered without any break, and the poverty and lack grew to such a point that many Jews died of hunger - Father told me that all options are closed, and commanded me to sneak across the border and escape to Hungary.

I recall very well when the Germans did to the Jews in our town from that Tuesday, July 1, 1941, about a week after the beginning of the war with the Bolsheviks... Our food situation worsened. The Ukrainian farmers, who had been growing wealthier, brazenly demanded inflated prices for every small item. All Jewish businesses were closed. It was forbidden for the Jews to do business with anything - everything was in the hands of the Ukrainian cooperatives. They even expropriated the houses of the Jews and removed them from their hands. Any Jew who still had money, hidden merchandise, or household objects in his house could still purchase something. Everyone else literally died of hunger.

... Every Jew had a food card of the German authorities. According of the plan, every individual was supposed to receive nine dekagrams of bread per day. However, the Germans did not want to give the Jews any flour at all. The *Judenrat* had its own bakery and a cooperative store to distribute provisions. However, for the most part, they were not able to distribute to everyone - aside for the 100 to 200 forced laborers - other than twice a week. It was a holiday for all of us in the town when we found out that the *Judenrat* had received flour for the bakery.

At the beginning of the winter of 1941, the Germans still distributed half a metric measure of potatoes (50 kilograms per person). When the potatoes were used up, the hunger was terrible. I saw our neighbor Meir Ch., who owned a large house and had been very wealthy before the war, eating potato peels with his family. This is what everyone did: They would first rinse the peels well in water and cook them in salt. Then they would grind a bit of oats with a hand grinder, mix the oat flour with the peels, and make a type of edible wafer from the mixture. In the home of another neighbor, Leizer T., a builder and a monument engraver, they would eat grass. There were seven small children in his house, the oldest of whom, David, was my friend.

[Page 267]

I would help him cut that grass, called "Lavada," a cattle food. My friend David's mother would cook a pot of grass each day in a large washing basin. She would prepare a type of patty from the cooked grass, like spinach. Eating grass affected the bodies of the children of our neighbor in a terrible fashion. Other Jews died from this reason. At Passover time, we would have four or five funerals a day - almost all of people who died of hunger.

*

Immediately, tribulations worse than these fell upon our heads, until we forgot even the hunger with everything that was happening. The German authorities were approaching. The men of the border guard moved to the border village of Sianki after having camped for four or five months in our town; and an entire group of 15-20 German gendarmes settled with us. Their commander was Feldfevel Strottman, and his deputy was Corporal Shlaumilch, who was more evil than the commander himself. In the meantime, a new command of the assisting Ukrainian police arrived from Stryj, whose name was Vanchun. He too tried to torment the Jews in any way that he could. The *Judenrat* was forced by the authorities to set up a cafeteria in the communal building. Any German or Ukrainian who came to visit Turka was to be provided with all his needs. Even when the head of the Gestapo of Drohobycz, Uber-Lieutenant Ginter, came to town for an inspection, he would take his meals at the *Judenrat*, and they would get drunk and boisterous there. They would order and force them to bring them the best and most expensive that they had: Hungarian liqueurs, champagne, sardines, and the like. After they had drunk to the point of inebriation, they would go out to the street and beat Jews. That Gestapo head Ginter would come to Turka often to visit his mistress, a Polish girl named Wanda. It was rumored that he would say that all the Jews must hide in their houses when he would come to town, for he could not tolerate the appearance of a Jew on the street, he would extort a great deal of gifts from the Jews, and his mistress would receive the finest of gifts.

On one occasion in the winter, at the end of December 1941, the Gestapo head along with a group of 30-40 *sturmeisters* came to town, and a command was issued that all the Jews had to give over their furs to the German Army, which was fighting on the Russian front. Fur clothing, hats, gloves, scarves, and even felt boots were included in this edict, in a way that no fur products would remain in the hands of any Jews, even if its size was only one centimeter. Ten Jews, including several members of the *Judenrat*, were imprisoned as hostages to ensure that all fur products, up to the last hand band, was given over. This activity lasted for about a week, and more than 1,000 fur products were collected at the *Judenrat*. There were Jewish fur merchants, and they had to give over all of the merchandise that they had. Many Jews who gave over their winter coats froze from cold due to the lack of warm clothing. When this activity was finished, the Gestapo leaders chose the best of the furs for their wives, and sent off the rest of the collection.

[Page 268]

*

... Thus did matters go until the first slaughter, called an *aktion* by the Germans, was perpetrated. This took place on Wednesday, January 8, 1942. First, the Gestapo men, headed by Ginter and Krauze, came to the *Judenrat* building, gorged themselves with the best foods and drinks at the community cafeteria, got drunk to the point of boisterousness, and then informed them that an order had come from Krakow regarding an *aktion* in Turka. They did not prepare a list of names. Rather, anyone who crossed their paths on the street would be snatched and placed in prison. In this manner, about 400 Jews - men, women, and children - were brought in. The next day, Thursday, January 9, all of the imprisoned Jews were loaded on transport trucks in groups of 25, and dispatched to a field outside the city known as "Na-Lipach." There, every group was shot dead. As one group lay dead, another group was brought, until all 400 Jews had been shot. Only two people survived by miracle. One was Sarah N., a butcher. She later described how the event unfolded. When they pushed them out of the transport trucks, she saw an open pit nearby with a pile of corpses, who had been shot. She immediately understood what had happened, and she jumped into the open pit. The German gendarmes were so busy with the killing that nobody realized this. As she lay in the pit, she heard a succession of shots, and then the corpses were tossed into the pit. After the deed, the Germans were too busy or too lazy to cover the pit with earth, so they only covered it with boards. A miracle happened to that woman, had she succeeded in crawling out of the pit. They later nicknamed her, "The dead one." The second person who survived was a 15-year-old boy, Chaim Sh. He was an orphan who was raised in the home of his Uncle Kalman. He was one of the last to be shot. It was already dark, and the Germans did not realize that he had only been injured in his ear by a passing bullet, and that he was still alive. It was a few days until the pit was covered with earth, for the Jews were afraid to go to the grave. I still remember the names of several of the victims of this killing. The rabbi of Vanovichi who was more than 80 years old; my friend from public school, Yehoshua Longenor, 16 years old; Fani Artel, a wealthy woman, the wife and daughter of the pharmacist Monash. It was said that

[Page 269]

the Germans wanted to free the 17-year-old daughter of the pharmacist, Arika Monash, but she refused to part from her mother, and they were both shot.

*

After a few months - perhaps two weeks after Shavuot (June 1942) - the Gestapo perpetrated the "delegation of punishers" in our district. In the village of Sianki, literally on the border, 62 Jews were shot, and 100 Jews of our own of Turka were captured to be shot. This time, the Gestapo already had prepared a complete list of those taken to death. The Gestapo Lieutenant Krauze headed that *aktion*. The victims included: *Judenrat* member Berish Loberbaum, the militia man Goldberg, the lawyer Dr. Freundrich, and Mrs. Eigler and her two children. At first hey also arrested the *Uberman* (chairman) of the *Judenrat* Yehoshua Nachman Meiner but they freed him at the last minute. For some reason, the story of the delegation of punishers became known. At the Sianki border point, a group of Jewish forced laborers from Hungary, called " *Munka Tábor*" in Hungary, were camped, working on the paving of the road next to the border. They were housed in barracks over the German border. When the Jews of Hungary found out about the terrible poverty in which the Jews of Galicia found themselves, they asked their director, a Christian Hungarian captain, to give permission to the forced laborers under his command to share their bread with the starving Jews in the village of Sianki. The Jews in the Hungarian work battalions were treated much better than those in the German labor camps. They were given bread and good food, the work was easier, and they were given the entire day of Sunday off work. The commander Hamyor had mercy on the Jews and averted his eyes from the people helping each other. Each day, 500 forced laborers would leave behind a portion of their food allotment in the kitchen of the barracks (they had decided to leave over 1/3 of their bread allotment), and Jews from the village of Sianki and neighboring villages - men, women, and children - would come every evening to benefit from the taste of nourishing porridge. This continued for several weeks. The organizer of the assistance activity was one of the Hungarian Jewish forced laborers from Chust. When the Gestapo found out about this, they sent the delegation of punishers, and shot to death 65 Jews.

Translator's Footnote:

80. There is a footnote at the bottom of page 266, as follows: The article was published in the "Knesset" anthology, published by Mossad Bialik, 5703-5704 (1943-1944).

[Page 270]

In the Holocaust

by Esther Brand (nee Longenor) of Kiryat Bialik

Esther Brand

A memorial candle to my mother Kreinchi Longenor, nee Kleist, my sister Rozia, and my brothers Yehoshua and Shlomo, may G-d avenge their blood.

As is known to the world, the Holocaust did not fall upon the Jews of Turka and its area at one time. It was preceded by daily fear, hunger, physical and spiritual suffering, and persecution by the Ukrainian population - to the point of the loss of the image of G-d. The aktions that were perpetrated in our city left a deep wound on every family. They diminished the Jewish community, which was eventually deported to the Sambor Ghetto in the name of the "final solution."

The Germans captured Turka at the beginning of July 1941. As in all cities, the first task was the appointment of the Judenrat, through which the edicts would be transmitted to the Jews of the city. The city notables, such as Yehoshua Erdman, Yehoshua Nachman Meiner, Elimelech Wizner, and others belonged to it. The first edict was that a white patch with a blue Star of David must be worn on the right arm. Now, a Jew would be noticed from afar. Failure to follow the edict was punishable by death. Later, everyone had to turn in their furs. Whoever left a full fur in his house would pay with his life. A few more weeks passed, and we were forced to turn in our gold objects, including wedding rings. Indeed, we became accustomed to such orders, and did not oppose them. We prayed to G-d that the situation would not worsen.

The First *Aktion*

January 7, 1942 arrived. It was the height of winter. My brother Yehoshua went out to stroll on the street with his friend Mendel. Not far from the *Judenrat* building, they saw Germans arresting Jews and hauling them to the Ukrainian police station. They entered the *Judenrat* building, hoping to find a safe hiding place there. However, immediately upon entering, my brother was told to join Avraham Barth, who was already there at that time, to go out to work, since the Germans needed two workers to unload a shipment of kerosene barrels from the wagons and take them to the cellar. The request came from the head of the *Ordnunsdienst*, Elimelech Meiner. My brother pleaded before him and said that he saw with his own eyes that the Germans were capturing Jews and taking them to the police station. Elimelech Meiner urged them and promised that nothing bad would happen to them, since he himself would accompany them and take full responsibility for them. The three of them went out to do the work, but only the responsible person Elimelech Meiner returned from there... My brother Yehoshua and Avraham Barth never returned. They were shot along with 500 Jews by the brick kiln (*Cygalnia*). They succeeded in working with the Germans until noon. On the way home, they met a Ukrainian policeman who hauled them to the Gestapo. Their pleas and requests were to no avail. Elimelech Menier, who begged for his own life, was freed. This was the first *aktion* in the city of Turka. It left behind many orphans and widows, and sowed fear and death amongst the survivors. The death of my brother left a deep wound in our family. He was among the first victims in our city, and he was 15 years old at the time. May G-d avenge his blood.

[Page 271]

We did not only lose my brother in this *aktion*. My grandfather Moshe Leib Kleist, my grandmother Gittel Kleist, and my mother's sister Chava Kleist were among these victims. Whoever thought that the Germans satisfied themselves with shooting alone is mistaken. They and their Ukrainian helpers beat the victims with sticks until blood flowed before they carried out what they had planned. I heard the details from my mother of blessed memory, who was caught up in that *aktion* and survived by a miracle. She returned home at 3:00 a.m. all confounded, to the point where she could not utter a word. When she calmed down, she told us how the policemen gathered the Jews in the police warehouse in Artel's building. Most of those gathered were elderly men and women who were beaten with rubber batons before being forced into the warehouse. My grandfather protected my mother with his body, and endured merciless beatings. She told us how the rabbi of Vanovichi was brought into the warehouse with beatings. A Gestapo man approached him, put a gun to his nose, and said, “Smell this and pray to your G-d to help you.” He continued beating him without stopping. The rabbi was silent. Everyone was ordered to sing Russian songs. “A Jewish Communa,” shouted the Gestapo men, and anyone who did not sing was beaten. In the meantime, groups were taken to the upper storey. There, everyone endured a body search and a classification. My mother was among the few who were sent home. She had indeed endured a search, but they did not find anything with her, even though she had several hundred marks in her stocking. As was customary, every Jew carried the majority of his property on his body. On the third day of the *aktion* they loaded all the Jews on vehicles and covered them with tarpaulin. Ukrainian policemen sat on the tarpaulins, singing jolly songs. In this manner, approximately 500 Jews were taken behind the brickyard and killed with shots. They were buried in two large graves. The fear of death overtook us. We did not leave our house for a few weeks.

[Page 272]

*

After these things, the *Judenrat* transmitted an edict from the authorities to us, that every Jew was obligated to work and carry a certificate stating their work location (*arbeitsausviza*). Everyone attempted to find work. Young people found work in the quarry that belonged to the German firm "Hess Brothers of Breslau." The work was backbreaking, and lasted from 5:00 a.m. until late at night. My mother's four brothers, Yosef, Yisrael, Shlomo, and Shmuel worked in this quarry.

Another *Aktion*!

Days and weeks passed in this manner until August 2, 1942 arrived. We were awakened at 5:00 a.m. by a noise. The noise was the screaming of Jews who were being hauled away in open vehicles, as the Germans were beating them over the head with the butts of their rifles. At 5:30, Jews from the *ordnunsdienst* passed through the city and declared in a loud voice that everyone must present themselves at the railway station at 7:00 a.m. to be transferred to a different city. Each person was permitted to take up to 20 kilograms of luggage; therefore it was recommended to take only the most valuable belongings. Our family decided to not follow this edict, but rather to go up to the hiding place in the attic. This hiding place was constructed with great care by my younger brother Shlomo of blessed memory, who was only ten years old at the time. My aunt Lipsha Kirshner, her husband Yosef Ber and their six-year-old son Aharon, who had escaped from the village of Bukla out of fear of the Ukrainians, were with us in our house at the time. Also with us were my aunt Manya Kleist, with her four-year-old son Salek and 6-month-old baby Benek. The Artel and Stern families also joined us. This group of approximately 20 people went up to our hiding place. We brought the ladder inside, and closed the cover, which appeared as an extension of the wall, behind us. We waited for what would come. We lay quietly for three days and three nights. Throughout this time, the Germans brought hundreds of Jews to the railway station. The trains, loaded with men, women and children, departed from the station twice a day. In accordance with the command of the Gestapo, the men of the *ordnunsdienst* removed all the furnishings and kitchen utensils form the abandoned houses and the synagogue. Jews who succeeded in avoiding the *aktion* returned to their houses, finding them completely empty. On our third day in the hiding place, we went down to our dwelling to stock up on food. My task was to look through the window and inform everyone of any suspicious movement. My mother had just managed to light the oven when I noticed our Polish neighbor Drangowiec bringing two Gestapo men in our direction. We left the oven lit, along with all the preparations, and jumped back to our hiding place. We brought the ladder in and closed the door behind us. My aunt gagged her baby so that he would not utter a sound. We lay quietly and listed to the footsteps of the Gestapo men. They searched in every corner, felt every board and plank, and finally left our house in a huff, spewing curses: " *Verfluchte Juden*" (damned Jews).

[Page 273]

We heard the whistle of the train. This was the final shipment. The *aktion* concluded. To where did they take the 4,000 of Turka? The *Judenrat* paid two Christians to follow after the train. They returned and informed them that the final destination of the train was Belzec.

New *Aktions*

Few people remained in the city of Turka. The Germans promised the *Judenrat* that nothing bad would happen to those that remained, on the condition that every Jew would work. They kept their promise for only two months. On a Saturday in the middle of October, the Germans gathered the Jews from their workplaces and transferred them to a train destined to Belzec. At the end of October, another *aktion* took place, organized by the Ukrainian policemen. They passed through the roads of Turka in vehicles, and when they saw a Jew, they stopped the vehicle and brought the Jew inside. They commanded him to lie down, so that nobody would figure out what was taking place. Children were also taken from the yards as they were playing. They snatched them by their arms or legs and tossed them into the vehicles like balls. They were all shot in the suburbs of the city. I recall that Avraham Loberbaum and the lawyer Freundrich were among the victims. During the *aktion*, I was with my mother on the street, and we did not succeed in reaching home. We fled to the cemetery and hid among the gravestones. We were jealous of the dead who were lying in peace, not feeling anything.

*

At the beginning of November 1942, an additional aktion was perpetrated by Jews who were members of the *ordunsdienst* from the city of Sambor. Apparently, Sambor had not succeeded in collecting enough Jews, so they received permission from the *Judenrat* of Turka to fill their quota. At 2:00 a.m., they passed through the houses with a list prepared by the *Judenrat*. They gathered the Jews in the Ukrainian police building, and transferred them to the railway cars in the morning. Noise from the neighboring houses woke us up during the night. We did not suspect an *aktion*; however we instinctively grabbed blankets and ascended to the hiding place. There were six of us in the hiding place at that time: my mother, my sister, my brother, Henia Shreiber, and Mrs. Steininger who lived with us after they lost there families, and I. We did not have enough time to inform the other residents of the house, and they remained in their dwellings. My uncle Yosef knocked two members of the *ordnunsdienst* to the ground and succeeded in escaping to the fields. My aunt Manya Kleist, her son Salek and her baby found a hiding place in their dwelling. They were discovered and taken to the Ukrainian police. They beat the six-year-old Salek cruelly to urge him to disclose the hiding place of our family. The child did not give in. At 6:00 a.m., they were all on the trains. Before the train set out, they came to us for the fourth time that night. According to the list, they were certain that we were somewhere in the house. They ascended to the attic, knocked on every plank with sticks, went down, came up again, and eventually left the house. We heard them saying that if they did not find us, nobody would. The Angel of Death passed over us that time as well.

[Page 274]

*

Several days passed, and announcements were posted in the outskirts of the city of Turka that on December 1, 1942 at 8:00 a.m., every Jew of Turka and its area must be at the railway station. The train would take them to the Sambor Ghetto. Any Christian who would dare hide a Jew would be liable to the death penalty along with his family. This was the final phase before Turka would be *judenrein*. There were some Jews, especially young ones, who prepared to go out to the forests. The preparations had begun a half a year earlier. These lads worked in the quarry during the day, and in preparing bunkers in the forests, transferring food and acquiring weapons, which were very hard to find at that time, at night. My mother's brothers were among them. My mother, tired from all the tribulations, decided to go to the ghetto...

At 8:00 a.m. on December 1, 1942, the train laden with Jews, including the *Judenrat*, departed for the Sambor Ghetto. The Jews were weary and broken in body and soul. Several Jewish families remained at the recommendation of the Germans. These were professionals who were needed by the Germans. These included the Zeiman family, tailors; the watchmaker

Wind and his family; and the shoemaker Zeifert and his family. However, they too were shot at the time of the liquidation of the Sambor Ghetto.

Thus was the Jewish voice silenced in the city of Turka.

[Page 275]

In the Atrocities of the Times

by Dr. A. Hamermash of Ramataim

We knew that difficult years lay ahead of us, but we never would have imagined that things would come to such an all-encompassing Holocaust.

During the first days, the Germans snatched Jews for work. They were barely given any food. Later, an edict was issued for Jews to give over all valuables that they owned: gold, silver, and diamonds. The Jews gave over everything to save their lives.

It was the winter of 1942 - a January month in the Carpathian winter. An edict was issued by the *Judenrat* to give over anything called a fur for the brave soldiers at the front. Of course, everyone ran around in fear, hurriedly giving over all the furs.

One clear day there were rumors... The Jews had violated an edict, and the punishment was to come. Thus, one day toward evening, a panic broke out: they were capturing Jews. The first victim was V. B. Rozen. Everyone ran away, especially the men, for it seemed to be directed at them. I lived with Mr. Avraham Fieler, and next to him was his brother Leib Feiler. His son-in-law Mr. Rozen, A. Fieler and I escaped in the direction of Borinya. We reached Lipa with difficulty due to the snow and ice. Rabbi Youlis was already there in a small, poor house. We waited for news. After a brief time, a messenger arrived with a warm coat for the rabbi, along with the advice to not remain there, but rather to proceed in the direction of Jablonka. The messenger told us that they were capturing Jews in Turka, especially men, and bringing them to the prison in the police yard.

Mr. Feiler and I were very worried about our families, so we decided to return to Turka. My wife Helena Hamermash (nee Rosenberg) was in her final months of pregnancy. Along the way, a wagon appeared before us, with uniformed Germans inside. We succeeded in jumping into a sewer at the last moment, and they did not see us... We were saved by a miracle.

We arrived home with great difficulty. In the meantime, the matter was clarified completely: Jews were brought to the police station and were beaten with deathly blows. Mr. Feiler decided to hide in a certain pit that had been somewhat cleaned, and I remained with my wife.

We were awake all night. We were not daring enough to put on a light. Around, there were screams and wails. In the morning, we found out the details: at night, they continued to capture Jews and take them to the police. Then, we saw the police approaching the house of A. Fieler, on the street that leads to the railway station. Without giving any thought, Leib Feiler, his brother-in-law, Rozen's daughter and I jumped into the cellar. My wife managed to toss something onto the entrance of the cellar so that they would not see its cracks... Suddenly, there were screams above us... Our blood froze in our veins. What happened there? Perhaps they kicked my wife's stomach or captured people from the Feiler or Pikholtz families. We waited and waited... After approximately a half an hour, they took us out of the cellar. We found out that they had been searching for me and Mr. Feiler. They needed us to fill the Gestapo quota... My wife said that the doctor (referring to me) went to a sick patient, and Leib went to work. Having no other choice, they took the old woman, Mrs. Pikholtz, a semi-paralyzed woman. The screams were from her. They also took the daughter of Rabbi Youlis. Mr. Breuer, a member of the *Judenrat*, came to us secretly and told us that the quota had already been filled. There is already a surplus...

[Page 276]

Suddenly, we saw a passing truck filled with naked people covered only with a tarpaulin. It was headed toward Jablonka. Toward evening we already found out that the captured people had been taken to the brick kiln on the route to Jablonka, where a pit had been prepared. The people were killed with volleys of shots and covered with pitch. The earth was still quaking on top of them... Two people were saved by entering the brick kiln: Mr. Chechkes and Mrs. 4.

*

My wife went into labor. We were faced with the choice of giving birth at home with the possibility of complications or going to the hospital. Toward morning on January 9, 1942, we set out in the direction of the hospital... Along the way, we found German soldiers who displayed indifference because they had too much "work," and they allowed us to pass. Toward evening, a son was born to us.

In the meantime, the tally of the *aktion* became known: 800 Jews, from among the most honorable, had been buried in the pit. A sign was placed atop the mass grave: "Here are found the Communists from the city of Turka." Indeed, a completed job.

*

This was only the beginning. Life continued on somehow. The poverty increased, and there was no bread. The *Judenrat* faced massive and increasing demands from the Germans.... People died sitting down, lying down, or standing... The dead were fortunate - for them, everything was finished.

It was the summer of 1942, a Sunday in July. The infirmary ("Jewish Polyclinic") in which I worked was located in the house of Nachman Meiner next to the *Judenrat*, close to the cemetery.

[Page 277]

There were rumors once again. As usual, the *Judenrat* did not know any details. In the meantime, our comrade Dr. Philip Schechter of Krakow, a refugee like me, died. We concerned ourselves with arranging the burial and waited for the wagon with the deceased.

It was 10:00 a.m. I set out for the main street. A child said to me, "Doctor, do not go - they are capturing Jews, the Gestapo is in the city!" If a child speaks, one must listen! I returned to the infirmary. A wagon appeared with a coffin and the deceased, but without a wagon driver. The wagon driver had been captured by the Gestapo along the way... Next to the wagon was Mrs. Schechter, wearing black. She was not dressed as a Jewess... Everyone escaped, and there was nobody to take care of the burial. The only one who volunteered to do so was Yisrael Avraham Kraus. He arranged everything, including the preparation of the body, the preparation of shrouds, the digging of the grave, and the arranging of the burial in accordance with law and custom.

The cemetery was located on a hill. From atop the hill, one could see frightful panoramas as if on the palm of the hand: Jews were being loaded onto trucks. There was fear and trembling. I somehow managed to reach home along the path near the river, and between the alleyways. I found my wife filled with worry and concern.

*

Continuing...

At the end of July, I was sent to Wysocko to inoculate Jewish children against smallpox... The Germans were concerned about the health of the Jewish children... However, it quickly became clear that this was merely a cover for the next *aktion*, which was not long in coming...

It was the beginning of August 1942. All the Jews of Turka and the area were being gathered in an area near the sawmill. Rumors were circulating that only Jews who possessed a work certificate for some enterprise would be saved this time. The gentiles took advantage of the situation and sold work certificates in exchange for large sums of money. Only very few people had the money...

It was the morning of August 5. My neighbors awakened me, "Doctor, they are capturing Jews!" They were being taken in the direction of the railway station that was near our house. My wife's parents were also in our house, hiding in a camouflaged room. I went out to the main street to find out what was happening. The gendarme commander noticed me from afar and shouted, "Halt!" Shots began. I managed to arrive home through a side route. At that time, I was living with a gentile. He placed a cross on the window and answered to any gendarme that was passing by, "Ukrainians live here." This saved me that time. The next time, the gentile was not prepared to endanger himself anymore. We sat and waited in silence.

[Page 278]

We no longer dared to burn fire in the oven to cook food for the baby. In our house, there was another child whom we had gathered from the street. There were shots and screams in the area. My father-in-law hid in the garden; my mother-in-law and sisters-in-law in the cellar. Suddenly there was screaming. They took out my mother in-law and her daughters from the cellar... They were taking them in the direction of the train...

It was evening. The screams died down. I went out to verify the situation. Suddenly, the well-known Ukrainian slanderer Matkovski appeared between the rows of houses on Cokrowa Street accompanied by a German soldier. I began to give an excuse why my family and I did not go to the *aktion*. The German soldier was weary of blood and atrocities, but Matkovski pressured him - and they went toward my house. My wife managed to jump out the window. The baby was in the cradle. The slaughterer took out a revolver and was about to shoot him. With the aid of a gold watch, I convinced him with difficulty to not do so, and I promised to present myself with my wife and child at the next *aktion*...

*

Aside from the quarry workers, a handful of Jews remained in the town to perform the cleanup work after the *aktion*. I had to concern myself with bread and a work permit. My wife and the baby were hiding in the cellar - they no longer had the right to exist... I received a work permit as the physician of the quarry. However, at the first opportunity, a young priest from Jablonka approached me and warned me that the entire new order was nothing more than a blindfold, and that I must make efforts to escape to Hungary.

Easy to say, but hard to carry out...

Sianki

[Page 279]

A Young Man in a Nazi Work Camp

-- A Record of Events

by Shalom Braier, Bat Yam

Shalom Braier

The Camp

It was in the Kostopol[1] Camp. The entrance to the camp was on a side street on the eastern side of the city, and was accessed through a short alleyway. The building of the Ukrainian police was on one side of the alleyway, and the building of the German military command on the other side. The central building of the camp was large, with four stories and three entrances. A river flowed on both sides of the building, and there was a sparse forest on the other side of the river. On the south side of the building, there was a concrete fence, with a four meter high wire fence on top. On the north side, however, there was a regular wooden fence, connected with the field latrines, which border on a tall cliff. The railway tracks were located on the other side of this fence, at a distance of 8-10 meters. They cross the river over a tall bridge. On the other side of the tracks there was a large wheat field, beyond which was the road that leads to Janowa and Dolina.

People and Their Work

Jews from near and far were concentrated into the camp. There were Jews such as me whom the Germans captured in Volhyn, to where they had been brought previously by the Russians. There were Jews from the area: from Berezany, Stepan, Kostopol, and even from Rowno. However, there were also Jews from Warsaw who had escaped to Russia and were captured by the Germans as they attempted to return to their homes...

Most of the people of the camp were middle aged. There were few youths. We were divided daily into work groups, in accordance with the needs of the various German divisions. There were certain permanent work divisions, such as the group that worked at loading blocks of wood at the railway station.

[Page 280]

These blocks were 15 meters long and used for building bridges. This group was guarded by 15 Germans. Another group worked for Reichskommissar Ginter, may his name be blotted out, building a pool for his wife who was about to arrive in the district. The luck of the people of this group was poor. A spring flowed out from the place designated from the pool. They had to draw the water away and pave the area with the gravestones from the Jewish cemetery. There were various other groups.

I was not interested in any special type of work. My sole desire was to work together with my father of blessed memory, who was also in the camp. I worked for a time for Ginter, where one workday seemed like an entire month.

At 6:00 a.m. we received a cup of "coffee." We then arranged ourselves for roll call, from where the Jewish guards would take us to our work places. There, we were received by the Ukrainian or German guards who were responsible for us. After various attempts, I succeeded in joining the group in which my father worked, numbering 40 "Juden". We worked for a German engineering group. The command language for issuing work orders was... shots above our heads. The work, which was carried out with incessant fear, was loading large wooden boards at the Mokvyn train station to be sent to the front.

One rainy day as I was loading the wood, I could not reach the appropriate height. My hand let go of the board, and I began to return to my place. I suddenly heard the German shout "*Achtung*" (a warning call). The board was also too much for the other weakened Jews, and it began to tumble downward. I was not able to escape, but I was able to jump high at the last moment. The board passed beneath me and I remained alive...

At that moment, the angry German foreman appeared before me. I generally wanted to avoid his attention for an entirely different reason: I had once worked at an entirely different place under his supervision as a "Ukrainian" lad. At the urging of my father, the Ukrainian foreman agreed to take me on as a wagon driver at the work place, where I excelled greatly. At this point, I did not want him to recognize at my present work place...

The German came to me... "Are you a Jew?" he asked with great astonishment, "are you not the good wagon driver... Why did you not tell me previously that you were a Jew?..." I took my life in my hands and answered, "Had you known the truth, you would have killed me a long time ago, when the person in charge of the forest first met me." His answer was not long in coming, "Right, you are correct..."

[Page 281]

Why We Did Not Rebel...

Incidentally. I will not rehash everything that happened to me when I worked with the aforementioned forest supervisor, on my expertise as a wagon driver, on my ability to hitch up and take control over wild horses that had never previously been harnessed. I served as a translator between the Germans and the Ukrainians. An incident took place to me there that will allow me to answer and explain the eternal question: "Why did we not rise up against the Germans and go as sheep to the slaughter?" This is what took place: One evening, I approached a Ukrainian village with a German. The German turned to the head of the group, responsible for ten people, telling them that they must go out to cut down trees. I translated their words. The head of the division responded, "We do not have any time now, for we are busy tilling our soil." The German response was a volley of machine gun fire that pulverized the Ukrainian. There were about 50-60 gentiles around us, and I began to tremble with fear. I searched for a way to escape. However, the entire crowd did not move – they were afraid to touch a German...

Exceptional Germans

There were German work directors who related to us properly and with secret appreciation. Aside from the aforementioned German who asked me why I did not tell him that I was a Jew, and who later frequently related to me at various opportunities with mercy, and who even scolded others who behaved cruelly to me; there was another German there, called Kurt, who even told us that we would be soon taken out to be killed. We did not believe him... He offered us weapons and advised us to flee. Even during the work he did not shoot over our heads, but did show himself as shouting at us...

A small amount of weapons were smuggled into the camp. I did not know all the details, for I was a "minor". These weapons were given to my father and Yaakov Lerer, for we all wanted to take a stand and believed that we may be able to pass through the times in peace – "for the Germans need us to work for them..." We received a daily ration of 1½ kilograms of bread for eight people, and water without restriction... We waited for salvation. However, that is not how things worked out.

Signs of Bad Tidings

This took place in the month of Elul, 1942. We returned in a group from harvesting in the large plains. My father, who was known as an excellent worker, was there. He was revered for this by the gentile work directors to the point that they gave us permission to go to the nearby village to seek food. When we returned in the evening, we saw many S.S. men on the road leading to the ghetto and the camp. I turned to my father, "I do not like this; they have come to liquidate us." My father, as was usual under such circumstances, was silent and did not answer. "Stand – Who are you?!" The Judenrat guard who was accompanying the S.S. responded, "They are returning to the camp after work." They asked us a few questions and allowed us to pass.

[Page 282]

When we arrived at the camp kitchen, I sensed the electric atmosphere. We recognized signs of bad tidings. This started in the kitchen, which gave us a relatively good soup that time, containing 6-8 broad noodles, and continued with the continuous arranging of people. Everything hinted to tension. Then the head of the Judenrat appeared and said, "Do not heed the rumors, for I am promising you peace and quiet. Not one hair of your head will be harmed." Nobody believed him. We were arranged in rows of three, and we set out to the other side of the camp, located on the other side of the city. As we passed through the main road, I noticed many strange glances from the windows of the houses, some of pity and others of curiosity. Everything foreshadowed the end. My heart told me that I must escape immediately.

Death From the Windows

We entered the camp, where other Jews who had retuned earlier were waiting for us. They asked us about the situation – but who was able to give an answer? We felt only that our end was approaching. We could feel it with our hands...

I then clearly saw how they are placing us into a long, wide grave with steps that lead to the World of Truth. I very much did not want to go there before at least bidding farewell to my mother... And behold, my mother was informed of my death, and I saw in my imagination how she was weeping over our bitter fate...

Night fell in the camp and I lay down. I was awake and not sleeping. Then I saw that my Father was speaking with Chaim Gross and Yaakov Lerer of Rarnowa, as well as with Itzi the brave man, one of the refugees from Warsaw, his friend Martin the eternal pessimist, and several other of his friends. I got up, approached Father and told him, sort of quietly and sort of loudly, "Come, let us cross the river and sleep in the forest. If it is quiet here at night, we will return to the camp early in the morning." As I was speaking, a delegation of two Jewish policemen appeared. They turned directly to Father: "Mr. Braier, the Jewish police requests that you do not foment revolt among the community. It will be quiet, and there must be quiet, because if anyone is missing from the night roll call, other innocent people will be killed on your account..."

[Page 283]

The words were spoken with simplicity, and of course, they influenced my father to refrain from escaping. I did not want to move without him. I entered our sleeping quarters, which contained 50-60 two story beds, and I lay down. I did not remove my shoes. I only tied the laces around them, so I could remove them quickly if I needed to grab hold of a tree, or for some other reason. At 9:00 or 10:00 p.m., I heard the voice of Shlomo Katz, "I hear German commands from the ghetto. I smell the odor of burning!" I jumped quickly outside through the window. People were running outside, but complete silence pervaded. I once again met my father and once again urged him that we should escape. However, he stood his own, "We are not escaping now."

"Jews, We Are Being Destroyed!..."

We returned to the building. I calmed down a bit, and apparently a light sleep overtook me. Then I heard the voice of Martin, "Jews, we are surrounded, Jews we are being destroyed." I attempted to jump out of the window as before, but a shot awaited me... It was the same at the second window... Ukrainians began to break in and chase people outside... I jumped into the heating chimney and from there I heard that my father had already been chased out. I decided to join him and be killed together with him. When I exited the corridor, I saw that they were beating people with rubber batons, so I decided to flee to the cellar. There, I noticed that 8 – 10 people had already preceded me. As they were objecting to my joining them lest they be revealed because of me, a Ukrainian guard came down the cellar, and lit it up by setting a flea-infested mattress on fire. However, one of the group jumped upon him with an iron bar that had been there, apparently, from the time of the Polish army. The guard remained there... I ran through another room, and with great difficulty, I reached a ground-level window. I went outside and joined the entire crowd. I decided to shout loudly, "Father, Father!" until someone told me that he had seen him in the other side of the crowd in the camp. I could not reach him due to the large volleys of cross-fire that were being shot by the Germans from all sides of the crowd, so that they would not escape. The noise and shouting was great. Jews were running around without pants or anything to cover their nakedness. I shouted incessantly, "Jews, escape!" Then someone lifted me and threw me behind – my father! I fell upon his neck and we kissed farewell kisses. My father held me with his hands between the other friends who were all holding hands. I saw Yitzchak, one of the refugees from Warsaw, Yaakov Lerer, Chaim Gross, Meir Fuchs, and Shalom Katz next to me.

[Page 284]

The S.S. men were around us. I saw very clearly that the commander of the operation was short, armed with a revolver and a rubber baton, wearing a high hat with a visor, riding pants and shiny boots. He then began to speak to us, "Since the automobiles that went out to pursue the Russian paratroopers in the Lodopol district got stuck in the mud, we must extricate them at any price... I am hereby issuing an order to arrange yourselves in threes, and anyone who does not listen to the order will be shot like a dog! One, two, th..."

However, the three was not completed quietly. My father, who had spoken to his friends before this, began to shout "Hura, Hura!" with the entire group. I lost sight of him within a moment. Everyone began to run and escape. The machine guns began to operate, and Jewish blood flowed from all corners. I could not move, for I was in the middle of the crowd. I did not see my father. Only the shouts of Hura still echoed in my ears. I jumped over a fence and fell atop the body of Chaim Gross, who had just been hit by a bullet. From there I could see clearly how the Germans were chasing after the escapees and pursuing them from the right and left. Many were wallowing in their blood, and many continued to escape through the volleys of fire emanating from the machine guns. As I was lying on the ground, I wanted to approach the well, to jump inside, and wait until the wrath would pass. I stood up, and a tall German shot in my direction with his revolver. I fell, and the German approached and kicked my right side. I turned over and stared at him with alert eyes. Apparently, he took me for dead and abandoned me, as he ran toward another group of escapees.

*

During my wanderings after my escape I found out that my father of blessed memory was not killed during that revolt. Later, he killed the commander of the aktion, and captured his gun and hat. His friends also displayed bravery, allowing many people to escape, a few of whom succeeded in surviving and reaching the liberation.

Translator's Footnote:

13. See http://en.wikipedia.org/wiki/Kostopil where the story in this article is transcribed in brief.

[Page 285]

Inhuman Suffering and Horrors

by David Schwartz of Ramat Gan

On June 21, 1941, the Hitlerist gangs attacked Russia. The Red Army retreated from our area in great disarray. The Jews remained helpless. A very small group of the youths went along with the Red Army. The confusion was great. There was no time to decide.

When they left Turka, the Russians left behind two soldiers to preserve order in the city. Soon, the Ukrainians began to act like they were in charge. Of course, their first task was to rob and beat Jews.

The Ukrainians shot one of the remaining soldiers. They took Jewish men and women and ordered them to take the corpse to the Jewish cemetery and bury him there. The men and women were forced to kiss the corpse and sing proletariat songs. Two days later, the Germans entered the city. I do not have the ability to describe what our brothers and sisters endured during those times, other than describing a few incidents that are etched in my memory.

*

The first time that they took men and women to work, they barely gave them anything to eat. A worker received 180 grams of bread a day. Furthermore, the work was very difficult. A few weeks later, the Germans issued an order that the Jews must give over their gold, silver, jewels and diamonds to the German authorities. The edict included the threat that any Jew who was found with would be shot on the spot. The Jews gave over everything that they owned. The Germans went around with bloodhounds that dragged away any item that still had some value.

[Page 286]

One day, the Ukrainians and Germans found hidden pictures of the Soviet leader. They gathered the Jews together and ordered them to carry the pictures; this was a sort of procession to the Jewish cemetery. The Jews were forced to sing and endure terrible blows throughout the entire way. Then, they buried the pictures. The Germans ordered the Jews to dig graves for themselves. There were 300 Jews in the cemetery at that time, and the murderers prepared to kill them. Miraculously, this did not happen... suddenly, the commandant of the city, who was a German Austrian, appeared and ordered that the Jews be set free. That time, they were saved, but not for long.

*

An order was issued that the Jews must turn over all fur garments in their possession to the Germans. They Jews gave everything over. They remained naked, hungry, and broken. However, our martyrs always hoped for a miracle. Nobody knew when their tragic end would be at hand.

On January 4, 1942, Gestapo men with Ukrainian assistants appeared in Turka. They began to capture men, women, and children. They gathered together about 800 people and imprisoned them in several points in the city. They beat them terribly. The Jews who were still free turned to the *Judenrat* to ask them to try to ransom the Jews. The Germans promised to free the unfortunate people. They gave over to them the last things that were found in the Jewish homes. The Germans took everything, but they tossed the Jews onto transport trucks, as if they were tossing lumber. They seated Ukrainians atop the victims who sang in loud voices so that they would not hear the crying and shouting of the Jews. The wild murderers took our tormented brothers and sisters to a place behind the city, where they had prepared mass graves. They shot them all, or tossed them live into the graves.

[Page 287]

Out of the 800 people, one woman survived. She related how the people were murdered.

The Jews who were still living in Turka at that time suffered from debilitating hunger. They no longer possessed anything. The Germans had stolen everything from the Jews. They had to give over their last shirt for a potato or a bit of flour. At that time, the Germans issued an edict: If they catch a farmer selling provisions to a Jew, he would be shot immediately along with the Jews.

Jews swelled up from huger and died en masse. The holy, weary souls departed. Those who still survived were jealous of them... Fifteen to 25 Jews died a day, aside from those in the villages around Turka. The Jews who died at that time were unable to be brought to a Jewish burial, for the Jews were forbidden from traveling from one place to another. A Jew was not permitted to go out on the street other than on specific hours of the day. If a Jew was seen on the street, he would be shot on the spot. Every Jew had to wear the badge of shame. If a Jew was found without that badge, even close to his house, he would be shot immediately. It is hard to believe today that a person could survive all this.

*

The most terrible thing came: on August 1, 1942, the Germans ordered all the Jew of the province to gather in Turka. They were ordered to set up a ghetto there. In the meantime, the Ukrainians organized the farmers in every village, so that they would not let the Jews out of their houses, until they were loaded upon wagons under a guard and hauled to Turka. The entire city was surrounded by the Nazi murderers. Trains were prepared. They loaded all the Jews and sent them to Belzec. There, they were all murdered. Several Jews succeeded in surviving at that time. Their fate was no better, however. Later, they were all tragically murdered.

[Page 288]

The Children's Aktion in Turka

By Chaim Pelech

The children's aktion that the Nazi German beasts perpetrated in Turka was cruel in the full sense of the word. The bizarre grabbing of children from the streets, homes and hiding places was so sly as to be unparalleled.

The murderers rode around on automobiles and snatched the children as they were playing. They tossed them into the autos as if they were stones and beat their heads. One automobile drove from the Lakicz and found children playing near Aharon Leib Weicher's house. They snatched Shua Ajchenbaum's girl by the legs and tossed her into the auto. An outcry arose, and the child's mother came out running, and wanted to take back her girl. The Germans shot the mother on the spot. The grandmother, the mother's mother came out and began to shout, “Murderers, why did you shoot my daughter?!” They shot the grandmother. The outcry and panic on the street were indescribable. Fear enveloped the entire town. The despair of the mothers and fathers reached the highest degree.

At the same time, the German police and their assistants went from house to house. They snatched the children who were hiding in the houses and drove them to a designated place where they shot them.

A young woman, Esther Weiss, the daughter of Avraham Weiss, went to the Olica near Avrahamche Langenauer's place, with her child in her hand. Two S. S. men approached and violently ripped the child from her hands. She held her child tight, and did not let him be taken from her hand. The S. S. men shot the mother, grabbed him by the legs, banged his head against the wall, and tossed him dead onto the sidewalk...

When I was in Sambor in 1945, a Jew from Turka told me a shuddering story that took place in his home during the children's aktion. They drove Chaim Feiler, the son of Shlomo Feiler the butcher, to the designated place. The child cried and sobbed so strongly that it would rend the hearts of sticks. As they were going through the Olica, the boy threw himself onto the earth and screamed: "I do not want to go, you are going to shoot me. I want to live. I don't want you to shoot me. I do not want to go. Let me be. I want to flee to my hiding place..."

The man related further: "This went on for a long time until they calmed the child. Then he was taken weeping to the designated place, where they immediately shot him..."

I sat on the bench as I heard this. I felt as if my body was burning on fire, and I felt as if I myself had been hauled out of that house. I ran through the streets of Sambor as if I had been poisoned. I was broken and wounded.

My only child Avrahamele was shot during that same aktion...

The main street (Legjonow) The "Olica"

[Page 290]

Bloody Episodes

Told by David Binder

A. Chava

We were about 150 Jews of Turka working in the Blic quarry at that time. During one of the last large *aktions*, they took us too from work and placed us the transport wagons to be dispatched to the camps. Before that, we again had to stand at roll call, as was fitting for the Germans, as they incited a large hunting dog against us. Blic's wife was also killed during that roll call.

In one of the wagons I met my sister, who had been captured in the *aktion* and hauled here. She was very worried and told me that she had been captured as she left her house to arrange some matter. Before she went out, she placed her daughter Chava into a hiding place and locked her from the outside. Now, when they are taking her to the death camp, what would be with Chava?... She will suffocate there!

In the meantime, it became clear that more people were captured than were required by the quota. The director of the quarry appeared immediately and brought back from the wagons many Jews who were workers at the quarry. I was among them.

Parting from my sister was distressing. It was the parting of a brother and sister sentenced to death - one of them on an earlier date and the other a bit later... When I left the wagon, I immediately began to think about freeing Chava from her prison. Somehow, I succeeded in getting to my sister's house and freeing her, but my sister, of course, was not able to know that her daughter had been saved...

However, with this, the Chava's adventures had not ended. Difficult days lay ahead for her.

Her father and other Jews of Turka were sitting in a bunker that had been dug for them in Simunka. A gentile informed on them to the Germans for a kilo of sugar and a liter of vodka. The Germans arrived, but during the liquidation and the killing, Chava, who had also been in the bunker disappeared. She arrived barefoot and tattered to some farmer at the edge of the village, and remained there. I found out about this when I was already wandering in the forests of the area, along with other Jews of Turka. I immediately offered her assistance and food. Chava survived... She succeeded in making *aliya* to the Land of Israel after the liberation.

[Page 291]

B. Parents Kill their Children

When we, the last Jewish workers of the quarry, realized that our hope of remaining alive was in vain, we decided to go out to the forests. We found a place for a bunker behind the Jawoda sawmill. However, after our first attempt, we found that it was not all that fitting. We still worked in the quarry while six of our people dug the bunker. Every evening, about 20 of us transferred wheat and food to prepare for life in the bunker.

Among us was a certain family from Turka who also wanted to go to the forest. However, they had a three year old daughter... At first, they gave her over to a gentile, but for some reason, the gentile quickly returned her. The decision of the parents was frightful: With the active assistance of a friend of the family, they suffocated the girl! It happened that in the first German attack on our bunker to which we fled, after Turka had been declared *Judenrein*, this third friend was the first to be killed...

C. In the Forests of Opolinik

Life in the forests was difficult and unbearable. Having no other choice, we lived from robbery. We would attack farmers who collaborated with the Germans - and thus we succeeded in surviving as our numbers continually dwindled...

Once, we were told about such a collaborator in a certain village. We attacked him and stole everything that we could: property and clothing. After some time we found out that we had made an error in the address: this had been a gentile that was good to the Jews. Mendel Zeifert and his wife were hiding there. We then gathered together all of the items that we had stolen, including those that we had already distributed to some people, and returned them to the gentile. On that opportunity, we also met the Zeifert family there, and the joy was very great.

*

The Germans and their collaborators gave us no rest. We were frequently hunted. Once, the Germans attacked us. The person on guard kept the Germans at bay for a long time. He paid with his life, but it was possible for the entire group to escape and disperse.

[Page 292]

Two daughters of the Weicher family, one eight and the other ten, were in the group. One of the girls did not have enough time to put something on her feet, and she ran barefoot in the snow and ice for an entire day. The girl got sick, and the pains in her feet were unbearable. We decided to go to the village and place her in one of the houses until she would recover. We knocked on one of the houses, and found an elderly woman there. We commanded her: "Behold, the girl is sick. Her feet froze. We are leaving her with you and you must do everything you can to cure her. After a short time, we will return to fetch her..."

Ten days later, we went to check on her. We were five people, including her uncle Anshel Weicher. The woman told us that despite all her efforts, she did not succeed in curing her. If we have god in our hearts, we must kill the girl, for her suffering is unbearable.

We answered her that we must consult with the entire group in the forest. The "forest" decided to kill the girl. The five aforementioned people were designated to carry out the act. Several days later, we returned to the woman in the village, and saw a miracle - the sick girl had recovered! A few weeks later, the girl returned to the forest.

*

In 1949, five years after the liberation, I visited my friend in the city of Wroclaw in Poland. When I entered his place of business, I saw a young girl who smiled at me and did not stop. I asked her, "Who are you?" She responded, "The girl who was sentenced to death..." She was already 17 years old.

[Page 293]

The Escape from the Open Grave

by Moshe Hager and Genia Liberman of Netanya

This was the second year that we were hiding in a bunker in the Sianki Forest near Turka. A gentile who had been a childhood friend brought us potatoes and a piece of barley bread twice a week.

One day the gentile, may he be remembered in a positive way, appeared and told us that a cross-border smuggler came to him and asked if he knows of any hidden Jews who are interested in crossing the border to Hungary - in exchange for a proper fee, of course.

W agreed to take a risk, and we went with the smuggler through the forests for eight days until we came to the city of Uzhgorod on the Hungarian border. This was the eve of Rosh Hashanah. A Hungarian Jew agreed to take us by train to Budapest in return for a payment. We did not know the language of the country, and they were searching for refugees along the way.

A search was conducted by the Hungarian police along the way, and we were caught without documents. We were removed from the train and returned to the Polish border, where we were given over to the Gestapo in

Sianki. There were 19 other Jews with us who had been caught on that train. All were later shot by the iniquitous hand.

The Germans imprisoned us in a cellar and sent for the Ukrainians to dig a communal grave for us. Indeed, fate mocked us, for that same Ukrainian had worked in the fields of my father Yosef Heger. Now he was digging a grave for us with a faithful hand.

They brought us to the grave toward evening. This was on the first day of Rosh Hashanah. We all stood in a line around the grave, and our hearts were heavy: was this our Day of Judgment? The judgment against us was so harsh - and we were still so young... We were ordered to strip down to our shirts, and we were placed in a line. By chance, we were standing at the end of the line, and each of us was saying to the next one that he wanted to die first, so that he would not see the death of the other. However, as quick as lightning, we decided - to escape! Not in order to save ourselves and survive - for we did not hope for this - but rather to take the bullet from the back, without waiting for it with alert eyes, without seeing how we would be shot and fall.

[Page 294]

We decided to run, each of us in a different direction. The destination was the forest, which was very close. We heard shots from behind. We heard the blood-curdling sound of dogs sent after us: to be torn apart by hunting dogs was worse than being shot with a bullet!

The forest drew nearer. We reached it and continued to run. The Germans were afraid of entering the forest out of fear of hidden partisans. Then a miracle occurred! It cannot be believed if we tell it - the barking of the dogs stopped. Perhaps they lost our trace. In any case, this remains a puzzle for us to this day.

We continued to run without knowing to where. Fear quieted any thought. Thus did we wander about the forest for a week, hungry and thirsty, wandering without a path or a road. Our sole objective was to reach the gentile who had at one time dug the bunker for us.

This was the month of September, as has been noted. The cold froze our bones, but we continued to survive. It is difficult to explain this with logic. We reached the home of the gentile on the eighth day. He was very afraid to take us in, for news of our escape had echoed throughout the entire region. Searches for us were being conducted with great diligence.

The gentile gave us digging tools, and we dug a new bunker in the forest with our meager energy. There, we sat hungry and frozen until the Russians liberated us.

*

After tribulations and wandering, we succeeded in reaching resting place and inheritance. We arrived in Israel on the eve of the War of Independence. How great was our joy when we found our four-year-old daughter, whom we had sent to Hungary!

A son was born to us who bore the name of his grandfather. Who would have imagined that we would yet merit to play with his pleasant grandchild on our laps!

Indeed, many are the thoughts in the heart of man, but the desires of G-d will be fulfilled!

[Page 295]

We Were Refugees in Soviet Russia

by Michael Heisler

The War Began

It was the autumn of 1939. The small war between Poland and Germany, lasting a few days in total, spread throughout the entire land, and to our small corner as well. At that time, I was living temporarily in Turka. Young people, Jews and gentiles, quickly took leave of their families and went to their military posts. Many never returned. I was one of the lucky ones who had a blue military slip and who did not have to enlist in the military. I remained at home.

The first bombardment caused a panic in the town. The shops quickly hid their merchandise in the cellars and there was a shortage of food. The Jewish youth in the city organized a self-defense organization to protect against the eventual attack of Ukrainian nationalists. Some Jews, I and my family among them, fled to relatives and friends in the neighboring villages. There, the panic was no less than in the city... The gentiles had already begun to gnash their teeth and sharpen their knives for the Jews. It seemed like the Germans would come in slowly but surely and slaughter us all. The hours were numbered, and the tension grew.

Russians!...

Great was the joy when, instead of the Germans, the first patrols of the Soviet Army were seen... Jews calmed down and began anew to live and work. There were indeed a few unacceptable deeds perpetrated by the Soviets, such as deporting people to Siberia and nationalizing businesses - but this was quickly finished. Great tragedies did not take place in our region. It was the opposite, the Soviets related better to the Jews than to the gentiles, and placed greater trust in them.

[Page 296]

However, people had predictions that this was only temporary, and that it would not remain this way. Something gave them a bad felling that something would take place, and it would be bad.

We also used to receive news from the Jewish refugees who had already fled from the Germans. They all gave testimony that the time of a greater catastrophe was nearing. Even the Soviets themselves believed that a war with the Germans was inevitable, and was approaching with quick steps. They acted upon this with deeds, such as building fortresses and bunkers.

A few days before the German-Soviet conflict, the Soviets mobilized all of the Jewish youth to military service. The elderly, women, and children were almost all that remained. This time as well, as before, I had luck and I was not mobilized. At that time, I was on a mission to Lemberg.

The German-Soviet Conflict

On June 22, 1941, the day of the German assault on the Soviets, I was caught in Lemberg. I can never forget that day. I will never forget the terrorized faces of the helpless women, as they were running through the Lemberg streets with their children, not knowing what to do. I understood that everything was hopeless - there was no means of salvation. I felt a longing for my wife and children. My conscience bothered me greatly: why did I leave them all alone. I decided to reunite with them at any price.

I Go Home By Foot

I barely stopped at the destroyed railway station. I quickly turned in the direction of Sambor, and set out by foot. A stone was lifted from my heart - I was going home and I would see them soon. I wanted to fight the Germans; I wanted to slaughter them, tear them, bite them. I would not let my children be killed! I was speaking to myself, asking questions and answering them myself...

[Page 297]

Thus did I go the entire way, which lasted for three days and three nights, until I arrived at the Turka Mountain, on the way to Jawor, right near the Turka cemetery. From there, I saw all of Turka. It broke my heart - for I knew very well the misfortune that lay ahead for the poor town. I was greatly comforted that I was already in the town, and from there, it was a few kilometers to my home village. I had a strong desire to turn aside, here in the cemetery, to my mother, who had been laying here for a few decades already. I was here, and I wanted to pay my respects, perhaps for the last time.

I knew the way very well, and fell onto the grave, weeping. I told her everything, speaking from my heart - about the great danger that was hanging over us, about my children and my wife, who was already in her final months of pregnancy with our third child. Everything, everything I told her, as if she was standing before me alive...

I could barely go through the streets of the city. They were full of Soviet soldiers with tanks and cannons. Jews were running to and fro in a disorderly fashion, afraid and desperate, not knowing what to do. I did not stop or talk to anyone. Along the way, I met a few local Ukrainians. I greeted them and asked them what was happening in the village. They did not answer me, but rather smiled from under their visors and waved their finger over their neck, making the sign of a slaughterer slaughtering...

To Escape or to Remain?...

It was not long before I reached my home. The children were very happy to see me. My wife was pale and sorrowful. I understood her sadness very well: A pregnant woman at that time had what to be sad about. I calmed her.

[Page 298]

"I knew that you would come back, that you would not leave us alone and helpless," she said to me. "Look here," she pointed with her finger, "I have already packed some items and some food to take with us on the journey. I was only waiting for you."

"What do you mean?" I asked her with curiosity.

"I mean, that we must escape from her quickly," she said. "Have you not heard what my sister said when she escaped her from Krakow, barely with her life? Have you not heard what the Germans are doing with the Jews?! I do not want to wait willingly for death; if death wishes to claim us as victims, it will not be so easy, it will have to torment us, to pursue us..."

"We will travel to another village, to my brother - I said. There, the Ukrainians are a bit better than here, more friendly. They lived well with my parents and my brothers for so many years. There, we even had partnerships in fields with them. You will see that they will receive us well."

"Do not trust the haters!" she said. They are awaiting the moment when the Germans will arrive. Then, they will finish up with the Jews and steal their belongings."

The door opened and my wife's sister entered. She was an unmarried girl. I heard their debate - she turned to me and said -"If you would have seen what my eyes have seen, what the Germans have done with the Jews of Krakow, you would not tarry for one moment. Go rest a bit, for you must be tired from the journey. Do not worry, I am also going with you, and we three adults will not fail!"

In he meantime, my wife went out to all the neighbors and told them to escape.

"Where should we escape," they shrugged their shoulders. "They will go through quickly. Fool, you do not remember, a year and a half ago how great the fear was when the Germans were about to enter? - And there was peace. Aside from the few people who were killed in Turka under Petrikov, no more bad things took place. In the same way, it will be peaceful again. The Germans intend only for the Communists - what do they have to do with us?..."

[Page 299]

In the meantime, I woke up from my sleep, and saw how people were gathering and setting out on the way outside. On the road, I meant a Russian officer whom I knew. I asked him what was going on. "Not good," he answered. "We are retreating from the entire region with all the Russian officers. We are setting out very early tomorrow morning..." He told me this last piece of information as a secret, so that nobody would hear...

I barely slept the entire night. I prepared the wagon, made a booth like the Gypsies, and hitched up the horses. In the meantime, my wife and her sister prepared the children and loaded the packages. Not far from my house I saw a few young Ukrainians whispering to each other. They were already waiting, like dogs, to bite...

We Escape...

We set out. Along the way, we joined up with the entire company of Soviet officers and teachers. Several other Jewish families joined us, including Leib Teichman of Nyszny Wysocko, Yosef Shindler of Jablonow, the two brothers-in-law Berl Heger and Yaakov Feldman - all with their families. There also was Avrahamche Feljor of Nyszny Wysocko and his sister, Shmuel Zisha Furmans and his two children: all with horses and wagons. These were the few families of the entire Turka region who succeeded in escaping at the lat minute. Everyone else remained behind.

We really did not know where we were going, but we traveled in the direction of all the travelers. Tanks, cannons, various military formations and civilians were also traveling. The way was full of debris. This was not a normal journey, but rather a haunted journey. We were very chagrined... Indeed, we were civilians fleeing - but we were unprotected people with wives and children on the wagons. However, they?! The mighty Russian Army?! Where is their honor, are they not ashamed?!...

[Page 300]

Our group, particularly the Jews, stuck together and took care of each other so that nobody would be left behind on the way. If something broke in somebody's wagon, everyone would help fix it, and then we would continue on. We rested during the day and traveled on at night. My wife traveled the entire way as a woman of valor. She never complained. She took care of the children, and from time to time, she let me rest a bit and drove the horses herself.

In Russia

We traveled in this manner for approximately four weeks, until we reached the old Russian border at the Zbrucz River. When we were on Russian territory, the Soviets pointed everyone in their direction to their homes, but we Jews remained alone without a leader... After a brief conference, we decided to abandon the horses and wagons, and continue on the journey by train.

When I unloaded my packages and children from the wagon, I noted a heavy package that I had not yet seen. My wife had taken along my *tallis* and *tefillin*, a prayer book and a few other books. “I did not want the German and Ukrainian gangs to have something to mock,” she said.

Soon, a large transport of transport wagons arrived, which were full of Jewish and non-Jewish refugees. The transport did not even stop at the station, but continued on. As it was traveling, we threw all the children of our group onto all the wagons, and we jumped on. Many of our packages were left behind in the station, including my *tallis* and *tefillin*. We were happy to have our children.

[Page 301]

As we were traveling, we collected our children onto one wagon. We traveled on and on until we mixed in to the large sea of Jewish refugees fro various countries - Polish, Lithuanian, Latvian, Austrian, Bessarabian and Ukrainian Jews. We all shared in the bitter lot of the refugees.

On August 11, 1941, we received congratulations in the city of Stalingrad. My wife gave birth to a daughter. This was also at the time of the beginning of our tragic wandering through Russia.

In Besieged Stalingrad

After a short rest in a *kolkhoz* [collective farm] in the Stalingrad region, when the Germans were beginning their terrible offensive against Stalingrad, I was already no longer together with my family. The Soviets mobilized massive forces and sent them to defend the large city with its hazardous factories.

Some went into the army with weapons, and others dug fortifications and performed other strategic work under the supervision of military officers and supervisors. I was involved in such a group.

It was already late autumn. Aside from the difficult normal work and terrible hunger, the Russian cold froze my half-naked bones. People died of hunger and cold more than on the fronts.

The Family in a Foreign Place, in Great Danger

My family was far, in a foreign place and in great danger. The enemy was approaching them. This time, they were in greater danger than four months previously, when we fled from our home. At that time, it was still warm outside, and now it was cold and we had a young child. Who knew if there would be familiar people who would organize and help with the escape? My head was splitting with thoughts: I could not relax. I wanted to run to them, but I was 300 kilometers away. What could one do? - I thought. It was better to die at home together with everybody, than here in the Stalingrad steppes...

[Page 302]

After a difficult internal struggle, I decided to run, run. Perhaps this time, like the previous time, I would succeed in coming to them at the right time and to help them escape. I indeed succeeded, and I achieved my objective. After wandering for several days, I met them on the way to the railway station... In my life, I will never forget the moment of our meeting! I later found out that the escape was organized by Chana Furman, Shmuel Zishe's daughter from Borinya - who was only an 18-year old girl! She knocked on all the doors of the local authorities, asking that they help her evacuate the few families. The local authorities fulfilled her request. She herself did not leave the place until everyone had set out. She traveled on the last vehicle, together with us.

It was cold outside. It was raining and snowing. We sat in a deserted railway station, waiting hours for a train. The wagons were filled with war equipment, and all the trains were going in one direction - to Stalingrad. None of them wanted to take us on, especially with young children in diapers.

After begging profusely, a Soviet officer had mercy upon us and permitted us to occupy a small place in his loaded, open platform. Thus did we travel. To protect ourselves from the snow and wind, I made a booth out of pieces of lumber, and covered it with twigs and straw. We all gathered inside. In this way, we were able to nestle together and warm our children. At that time, the oldest was six years old, and the youngest was three months.

A normal journey to Stalingrad would have taken a few hours. We traveled for four weeks. We wanted to cross the Volga through Stalingrad.

[Page 303]

On the other side of the Volga, there was still free traffic in the large, wide expanse of Russia, to Siberia, to Kovkhoz, to the Far East, and also to the Middle East. Together with the entire stream of refugees, we entered Stalingrad and waited for a possibility of crossing the Volga.

The Besieged City

Stalingrad was full of refugees. Tramways and cars could not go through... People pushed, tore through, and even fought for a corner where they would be able to protect themselves from the harsh wind and snow. Many were frozen, and squeezed themselves together.

After a few weeks of terrible suffering, and order was issued by the supreme authorities that the entire population, including the refugees, would be evacuated. For that purpose, the regime enlisted ships and small boats on the Volga. There was terrible chaos as the ships were loaded... the voices and warnings, the running and shoving - everything looked like a sinking ship full of people in the middle of the sea... Entire families were scattered in this admixture. Our intimate group, which had held together the entire time, was also separated there. We never saw each other or met up again.

After long and difficult months of wandering with various means of transportation, my family and I reached Central Asia, directly below the Himalayan Mountains. There, we met many families from Poland who had traveled there some time previously from Poland via the Soviet Union.

There, we felt secure and out of danger. We remained there until the summer of 1944.

[Page 304]

Saved by Righteous Gentiles

by Esther Brand of Kiryat Bialik

"Righteous Gentiles have a place in the World To Come" (Tosafot Sanhedrin, 13)

A great deal has been written about the Holocaust as well as about the anti-Semitic population that helped the Nazis carry out their plots. On the other hand, not much has yet been written about the righteous gentiles who often endangered their lives to save a Jewish soul. As one of the survivors of the Holocaust, I believe that I have not fulfilled my obligation if I fail to write in the pages of this book about one Polish family in whose warm home I found refuge during the days of the Holocaust.

*

It was November 1942. The winter was in its full strength. The cold penetrated the bones, as was usual in my native city of Turka. On Rynek Street, one could meet Ukrainian villagers next to their winter sleighs who came to sell the produce of their land, such as potatoes, rye flour, and other such items - all in small quantities. At times, one could notice a Jew wearing the Star of David patch, exchanging words with a villager, turning from side to side to see that there was no German around. In general, the exchange ended without results, for the farmer demanded astronomical prices in terms of clothing, kitchen utensils, and the like for a kilo of potatoes. The Jews who remained after the *aktions* were very few in number, about 500, broken in soul and lacking of means. A Jew who failed to wear the patch would be punished with death. Despite this, I endangered myself and sometimes went on the streets without the patch. My Aryan appearance helped me. However, as I was walking on the street that time, I was overtaken by fear for some reason and I wore my patch on my arm. I approached one of the farmers and asked him if he would like to purchase kitchen utensils from me in exchange for food. The farmer agreed, and followed me to my house. I showed him all types of pots and dishes. He looked at them, but instead of asking for their price, he invited me... to accompany him, for he was willing to hide me until the end of the war. He said, "I saw announcements that you must be prepared to go to the Sambor Ghetto. We have no children at home, and we want to perform a good deed in this world and save a young soul from extermination." His offer enticed me greatly. I told this to my mother, who of course agreed. We agreed to meet next to the Cygalnia (brickyard). I was to dress like one of the Ukrainians, to set out on my way and stop the sleigh in which he would be sitting, and ask the driver to take me to Wysocko-Wyszna.

[Page 305]

*

It is easy to imagine how difficult it was to part from my home and my family. Indeed, we knew that there was no hope of surviving in Turka, and there was no ray of light for salvation, but we still wanted to remain together. We wept, wailed and comforted each other. We said in our hearts that G-d only knows if we will see each other again. My younger brother Shlomo of blessed memory, who was ten years old at the time, asked and begged to join me. He was only comforted after I explained to him that he was the only male in the family, and he must protect everybody. Accompanied by my friend Henya Schreiber, who lived with us after the death of her family, I left our home and set out on the journey. We had to cross the river, with the fear of the Germans who used to wander over the bridge. The road led us to the meeting place. From afar, I saw the approaching sleigh. I signaled it to stop by raising my hand, and asked the sleigh driver to take me to Wysocko-Wyszna in return for payment. The Ukrainian acceded to my request. I sat down and glanced back to my friend Henya, who had set out in the direction of the house to inform my mother of my departure.

We sat in the sleigh: a Ukrainian police captain who was the sleigh owner, the Pole in whose house I was to remain for the remainder of the war, and an elderly Ukrainian woman. The woman explained while weeping that the *Volksdeutchen* had conduced a search in her house and taken all of the belongings that she had purchased from Jews. The Pole told me the same thing, and I found out that all of the kitchen utensils and blankets that my mother had given him had been confiscated by the *Volksdeutchen*. Along the way, the Ukrainian wanted to talk to me in German, boasting that he had succeeded in learning the language during the course of his job. I pretended to not understand even one word, and he translated the discussion into Ukrainian for me. To me, the entire matter seemed like a joke suffused with pain.

We passed near the Ukrainian police in the village of Borinya; however, nobody came out to greet us. We reached Wysocko-Nyszny, and even then they did not stop us. We were all surprised. The Ukrainian captain explained that the police had found a Jewess a few days ago in this place who had been hiding in a coffin that was being transported by a villager. The villager was cruelly beaten and then turned over to the Ukrainian police. Of course, the villager also received his punishment. The captain said, "It is interesting that now, when there is no Jewess with us, they are not conducting a search." Everyone burst out laughing. They laughed and joked. I also laughed with my voice, but inside I was weeping bitterly, in accordance with the words of the prophet, "My soul weeps in the hidden recesses." I thought about how downtrodden our people were, how we had become an object of mockery and derision - were our sins really to great to bear?! Sadness overtook me and a spirit of depression fell upon me, but I quickly recovered and continued to laugh... I recalled the words of the wisest of men, "There is a time to weep and a time to laugh"[1]. We continued to travel on, as we were chatting and laughing.

[Page 306]

Suddenly, I felt a light kick from the foot of the Pole. I understood that this was where I was supposed to get off... I paid the Ukrainian four zloty and got off. The Pole also got off and politely "offered" to accompany me because of the darkness. "I agreed" and after a tiring half-hour walk in the deep snow, we arrived at his house. This was a typical village house. His parents and three sisters lived in one part of the house - and they did not know about my arrival and my presence in the house until the liberation! He and his wife lived in the second section. When they saw me, his wife expressed her joy and welcomed me warmly. She served me supper and made my bed. This was my first night in this house in which I spent close to two years.

The sawmill near the Stryj River

[Page 307]

The next day, which was a Friday, the Pole, whom I had started to call Mr. Wlodomierz, joined his *Volksdeutche* neighbor, and they both set out for Turka. I gave him a letter for my mother, in which I describe my success. Among other things, I asked her to give him belongings that they were not going to take with them to the ghetto, and to try to convince him to take my sister along as well. This was one day before the transfer of all the Jews of Turka and the region to the Sambor Ghetto. The villagers knew about this, and therefore they all came to the city in order to purchase anything that the Jews had. Indeed, Mr. Wlodomierz returned late at night with a chest full of all types of items - but he did not bring my sister. In his words, he was afraid of the *Volksdeutche*. The next day, Saturday November 28, 1942, corresponding to 21 Tevet, 5703, all of the Jews of the villages were deported to the ghetto. I stood next to the window for hours looking outside. I saw Jews - men, women and children from the villages - walking with suitcases, packages and sacks. Some wept, and others were just sad. From time to time, they peered backward, as if to cast a final glance at their houses in which they and their ancestors had lived - and who knew if they would see them again. I then thought about my family and was sad that we were not together and that we could not comfort each other.

*

I spent my first week in the village in a closed room. Then, I entered the hiding place and remained there for the entire winter. The hiding place was a crate with a double bottom. There were potatoes on top, and I slept on the bottom. I was not able to sit. I only left my hiding place once a day, for a half hour at midnight, in order to attend to my needs and breathe fresh air. Mr. Wlodomierz and his wife Maria called this crate, "The Ark of Moses." Frequently in the evenings, neighbors gathered in our house and discussed various issues. I heard conversations about the advance or retreat of the army, about the conquest of cities, about the capture of Jews, about Jewish partisans in the forest, and about everything that was taking place in the world. I paid attention to all of these conversations, and listened quietly without moving. Once, I heard a light knock on the window and I realized from the discussion that somebody was asking for food. The next day Maria told me that a young Jewish girl from the Fejler family of Turka was hiding with her father in the forest. She would come to her window from time to time to request some food. Of course, she was never sent away empty handed.

I lay in this crate until the spring. They had to liquidate the crate when the stock of potatoes ran out, in order to avoid arousing suspicion. Mr. Wlodomierz, who supported himself by building ovens, dismantled the old oven and built a new one with a hiding place for me. Now, it was more comfortable for me. I was able to sit, embroider, write and read. This hiding place was also less suspicious than the previous one. Thus passed days and nights, that merged into weeks, and the weeks into months - until June 1944. The German Army suffered defeats in all places and retreated from the fronts. The Bandera gangs attacked the villagers, burning, pillaging their property, and spreading ruin and destruction in every place that they passed through. Fear and trepidation fell upon the residents of Komarniki.

[Page 308]

One day, my savior decided to remove me from my hiding place for my safety. They transferred me to a field and put me in a haystack. I remained in the haystack for three months. They would visit me daily and bring me food. At night, I was overcome with fear of the rain, thunder, and barking dogs. Once, Germans came to get some hay. They went straight for my haystack, but Mr. Wlodomierz, who was working in the field at that time, directed them to another haystack, explaining that this particular haystack had rotted from the rain. One night in the month of October, they brought me back to their house and hid me in the attic. However, I remained there for only one night - the Soviet Army arrived the next morning!

My saviors did not want to reveal to the village residents that they had been hiding a Jewish girl. They only told this to their relatives who lived in the other part of the house. When they came to see me, the looked at me as if I had fallen from another planet. They did not believe the sight of their eyes. The next morning Mr. Wlodomierz took a loaf of bread and a bottle of milk, and we set out on the road leading to Turka. We walked on foot for eight kilometers and arrived in the city. It was difficult to recognize the city of Turka. It looked as it had suffered a bombardment. We did not find even one intact Jewish home. Not only had they removed the windows from the Jewish homes, but also the ceilings and floors. There were also homes without any remnant. We did not find even one intact room in our home, the Kleist home in which five families had lived previously and which consisted of approximately 20 rooms. We wandered through the streets of Turka, and I recalled Turka from before the Holocaust... streets that had bustled with Jews, tradesmen, merchants, wealthy people, poor people, and members of the middle class; coffeehouses and other such places. All that was left from all of these was a heap of ruins, without any Jewish remnant. I was very depressed that we did not find my family. I thought, was it possible that I remained alone in the world?! I was overcome with despair. I was encouraged somewhat when I met a few people who had just returned from the forests. These included the Bruner family, David Binder, Moshe Meiner, Moshe Kirszner with his brother Yosef, Tova Pesi and Moshe Shreiber, Shalom Erdman, Hillel Erdman, Avraham Liberhart, Chaya Goldreich and her mother, Esther Shein, Shaul Kleist, Ben-Zion Bronanka and his brother, the Ringel family who had come from Sambor, the Kris family and others.

[Page 309]

A few weeks passed before I succeeded in setting myself up with work. In the meantime, I received assistance from Wlodomierz and Maria Komarnicki, in whose merit I had survived. I express my gratitude to them.

Myckowicz Street

Translator's Footnote:

81. Ecclesiastes 3:4. By tradition, Ecclesiastes (Kohelet) was written by King Solomon.

[Page 310]

Dream

by Y. M. Zeifert of Los Angeles

We are lying beneath the hay in the attic of the stable, hiding
From the Hitlerist murderers and from death;
From one morning to the next, we wait for the liberation,
To redeem us from tribulations and need.
As we count the days and nights in this mannerAlready a full year has passed... For us, it is incomprehensible evil,Bearing nothing that was light.
The month of November has already passed,December has come for the second time...The night is long and frightfulThe day is boring as it passes by.
It does not want to remain quiet for longIn its anger, the stormy wind...And from cold - the household dogStarts to bark in his doghouse.
Near me, my child tells of his dream:I do not see her face, her expression - I only hear: "Daddy, we are now happy, there is already peace,Are we also going to go home to Palestine?..."
[Page 311]

And when she wakes up in the morning,
She said that in her imagination -
She heard joyous voices outside,
As the woman householder, our gentile, came up
And said, "The war is over,
The confusion has ended,
You can come out of your hiding place now -
Hitler has suffered his downfall..."
"My child, would it be that your dream would come true,And that we would hear this news in truth..."Hope and aspirations cross through the mindWith the thought - would we survive to see it?

Melniczne
December 7, 1943

Editor's notes: The girl who dreamed - today Shoshana Rothschild - is a teacher in Tivon near Haifa.

[Page 312]

Remember

by Dr. M. Dvorzhitzki

Remember the Holocaust of the Jewish people, remember the loss and bitterness. It should be for you a sign and a lesson for generation after generation.

May this memory accompany you always - when you walk on the way, when you lie down, and when you arise.

May the memory of brethren who are no longer here be bound to you forever.

Let the memory be on your flesh, your blood, and your bones.

Gnash your teeth and remember; as you eat your bread - remember; as you drink your water - remember; if you hear a song - remember; as the sun comes out - remember; as night falls - remember; on a holiday and festival - certainly remember.

If you build a house, leave a part unfinished so the destruction of the House of Israel will be before you always.

If you plough a field, set up a mound of stones - as a witness memorial to our brethren, who were never brought to a Jewish burial.

When you lead your child to the wedding canopy, bring to the forefront of your joy the memory of the children who will never be brought to the wedding canopy.

Let them be as one: the living and the dead; the victim and the survivor; those who went on their journey and are no longer, and those who remained alive.

Hear, oh member of the Nation of Israel, the voice calling to you from the depths; do not be silent, do not be silent!

[Page 315]

The Holocaust in the Surrounding Villages

Murder in the Villages around Turka

Meir Seeman of Tel Aviv

Translated by Jerrold Landau

a) "Eicha Yashva Badad" Oh How Does it Sit in Desolation[1]

Oh, how does the city of Turka and its environs sit in desolation over its Jews. All of their friends, the Ukrainians, have dealt treacherously with them – behaving like enemies to them. The children went to the crematoria or were murdered locally. They went about without strength before their enemies, the Ukrainians and the Germans, may their names be blotted out. Their enemies have seen them, and mocked at their desolation.

The Jews gave up all of their valuables for food, to refresh the children of Turka and the area. The elders perished for want of food to restore their souls.

Outside, the sword ruled, and inside the house – death. All of their enemies, of Turka and environs, opened their mouths to them, they whistled and gnashed their teeth: "We have swallowed up, this was they day that we waited for – we have found and seen". Indeed, they slaughtered and had no mercy.

My eyes shed streams of tears over the destruction of the Jews of Turka and environs: Those who used to eat fine food gasped outsideÉ and cleaved to the garbage heaps. Those who were victims of the sword were better off than the victims of hunger.

b) The Destruction of Husna Vyzna[2]

On a summer Sunday in 1941, we heard in Husna that Hitler, may his name be blotted out, went out to war against the Russians. On the Friday of that week, five days after the beginning of the war, the Russian soldiers left the village. Three hours after the departure of the Russian militia, the Ukrainians were already breaking the windowpanes of Jewish homes. On Saturday morning, one could already see Ukrainians with rifles, as they rounded up Jews from Husna and Kryvka to hew rocks on the streets of Husna...

And further: Already on Sunday, placards were posted indicating that Jews must wear a patch with a Star of David; Any Jew who disobeys the edict was to be sentenced to death. Furthermore: the Ukrainian population must not come into contact with Jews. No Germans were seen yet; however a few Hungarian soldiers from the border guard found their way into Husna in order to fulfill their commandment[3] of robbing Jewish houses...

The following Friday, the resident Tzvi Sternbach, who worked in Barinya for a baker, came running into Husna, black with fear. He told the following: In Barinya, the Germans and their Ukrainian assistants rounded up twenty Jews, who had to take spades and dig pit on a hill in Barinya... The Germans shot ten Jews. The rest of them were forced to cover the grave and dance on top of it, after those that were shot were tossed into the grave... However, the Jews of Husna did not believe him. They cursed him for causing trouble...

Jews were forced to work. Two weeks later, again on a Friday, we heard a taxi coming. In Husna, a taxi had never before been seen... We realized that this time, Germans were coming. I quickly remembered the story of Barinya, and I jumped out the window and hid by the edge of the river. The Gestapo entered our house, and found my parents and a young sister. They sternly commanded my sister to run to all of the Jews in the village and tell them that they must come with spades in their hands – to work... If she does not do this promptly, my parents would promptly be shot. My sister ran and fulfilled the order – however all of the Jews fled to the nearby forest... The Germans and Ukrainians realized that they were left with only three Jews, so they abandoned the entire enterprise. That Sabbath, all of the Jews of Husna and Kryvka remained in the forest.

A few days later, 24 Germans arrived in Husna. They set themselves up as border guards in a special, large guardhouse that the Russians had recently built, also for the purposes of border guards. A few days after their arrival, the mayor4 Husna called all of the Jews together and announced that, in accordance with an order of the Germans, the Jews of Husna and Kryvka must appear each day at the German command. Their task would be to provide wood, and to draw water from the well at the border house. At that time, the well was operated by hand (earlier, it was operated by horses).

Things went on and on, each day coming with new edicts... All cattle and fowl had to be given away...All heirlooms and gold were given away... People gave their belongings away, believing that this would be the end: that they would be allowed to keep their lives...

Hunger, want and terror grew stronger day by day. Jews of Husna and Kryvka went around with wooden shoes, torn and in shackles – and starving. They went to their work with the Germans day by day. Each day, they had to fill up the tankers with 3,000 liters of water. The Ukrainians did not even let the Jews grind a small amount of oats in the Husner water mill, which had previously belonged to the Jews Tzvi Goldreich and Yitzchak Hanes of blessed memory.

Terrible news came from all sides... This was the situation until the final liquidation in the summer of 1942.

Translator's Footnotes:

82. The three-word title of this section are the three words of the first verse of the biblical book of Lamentations (Eicha). The entire first section has words interspersed from the book of Eicha in a semi-poetic fashion.
83. I was unable to definitively identify this village using the Shtetl Seeker of http://www.jewishgen.org, or my atlas. I assume that Husna Vyzna and Husna Nyzna are tiny villages near Turka. Other towns in the article, Turka, Kryvka (actually Kryvka in the text, but spelled with the v), and Borinya (or Borynya) were identifiable.
84. An obviously sarcastic commandment. The Yiddish / Hebrew word used here is 'mitzvah', signifying a Jewish religious commandment.
85. The word here is not clear 'saltim'. I translated by context.

[Page 318]

The Destruction of the Jews of Borinya

by Helena Ringler (Gissinger) of Netanya

Helena Ringler

Borinya, one of the villages in the district of Turka, had a population of several hundred Jews at the time of the German invasion of Poland in 1939.

Confusion and fear overtook the Jews of the village when the Nazis entered. This was despite the fact that several Jews remembered the Germans from the era of the First World War. They could not imagine that such cultured people would be able to perpetrate such base, murderous deeds!

In the meantime, the local Ukrainians pillaged in Borinya. They beat the Jews and stole their property to their hearts content. When representatives of the German authorities entered, "normal life" pervaded in the village, so to speak.

Their first command was that the Jews must place a white band on their left arm so that they could be recognized. The men had to appear for work daily. This was, of course, gratis work, under the "supervision" of the Ukrainian guards. Those Ukrainian guards tormented the hungry, weakened people in a cruel fashion. Women were sent to clean various communal institutions.

Nevertheless, despite the difficult life and the social, moral and economic tribulations, the Jews continued on with their dismal, difficult lives. A spark of hope and an illusion that the terrible time would pass remained in the hearts of everyone, for it was difficult to believe that even more difficult times were to come, and that there was no bounds to the tortures.

I recall that my brother Shmuel Gissinger returned home perplexed and harried a few days after the Germans entered the village. When he came home, he stumbled upon a German captain who was passing in front of him. The captain stopped him and asked him why he, a Jews, dared no greet him, the German captain. "Since I do not know your honor," was his answer. The Nazi slapped him over the face several times and stated, "How do you dare speak to me in such a fashion, Jew?!" This incident, not one of the most severe, instilled fear upon the entire Jewish community.

[Page 319]

The Gestapo men arrived after some time. None of us imagined that the meaning of that word was – death. This time, they were looking for people named Furman. They captured approximately eight men and took them to the police. Aside from them they took 30 men to a field outside the village and commanded them to dig a grave. The following people were among those arrested at that time: Ben–Zion Furman, his daughter Golda and her husband Moshe, Yitzchak Furman as well as his wife who was also named Golda, Zusia Furman, his wife, and several other members of the Furman family whose names I do not recall at this time. They were brought under guard to the field next to the grave. They called out the name of each one of them, and they approached the grave, one by one, under guard, and were shot. They also read out their verdict and the accusation before them: There were German settlements in the vicinity of Borinya. Before their retreat, the Russians arrested and killed the owners of these settlements, and since Furman's daughter worked in the kolkhoz [collective farm] that was set up in one of these settlements – anyone with the name Furman was sentenced to death. According to their calculations, they had to kill ten people. Since there were only eight Furmans, they captured two others Jews, who were the youngest of those that dug the grave, and murdered them as well. Their names were Dolinger and Meir Jager.

The diggers of the pit were witnesses to the murder perpetrated with German precision. The victims were first beaten with murderous blows. The area was surrounded by German and Ukrainian guards, and it was impossible to even think about any sort of escape... Jager's older brother was among the diggers. As I had said, they murdered Jager along with the Furmans. They had to cover the grave over him and the rest. Since the earth pulsated about the bodies of the people who were buried before they expired, they were ordered to put stones atop of the pit...

Not only did the bereaved families not dare to complain, but they were even afraid to weep over their dead.

*

The hunger afflicted everyone. The farmers no longer knew what to demand from the Jews for a handful of barley or several potatoes. In general, they were in no hurry to sell food to the Jews, for they knew that in any case, all the fortune of the Jews would fall into their hands for free...

On the night of February 2, 1942, the Gestapo and Ukrainian guards surrounded the houses of the Jews and removed all people that they found there. Among them were Shmuel Gissinger, Moshe Rozen, Muno Sofer, his sister Mani, Nusia Friedman, Ben–Zion Liberman, his two sons Yisrael and Avraham, Yehuda Liberman, his brother Shlomo, and others – 36 people. After they beat them all night, they led them naked and barefoot in the cold, and bound them two by two behind the village, where three graves were waiting. Some of the Ukrainians tried to save Shmuel Gissinger, but when the Gestapo was informed that he was a lawyer, they refused to free him.

[Page 320]

After the act of murder, the German policemen from Turka broke into the house of Shmuel Gissinger, where his widow and two orphaned children were located. One of the policemen, named Vikki, asked Regina Gissinger (nee Taffer) with satanic laughter if she knew where her husband was. She did not know that her husband had been murdered, and she answered that they had taken him at night. Then Vikki "explained" to her with full seriousness that her husband had "travelled to heaven." He commanded the Ukrainian policemen to take everything that was in the house. They removed all the furniture and bedding, and even the small amount of food. The same thing was repeated in the home of Moshe Rozen, the brother–in–law of Shmuel Gissinger, who lived in the same house. Rozen had left behind a wife in her final month of pregnancy, as well as a three–year–old child. He was a native of Turka, the son of Chana and Mendel Rozen.

After this aktion, there were other "unofficial" snatchings and murders. In December 1942, the remnants of the Jews of Borinya who were still alive were transferred to the Sambor Ghetto.

At that point, Borinya was Judenrein.

[Page 321]

Episodes from the Great Misfortune in Borinya

by Yosef Brenes of New York

Yosef Brenes

When the Polish army was defeated, all of the soldiers fled to their homes. At that time, the Germans (the so called "Shtraf Ekspeditzia") found a group of people, including Jews, returning home to Borinya, and shot them on the road leading to Jaworów. There was great chaos at that time. Many Ukrainians began to come to Borinya from all the surrounding villages, because a rumor was spreading that Jews were responsible for the shooting, and that all those running about were prepared to pillage...

However, one of the gentiles appeared in the middle of the market and announced, "It was not the Jews who were guilty. I have seen myself that there were Jews among the dead..." The words had their effect, and the first pogrom was averted.

It was Rosh Hashanah at that time, and we were worshipping in the Beis Midrash. An order arrived from Zalman Frajdman that the Jews must attend the funeral of the fallen Ukrainians. Of course we went for the sake of peace.

*

When the Russians retreated, they announced that anyone who wishes to come along with them can do so. However, very few went with them. First, we did not have any good experiences with them. Second,

[Page 322]

good reports were coming from Krakow that life under German rule was normal...

Those girls and boys who retreated with the Russians had earlier been members of Komsomol1 and were active with the Russians. They no longer had any choice. The Furman family, a certain Heger and others were among them.

*

When the Germans entered Borinya, they immediately gathered the remaining members of the Furman family along with about 20 innocent Jewish youths and shot them. They were tossed into a mass grave that we had to dig in advance. We had to dance on the grave until the victims were silenced... We the gravediggers were told to not tell anyone about this. Otherwise, we would meet the same end...

*

Shortly thereafter, the Germans took over the administration from the Gedula Firm, and imposed set quotas upon the Jewish men and women regarding how many cubit meters they could till. They also promised to give certain provisions for the work.

The quotas were very difficult. People, even if ill, had to go to work. Rumors were spreading that people were being snatched from the houses to be shot – which was better than going to that difficult labor.

We discussed escaping, but everyone had reasons to remain. One had young children, another had old parents – how could one escape? As the manager of the work in the forest, I had the ability to go from one forest to another. I began to dig a bunker. I thought that we might need it later.

[Page 323]

Ukrainian bands took advantage of our situation. They offered to transfer people to the Hungarian border in exchange for money. They would take their victims to the border. Then they would obtain notes from them stating that they were in the best condition – and after that they would murder them in a bestial fashion.

*

An edict came: All men, women and children must go to the ghetto in Turka. Each family can take along food and clothing, and everything that the possessed. Chaos broke out as everyone moved through the city. In the city, everything was taken away from them. The people were confined in old barracks without food and drink. The next morning, with force and threats from the Germans, everyone was led to the railway station, loaded up like animals, and sent to death camps. Anyone who attempted to escape was shot on the spot. My brother Tzvi was shot near the station by his one–time classmate with whom he had studied together and who had been a frequent guest at my parents' home. The scene that unfolded that day is beyond description.

*

There were 50 working people in Borinya. We continued to work in hunger and need. Things continued on in this fashion until December 19442, when announcements were posted that Borinya must become Judenrein, and all the workers must transfer to the Sambor Ghetto. It seemed that everyone could take what he could, and could travel by train.

At that time, many young people began to escape to the various surrounding forests, or to hide with neighbors. My late wife and my sister–in–law Esther, who is now in New York, had a few agreed upon places to hide with gentiles. At that time, it seemed that the war would last at most six more months. However, at the end, all the gentiles who had promised to hide us were afraid, and we were left in our desperate situation.

Translator's Footnotes:

14. See http://en.wikipedia.org/wiki/Komsomol
15. I suspect that this date is off by one year, and 1943 was intended, as the area would have been in Russian hands by December 1944.

[Page 324]

The Story of Dzvinyach in the Holocaust

by Shlomo Katz of Haifa

Shlomo Katz.

Life of Calm and Tradition

The village of Dzvinyach extended along the San River. It was bordered in the east by the village of Tarnowa Gizna, and in the west, by the village of Didyova. For the most part, Ukrainian farmers lived in the village, as well as about 30 Jewish families who were also occupied with agriculture and small–scale commerce. Most of them were related through marriage, and therefore were like one large family.

All of these Jews were observant and lived traditional lives. They wore the *streimel* and *kapote* on Sabbaths and festivals, and worshipped in the synagogues that met in private homes. The youths would gather together in the hall of the Mizrachi Movement on Sabbath afternoons in order to hear lectures on Zionism, etc. Some of them went on *hachshara* and hoped to make *aliya* to the Land. The Jews lived peaceful lives in this manner until the outbreak of the Second World War in 1939.

The Germans for the First Time

A few days after the outbreak of the war, the Germans reached us from the west. Their first command was to gather all of the men in the *gmina* (governing house), but the Jews hid in the forests and did not appear at the roll call. The rumor had already reached us that the Red Army was also approaching. Indeed, that same day, the Russians approached and arrived at the San River from the east. Thus, there was a division between the Germans and the Russians: some of our houses were on one side of the San and the others on the other side. Most of the Jews left their houses on the German side and streamed to the Russian side. Both sides set up sentinels, and crossing the San became almost impossible. After some time, an exchange of property and population between the Jews and Ukrainians took place, and all of the Jews moved to the eastern side.

[Page 325]

Evacuating the Civilian Population

Already by the middle of the winter, the Russians issued a command to evacuate the civilian population from the border district, and move them to the interior of the country. The Jews of Dzvinyach were moved to Malinsk in the district of Rovno. We moved there by train. Every family was given a dwelling as well as employment in accordance with profession. All of the Jews of our area organized themselves and set themselves up in one district with the approval of the authorities. We were once again a large unit. We worked in the fields, in porting, and in transporting and cutting trees. The Russians treated us well, and we lived a renewed normal life.

1941 – The Germans Return!

At the outbreak of the war between Russia and Germany, the Russians began to retreat. Some of us retreated with them, but the numbers were small. Families with young children or elderly parents did not move. Thus, after a brief period, we again found ourselves under the Nazi boot.

Their first command was to wear the yellow patch so that the Jews could be recognized immediately. A command was issued to collect money as well as valuables to give over to the Germans. Immediately, various persecutions of the Jewish population began. They cut off half of the beard of Binyamin Breier, an honorable Jews from Tarnowa. They confiscated horses and cattle that we had brought from home, and drafted us to forced labor, especially in repairing railway lines that had been destroyed with the retreat of the Russians. We worked at harsh, backbreaking work without receiving anything in return.

The Berezna Ghetto and Work Camp

After fixing the railway line, the Germans deported us to the Berezna Ghetto. There, they separated between men who were capable of work and other family members. There, we were required to give over the small amount of property that we somehow still had. We were now empty of everything... Men who were fit for work were transferred to a Work Camp in Kostopol that was under the supervision of the S.S. and the Ukrainian police. There were about 300 of us Jews there, including the following people from our region: Avraham Yaakov Breier and his son Shalom, Shalom Katz and his son Shlomo, Gedalia Erlich, Chaim Parnas, Gedalia Kesler, Yosef Neuman, the brothers Chaim, Shlomo, and Lipa Rand, Meir Fuchs, Yaakov Lerer, his brother-in-law Avraham Breier, and others. Our job was to load trees on the train cars. The work was difficult. Food was not given to us. Rumors about actions and murders circulated daily. We also saw Jews being hauled to places of murder following the actions. We were in constant fear that our turn would certainly come.

[Page 326]

Then, one night in the month of Elul 1942, we saw that we were surrounded by the S.S. men and a growing number of Ukrainian police. We immediately understood that our turn had come. At 2:00 a.m., they took us out to the center of the field of the camp. A heavy guard with automatic weapons surrounded us. Now, we had no doubt regarding the aims of the murderers.

In the yard, we attempted to crowd together and remain together – especially our group – as we waited for what was to come. When the command was issued to arrange ourselves in rows of three, Yaakov Breier, who had been a Jewish captain in the Austrian Army, began to shout, “Jews, we are being brought to slaughter! Hurra! Flee for your lives. Escape to wherever you can!”

A tumult broke out with shouts of "Hurra!" We began to flee for our lives in all directions. The guards began to shoot at us, but we had nothing to lose. Whomever fortune shined upon escaped. Those who remained in the place or were caught during the escape were taken out to be killed the next day.

A. Y. Breier, Shalom Breier, Shalom Katz, Shlomo Katz, Gedalia Kesler, Avraham Breier and several other Jews from other areas survived from our group.

However, most of them eventually died there. May their memories be a blessing.

[Page 327]

With Village Jews under Siege

by Zerach Katz of Kiryat Chaim

Zerach Katz

In 1940, the Russians transferred us from Dzvinyach Gruna on the San to Malinsk, a town on the railway line between Kostopol and Sarna. We received a house about two kilometers from the town. My father and older brother traveled to Malinsk every day to work at the railway station in transporting lumber or loading lumber onto wagons. My sister, brother, and I went to the school that was next to the station. Our neighbors around us were Poles or Ukrainians, and related to us in a sufficiently positive manner.

When the war between Germany and Russia broke out in 1941, the Germans had been with us within two weeks already. The Germans employed the older people at fixing the railway tracks that the Russians destroyed during the time of their retreat. The Jews knew that the Germans would not let them remain scattered, but rather would finally gather them into a ghetto. Therefore, our mother of blessed memory made sure that the young children would remain with Polish residents in the area. During the time of the deportation of the Jews from Malinsk to the Berezne Ghetto, my two sisters Fania (Talila) and Chana and my brother Peretz remained with the Poles.

When they brought us the Berezne Ghetto, we tried to keep the entire family together. However, after a short time, they took Father and my older brother to a work camp in Kostopol. The economic situation continually worsened. I decided to return to Malinsk to find something to eat. One day, as they were taking the Jews out from the ghetto to work, I went with them. I did not return at night, and I continued along through the Ukrainian villages to Malinsk. The distance was about 30 kilometers. I arrived at my brother, who was with a farmer, and told him that the children are hungry for bread. He gave me some flour. I also approached my sisters and there too, I received a portion of wheat from the owner of the house. I returned to the ghetto with this double portion. I did this at night, but the problem was: how to enter the ghetto with flour on my back? Somehow, I succeeded in sneaking in toward morning, while the residents were still sleeping.

[Page 328]

I remained in the ghetto for only 24 hours. Toward morning, I set out on the way to a farmer who lived near Malinsk who promised me at one time to take me on as a cattle herder. I made this journey to the ghetto and back two or three times. Along my way from the Berezne Ghetto to the village, I also snuck into the train station in Malinsk. I met Father and my brother Shlomo there, and gave them greetings from Mother.

*

When I reached the ghetto for the last time, they told me that something was about to take place. I left the ghetto that night and returned to work with the farmer. The next day, I was already in the pasture with the cows. At night, I sat and thought about the journey that I had undertaken (every time I made this journey to the ghetto and back, all types of unpleasant surprises took place). They told me that my brother and two sisters had come to me, for the farmers were afraid to keep them. Thy told me that all of the Jews from all of the surrounding cities in the area had been killed. My householder, an elderly Pole, told us to enter the barn for the night, and to hide the next day in the bushes in the area for a few days until the wrath would pass. This was on the 21st of Elul, 1942. At night, we snuck into the piles of fodder where we made caves and fell asleep. During the day, we hid in the bushes. We knew that other Jews, including relatives, were hiding in the surrounding forests. However, we were afraid to search for them in the forest. They also knew that we were hiding in the bushes in the area. One day as we were sitting among the bushes, we heard two people approach us. We recognized them. They were Gedalyahu Erlich and David Lipa of blessed memory. They took us to them. There, we met other uncles and aunts. My grandmother and sister Lea all escaped from the work camp in the area at the time that they came to take them back to the ghetto.

*

I found out that Father, my brother Shlomo and other Jewish families were hiding in the forests around the village of Polonne. I decided to go out and search for them before the snow would fall. The distance was about 20–25 kilometers. I went out on the journey toward evening and walked at the side of the road. I hid every time I saw a form approach me. More than once, the form that I saw also disappeared and did not pass by me... I was very frightened. The problem was, how to find the place where Father and my brother were hiding. I wandered around all day at a distance of 200 meters from them and did not find them until I chanced upon a path and continued to walk along it and reached the place in the evening. They did not believe their eyes, and I too did not believe. There I met, aside from Mother and my brothers, Avraham Yaakov Breier with his two sons, daughter and niece, the Kesler family with three children, and several other local Jews (that means, they had lived there for many years). The next night, we returned to my sisters and brother in our forest.

[Page 329]

As time went on, we heard that Ukrainians had murdered Sara Kesler, her son Hirsch, Avraham Yaakov Breier with several other Jews, Breier's children, and Gedalyahu Kesler with his son and daughter of blessed memory. They came to us in the forest. Since we were a large group, it was dangerous to remain in one place. We had to exchange ourselves at all time so that the local residents would not know exactly where we were. We were afraid of the Germans as well as the Ukrainians. During one attack of the Ukrainians upon a group of Jews, Gedalyahu's daughter Mania Kesler and my aunt Mindel Rand (nee Parnas) were killed.

*

With the liberation of the area by the Russian Army in February 1944, we left the forests where we had been hiding for a year and a half and returned to Malinsk.

In March of that year, I reached Berezne with a group of six youths whom the Russians promised to send to school in Russia. We arranged all our required papers, and set out by foot to the nearby railway station along with a large group of Ukrainians whom the Russians had drafted to the army. Along the way, we had to stay over in a Ukrainian village. The Russian who was responsible for the entire group arranged for us to sleep in one of the houses in the village. We all slept with our clothes, only taking off our shoes. They woke us up toward morning and told us to go outside. I looked through the door and saw and saw that a Ukrainian was standing there with a gun, urging, "Hurry, hurry." That moment I approached the opening of the window. The Ukrainian jumped and dragged me back. At that time, four youths managed to jump out the window and began to escape in the direction of Berezne. The Ukrainian managed to capture one youth (Eliahu of blessed memory, the son of Gedalyahu Kesler). He dragged him to another room which did not have any windows. Instinctively, I crawled back to the room (before the Ukrainian managed to close the door). I jumped out the window and began to run in the direction of the city of Berezne. I met the four youths on the way to the town. We reached the town and called upon the Russian Army for help. We returned to that village, but found neither the Ukrainian nor Eliahu there. We could not find out where they took him.

We returned to Berezne, and from there to Malinsk.

[Page 330]

Harried and Afflicted[1]

by Shalom Katz of Tzfat

Shalom Katz

After the great slaughter in the Kostopol Camp, when a few Jews, I among them, succeeded in escaping, I did not know who had remained alive. I ran wherever my feet took me. I ran to the forest. As I was running, I threw off my coat that I still had from the Russians, so that it would be lighter for me as I ran to the forest. I heard a shout, "Father, where are you?" This was my son Shlomo, who had found the coat as he was running, and recognized it as his father's garment.

That is how we met up in the forest. There, I we found three other Jews from our camp who had fled. They were from Stepan. We were together for a bit of time, and then we were separated. My son and I wanted to go to the town of Berezne, where the rest of our family were in the ghetto. Along the way, as we were walking among the fields, a gentile showed us the direction to go to Berezne. When it was already day, we came up to a house and again asked the way to Berezne. Seeing that we were Jews, the gentile answered that we should not go there, for the Germans were killing the Jews there.

[Page 331]

From that gentile, we learned that a Ukrainian from Dzvinyach was there in the village. We secretly went to him. The Ukrainian received us nicely. He gave us food and told us to rest in the stable. After a short time, he came to us in the stable and told us to go on further, for he was afraid of the neighbors.

Our pleading was to no avail, and we had to leave his house during the day. We went to a second and third gentile acquaintance. Nobody let us in.

In Strange Fields

We left the village at night and wandered in the fields in an unknown area. Finally, we went to a gentile who lived far from a settlement, near swampy fields bedecked with bushes. There was no forest there. There, we found out that some Jews were still alive in the area, and that they were hiding. We worked for the Ukrainian for two months. We rested in the stable during the day and hid at night.

When the gentile no longer wanted to keep us, we went on further. In a different village, we were approached by a Ukrainian who offered to keep us for work. I went outside to rest a bit, and my son remained waiting in the house for a bit of food. In the meantime, a young Ukrainian entered the house and recognized that my son was a Jew. He took him to turn him over to the Germans. I saw everything, and could do nothing to help him... Fortunately, my son managed to escape from him along the way, and we were reunited at night.

*

We wandered further, hiding in the fields. We met a Jew from Berezne who was familiar with the area. From him, we found out about many other Jews who were hiding there in the surrounding fields. Together with him, through snow and water, we entered the forest.

[Page 332]

There in the forest, we met a few Jews from our area: Avraham Yaakov Breier with his four children, Malka Breier, and Gedalia Kesler and his family. There were also some Jews from Berezne. There, we found out that my other five children were alive, and were hiding in another forest about 30 kilometers from here. Two days later, my son Zerach came to us in the forest, not knowing that we had come there. He was the go-between for the Jews in both forests.

Zerach told me about everything that taking place in the area. The three of us went to the other forest where the other children were located. My wife, my youngest daughter, as well as my father were killed in the Berezne Ghetto on the day of the last aktion.

Life in the Forest

I was now together with my six children. Now we had to find a way to continue to survive. I found other relatives there – my sister-in-law who was already 70 years old: Hendel Rand. Her two sons and her daughter Mindel with her husband, and a daughter-in-law were with her. Our good neighbor from our home, Gedalia Erlich, was also there.

We made a bunker, and exchanged it from time to time out of fear. At night, we would go to the nearby villages to beg for food from the gentiles. We cooked in the bunker at night, so that nobody would see the smoke.

*

In the meantime, a misfortune took place. A pot of hot soup fell on my daughter, and her life was in danger. We were helped there by Gedalia Erlich. Together with my sons took a bed sheet, swaddled my daughter, took her to a gentile acquaintance and laid her down there atop the oven. She remained there for a month together with my oldest daughter. There, she healed her sick sister with linseed oil and gave her food. At the same time, my older daughter knitted sweaters for the gentile. Then, they both returned to the forest.

[Page 333]

That same Erlich helped me greatly with life in the forest. This was in the winter of 1942–1943. The salvation did not come in the summer either. My son Shlomo went out to the partisans, and I remained in the forest with the younger children.

Banderovches

In the forests, there were Banderovche Ukrainians who were seeking to murder Jews. The fear of them was greater than of the Germans. The Germans were afraid to go into the forests. The Banderovches also murdered entire villages of Poles – and their workshops remained empty. Therefore we would go at night and take some food. We took wheat and potatoes and hid them in barrels in pits that we dug in the forest. We hid them in many places and made markers. We prepared for a new winter. We built new bunkers, for we moved our places.

Liberation

We began to hear the artillery of the approaching Russian Army. In February 1944, the front came through our forest. For security reasons, we remained in the bunkers for the entire week. After that, we sent out three people to find out about the situation. They returned and told us that the Russians were already in the villages.

Translator's Footnote:

12. There is a footnote in the text here, as follows: See: Shalom Breier – A Young Man in a Nazi Work Camp, page 279.

[Page 334]

Surviving in a Bunker in the Forest

by Yosef Brenes of New York

The Morning After Judenrein

Life in the bunker began the morning after Judenrein – that is, when we had to transfer to the Sambor Ghetto. We had to connect with somebody who could bring us something from time to time. However, all of the gentiles who had made promises now had regrets: nobody wanted to help us. Having no other option, I turned to a farmer who had at one time worked for me, transporting wood and other things with my horse. His name was Ichnat Sokol. That farmer responded to me, “Go into the bunker in the forest, and I will help you with what I am able.”

The bunker had been prepared several weeks earlier. It was a hole in a hill, dug large enough for three people to lie down and sit. One could not stand up in it. I could not dig any further in the rocky ground. Furthermore, I had intended that it be small so that it will be warm in the winter. It turned out the opposite: It was very warm in the winter, but we froze from cold in the summer. On some occasions, we had to go out of the bunker to warm ourselves up in the sun...

Nobody could notice the entrance to the bunker. It was made under an old, fallen tree trunk that had been broken off by a wind perhaps 50 years earlier. The trunk was more than a meter thick and perhaps 20 meters in length, and a great deal of moss was growing around it.

Morsels of Food

I worked out with Sokol the farmer that we would meet under a certain tree once a week. I dug a pit by the tree, where he would be able to leave some food if for some reason we could not meet. The place was an hour walk from the bunker. More than once the journey was fruitless, or I did not find the way. I wandered around an entire night and returned to the bunker.

[Page 335]

Later, I decided to make markers on the trees, so that I would be able to find the way. I worked for several weeks making cuts in certain trees. I also got used to seeing in the dark. All of this was in order to remain in contact with that farmer to obtain some food.

We lived under terrible conditions, but with an urge to survive. Nothing was too great to help us to maintain ourselves. We searched for berries in the forest, and picked nuts from the trees. Winter approached, and the gentile informed us that he would be unable to come in the winter. We prepared a hole not far from the bunker, and filled it with potatoes, turnips, and beets that could last us a long time. We fasted every Monday and Thursday... The farmer also brought us 200 kilograms of rye and a small coffee grinder to mill it. We would mill it and put it in the soup, so that we would be able to sustain ourselves.

Sick and Hungry

The entire time, we were sick more often than healthy. We would sleep for entire months and endure the tribulations. There was a rock in the bunker that I was unable to uproot while digging. It indeed caused us difficulties: it hurt my stomach which was always lying upon it. Eventually, I became accustomed to it. When I was later free, I could not sleep unless I put some hard and uncomfortable object there...

[Page 336]

Our dream was to go outside, wander around freely, and eat a morsel of bread... The farmer indeed finally brought more to eat: bread, butter, and marmalade – what had happened? Perhaps he wants to be free from us? We realized, however, that this was for another reason: The Germans had begun to retreat from Stalingrad...

In the meantime, the front approached us. We already heard frequent shots in the area. The forest started to fill up with soldiers and other strange people. We had been lying there already for 19–20 months. The fear was greater, but hope was also growing —perhaps we will indeed succeed in surviving.

*

In the meantime, we were hungry. I would go out of the bunker in the morning to fetch a bit of water. Once, I saw a shot deer not far from the bunker. The Germans probably hit it with a bullet. However, what does one do with such a large animal? First of all, I removed the lungs and liver with a small knife and cooked a good meal. Then we began to search for a way to utilize the flesh. We dug a pit, filled it with snow, and laid the dear in it. We ate of its flesh for two months.

We also had a hidden stove made of two stones. The smoke was directed 20 meters below the ground. In this manner, we managed to hide the smoke. Inside, we had a small lamp. One liter of kerosene lasted us for two months. We did not burn it regularly, just in times of need. We lit fire by rubbing two stones between dry, rotting wood, which would ignite...

*

I recited my prayers every day sitting on a tree. Once, sitting on the tree, I suddenly heard a voice approaching me. I quickly got down from the tree and entered the bunker. The voice was from two or three Germans who were sitting not far from the bunker. We held our breath and my hand grasped the hand grenades that the farmer had provides us with. In such a case, they might be useful. The talking lasted for a half an hour, or perhaps an hour, and then things became silent. We breathed a bit more freely, but the fear was so great that our feet would not move... After several hours, we regained our composure and finally crawled out of the bunker. We found a bit of liquor, some meat, a piece of bread, half a box of sardines, and even a piece of chocolate. We even found a leaflet that was an appeal from the German General Paulus1, who had surrendered in Stalingrad. In the appeal, he warned the German Army to refrain from spilling blood cheaply. Hitler had lost the war. Now he will kill the German people.

[Page 337]

*

The front approached closer and closer. We heard shots and airplanes. Food was available again – would we survive? I went out on a Saturday afternoon to fetch water. I heard loud talking when I approached the bunker. This was our farmer, who had come to tell us the news: the Russian Army was already in our area – we were free!

Translator's Footnote:

11. See http://en.wikipedia.org/wiki/Friedrich_Paulus

[Page 338]

Wanderings During the Holocaust

by Yitzchak and Avraham Schindler of Kfar Ata

The Germans Arrived...

The Germans arrived in our village of Krasne near Turka in 1941, and immediately took ten of our best and finest young men, brought them to the top of the mountain, and killed them one by one by shooting. After several days, the Jews were taken to harsh labor. Many were sent far from their houses. Indeed, letters arrived from them, but they were infrequent.

We and our family members were given work in cutting down trees in the forests of our region. Our payment was two kilograms of black bread per week. Our family still had food... However, there were many families who were left with nothing, and did not even have bread. This work continued for a year. We lived in fear; for news reached us that they were murdering Jews in all places.

At that time, Gestapo captains reached our village, accompanied by a Jewish captain whose name was Baruch Aharon Rosen. They traveled from city to city and from village to village in the black automobiles in order to proclaim the edicts of the German Army. The current edict included the removal of property, including blankets, gloves, pillows, all clothing, work implements, plows, as well as food. They were to be taken outside and given to the Germans. They also requisitioned the animals.

The Ukrainians Begin to Act...

After a few days, a curfew was imposed upon the Jewish residents. It was forbidden for a Jew to be seen on the street after 6:00 p.m. One day, an edict was issued by the Ukrainians in the village that all Jews were to gather next to the school on Friday. Our family, who came early, did not find any living person there yet. Therefore, we went to chat a bit with some family members who lived nearby. The Ukrainians suddenly appeared and imprisoned us in one of the school rooms under the pretext that we were involved in politics. We sat in that room for nearly four hours until they freed us. That night, the local priest came to us and promised us that nothing will happen to my family. This was in exchange for the assistance that I extended to him when the Russians were in the country. I was on the committee at that time, and I helped him.

[Page 339]

In the meantime, the situation of the Jews became more severe. They were forbidden to gather in groups. The Ukrainians broke into the houses and pillaged anything that came to their hand. They took a great deal of property, and especially food. They also took care of people on the streets and did whatever they wanted to them.

To the Ghetto:

After a few days, an edict was issued by the Germans that within three days all of the Jews to gather in one place, since they had set up a ghetto in Turka, and all of the Jews were to go there. We were very afraid, since we knew that a ghetto is no simple matter that passes quickly. We heard that they kill Jews and work them hard. Mother, who had relatives in Smozhe, was able to move there since she had been born in that town. We packed everything possible, including some furniture that we dismantled and bedding, and gave them to our gentile neighbors. We gave six good outfits to our Christian maid.

At midnight, we moved mother to her relatives in Smozhe. The next day, we went to the gathering place that was designated for us. In the meantime, we found a Jew named Michcha Steininger who told us, “You have no place to go.

They are murdering Jews in the ghetto, and you are literally going to meet death by bullet." After my brother and I heard this, we succeeded in escaping to the nearby forest and hid there through day and night.

In the forest we were secure from the Germans, but open to beasts of prey. This was a thick forest, through which nobody dared to traverse alone during the day, and certainly not during the night. It is easy to imagine our fear when we were forced to spend and entire day and night there. Therefore, we decided at night, to go to our mother to see how she was doing, and to decide what to do further. The family with whom she was staying could not take in us as well, for this was absolutely forbidden. Mother, whose hometown this was, was permitted to be there. Not so with us.

When we told our uncle the situation, he told us that he had heard that those people who had worked before and now went to the ghetto received permits that allowed them to return to their former employment, and would not be bothered further. We again decided to go in the direction of the city... A brigadier named Yehoshua Langnaur joined us on the way. That Yehoshua had some sort of identity card from the Germans, and he was certain that they would not capture us. We already knew Yehoshua previously. He had worked with us in the forests. He told us that when difficult days come, he wanted to join us. He would dig for us a comfortable place to hide, and since he had a certificate, he would be able to provide us with food.

[Page 340]

Finally, this Yehoshua was caught by the Ukrainians. On the way to the ghetto he freed himself from the chains and escaped across the forest. The watchman, who did not recognize him, turned him over to the Germans who shot him on the spot.

We continued on our way to the city. This was in the early morning. An old acquaintance named Yehoshua Szpilman appeared before us and told us what was taking place in Turka: They were murdering Jews on the streets. Everyone was dying or being taken to the camps. He advised us to not go there.

Persecutions

We turned around once again and returned to Mother. Our journey went through a thick forest at the ridge of a large hill, where in general no person set foot. We went along this route all night. When we reached the peak, we sat down to rest and fell asleep... We woke up at daybreak. We were very perplexed, so we went deeper into the forest and sat there. At night, we returned to the village where Mother was staying. We ate there, and returned to the forest. Thus went our life for two weeks. During the days we sat in the forests, at times under heavy, torrential downpours. At night we went to see

Mother and to eat a bit. The rest of the Jews in the village barely dared to allow strange Jews into their homes, for the Germans would murder the entire family if a Jew from another place was found.

One day we heard that the wood factory in Smozhe was accepting Jews for work. Anyone who obtained this work would receive an identity card that would protect him from being snatched to the ghetto and the like. I, who had previously worked in this factory, went there. I requested work from the work director. His name was Levincki. He was a pleasant, polite gentile, and he said that he was prepared to help me. I gave him the two gold watches that I had, but he did not want to take them. He took us on for work without any repayment. We began to work.

One day, S.S. scooters and closed cars arrived at the factory. The Nazis talked with the director of the factory. Immediately thereafter, the director told us that we must leave the place, since they are taking the Jews to the ghettos in the village of Krasne. My brother and I wanted to cross through the town with the hope of saving Mother and taking her to the forest, but when we reached the mountain and looked from above, we saw that they were already hauling tens of Jews. We were too late... We later found out that Mother was in the field at the time that the Gestapo captains arrived. She sensed the approaching danger, and ran home in order to escape to the forest – but they caught her and took her to the ghetto along with the rest of the Jews. According to the news we heard, they already murdered her along the way. At night, we stood outside and saw how the gentiles were pillaging and taking everything that they wanted from the house.

[Page 341]

We returned to our village of Krasne, for we had heard that the mayor had designated one of the houses for all Jews who succeeded in escaping from the ghetto. When he saw my brother and me, and another family member with a wife, two daughters and a son, he decided to give us our own house. We worked for various gentiles at various jobs until one day; a certain gentile took us to himself for regular work. We were like his slaves, but he treated us in a decent fashion.

In the Bunker

One day, a command arrived to turn over all the Jews. A few Jews escaped immediately, and some others were captured. The gentile with whom we worked wrote a letter requesting that they leave us with him. In the letter, he took it upon himself to kill us with his own hands if he would find out that there are no more Jews in the entire world... But the authorities did not agree, and we were forced to escape. This gentile promised us that if we would survive until December 13, we would continue to live always... In the meantime, my brother, another relative and his family, and I went to the forest. There, we decided to separate, and to meet on occasion at a certain gentile. However, they captured and murdered that relative and his family.

My brother and I dug a large bunker and decided to find shelter for a certain time. In the meantime, we approached a different gentile acquaintance, and requested a bit of clothing and food. At an earlier time, we had given over our property and clothing to him. He gave us pants and other such items and said that we do not need any more, for in any case, we would not live long... He wanted to give us a sack of potatoes, but we did not take it for we were afraid that this would make it more difficult to escape.

We remained in the bunker until December 13. We ate and lied down the entire time. At the designated time we exited the bunker, went again to that gentile, and asked him to give us more clothing and food. However, he refused to give us, saying that we would die soon, and it would be a waste. In the meantime he got dressed. When my brother asked him why he was getting dressed, he responded that he was preparing to accompany us, for the gentiles would murder us on along the way... We realized, however, that he was intending to turn us in to the authorities. We thanked him for his "good heart" and disappeared to the bunker.

[Page 342]

The snow melted the next day, and it was a nice day outside. The sun was shining and the birds were singing... We left the bunker to rest a bit. Suddenly, we heard footsteps approaching. We immediately returned to the bunker and began to shiver with cold. The voices came closer, and we realized that the gentiles had indeed come to the forest to murder us. We heard them discussing this. One of them said, "Indeed, why are we searching for them now, to kill them? One day the war will end, and we will be able to kill them on the street." The other responded, "If you say this, and many others say this – it will turn out that many Jews will survive, and then, woe will be unto us." The rain and the wind that started up suddenly chased the gentiles away from the place. Even though we were hungry, we did not go out to search for food that night.

Thieves for Hire...

The following evening we went to a different gentile, named Roman, who had once promised us that if things were bad for us and we were in a difficult situation, we could come to him. We arrived to him at midnight. He was happy to see us and said, "G–d had sent you to help me, and I will help you." It seemed that he did not have bread at home, and therefore he gave us milk to drink. However, if we would obtain hay for his cows, he would be able to plow other people's fields, and then there would be food for him and for us... We took two blankets, went to the gentile Lorenz, stole two bundles of hay, and returned...

This continued for 18 nights. During the day we slept in an attic. This continued until Lorenz realized that hay was being stolen from him, and he hid it... We returned without anything and realized that now we would have to return to the forest. But that gentile told us that the hay that we had brought him would last the cows for one month, and we could stay with him.

In the meantime, we received 20 dollars from a Jewish lad who wished to join us. However, since we were filthy and lice–ridden, he regretted this. He forfeited the dollars. We gave the dollars to that gentile with whom we were staying during that period, and remained there for a sufficiently long time. We performed various jobs for him. My brother set up a good wagon for him, but it was missing two front wheels. That gentile who was passing through the town "by chance" saw two wheels that would be very fitting for his wagon and asked us to go and steal them... This was on a Friday. We told him that we would not go that night, but we went on Saturday night and "took" the wheels. The people who were guarding the fields almost caught us. As we were returning, we passed through a forest and heard voices. We turned around, and the two wheels on our backs banged against each other and made a ringing sound... The gentiles stood and said, "Some sort of demon is making strange sounds at night. It must certainly be Jews." We stopped moving for some time, and continued along our way when the gentiles disappeared from the horizon.

[Page 343]

The next day, we went to steal bundles of hay, when we suddenly heard a shout "Stop." We were startled. We dropped the bundles and fled to the forest. We remained there for two nights and returned to that gentile. He told us that he was afraid to keep us any longer, despite the fact that he had food for an extended period, since those gentiles who saw him had figured out that we were the children of Rachel, from the lice–ridden sheets that were covering the hay that we wanted to bring to spread in the cave in which we lived...

Preparing to Cross the Border to Hungary

We then decided to go out and ask for help from that Lorencz. He told us that he could bring us across the border to Hungary. He also promised to clarify how we could arrange ourselves there. Jews from Hungary sent everyone 100 Pengő (Hungarian currency) two shirts and 100 cigarettes. They said that it would be possible to stay with a Jew named Mordechai Gutman.

My brother, Shmuel Freilich, his wife and three daughters, two of them married, and I gathered together and decided to cross the border to Hungary. Two daughters, who did not want to go without a guide, decided at the last minute to return to the forest. I returned to the village to fetch my brother's *tefillin* bag, the only property that we still possessed. The girls parted from their parents with bitter weeping. We recited the Wayfarer's Prayer [*Tefillat Haderech*], and requested from the Holy One Blessed Be He that He do good to us and make our journey successful. We set out on the journey.

Of course, we only traveled at night until we reached the river. Since the river was not yet completely frozen, we were forced to cross it by walking through the cold water. We got undressed and crossed. We reached the mountain and ascended it. Then Shmuel realized that he had made a mistake on the route and did not know how to continue. His wife began to scream and wail. Then we decided that, since there was a village on the descent of the mountain, my brother would go down there and ask the name of that village. I parted from my brother with bitter weeping, not thinking I would see him again. He went down. He went to the first house, where he saw a woman outside, and asked her the name of the place. The woman responded, "Who are you that you do not know where you are?"... My brother Yitzchak immediately made up a story that his brother, a tobacco salesman, had been captured in Hungary, and now he wanted to go to save him. The woman believed him, took him into her house, gave him food, and showed him the way to Hungary. He returned to us in peace, and we began to walk in the new direction. We had to cross the river again and traverse the mountain. When we reached the border, we lay down for a long time at the side of the road until the road was emptied of all vehicles of the border guard.

[Page 344]

In the Designated Village in Hungary

After Shmuel and I scouted out the area, we reached the designated village. We went to Mordechai, and knocked on the door of his barn. A voice was heard from inside in Yiddish, "Who is there?" Shmuel responded, "I, Shmuel Freilich." No response came, and the door did not open. We entered the pen and froze there from the cold of the snow that stuck to our clothing. The next day that Mordechai came out and gave us coffee and a piece of bread. Of course, this did not satiate us. They sent Shmuel and his wife to one attic, and his daughter, my brother and I to another attic. The attic was open, and therefore a fierce wind blew in it. We froze from cold throughout that entire day, and our teeth chattered as if they would break.

At night, he took us all down to the potato storehouse. There it was hot, and the air was clear. We had to sleep on the wet potatoes. Our bodies were filled with wounds. The swarming lice began to itch and hurt. Our entire body hurt. We lived under such conditions for two weeks. Then, Mordechai transferred us to a Jew named Tuchman, who was Shmuel's cousin. He received us very politely.

It was Friday night. We all sat down and ate in a fashion that we had not known for a long time. We remained there for a week until they (a Jewish group) decided to transfer us to Budapest. There, we were to obtain papers and identity certificates with Christian names. The Jews who had transferred us placed my brother and me in one place and Shmuel and his wife in a different place. They told us that if we were to be asked for papers on the train, we should respond that a soldier had purchased our tickets.

In Budapest as Christians

We arrived in Budapest in peace, and went to the restaurant where the refugees gathered. This was on 11 Kiri Street. We ate and drank to our fill, but they did not give us a place to sleep since we were dirty. He continued from there to the synagogue. We lay down there to sleep, but the *shamash* did not permit this. From there, we went to a certain Christian hotel, where we received lodging for one night. They did not want to accept us for more than one night, since we did not have Christian papers, and it was possible that we might be caught.

The next day we went to the city hall to receive Christian papers. They photographed us and we filled out various forms. We received our certificates six days later. They called my brother by the Christian name Ignac Koblaski, and I was called Edvard Koblaski. I was constantly afraid that I would forget the name of my father and mother, and the name that they called me... I registered as a farm worker and my brother as a smith. They sent us from there to the work in the city of Neidvarok. We were received there by Naftali Adler, who was the son-in-law of the Rebbe of Visznitz. He arranged for us places to work and eat. We received 45 Pengő while still in Budapest, with which we purchased new clothes and food. This Naftali made sure to find us a workplace where they did not work on the Sabbath. This was in a factory for weights, owned by Lichtman, a G–d fearing Jew. My brother received work in the smithy, but there they did work on the Sabbath. Each week he found a different excuse in order to not go to work. However, out of fear that they would finally suspect him and capture him, he left the workplace and transferred to a suitcase factory. We set ourselves up properly, we ate well, and our economic situation was good. Everything was like this until the Germans entered Budapest on March 20, 1943. A great fear overcame the Jews.

[Page 345]

One day, the owner of the factory called me and told me that he knows my origins – that I was a Jew. He probed and asked many questions. When did I escape and leave Poland? What was the situation of the Jews in Poland during the time of the German invasion? I answered all of his questions in brief, and explained the situation to him. He invited me to his home for Sabbaths. I lived with him for more than a month.

In the Neidvarok Ghetto

A ghetto was established in Neidvarok on April 5, 1944. We begged and pleaded for the Jews to leave the city while it was still possible to do so. I told them everything that had happened to us, about the myriads of Jews who were slaughtered – but they did not believe us and did not listen to us.

Then, one day, a Jew was captured on his way from the synagogue. Of course, this immediately caused many echoes, and people began to be afraid. However, even then they did not escape. They trusted that their money and all their friends in the police would help them. After a short time, 30 Jews were captured. In exchange for them, the Germans demanded 30 fully furnished rooms. They received their rooms immediately, and the captured Jews were freed. All of the Jews were brought into the ghetto that was established. That factory owner with whom I pleaded and begged so much to leave and escape from the city, and who trusted in his remaining money – met my brother in the ghetto and begged from him a box of cigarettes and a liter of milk...

[Page 346]

We were about 60 Jews with Christian papers. We lived in dwellings outside the ghetto. My brother and I did not have entry certificates to the ghetto. The factory was closed for about two weeks. Then, it was reopened after the ownership was transferred to a Hungarian gentile. We all returned to work. We lived in relative calm for quite some time, until we heard knocks on the door of our dwelling one Sabbath. We were very surprised, and we opened the door. Policemen stood at the door. They asked us if the Koblaski brothers and two other youths lived there. We responded affirmatively, and they asked us to come down.

All the Jews with Christian certificates were gathered downstairs. We were arranged in rows, and the guards passed by us to determine who was a Jew. I was one of the first to enter the room, and I was asked to pray. I crossed myself and prayed with "devotion". Then a physician examined me and determined that I was a proper gentile... I was afraid that my brother would stumble, since he did not know the "blessings." However, to our good fortune, they asked him if he was the second Koblaski. When he answered affirmatively, they immediately transferred him to my side. Everyone except for two people passed the examination.

Escape to Romania

However, from that time, we no longer felt secure, and we decided to escape to Romania. We got in touch with Miklos, a gentile who transferred many Jews from Hungary to Romania. He asked for 1,300 Pengő. Of course, we did not have such money, so my brother returned to Budapest to sell various belongings of Jews that were left with us. We arranged with that Miklos to meet us in the railway station and to take us. We were four people, but when we got there, we found another 18 people whom he also agreed to transfer. We traveled in a train full of German captains, but everything went in peace. We traveled until the Romanian border depot. There, we got out and went through the fields. We walked all night, and we arrived in a Romanian village toward morning. We entered a house, ate and drank, and set out on our journey at night. My brother and several other people who were at the head of the group walked with the guide, and I walked behind with the wife of Yisrael and another gentile. Suddenly, that gentile decided to return to the village. We attempted to convince him to continue on the journey with us, but he refused. In the meantime, all of the first ones got father away from us, and since it was dark, we could not see the route. We continued alone along the straight path until we reached a crossroads. We did not know which way to turn... We screamed and called out, but this did not help. Yisrael ran after that gentile to ask him which way to go. In the meantime, dawn broke, and we, the woman and myself, stood in an open field. We entered the nearby forest and sat there all that day. We returned to the village in the evening.

[Page 347]

We entered a house, ate to our fill, and asked the master of the house to take us to the city of Arad. He agreed on the condition that we give him a suit, which we gave him. However, the gentile lied to us and did not bring us to the city. In the meantime, rumors spread through the entire village that there were refugees there. We went to the local police, since there was no choice, and it was no longer possible to escape. At the police they told us that the first group was also caught, since "their" gentile also escaped and left them alone, not knowing the route... They interrogated all of us and sent us to the police in a different city, the city of Tinca, where they were treated us harshly and beat us cruelly. They took all the property and food that we had. We met a Jew there who promised to bring us to the guards at the Hungarian border, where they would free us.

Interrogations and Suffering

They brought us to the Hungarian–Romanian border, and warned us that if we were ever to return to Romania, they would kill us. This warning was repeated several times. The Romanian police showed us the route to go to Neidvarda. The journey was at night, so it was comfortable. However, since we were about 30 people, we were afraid that they might capture us – and then we would be goners! Therefore, my brother, Chaim and I went in a different direction. We walked all that night until we noticed houses, fields and people toward morning. We did not know whether we were in Romania or Hungary...

We approached one of the houses and asked the way that leads to Neidvarda. The gentile told us that the railway station was close by and we could travel on it. He told us to wait, for he wanted to go with us. Not even five minutes passed when he returned with... a policeman. The policeman interrogated and questioned. We told him that we lived in the city of Neidvarda and worked in the factory, but it was closed when the Jews were taken to the ghetto, so we went to seek agricultural work in the villages. We lost our way at night, and reached the village toward morning. Then we asked him for directions to return to the city. The policeman took us to the military police where they interrogated us thoroughly. We had to give over all of our property: money, clothing, etc. They did not beat us, but they shouted at us and placed each of us into a separate cell. They called us out for interrogation every two hours.

The interrogations were accompanied by death threats. After several interrogations, they called me. The policeman said that they had killed my two friends, so I now can state the truth. When I heard this, death did not matter to me, so long as I would not state the truth. I got up, raised my hand, and said that I was prepared for death. The policeman saw this and told me to sit down. Another policeman who was present in the room went and called my brother and Chaim... The end of the matter was that the police wrote a note of confirmation to the civil guard that we were gentiles who had gone out to seek agricultural work – and we had been caught by chance...

[Page 348]

We were transferred the civil guard, who also interrogated us. We repeated our story again and again. We remained in that police station for about four days, until... we were summoned to a new interrogation. We were put into a cell where there were criminals, murderers, and robbers. They provoked us in various ways, to the point where we were forced to ask to be transferred to a different cell. We were transferred. We were freed after the interrogations, and we finally returned to our place of residence of Neidvarda. We began to work in the factory, and amassed money.

After some time, the ghetto was liquidated, and all of the Jews were taken to be murdered. The danger increased.

Return to Romania

We once again paid a significant sum to a gentile, who agreed to transfer us to Romania. We arrived at a village in Romania. When we were in a room there, we found various notes and letters from Jews who had been there previously. Our acquaintance Shmuel Freilich was among them. The next day, the person who transferred us, a mute youth, sent us to be transferred to the nearby city. At first we suspected him, but then we went. When we arrived there, we found the Jews who had escaped before us. All of us stayed with one *shochet.* Since we were more than 50 people, he was not able to keep us all. My brother and I went to a certain family. This was on the Sabbath. They were poor, but they still gave us food. We were very tired, and fell asleep quickly.

In the afternoon, they came to tell us that a car was waiting to take us to Arad. Of course, we quickly went, and drove with them. Along the way, the police caught us and began to interrogate us... They decided to transfer us to the police in Tinca, where we had been previously, and who had warned us not to return to Romania, or we would be killed. We began to fear for our lives. However, a certain Jew promised to save us. He bribed the young men and women of the village to each keep one of us, and then it would seem that we were guests. He told the Tinca police that we were tourists.

[Page 349]

We returned to that *shochet* in Dionto, and remained there for several days. After some time, they again gathered all of the people in a large transport vehicle and took us to the city of Arad. From there, we were transferred to Bucharest, where we received Polish papers. We were no longer afraid. By then, the Russians had conquered Romania – we were free!

*

After about two weeks, I received a notice to travel on the Solahatin Ship to the Land of Israel. I arrived in the Land on Chanukah, 1944.

A Nazi Murderer Met His Death in a Fight with Two Jewish Girls

by Tzipora Zelmanovitch (Katz)

The family of my uncle Shlomo Bruner numbered 11 souls. Aside from his wife Rivka, he had nine children: Esther, David, Leah, Ben-Zion, Sheindel, Avraham, Udes, Shmuel, and Chaya-Sara. The family hid in a bunker that was dug in the forests of Rosokhach. About two months before the liberation, the Germans uncovered the tracks of the gentile who brought them food, and reached the bunker. Two of the girls fought valiantly against the Nazi murderer who wanted to capture them, and succeeded in killing him. However, they were shot by the Nazi friends of the murdered man as they were escaping. My uncle, aunt, and all the rest of the children were murdered by the Nazis when they were captured.

[Page 350]

The Destruction of Ilnik

(Story from a survivor)

by Yeshayahu Schwartz of Netanya

Yeshayahu Schwartz

When the Germans came to us in 1941, the tribulations began immediately. The Ukrainians began to pillage Jewish property. A little later, they also began to murder Jews. The Germans issued an edict that every Jew must wear a white band with a blue Star of David so that people could see from afar that a Jew was passing by... Anyone who did not follow the edict would be shot.

Plunder

Later, the Germans began to take Jewish property. We received an edict that we must give over our animals, grain, and everything that we had in the storehouse. I saw how the Germans were purchasing our animals from the Germans at an auction. Their joy was great when they could get everything dirt cheap. An edict was issued that every Jew who had animals, hens, grain, and the like would be shot. My mother and sister wept bitterly as we gave everything over. They could not imagine what type of a misfortune was still awaiting us.

Later, the Germans took our furs, and we were left naked, barefoot, and hungry. They issued an edict that all Jews must cut off their beards and *peyos*. The Jewish women were pulling their hair from their heads. I think about the great misfortune that afflicted my father: his beard and *peyos* were his pride.

[Page 351]

Murder

One night, the Ukrainians came and arrested my brother Ben-Zion. They held him under arrest, beat him, and did not give him any food. We brought him some food from home. They took it from us, told us they would give it to him, but did not give it to him. Later, they took him out to the forest, beat him murderously, and murdered him. They did the same thing with my cousin Eliahu Katz. They took all the young lads from Ilnik at one time and murdered them. These included Shmuel Lauterman, Itamar Rosenberg, Sender Fuchs, and Yitzchak-Izak Fuchs.

Hunger

Hunger began to prevail in Turka as well as in Ilnik. People began to suffer from the effects of hunger. Anyone who noticed that his foot was swollen realized that he was going to die... Today one could be talking with a person – and the next day he could already be dead. Anyone who had anything to sell tried to do so for a bit of oatmeal or potato peels. People cooked grass and mixed it with a bit of oatmeal to bake small cakes. The children were excited about such a piece of cake...

I went to work with the gentiles. I drove the horses and dragged the plow, as I toiled for 14 hours. In return, I received a bit to eat. I brought half of the portion home. In the meantime, the entire work with the farmer became improper – if they caught me they would shoot me... Later, an edict was issued that all Jews must have a work certificate. My father and I obtained the certificates, but my mother, sister Reizele and brother Hershele were unable to obtain them. When an edict was issued that all Jews who do not have such a certificate must present themselves in Turka, and register there to obtain certificates – I already knew that they were just fooling us. I already knew their dark methods...

[Page 352]

In Concentration for Annihilation

My brother, sister and mother went away to concentrations points in Turka. I went along with them. All the Jews from Ilnik and many villages around Turka were there. I saw thousands of people there, including our entire family from Bikla, Yavorov, Jablonka, Walsza, Libechiv and other places. We kissed and embraced, and asked, "What will be here?" Nobody knew how to answer.

My father and I returned to Ilnik. We did not sleep the entire night. In the morning, we took a bit of food and wanted to bring it to the city. However, as we were leaving the house we met several gentiles who informed us that the Gestapo had taken all the Jews. Food for the family was already too late...

The Nazis surrounded the Jews with dogs and wild shouts, pushed them onto wagons like stones, and transported them to Belzec... We wept for them day and night, for we already knew the dark truth. We worked in the forest with 100 grams of bread per day. I did not have the energy to haul the thick beams. My father did everything to lighten my workload.

And again a dark end. They surrounded us in our house at night and captured us all. They did not even let us put on our shoes. I stuck my feet in my galoshes and went outside. They seated us in the snow, and Ukrainian police began to beat my father. I could not help at all. I then had an opportunity to escape. My father was so badly beaten that he could not move. They pursued me, but did not succeed. I never saw my father again. Feiga Rosenberg later told me that when they were later taken to the camp by train, my father told her that he was happy that I had escaped. Perhaps one of the family will survive. Feiga later jumped off of the train and survived.

[Page 353]

Wandering in the Forests

I entered the forests naked, barefoot, hungry, and alone like a stone. Later I met friends who helped me. We began to make bunkers and prepare for the winter. In the meantime, we received information that the Germans knew about us and that they were preparing to attack us. We lost our bunker in the fiercest snow and storms, so we looked for a hiding place in a second forest. We remained there until the end of the winter.

During the summer, we met other Jews from Turka in the forests. There were also Jews from Sambor who fled there during the time of the liquidation. I met Avraham Feiler, Avraham Libhart, Yosha Szleicher, David Laufer, and others. We were a large group and this strengthened us a bit. We no longer had to ask for a bit of bread from the Ukrainians – we would take it by force. We brought an animal into the forest and had some food to eat. I found some clothing from somewhere, and living became a bit easier. We began to prepare for a new winter in the forest.

Battle with Germans

For the second winter, we prepared two bunkers, 50 meters apart. Each bunker had two "stories," an upper and lower. It was quite warm in the top story. In the lower story, where I slept, it was very cold. Cold and hunger were constant. We would always remain on watch and guard.

Shlomo Yitzchak Entner was standing on guard, when he saw hundreds of Germans coming from afar. We all left the bunkers. We did not see them well, because the bullets from both sides were hitting the branches, stirring up the snow. I was running around the mountain when I saw that Mrs. Shuster had been wounded. She shouted at me to help her. Unfortunately, there was nothing I could do for her. When the shooting between the Germans and us stopped, the Germans broke into the bunkers. We thought that they would surround us, and we were prepared for our final battle. However, they apparently had regrets. They were afraid of entering deep into the forest.

[Page 354]

*

Yitzchak Oferman shouted to me, "Are you still barefoot!" Only then did I notice that I was barefoot, until then I did not feel it. My feet were red like fire – for how long can a person stand barefoot in the snow? I was wearing only a shirt. That was the way I had left the bunker. I begged my friends to shoot me, for I had terrible pains in my feet and I knew that without shoes, I would not be able to manage. Of what use was it to suffer?

Mendel Fuchs from Ilnik had a blanket with him. He tore it into two. He covered my shoulders with one half, and bound my feet with the other half. Someone had a bit of string, and they bound me up.

I wandered around in the wind and deep frost until night. At night, my friends went out to procure food. I tried to go along with them, but at the end they left me behind.

Hungry, thirsty and in great pain, I entered a sheep pen and fell asleep. However, when the gentile came to feed the sheep, he saw me and shouted at me to leave immediately. All of my pleas had no effect. He grabbed at me wildly and tried to stab me. I left the pen and began to return to the forest. I leaned against a tree and wept...

[Page 355]

The thought came to me to pass through the mountain and go to Ilnik, where I had gentile acquaintances. With my last strength, I climbed up the mountain, dragging along my rags in the deep snow. I saw a hut at the summit and entered it. The gentile sat me down near the oven, and gave me hot milk. I swaddled my swollen feet. The gentile comforted me and kept me for two weeks.

[Page 355]

David Laufer, the Hero from Ilnik

by Yeshayahu Schwartz

David Laufer

When I write these words about you, David Laufer, my heart is broken. Why did you not survive to see the downfall of the German murderers? Even more – why were you not permitted to witness the freedom of the Jewish people?!

When you used to speak to me – your aspirations were for your freedom and to come to Israel. You were the one who always comforted me and never let me become discouraged. You always said that we would survive everything. When you had a morsel of bread, you would share it with me. You always carried yourself like a soldier, and your weapons were in your sack. When we would go to a village to fetch some bread, you would always look at me – to see if I was going with courage, was I not falling down, or was I perhaps rolling around in some pit.

[Page 356]

This went on until the dark day came when the Germans and their Ukrainian assistants attacked our two bunkers and fought against 60 Jews. Shlomo Yitzchak Entner was standing on guard. When he saw them, he shot at them, and we left the bunkers.

The Germans then shot at us with machine guns. It was dark. The snow fell off of the trees, for the bullets hit the branches. Not far from the bunker, a battle was raging to the last bullet, and you yourself took care of so many murderers. I saw how you crawled on your stomach in order to distance yourself from them, but you could no longer crawl in the deep snow, so you remained lying there.

We fought against them, but unfortunately, we could not hold them off. They approached you and shot you in cold blood.

You, David Laufer, were a true hero. You are no longer with us, but your heroism will shine its light for generations.

[Page 359]

There are no more Jews in Turka

From Atop the Roof I See You

by David Y.

From atop the roof I see you Turka
So clear and fine,
With your smile
Without sorrow, without weeping…
I see the winding alleyways The curved small
houses, With fallen roofs – Why so afraid?
And why? The Szymunka with its prideLaughs at
me and says: "There is no more a shtetl! There is
no more a Jewish home"…
Mizera, Elul 5724 (1964)

[Page 360]

In the Empty City…

by Michael Heisler

In the autumn of 1944, fate brought me once again face to face with the city of Turka. Already on the second day post liberation, I once again found myself on the Turka mountains, in the same place where I had lived some three and a half years previously, close to the Turka cemetery, from where I could see the entire city in all its grandeur. From afar, I could still hear the firing of the Soviet cannons, accompanying by the fleeing of the Germany Army.

The city was empty and quiet. Not a soul was around. It seems that the houses were smaller than before, shrunken, black, dismal, without windows, without doors, without people... The streets were filled with yellow, rotting, leaves. The railway bridge was ripped apart, and its stones were scattered throughout the city. The rails were curved and flattened. Not long ago – in fact, it seemed like yesterday – Jewish life bustled in every corner here. And today?... Today everything is dead.

I did not weep. Why should I weep?. Was I seeing the first dead city?... Over the entire past three and a half years, I wandered over ruins, over dead, murdered cities and villages, until I arrived in Russia. I had wept so much that my nerves did not react when I saw my own city of Turka in the same situation as thousands of other cities and towns.

I wanted to find a living witness who would tell me details about the tragic death of the Jews who had lived there. I entered the city. Along the way, there were broken gravestones, tossed into the mud and the ditches, trampled by tanks. I attempted to find my mother's gravestone, but it was not possible. In the cemetery I met an old Christian who was leading a sheep on a leash. She led me to a place and pointed with her finger – here is where the Germans shot very man Jews from the city, and her is the place where they lie. The grave was already overgrown with grass... "Where are the rest of the Jews?" – I asked. "The Germans sent them all away," she responded.

[Page 361]

*

I set out for the villages to look – perhaps I would find someone alive, or a sign of their murder. I walked to almost every village. It was the same emptiness everywhere. The houses were burned or occupied, and the soil was plowed. Not even a marker remained.

I asked the local residents about how all the Jews had been murdered. The told me that the Germans led them all away to the gas chambers, and that no Jews were murdered here. However, I found out from reliable Ukrainians that many murders were perpetrated on the place itself by the Ukrainian bands. Throughout the entire time of the war, the primary employment of the bands was to search for Jews and murder them, or turn them over to the Gestapo for a "high" payment – a kilo of salt for a Jewish soul...

[Page 362]

In Turka After the Liberation

By Chaim Pelech

Translated by Jerrold Landau

Donated by Boaz Ben-Pelech

I was in Russia. The end of the war was approaching. I read in the newspaper that the Hitlerists were already retreating in the Carpathians. I was anxious for Turka to be liberated, but it was not happening. Difficult weeks passed until Turka was finally liberated. I quickly wrote a letter to my wife in Turka, but I received no reply...I already understood that it was bitter: there was nobody left in Turka... I wrote another letter, this time to the Turka community. After a long wait, I received a letter from Avraham Hanz from Radicz, near Turka. He told me that the bandits murdered all of the Jews of Turka and its environs. No trace was left of my family...

That meant that I was alone. What should I do now – no wife, no child, no brothers, no sisters. I was sitting here in dark Lapatino, deep in Russia, knowing nothing about what was going on in the Jewish world... How was it that the Jewish world could have allowed so many Jews to be murdered? I asked many questions at that time: Why? However, nobody was able to give me an answer...

I began to make efforts to travel home, to Turka, so that I could witness with my own eyes the great misfortune.

I arrived in Lemberg after twelve days. I slept there with my former classmate Shreier, who had survived. I traveled on. I went to Sambor, for no train went to Turka. I arrived in Turka early on the second day.

As I arrived, I stood still and did not know where to go... The entire city was a ruin. All of the houses were broken. The only ones that remained whole were the town hall and Chaim Hirsch's house. In the Olica, there was also Moshe Hirsh's house and a number of other houses. The others were broken and run down to the ground. This was my native town, where I spent my entire life! My spirit was downcast, and I remained standing there in a bewildered state...

A loud shout woke me out of my thoughts: 'Chaim, when did you arrive?". This was a Jew from Turka. He took me to Chava Brandelsztejn, who remained alive. A Turka Ukrainian, Kamarnichki, hid her in his cellar. Chava was very happy to see me, as she was our best neighbor. She told me everything that took place in my home. She told me when and how my dear ones were killed: my son, wife, sisters, brothers, and stepmother. As she talked, my gaze was fixed upon the floor. I could not look her in the face... How could I have left everyone behind to wantonness, and saved myself alone?!

I listened on.. A letter came from Stryj informing that they shot my brother Shlomo Pelech there on July 1. A letter came from Przemysl that they shot my sister Bracha Pelech, also on July 1. My stepmother was shot in Turka on July 1, all in one day! When the children's aktion took place, a Jewish policeman, Chaim Meinbach, entered the house and took my only son Avraham. He was shot that same day.

Thus did I sit and hear about my downfall...

[Page 364]

In the Destroyed City

by Asher Brandelstein of Haifa

Asher Brandelstein

I returned to Turka in August 1945. I had been away from the towns in which I had been born and had spent my childhood and youth for four full years. I had spent four years in Russia. I came with my wife, with whom I had lost my home during the first days of the war, and with our young daughter was born in Bashkiria1. I left behind a town in which a few thousand Jews lived. When we returned, we found approximately 20 to 30 souls... The town had almost been completely destroyed. All of the Jewish homes had been destroyed and burnt.

My Mother Lives!

A special surprise awaited me when I arrived in Turka – I found my mother alive, one of the survivors from the town. She survived thanks to a Ukrainian family that hid her. My mother was a midwife, and, before the war, she had helped the family who hid her. My mother was known in town as someone who helped poor women in childbirth, both Jewish and Christian – and in her own need she found a savior.

She went through her hell. She could only tell me that my father had been shot immediately during the first aktion. My wife's parents with four young brothers were murdered during the large aktion.

[Page 365]

I Searched for Acquaintances...

Those who survived had hid in the forests. A small number had hid with gentiles. However, almost all immediately left for Poland (Turka already belonged to Ukraine). The rest were preparing to do so.

I, however, could not set out on the journey because my mother required an eye operation. When the operation was finally completed, I was already too late – it was no longer permitted.

[Page 366]

The first weeks after my arrival in town were difficult for me. There were moments where it seemed that I would go out to the street and meet my friends, acquaintances, and other dear faces from our youth and childhood. Even though the situation indicated otherwise, I would run – perhaps a miracle would take place?... I would have to go alone...

The first families who arrived in Turka after the war

A Jewish Teacher in a Strange School

At the beginning of the 1945 school year, I began to work as a mathematics teacher in the Turka middle school. It was difficult to be a teacher. More than once it seemed to me that the students who were now answering my questions – had perhaps shown the German and Ukrainian policemen where an unfortunate victim was hiding during the aktions. We often discussed such facts.

It was difficult, very difficult, to be a Jewish teacher in a school in which many Jewish children should have been sitting – and where are they?...

In 1951, I was nominated as principal of that same middle school. Every year, I conducted formal matriculation ceremonies. Those ceremonies caused me great vexation. I would come home sick and broken. Once again: where are our children who should have received the same certificates today?!...

A few Jewish children, from the three Jewish families in the city, studied in that school. This gave me a bit of happiness. I frequently dreamed of being a teacher in a Jewish school. In the meantime, this was indeed only a dream.

In the meantime, I frequently had to listen to anti–Semitic speeches from teachers (for example, during the Doctors Trials[2] during the Stalin era), and to anti–Semitic proclamations from students. I also had to organize ceremonies marking the 300th anniversary of the arch–pogromchik Chmielnicki.

This is now past, as my dream of Israel has come true.

Translator's Footnotes:

86. See http://en.wikipedia.org/wiki/Bashkir_Autonomous_Soviet_Socialist_Republic
87. See http://en.wikipedia.org/wiki/Doctors'_plot

[Page 367]

The City Sits in Desolation...[1]

by Bronia Brandelstein of Haifa

Bronia Brandelstein

In the valley that is surrounded by a ridge of tall mountains, thick forests, and the lovely Stryj River, lies our native town of Turka. One's native town is precious to every person, but to me and all other natives of Turka it is sevenfold precious. Our town was something special and close to our hearts for us. Indeed, there were wonderful youths in our town. Now, when I think back from some distance, I am filled with wonder – how could such wonderful youth as were in those days have lived their lives full of content and sublime aspirations, without having any chance at all of fulfilling these dreams and hopes. Indeed, each person forged his path in accordance with his possibilities.

The war destroyed all of these aspirations and hopes. Everyone was afflicted in a different fashion. Some succeeded in finding refuge in the Land of Israel. Others were exiled to Siberia during the maelstrom of the war. However, awaiting the vast majority were the gas chambers, which opened their muzzles and swallowed millions of Jews. They swallowed those nearest and dearest: parents, brothers, sisters, relatives, and friends.

Fate had it that I somehow managed to survive. I traveled to an unknown place, to endure the difficult war in far–off Bashkiria, to endure the hunger, cold, and other tribulations, to give life to my baby under the most difficult of conditions, and to protect her life. Even though vast distances separated me from my native area, in my thoughts and imagination I remained with my dear ones in Turka.

The cruel war ended. Weary from the difficult tribulations, we decided at any price to return to the area of our native town of Turka – perhaps fate would turn out positive, and we would find some of our relatives who perhaps survived.

*

[Page 368]

We neared Turka, and found out with clear understanding about the terrible tragedy that befell us, and afflicted us personally as it did our nation. Our hearts palpitated. Here were the serpentines, through which we used to slide in sleds during winter nighttime excursions. Here is the Christian cemetery – and we arrived in the town.

Even were I to be blessed with the most talented writer's pen, I would not have the strength to write on paper about the great pain and terrifying impression that my devastated town left upon me... I walked through its streets and alleyways astonished from agony. Every stone, every pathway, reminded me of my happy, carefree, childhood days, and the years of my youth filled with enthusiasm and faith in a better tomorrow...

The town was empty of its Jews. Every house reminded us of the dear ones who had recently been murdered. The houses were ruined and destroyed. The empty windows and broken panes frightened me in particular... It seemed to me that death was peering out from each of them... Here is the house of Engelmajr – my friend Salka is no more... Here is the house of Beret – Marcha is no more... Here are the ruins of the house in which Esther Kesler and Salka Nistal lived... Mighty G–d, if you exist, how could you have allowed your chosen people to have been tormented so much?!... "Why, and how?", asked the agonized mouth, but no answer was forthcoming... Remaining were silence, destruction, pain, and wounds that time could not heal... I asked myself – is this not a big joke that I remained alive to be one of the few survivors, to go through my native town to weep for them all?... I walked through Turka during the years 1945–1957 with the feeling that I was trampling over graves. For me, the town was a cemetery saturated with the blood of those most dear to me.

We, the Jews who survived, were a rare sight in the eyes of the local residents... More than once did I notice an astonished look in the eyes of the Ukrainians at the sight of those of us who survived... There were those who justified themselves to me. Others attempted to pass by us with eyes lowered in shame. At times I felt great satisfaction that those who had collaborated and dipped their hands in innocent Jewish blood were seeing me alive... Certainly, this was a vexing thing for them...

*

We were several Jewish families in Turka: Brandelstein, Shein, Kenernstein, Meir, and others. My mother-in-law Chava Brandelstein survived. Can our great joy at this wonder be described?... Before our eyes was the picture of despair, the shadow of a mother who endured the Hitlerist hell. A Ukrainian family hid her. She spent months in dark cellars, where she partially lost her sight and was a witness to the terrible happenings in our town.

[Page 369]

The following was typical: Anyone who survived came to take one more look at Turka, the city of memories, in general only for a few hours. They came, and fled from it as quick as lightning without making themselves known. Any Jew who appeared in town was directed to us. I do not want to neglect to mention one episode that brought me to tears of laughter. At that time, the mayor of Turka was Vasyl Rohach. On one occasion, a Jew from the area of Turka came to him. Rohach met me on the street and wanted to tell me that someone came to him, but was afraid of calling the person a "Jew". He said in Russian, "With apologies to you, one of your nation was with me and asked me about the local people of his nation."... Indeed, I laughed to the point of tears at the unusual politeness with which he related to Jews.

Yaakov Entner came to Turka and told me that his sister had been murdered by a Ukrainian and had been buried in a garden on the Stryj. Yaakov removed her body from there and buried her in the Jewish cemetery. I will never forget Yaakov as he sprawled over the lovely grave of his sister and wailed out loud. He did not know how jealous I was of him at that moment. He knew the resting place of his sister's bones, whereas I did not. Indeed, even that type of jealousy existed at that time... One more victim was swallowed up by the Jewish cemetery, upon which the goats, cows and horses were able to trample. To our great sorrow, after the war, the Jewish cemetery turned into a pasture area for horses, cows, and the like.

[Page 370]

Frequently, fate laughs at a person. My husband Lemel Brandelstein, Fania Kenernstein and I worked as teachers in the high school. Fania and I completed our qualifications after the war, and it fell upon our lot to teach the children of those people who were unable to satisfy their lust for Jewish property, houses and victims. They fell upon their victims and their property like bloodthirsty eagles. Indeed, the children were innocent, but despite all of our intentions, the thought kept popping up – for whom are we toiling and giving over our energy and knowledge?... Is it not to future anti–Semites?... At time, when I was in class and I looked at the faces of the Ukrainian children, Jewish children from our town would pass before my eyes – children whose thread of life had been prematurely snuffed out. How hard was this on the heart! I paid a high price for remaining in Turka after the war!

Anyone who did not see Turka after the war – could such a person imagine that entire lanes had disappeared? Is it possible to imagine a greater desecration of the Divine Name than the paving of Legionow Street until the hospital with Jewish gravestones?! These gravestones were uprooted during the wartime period in accordance with a command of Mayor Pysanczyn, and placed with their inscriptions facing upward. To our great dismay, all of our entreaties to the Soviet authorities yielded naught, and the gravestones were not returned. It is possible to believe that an electric station was placed in the synagogue of Turka? This place, which was honored and holy to everyone, without difference in outlook; a place of supplication, where our parents prayed to G–d for livelihood and long life for themselves, their families and relatives; where they laid out their requests for a better tomorrow and peace throughout the world – that this place has become a receptacle for machines!

*

The Soviet authorities decided to arrange for the city to be cleared of its ruins, and to beautify it by planting trees and flowers in the destroyed areas.

[Page 371]

One of the areas that was designated for clearing of ruins was the place where the house of Kesler–Nistal stood. A few classes of our gymnasium with their teachers were drafted to help the town council in this task. Along with my students, I cleared the place where my two beloved friends Estera Kesler and Salka Nistal lived. My eyes welled up with tears as I lifted each brick, can or shovel. Books and unfinished notebooks were scattered among the rubble... The children stared in surprise at the sight of their teacher weeping. Apparently, life had not yet corrupted the young creatures. They understood the meaning of the weeping and were politely silent. Thus, instead of precious souls, Jewish houses, streets and alleyways – trees, shrubs and flowers are growing. Nature was used to obfuscate the traces of the lives of our dear ones...

*

Every teacher had the duty to visit the homes of the students to understand their living conditions. I had many students from Targovitsa. Once when I visited the Sakevchak family, I was stricken by astonishment and stood fixed to the doorway... I noticed a cloth on the table with Sabbath prayers and blessings woven onto it. The current task of this tablecloth was to adorn the Sakevchak house... I was not at all surprised when I noticed that the pillows and blankets were literally piled up to the roof. They were not obtained through the sweat of the brow of the owner of the house... When the mistress of the house saw my astonishment, she justified herself by explaining that she had received many things from the neighbors in return for milk, potatoes, and other provisions. Indeed, many of the local population explained their recently obtained new property in the same manner.

Entering the house where I was born and in which I was raised along with my four brothers was an unforgettable experience. That was the place where I absorbed warmth, parental love, and education. I found a merchandise warehouse on the first floor, and some sort of office on the second floor. I went up the steps with an agonized heart, holding on to the railing with my hand – the railing upon which I loved to slide down during my childhood, to the great fear of my parents and others. I entered the kitchen quietly, and moved from one room to the next. I wanted to find something that could remind me of my childhood home... I went up to the attic. Among the piles of paper I found my picture, the sole piece of evidence that I had grown up and lived there... Indeed, not in vain was the adage said that a person is stronger than iron, otherwise – how could one overcome this agony that pierces the heart and chokes the throat?! I, who grew up, studied, danced, and loved my dear ones here – slunk into my house on tiptoes, in fear and silence, as if to not awaken my parents and brothers from their sleep...

[Page 372]

Suddenly I was startled. A person approached me and shouted at me, asking what was I looking for there? This was one of the clerks of the office that was located in the house.

"What am I looking for," my trembling lips uttered," what am I looking for in the house in which I grew up? You ask: what are *you* doing here – I do not ask you... See: here we slept, sat, studied. Here my dear mother went around and prepared food for her five children. Here sat my beloved father as he was immersed in thoughts about how to provide livelihood for his fivesome..."

Everything came to life before my eyes... I suddenly saw the Sabbath table before my eyes: a sparkling white tablecloth, candles burning in the candlesticks, mother beside the table, father at the head of the table saying with a smile: at every corner I have a son, and at my side, for decoration, I have an only daughter. That is how he managed to give us a bit of happiness... The clerk was startled at my reaction. He must have considered me as one of the crazies who had entered the building.

*

A great miracle took place. We succeeded in leaving there and going to Israel. Here I am happy. I have found many dear friends living in Israel. They are very close to me, and each has a unique place in the recesses of my heart. They serve as a reminder and fine adornments from days gone by.

Translated from Polish by Ida Z.

Translator's Footnote:

16. A quote from Lamentations 1:1

[Page 373]

A Visit to Turka in 1957

by Moshe From of Haifa

In 1957, I traveled as a Polish citizen to visit Turka, which is today within the borders of the Soviet Union. I went there for two reasons: first, I wanted to visit the region where I was born and where I spent the majority of my youth, and where almost all my relatives and acquaintances were tragically murdered during the dark days of the Nazi occupation. Second, I wanted to visit the eight Jewish families who lived in Turka at that time, including my good friends for whom I had a special feeling, and with whom I remained in contact by letter.

I set out on an express train from the city of Szezecin, which is located on the Polish-German border, in the northwest close to the Baltic Sea. Twenty hours later I was already near the Soviet border, not far from Przemysl. The control formalities did not take long, and we transferred to a Soviet train. Very quickly, we were at the Lemberg railway station.

Lemberg in its Time

Lemberg, the central city of Galicia – who of us does not remember it?! The Hechalutz headquarters and the headquarters of all the youth organizations were located there. Thousands of *chalutzim* would come there to take care of their issues regarding *hachsharah* and *aliya.* Jewish students from eastern Galicia studied in the middle schools and the universities there. The large, modern railway station with its underground tunnels would be full, day and night, with Jewish passengers, who used to fill all the waiting halls and all the arriving and departing trains.

[Page 374]

My memory instinctively went back to the pre-war times, and it seemed to me that Zalman-Nachum Zolinger and Yisrael Pruker would suddenly come out of one of the tunnels, laden with packages. They used to come there at 8:00 every morning, and take care of various matters that the merchants of Turka had given over to him. One could purchase foreign currency through them. They purchased and brought with them all types of merchandise that people would order through them. At 8:00 p.m. they would already be back in Turka, where those interested would be waiting for them to take their packages. It seemed that the Turka merchants, and representatives of various business areas would soon be arriving, and each of them would be going to their businesses. Everyone felt even better and freer here than at home... Here, one was permitted many things that were impossible to do at home for various reasons...

And Today...

The microphone of the railway station, announcing in Russian arriving and departing trains every minute, brought to mind the pre-war times and reminded me that now I am seeing an entirely new Lemberg. Not even a trace of anything that once was remains today.

Late at night, at approximately 1:00 a.m. I departed by train for Turka. The train went from Lemberg to Uzhgorod (Ungvar) via Sambor-Sianki. Despite the fact that I was tired from the journey and from the many impressions along the way, under no circumstances could I close my eyes even for a minute. Even though it was dark outside, I looked at everything through the dark and attempted to recognize the region through which I was travelling, and which had been so familiar to me. We stopped in the former Jewish towns such as Komarno Rudki, Sambor, and Stary-Sambor. We traveled through known town in which no small amount of Jews had lived – Strelki, Jasienica, Rozluch, Jawora and others. A deathly silence pervaded throughout the entire way. Sometimes, I could see the light of a kerosene lamp through the window of a farmer's hut. We travelled through the Jawora Tunnel, and the train approached Turka. Here was the place where the large sawmill had stood. Today there is only an empty lot, which cannot even be recognized. Here is the place where there used to be large industrial enterprises that employed hundreds of workers, and from which Jewish families in town earned their livelihoods.

[Page 375]

Turka

With a wailing signal from the locomotive, we traveled through the last tunnel – and we already saw the second side of the viaducts that go through the width of the city, almost until the railway station.

A deathly silence pervaded in the railway station. A pair of weary Red Army soldiers were sitting in the railway station, and a few personnel were wandering about. It was before daybreak: they were just beginning their day. I looked about curiously and set out into the city.

My first steps were toward my friend Lemel Brandelstein, who at that time was working as the principal of the middle school and lived on the Palini near the large school building, opposite the Roman Catholic church. Lemel had returned to Turka with his family – a wife and two children – immediately after the liberation of the city. There, he met his mother, who had been hidden by Christians. She was the only Jewish woman of the older generation whom good Christians had taken in and hidden until the city was liberated by the Soviet Army.

[Page 376]

Chava the Grandmother

When I saw her, she made a fearful impression upon me. She looked very bad, much older than in reality. There was not one tooth in her mouth, she was hard of hearing, and her collapsed eyes could barely see. This happened to her when she was hiding in a cellar without air or light, which ruined her body. On the other hand, she retained her full intellect. When Lemel asked her if she recognizes me, she answered with humor and jest, "You ask if I remember him; I held him in my hands before his own mother saw him!"

Chava the midwife

It was indeed true. Which child in our town had not been brought into the world through the caring and delicate hands of "Chava the Grandmother"? For a long time, she was almost the only midwife in the region. Cruel fate had it that, specifically she, the one who was present at the births of all the children in the city and heard their first life call, and who announced their arrival to the world – should survive the terrible tragedy of their deaths. She saw with her own eyes how hundreds of children, who were so tenderly raised by their Jewish mothers and fathers, were murdered by the Germans and their Ukrainian assistants in an inhumane fashion, en masse and without a reason. And today, when she has lost her energy and when life has not much in store for her, she remains with a sole request to the Master of the World – that she could be brought to a Jewish burial. She spoke to me a few times and complained that the cemetery was neglected, the fences were broken, and the gentiles pasture cattle and goats there (as I myself witnessed later).

[Page 377]

The survivors

She later succeeded in leaving during the period of the repatriation to Poland, where she died and was given a proper burial in the Jewish cemetery in the Lower Silesian city of Wałbrzych. May her memory be a blessing.

[Page 378]

A Guest in Town...

News that a guest had arrived in town spread very quickly among the few Jewish families that lived there. Before I even had a chance to rest from the long journey, almost all of them came to Lemel's house. His wife Bronia decked the tables with drinks, wine, and various treats. We drank "*lechaim*" at the meeting of good friends.

Every one of us felt a pain in the heart. Our eyes filled with tears and the words were caught in the throat. Each person looked at the other, and nobody could utter a word. I felt like an orphan who had come to the cemetery, and was standing at a fresh grave without being able to begin the *kaddish*... In order to forget the tragedies a bit and and create a bit of creative humor, I drank several glasses of liquor. Until late at night, people discussed the miracles through which each of us had emerged alive from the terrible cataclysm.

In a Heavy Mood...

On the second day, I woke up with a headache and a heavy mood. I ate breakfast and set out for my first walk in the town. The weather was exceptionally fine. The sun emerged from the thick fog and beautified the majestic panorama of the Carpathian Mountains. The town was situated in the valley between the two tall mountains Shymenka and Kychera.

I walked along the street of the large school, near the building of the new courthouse. I went to the town square (Rynek). The path was largely destroyed, filled with stones and potholes. Since the time that I left the city fifteen years previously, it seemed that no renovations had been undertaken. The houses were neglected. Despite the fact that no wartime battles were conducted within the city itself, there were many houses, mainly Jewish ones, that had fallen down and had been dismantled.

[Page 379]

I wandered to the street of the synagogue. It was once called Ulica Bazsznyca. There was some sort of a strange feeling around, a mixture of memories and reflections. It was now the moth of *Elul*. At one time, it used to be packed with Jews who were going to services with their *tefillin* bags and *tallises*. Everyone was hurrying to worship with the first *minyan*, and then go to their businesses. One could already hear the sounds of the *shofar* blowing from all sides. It was already the time of *selichot*, and one could already sense the High Holy Days in the air.

All of the houses of worship were concentrated in that place. Hassidim from various "courts," each with their own *kloiz*, would hasten there. There were Belzers, Czortkowers, and Sadagorers. The Misnagdim would worship in the Great Synagogue or with the Golgower rabbi, Rabbi Eliezer Mishel of holy blessed memory. The butchers attended the synagogue of the businessmen together with the *Chevra Kadisha*. Even the tailors had their own minyan there.

If this was not sufficient, there were also a few private *minyanim*, which had no shortage of worshipers, such as with Reb Yudele the Samborer rabbi, and the Waniewiczer rabbi who had his own Hassidim in the city. The Zionists as well had their *minyan* in the national house. The professional intelligentsia of the city, consisting of several doctors and lawyers, worshipped there on Rosh Hashanah and Yom Kippur.

Devastation and Destruction

And today... Today, a deathly silence pervades here. One does not see a living soul. The *Beis Midrash* and the Czortkower Kloiz were turned into a warehouse for some sort of joinery cooperative. The Sadagoger Kloiz had been destroyed, without even a trace remaining. A diesel engine had been installed in the Great Synagogue, which is now serving as an electric station. A worker was killed at the time of the installation of the machinery – the gentiles said that this was a punishment from G-d...

[Page 380]

The densely populated quarter that was called "Behind the Synagogue" had been completely destroyed. The poor, wretched Jewish houses that were situated along the Jablonka River in the area of the bathhouse are no longer present. None of them was saved. They were destroyed along with their impoverished occupants.

When I would go before the war to the area behind the synagogue and look at the poor, wretched, little houses with their goat sheds, it seemed to me that for them the great Jewish artist Mark Chagall used that image for his characteristic pictures that illustrated the wretchedness of the Jewish *shtetl*.

The street that led to the "Lokacz" was a bit clearer and broader. There, almost nothing had changed. Beyond the bridge, the way parted into three sides: the right side led to the Targowicza [market], the left side let to the Skale, also a typical Jewish alleyway where lived the butchers Chaim Wolf Zeifert and Moshe-Yantsha Nistal with his wife Chana-Dvora "Tartak", who used to bring joy to every early morning with her juicy curses.

At one time, this alleyway was alive, when the headquarters of Hashomer Hatzair were located in Abish Nistal's house. Every night, the noise of the impromptu Hora dance, or the sentimental melodies of Jewish and Hebrew songs that the youth would sing to the light of lanterns or on the hill that was across the alleyway would permeate from there into the town. Saturday afternoons were especially joyous, for the Shomrim, dressed in their scouting uniforms and colorful ties, would march up the hill near Weissman's house and go from there to the Zwiriniec forests, or bathe in the Stryj River near the Jaworer Tunnel. In orderly rows and in cadence with jovial marching songs, they would march with pride; young children would run along the sides of the route, with great jealousy for them...

[Page 381]

Jewish houses still stand along the wide street even though their owners are no longer here... There was not even anybody to demand the inheritance. The houses of the brothers Volia and Yaakov-Hirsch Kanke, Yisrael Langenauer, as well as the bakery of Mordechai Erdman stood out. The houses of the street that led to the Targowicza remained whole. For the most part, they were occupied by military families who were stationed in the city, as well as by the Chinovniks1 who moved here from eastern Ukraine.

*

A strange feeling overcame me when I arrived at the Rynek. At one time, this was the main center of the city. The homes of all the honorable householders of the city were located around the large city hall, in the form of a square. During the First World War, all of the wooden houses burnt down there, and new, relatively better built, fine, strong houses were built in their place. Thousands of farmers would fill up the place around the city hall, sell their produce, and spend their money at the Jewish businesses, which provided them with everything that they needed.

Who does not recall the Wednesday market days in town. The town was full of people, and it was difficult to go through the streets. The businesses were full of customers until late at night. The stable boys and butchers ended their business at the taverns and guesthouses. They concluded their purchases over a glass of liquor, clasping their hands together – and the voices ascended to the heights of heaven...

Today, it is peaceful here... No memory of anything remains. Market days and fairs no longer take place here. In the Ring-Platz, between the city hall and the houses that belonged to Moshe Reiter, Hirsh Leib Shreiber, Leizer Stern and others – they planted trees and poplars that grew wild, both tall and wide, and formed a strange grove in which children of the passers-by who live in the houses of Shmuel-Nachum Shein and Leizer Stern would play.

[Page 382]

The courthouse is situated opposite, on the other side of the city hall, in the houses of Sender Goldreich and Moshe Shteiger. (The large building where the courthouse used to be located was turned into the barracks of the border N.K.V.D.) The house of Abish Artel, the son-in-law of Chaim Hirsh, was occupied by the city militia. The Gestapo was also located there during the time of the German occupation.

*

Otherwise, it was almost as if nothing had changed during the time... In the garden, which had been planted already in the pre-war years, there was a monument of Stalin. (Who knows – perhaps now in 1966 the monument is no longer there...) In the corner where the houses of Moshe Grossman and Shlomo Richter used to be, there is a tribute2 to workers who excel in high accomplishments with their work. To construct this, they removed the marble monument of Dr. Turnheim that had stood tall in the cemetery. They placed the black marble upon a platform, covered the inscription, and placed in a glass frame pictures of "*stakhanavches*"3, creating a cheap and primitive revolutionary point.

On the side of the Rynek, parallel to the viaducts, the houses of Shlomo Richter, Zeinwil Brenes, Hirsh Eigler, and my father's house where I lived until June 1941 all remain stating. The other houses did not survive the powerful detonations of the explosions during the blasting of the viaducts, and they collapsed.

The viaducts, which had been rebuilt, had lost their former splendor and beauty. They only laid stress plates over the remaining pillars, thereby completely ignoring the elementary requests of the architect. From the tunnel until the train station, barbed wire was sticking out from both sides, so that no living soul could approach the Jablonka River. Armed soldiers guarded there day and night. The route through the hanging bridge that leads from the Rynek to the other side of the town, known as the Ilyca, was clear.

[Page 383]

In Good Times

In the good times, before the destruction, the Ilyca was the center of the city. The majority of the businesses, extending for a long way along the main street, from the bridge until the Starostowa building, were located there. The shops, with a variety of merchandise, were one next to the other, and sharp competition existed among them. The merchants would fight for each customer, and this would often result in an argument or even blows. The farmers who used to come here from the surrounding villages would sell eggs, fowl, mushrooms, berries and other products. With the money, they would purchase salt, kerosene, shoes and other products. Frequently, they would barter one item for another, without using money... All week, there would be bustling and movement, and every Wednesday, which was the regular market day, one could not even go through the street. Farmers' wagons stood in all corners, and the businesses were filled with customers, among them some who did not come to purchase, but rather to steal a bit...

The businesses were closed for two days a week, Saturday and Sunday. On those days, the merchants would go out into the streets or sit with a cup of tea in the coffeehouses of Leizer Meiner or Hirsch Liberbaum and discuss politics.

On Friday night before candle lighting, Itzik-Aharon the *shamash* would appear on the streets with his wooden hammer and would knock on the doors of the shops to inform everyone that the holy Sabbath was approaching. Indeed, they soon closed, one after the other. The bakers had already sealed the ovens after putting in the *cholent.* Lit candles could already began to be seen in the windows. The town prepared to welcome the Sabbath.

[Page 384]

The next morning – how lively and joyous was it in town. Thousands of youth filled the alleyways in the headquarters of the youth organizations. Jewish children, festively dressed, happy and carefree, sprouted like colorful flowers on the mountains surrounding the city, and by the rivers, as they would play in the bosom of beautiful nature.

The older generation used to take a nap after the tasty cholent and fatty kugel. Later, they would go for a stroll in the grove near the pharmacy, or to the hospital area to get some fresh air and absorb some new energy for the new week, which would begin right after *havdallah.*

The socio-economic structure of the population here barely changed for generations. The chief sources of livelihood for Jews were business and a smattering of trades. The rest did not have any concrete employment. People lived from the "air" one from the other... There were brokers, village peddlers, wagon drivers, marriage brokers, teachers, and unemployed people. Aside from the few sawmills and the primitive brick kiln that used to be idle more than functioning, there were no industrial enterprises in the area.

Due to the fact that the town was surrounded by a large number of villages, it was able to serve as an administrative and business center. The Jewish population lived an impoverished, but comfortable life. Despite the lack of any great fortune and the lack of a perspective for a better future, people managed from week to week with nonchalance toward what fate might bring.

The Course of Fate

Fate took its cruel toll. During the course of three years, from 1941 to 1944, the Germans, with the assistance of the local Ukrainians, murdered the entire Jewish population of the city and the area. Not one family was able to save itself. Like hungry bloodhounds, they found all the Jews. Those who were able to pay the price of money and jewelry to hide with local gentiles also did not avoid the terrible fate. The gentiles would take all of their belongings, and then kill the people themselves or turn them over to the Gestapo.

[Page 385]

Only the Jewish homes remain, abandoned and orphaned, serving as reminder that there once was a large Jewish settlement here. Today the houses are settled by Ukrainians, no small number of whom played their role in the deaths of many Jews. Today, they utilize and enjoy the property of their victims, in accordance with the principle of "You murdered and you also inherited"4. From time to time, they encounter one of the small number of surviving Jews of Turka who live alone and forlorn in various cities in the Soviet Union. They bring here the concealed pining for a Jewish town in which they had been born and raised. They are driven by an unhappy inclination to see for themselves whether the destruction was as great and terrible as has been described and written...

As soon as they set foot upon the accursed ground and inhale the air that has been poisoned with murder and killing, the heart becomes aggrieved and the tongue becomes immobilized. They wish to go away, and escape as soon as possible from the terrible nightmare.

The voices of the Ukrainians whom one encounters on the street, looking at you as if you have returned from the other world... You are overcome by a strange feeling, as it seems to you that you must answer as to why you are among the survivors... From all sides, you feel wild strangeness and an non-understandable hatred. You feel alone, redundant and unwanted.

Every clod of earth here is saturated with Jewish blood. The walls are sprinkled with the brains of Jewish children, and the souls of the victims are fluttering around. You finally come to the realization that our Jewish town with its large Jewish society no longer exists – it is dead forever...

Translator's Footnotes:

13. A minor Russian official. See http://www.merriam-webster.com/dictionary/chinovnik
14. The term '*Erntapl*' seems to imply a sickle shaped monument.
15. See http://en.wikipedia.org/wiki/Stakhanovite_movement
16. I Kings 21:19.

[Page 386]

Memorial Corner
In Memory of my Father Reb Baruch Hirt

They were seven children – four brothers and three sisters. All of them were raised and educated in the spirit of Torah and religious tradition. My father of blessed memory was the youngest of them.

He was very punctilious about three things: love of his fellowman, giving charity in a hidden fashion, and the study of Torah.

He was never jealous of anyone, and never bore jealousy for anyone in his heart. He would give charity in a secret fashion to the extent that he was able. Regarding the study of Torah, he would say: Torah is our life, and a tree of life to those that grasp hold of it. Therefore, learning never departed from his lips.

He was a dedicated father to his children. He educated them in the spirit of love, with a full understanding to their new path in life. His aspiration was to make aliya to the Land, which he never merited to do. Three of his sons and Mother of blessed memory were murdered along with him.

May his and their memory be blessed

His son: Y. Hirt

In Memory of the Binder family

They had a small lot in Turka with a small farm: a few animals, a bit of agriculture, and a great deal of family warmth. Mother was literally a "Jewish Mother" – good hearted, able to instill ideas into all of her seven children that were in the home, as well as honor and respect for parents. She managed the house and business in good taste, even though the decisions always came from Father. Father was a G-d fearing Jew who observed the commandments. He was a farmer during the summer and a merchant during the winter.

I recall the warm Jewish home on Sabbath days. I recall the conclusion of the Sabbath, when the neighbors would gather in our home to conduct the *Melave Malka* meal, tell stories, and eat the special foods and the famous borscht.

Father was always ready to assist his fellowman – including visiting the sick and tending to the deceased. In everything, he saw an opportunity for a good deed and merits for the Garden of Eden in the World of Truth.

[Page 387]

Family life was conducted with Jewish understanding and values. I recall a picture that was etched in my mind: Father is sitting next to a kerosene lamp, with his spectacles on his nose, reading to mother a story of Reizele that printed in the daily newspaper. At times, the whole family would be together, and someone would sing. The comportment of the parents imparted in the children feelings of respect. When the Nazis came to take Father, mother left her hiding place and joined him. Thus, they were not separated in their lives and in their deaths...

Our eldest sister Rivka was also a victim.

Our sister Malka, the conscience and brain of the family – also fell at the hands of the enemy.

Our brother Yosef, graced with musical talent, also met his end in the crematoria of Majdanek.

Four of us remain – three in Israel and one brother in Belgium. Even though we have changed our way of life, many values from home remain with us.

The Hashomer Hatzair movement to which we belonged also imparted a great deal to us. It is good that there was such a movement that educated people to Zionism and aliya.

David Binder, Chaim Binder, and Hala Kushnir

In Memory of Menachem Langenauer

My brother Menachem the son of Rachel and Yisrael, was born in 1901 in Turka into a traditional, Hassidic home, and received a religious education. When the First World War broke out in 1914 and the Czarist armies burnt down the town, the entire family exiled themselves to the capital Prague. There, the lad studied in a night school for refugee children and began to display his talents as an artist. He continued expressing this talent in Turka after we returned to in 1917, at the end of the war. He would draw the sets for the various amateur theaters.

He went to the United States in 1929. There, he established a traditional Jewish family. His two children, one of whom serves as a military rabbi in the American Army and the second who is a physician, are involved in Jewish life in the United States. They and their wives are fluent in the Hebrew Language – and their homes are exemplary Hebrew homes.

Menachem participated in activities of the Hebrew movement in the United States.

[Page 388]

On the Death of Menachem Langenauer:[1]

The sudden death and the circumstances of the death of the dedicated Hebrew activist Menachem Langenauer of blessed memory had a depressing impact upon the Hebrew community of New York, which was dear to the departed. He was blessed with talent in drawing. He was the regular artist of the Hebrew Society of America, illustrating all of its artistic announcements, honorary scrolls for people of note, certificates for "The Hebrew Month," etc. A large group of relatives, friends and those that held the deceased in esteem gathered at his funeral, which took place on Wednesday, 9th of Nisan. Rabbi Tzvi Tabory, a member of the leadership of the Hebrew Society of America and the former president of the Moria chapter of Boro Park, to which the deceased served as secretary for many years, eulogized the deceased. We bring down here a selection of his words:

"... In the name of the Hebrew Society of America, in the name of the Moria Hebrew club of Boro Park, in the name of the entire Hebrew family of greater New York, I bow my head in piercing grief and deep sorrow over the sudden death of our faithful and dedicated member Mr. Menachem Langenauer of blessed memory. He was a comrade in ideas and a comrade in deeds, who girded his shoulders to work towards the revival of Hebrew. For many years, he invested his entire energy and essence on the altar of the Hebrew Language. The man did not labor solely for Hebrew, but rather for the Holy Tongue. His lips were always pure and holy. Our sages have taught us: "Be careful about a simple commandment as a severe one, for you do not know the reward of commandments"[2]. Maimonides expounds, 'A simple commandment, such as what? – Such as speaking in the Holy Tongue!'... The adage of Maimonides on specialization in one area is also known to us: 'Only one tradesman was ever victorious over me.' It is fitting for a person to excel in one thing, in which he finds the root of his soul. Reb Menachem the son of Reb Yisrael shone in all the commandments of the Torah, but speaking in the Holy Tongue was where he found his lot and his inheritance.

... He was the secretary of the Moria Hebrew club for many years, and now the man has been suddenly taken from us. Last night, he led his son to the marriage canopy, and today he has been called to the Heavenly assembly.

... Even though one is not supposed to comfort a person while his dead is still before him, we say to his wife: 'Let us bless G-d that Menachem merited to educate your children in Torah and to lead them to the marriage canopy.' He left behind children like himself, and whoever leaves behind children like himself does not die, but rather gathers unto his people. His children will continue along his path of life. May his soul be bound in the bonds of eternal life."

Translator's Footnotes:

12. There is a footnote in the text here: Hadoar, from 18 Sivan 5625 / 1965. Pirke Avot 2:1.

[Page 389]

In Our Homeland

[Page 391]

Our Aliya and First Steps in the Land

by M. and Ch.

Hashomer Hatzair in Turka

Despite all our communal alertness, our father, Reb Avraham–Alter Montag, did not at first permit us to make aliya to the Land. In these matters, he was satisfied to be on the side of Dr. Lewensztejn and not Dr. Cyper. Second, with regards to redemption and the kingdom of Israel, we are to depend on our Father in Heaven, and not to try to force the end...

However, the Hashomer Hatzair movement in Turka during those days, in 1920, thought otherwise. The preparations for *aliya* were in full force. Those were the days of Tel Hai and Joseph Trumpeldor1, and we were open to any news about what was taking place in the Land.

The most popular song at that time in Turka was "In Tel Hai, there in the Galilee, Trumpeldor fell." This song was written by a group in Turka, and I do not know how it turned out that this song became an Israeli song...

[Page 392]

Hashomer Hatzair in Turka. Top right – Abba Chushai

Indeed, we were warned that we were liable to be called upon for immediate aliya, and that we must be prepared in all ways, to the last detail, with the first call...

Abba Chushai headed the Turka chapter. Since he wanted to know who was prepared to make aliya, he summoned his people one night: "We are making *aliya* to the Land!" We presented ourselves at that time, and our level of readiness was determined in accordance with how we presented ourselves...

The pressure on the father of our household to permit us to make aliya increased. Having no choice, Reb Avraham Alter retracted somewhat – he permitted one to make *aliya* but not two together. The choice was made with decisive simplicity. A lot was cast, and I won...

The following people were in the first group, headed by Abba Chushai: Hela Reifler, Dvora April, Miriam Montag, Chava Berman, Chana Montag, Yehoshua Weiss, Elazar Weiss, Anshel Treiber, and Aharon Rozler. The following people joined us at the Lvov train station: Amnon Lin's mother Chava, and Yosef Fuchs from Zamosc. The lad and girl burst out in weeping. Their mother, who stood next to the train, said to her pioneers: "If you are weeping, come off the train."

Hashomer Hatzair in Turka. Top right – Abba Chushai

[Page 393]

We went by train from Lvov to Vienna to Trieste. In Trieste, we boarded the Japanese transport ship Nippon to Port Said. The journey took 21 days. We remained in the city for a day or two, and arrived in Jaffa a few days later.

*

After a week in Jaffa, they were about to send us to work. We demanded, and Abba Chushai was particularly insistent, that we be sent to the Galilee. The *aliya* absorption officers at first opposed this, especially for the girls, but they finally agreed, and we arrived in Rosh Pina.

It was summertime. We began to work on the Rosh Pina–Machanaim road. There were no showers, and we suffered from heat rash. Scorpions swarmed in the vineyard in which we slept. One night, Dr. Radovanski arrived from the settlement and woke us up from our sleep: "You are sleeping on scorpions!" Through his intervention, we later were given two rooms, and we slept on the floor. We barely had pillows for our heads... We worked very hard. We woke up at 3:00 a.m. so that we could finish our work before the heat of the day... We lived below the settlement,

Rosh Pina, 1920

[Page 394]

with Turkanicz, but our eating hall was above. Not infrequently, people did not show up for a meal because they did not have the energy to go...

*

Our first winter in the Land approached. Party activity was increasing in the land. The time of the founding meeting of the Histadrut [Workers' Union] was approaching

The first people of Hashomer Hatzair who made *aliya* in 1920. Standing Abba Chushai. Right: Yehoshua Weiss, and left Anshel Treiber

[Page 395]

Our group then entered a competition for the paving of the Haifa–Gedera Road. Later, we joined the Shomria group, that pitched its tents in the current location of Kibbutz Yagur.

*

Meir Yaari and a few other Shomrim were then in Bitania Illit. Abba Chushai and Mordechai Shenhavi began to organize the road workers in Shomria. We then forged connections with Bitania regarding the founding of a kibbutz.

Getting used to the hard labor was not all that easy. I remember on Yom Kippur, I was sitting on a heap of stones with regrets and thinking about ... home. I was at home, without furuncles, without eye problems. Indeed, I was dreaming about home...

In the meantime, we had to work! The Turka group sent 15 people out to work. There was a competition: who would build the largest gravel heap... However, warts broke out on our hands. Abba Chushai, who should have served as an example, was full of warts... We also had to prepare a meal, without fire, without wood – with some thistles – made of a bit of rice and raisons. At that time, the English paid work wages with food: fish, jam, and flour. People ate this food and licked their fingers! Indeed, there were good times, for the bitter days of unemployment were approaching...

*

The Haifa–Gedera Road

It was the first days of the Histadrut. We began to dream about settlement. Our group, the Turka group, stood out in every place. We had been forged into a unit and we had discipline. We also knew how to sing. With the arrival of additional people from Poland, we began to speak of Beit Alfa and Mishmar Haemek.

With the progression of the work on the road, the entire camp moved in the direction of Haifa. We camped next to the Kishon River. Once, the river overflowed its banks and flooded our tents at night, reaching our beds. Everything sunk in the mud. The group disbanded with the completion of the Haifa–Gedera Road. Some went to Beit Alfa and others moved to Haifa.

Translator's Footnote:

88. See http://en.wikipedia.org/wiki/Joseph_Trumpeldor . The song referred to in the following paragraph (although word order seems to be different so there may be a different version) is here: http://www.hebrewsongs.com/?song=bagalilbetelchai The author of the song listed on the aforementioned website is Turka native Abba Chushai, referred to frequently in this Yizkor Book. He later served as mayor of Haifa.

[Page 396]

Breaking Through the Shores of our Homeland

by Meir Hoffman of Ramat Gan

Uncaptioned. Meir Hoffman

It was July 1939. The relative heat of the Carpathian Mountains was oppressive. The youth, some of whom were "sitting on their suitcases" waiting for *aliya* to the Land of Israel, and some of whom were wandering around without anything to do, lacking in any means of setting themselves in any work, streamed to the other side of the river in order to enjoy bathing in its cool waters.

As if to provoke: It was specifically that week when I began my vacation that the awaited day arrived. I received a telegram from the "center" informing me that I was designated for *aliya*. We (including my wife and my sister) made our final preparations in accordance with the circular that we received. The brief instructions indicated that it was only permissible to take 25 kilograms of luggage. Another set of instructions, all in the negative, followed that. It was forbidden for anyone to know that we were travelling – for the *aliya* was illegal. It was forbidden to arrange farewell parties. It was forbidden to be accompanied to the train, even by one's closest relatives, parents included.

I will never forget that moment. It is as if it was just yesterday. The "taxi" (a wagon hitched to a horse) arrived. We loaded up the suitcases, and shook hands and gave a brief kiss to our parents. Despite this, a large number of friends accompanied us to the railway station. Our hearts were beating strongly, our hands were trembling – and the train set out... Through the window of the moving train I saw Father and Mother – who were full of concern due to the instructions and remained at home. They were only waving their hands gently, so that they would not be noticed – Heaven forbid.

I cannot forgive myself to this day – why, despite all this, did the farewell have to be specifically in such a manner? Father's last words still echo in my ears: "Who knows if we will see each other again... The situation in the world is unstable – who knows?..." Something unique was sensed in the city. One could hear the marching of soldiers during the nights. They were not preparing, Heaven forbid, for a specific invasion, but Poland was taking the opportunity to settle some sort of old account with Czechoslovakia, and was amassing its army on its borders.

[Page 397]

In Warsaw, a delegate from the Land greeted us for the first time. He was also to be the captain of the ship. There, we heard very serious words: the journey was difficult and fraught with mortal danger. The border was already closed in Romania. Only after a three day negotiation were we given the possibility of boarding the shop. The second group that we met along the way was sent back to Poland.

We discussed our ship extensively, but nobody could imagine the difficulties that would happen with the Tiger Hill, sailing under the flag of Panama, that transported 750 of the best *chalutzim* of Poland. It meandered through the paths of the sea for five weeks, unable to bring its precious cargo to the shores of the Land.

Who can forget the many days and nights sitting together on the ship in the midst of the sea?! The word "home" was woven into every sentence. Complete lack pervaded in every corner: no food, no drinking water, no medicine for the sick. Can anyone forget that terrible night: they extinguished the lights earlier than usual? Everyone was lying on the benches, and suddenly we heard some unique, strange activity. They were dragging "something." Then we heard something sounding like a eulogy, a casting into the sea – and silence... This is the way we brought our first victim to "burial." This was not the last.

Again, the sea and more sea. All sorts of rumors. The nervousness grew. Tonight we are going to go to shore. Again, we packed our sacks. We put out the lights, and approached quickly. We also saw hills... Someone whispered, "This is Haifa..." Suddenly a motorboat approached. We heard commands in

English and German, the rumble of machine guns – and the boat did a complete turnabout, and started to escape at full speed... We heard about the tragic situation: two additional victims. This was the "welcome reception" of the Mandate government.

Events developed quickly. On September 1, 1939, the radio informed us of the outbreak of the war and the Nazi invasion of Poland. Now, there is no longer any need to preserve the intactness of the ship – there will be no more *aliya*... There won't be any more people to bring on aliya. There will no longer be anyone to write to. We will not be able to calm our parents and to write to them that we will see each other again...

[Page 398]

The Aliya of those with Families to the Land

by Moshe Yisraeli of Kiryat Chaim

Moshe Yisraeli

With song, music, and enthusiasm, the people of the city accompanied the *chalutzim*, members of the youth movements, whose *aliya* began in 1920. This was not the pitiful situation of the elderly *olim* and those that accompanied them, at the time that they left Turka to make *aliya* to the Land. Those people had families with children who had not yet grown up. Those that accompanied them parted from them with mixed feelings. They even ostracized them.

Their *aliya* began in the middle of the 1920s and progressed very slowly. Unemployment was rampant in the Land at that time. The Mandate government did almost nothing to ameliorate the situation, and many young lands wandered about outside the cities without work for the day. It is clear, therefore, how difficult it would be for a head of a family – older people who were not used to physical labor, and who did not have appropriate means. From their perspective, this was a very daring and brave thing to do – to go to an unknown land with a different climate from their place of origin. Some of them came in the wake of their *chalutz* children. They struggled very hard and it took a long time until they somehow established themselves. It is fitting to dedicate some space here to recall these older *chalutzim*, who, through their *aliya* and suffering, added a serious layer to the upbuilding of the Land.

Zisha Feist

Zisha Feist was a working Jew, who lived his entire life from the labor of his hands. It is worthwhile to note that this nationalist Jew and his wife already knew then, at the beginning of the 20th century, to give to their children the possibility of studying secular subjects and books along with their Torah studies in the Hassidic environment of the *cheder*. Zisha Feist made *aliya* with his family, including daughters of school age, following the footsteps of his son, the first of the first of our town to make *aliya*. His son was none other than Abba Chushai, the well-known leader of the workers, today the mayor of the city of Haifa. I recall that when I went to greet them on the day of their arrival, I sensed, not only from the look on their eyes, their trepidation for what was to come.

[Page 399]

They suffered from no small amount of difficulties until they somehow established themselves in accordance with the conditions of that time. They were happy with their lot. Zisha and his wife died in Haifa at advanced ages, and left behind a large family that is involved in public life in Israel.

Abish Berman

He was an interesting personality among the human landscape of our city. He was a blend of Hassidism and fear of Heaven with worldly knowledge. He was a Hassid of the Admor of Boyan (of Rizhin lineage). Typical of these Hassidim was their boundless dedication to their Rebbe as well as to their external splendor. Abish Berman gathered the Boyaner Hassidim around him – few in number but graced with fine traits of Hassidism, the most important of which was a dedication to mutual assistance. Then, a half century ago, this trait was the main strand of their essence.

Abish Berman

His home served as a gathering place for like minded people. His nickname in town was "The Consul of Boyan." Reb Abish Berman was also fluent in the vernacular languages, especially German, the language of government. He was the only one of the like-minded people of the town who was a regular subscriber to the official newspaper of the Austria-Hungary Empire, the "Neie Frei Presse" – which was published in Vienna and for which Dr. Herzl served as one of the editors. All information about politics and news from the wide world had their source with Reb Abish. One could meet old and young people in his store every afternoon, debating and exchanging view on current events.

[Page 400]

Aside from his own business, Reb Abish was very knowledgeable about modern accounting in accordance with the principles of that time. He had a fine custom: Every few years he would accept a like-minded lad as an assistant in his shop. Through the work, he would impart knowledge of accounting to the lad, and thereby give him an important profession for life. In this manner, he established a generation of fine businessmen.

It was natural that Reb Abish, as a communal activist with an opinion, did not regard in a positive fashion the breaches in traditional life in the town. When the Zionist movement arose before and after the First World War, he actively objected to it. Later, when it absorbed the best of the youth, including many from Hassidic circles, he remained a very proper opponent. Discussions or debates with those anarchists, so to speak, were not accompanied by curses or disparaging remarks, in the manner of a "holy war." Rather, with calm and even mindedness, he tried to convince those enthusiastic youths that attempting to hasten the end is a sin against the G–d of Israel...

However, the irony of fate had it that Reb Abish made *aliya* with his family to the Land late in life. He went in the wake of his daughter Chava who made *aliya* with the first Hashomer Hatzair group, and died here in her prime. We young people, who remembered the opposition of Reb Abish to Zionism and *aliya*, welcomed him to the Land not with feelings of victory, but rather with great satisfaction that even people of his nature had begun to wake up to the national feeling.

Reb Abish slowly got settled and contributed to the economy of the Land, which was meager and poor in those days. With the passage of time, he established a group of like-minded Hassidim. I suspect that in the recesses of his soul, he often thought about the correctness of those Zionist youths in the city whom he opposed so strongly.

He died at an old age in Kiryat Motzkin. May his memory be a blessing.

Daniel Artel

Daniel Artel, his wife, and children also made *aliya* in the wake of their son Aharon, who arrived to the Land in 1920 with the first chalutzim of the "roads"[1] era. He was an important person and a serious communal activist in town. He also endured difficulties in acclimatization, especially in his transition from a wealthy situation in his home town to the new situation. However Daniel Artel, with his sense of humor and good nature that did not leave him even during difficult times, knew how to overcome and to establish himself in our Land. He was greatly respected in his environment, the environment of elderly people of his vintage.

[Page 401]

He died in Haifa and left behind a family involved in the life of labor and the workers' movement.

Moshe Nagler (Moshe Feibush's)

In this list of families I will mention Moshe Nagler, who also made *aliya* in the wake of his daughter, a member of Kibbutz Merchavia in the Jezreel Valley. Nagler, who was called Moshe Feibush's in our town, was an upright Jew. He had lived in a sort of Jewish suburb of our town, where livelihood was earned partially from business and partially from agriculture and farming. He raised his children in the spirit of Torah and labor. He also suffered from difficulties in absorption during that era, but he slowly established himself in a life of labor in the Land, and died at an advanced age. He left behind his children who are involved in teaching and labor, and are doing their part in the upbuilding of the Land.

*

I will mention Yaakov Gerstal in a positive fashion. He was an expert building contractor already in the Diaspora, and he quickly became involved in his profession in the Land.

*

The widow Treiber, who made *aliya* in the wake of her son Anshel, a member of Beit Alfa and one of the first members of Hashomer Hatzair in our city, settled in Haifa and struggled greatly until she somehow became established along with her children. She accepted everything without complaint, in the manner of G–d fearing women.

Meir Kleist

Finally, it is my duty to mention here our dear friend Meir Kleist, who fell victim to a work accident in the Itlit quarries, which provided building materials for the Port of Haifa. He was still in his prime.

Meir arrived in the Land during the early 1920s, after his return to our town after spending the days of the First World War in Italy. He often entertained the tent dwellers in the Valley of Olives in Haifa, natives of our town who were unemployed, with his joviality and the Italian songs that he had learned while living there.

When he became established after no small amount of suffering, fate was cruel to him. He was killed in a work accident. We will remember him with sorrow and agony.

Translator's Footnote:

17. Seemingly the era of road construction, as described in the article on page 389.

[Page 402]

In Memory of Those No Longer With Us
Manes Bernas

Manes Bernas

Manes the son of Feiga and Leib Bernas was born in Turka in 1903. After completing his high school studies, he continued studying in the high school for business in Vienna. He received the degree of Doctor of Economics from the University of Florence.

Upon his return to Turka, Manes joined the circle of his friends who were very active in Zionism. He was one of the founders of Gordonia, and later one of the active councilors of the chapter. He was a representative of his movement and party in the communal institutions of the town.

When he made *aliya* in 1935, he joined Kibbutz Kfar Hachoresh. He was forced to leave it for various reasons, and he moved to Haifa. He was a faithful and dedicated member of the Histadrut. He was a member of the Hagana, and was one of the first volunteers for the British Army during the Second World War, despite his older age. On account of his fluency in various languages and his academic credentials, he was placed in the air force, where he fulfilled important and responsible roles.

After his army service, he was accepted as an accountant in the Haifa Kupat Cholim. He fulfilled his role in that organization with great dedication. He was a member of the workers' council, where he was active and dedicated. Manes died in 1953, leaving behind a wife, Leah (nee Langenaur), a daughter, and a son.

L. B.

[Page 403]

Eizik Yitzchak Kurtz

Eizik did not merit witnessing the conclusion of this book. He responded to the editorial committee and wrote an article that is published in this book1. He witnessed the editing, but prophesied that he would not be able to witness the conclusion. A person knows what he foresees. Indeed, he left us before his time.

Eizik was a *chalutz*. He made *aliya* with the enthusiasm of Zionism. He participated in the upbuilding of the Land in a fine fashion, and loved every corner of it. All Turka natives knew him as someone who would help any new immigrant from his hometown, and therefore he was nicknamed the "Consul of Turka." He was one of the founders and active members of the Organization of Turka Natives in Israel, and was the living spirit of the meetings and memorial events of the natives of our town.

He constantly struggled for justice, righteousness and truth in the Histadrut and the government. He was willing to expend his money and energy for the sake of justice. He gave his life on the altar of this struggle.

He did not recover after the death of his wife. He weakened continually until death overtook him. May his memory be a blessing.

A. Shafer

Translator's Footnote:

17. See page 41.

Tovia Artel

Tovia Artel was born in Turka, Galicia, in 1911. He joined the Hashomer Hatzair movement during his youth, and was one of the active movers in the chapter. He spent a brief period with Kibbutz Massad in the Hachshara group in Lvov (he joined Kibbutz Tel Amel in Israel). He made *aliya* in 1939, and began working in aquaculture. He was modest and dedicated, always in good spirits, with a friendly spirit during his work. He joined the army a year and a half after his arrival, and he was sent to an artillery unit, in which he served for nearly five years in the Land and in Cyprus. When the brigade was founded, he joined it and was sent to Italy. He built his family while in army service, and had a son.

At the end of the war, Tovia returned from the army weary from his many wanderings. He desired to root himself in agriculture, and set himself in a permanent position. We also recognized his enthusiasm and desire to reconnect with a life of labor and society.

He was a quiet, modest man. He was dedicated to his family, loved his son, was faithful to the kibbutz, and forged his way of life there. He drew during his free time, and dreamed of the possibilities of developing

[Page 404]

the arts in kibbutz life. Through his art, he brought joy to the members during festivals and internal parties. During his final days, he dreamed about renovations of the reading hall, which he volunteered to look after. He fulfilled the plans in abundance.

Death overtook him. The evil hand afflicted him and took him from us. He died on the Black Sabbath[1].

(From a booklet published by Hashomer Hatzair, Tel Amel)

Translator's Footnote:

13. See http://www.jewishvirtuallibrary.org/jsource/History/Black_Sabbath.html and http://en.wikipedia.org/wiki/Operation_Agatha

[Page 404]

Yitzchak Zohar (Shein)

He was not one of the followers who respond Amen.

Itziu did not belong to those who are indifferent and comfortable, who let life pass by them. He approached the problems of our life by first weighing the worthwhileness of the matter. His entire essence was personal independence. He was constantly active in the storm of life. His categorical imperative was his conscience and the internal command such as is common with those forged of hard material.

Itziu was not easy with people. He often came into conflict with friends. However, at the same time, he was not easy with himself. He did not take upon himself the easy tasks. He was not concerned with the "unpleasantness" of stating the "truth" to a friend or to the entire kibbutz. He was always prepared to take the jabs of unpopularity and the danger of "injury" upon himself. He never hesitated to stand alone in his opinion. Alone, but not isolated, for even at times when he remained alone in his opinion, we recognized his spirit and knew that he was drawing from the depths of the clarity of his thought.

The art of pliability and adaptation were not his lot. However, he was graced with one fine trait: in his relationships with friends, he never left any sediment of bitterness – neither in his own heart nor in the heart of his fellow. He would accept the judgment of the majority with willingness and love. We granted him that benefit. Even though he was often in the minority, he felt that he was not speaking into empty space, but rather to the hearts of friends always open to meet him.

*

Itziu was among the generation of the founders of the kibbutz. He was one of the early builders of our Merchavia, to which he remained faithful. His early childhood between the Carpathian Mountains and the rivers of Poland wove the dream of the return to the homeland, to labor, to agriculture, and to the dream of a collective group.

[Page 405]

The fabric of our communal life is a living, building, creative, struggling, agonizing pattern. We do not create stones, stones in the arena of the farm, in the style of the collective kibbutz. Our group is made of cells, living cells; sustainers of the living organism.

Behold, one of those was taken from us. How can we fill the empty space that he left behind?

He drowned in the Kinneret.

(From a booklet published by Hashomer Hatzair, Merchavia.)

Necha Lerer

Necha Lerer

Necha Lerer, nee Bruner, has been taken from us here in Israel. Her revered image will remain etched in the hearts of her acquaintances who appreciated her, especially those who worked together with her.

Her activities already began at home, in the Hashomer Hatzair chapter of her native town of Turka. She left her studies in Lvov and returned to Turka, where she was one of the founders of Hechalutz in the city at that time, and was active as its secretary. At *hachshara*, Necha worked from sunrise to sunset with the knowledge that this is only the beginning of her pioneering actualization. Her name went before her – who did not know her energy and her good heart?

[Page 406]

Necha made *aliya* to the Land, where she settled in Kibbutz Nes Tziona. People enjoyed being with her in discussions and debates, and her opinion was taken seriously. She continued with her pioneering tradition when she left the kibbutz. Her work in the Committee of Working Mothers brought her renown in Nes Tziona. Her home was always open for advice and guidance.

Aliya absorption formed an important chapter of her life. She regarded this as holy work. She took care of all day–to–day affairs. She would leave the house and help absorb new immigrants. She left room for others to follow in her footsteps.

Bitter fate cut off her young, pleasant life in the middle, to the agony of her family and the heartbreak of all her friends and acquaintances in Israel

G. G.

Turka natives at a memorial gathering in Israel

[Page 407]

Addendum

[Page 408]

The Jewish Youth of Turka in the 1920s and 1930s

by Zerach Shein

Zerach Shein

At times, we, the Jewish youth of Turka in the 1920s and 1930s, began to become acquainted with friends from the neighboring cities and towns (Nowy and Stary Sambor, Drohobycz, Boryslaw, Stryj, Skala, etc.). "From where, from Turke (or Turka), from the place where the skies are covered with rags?" We used to listen with great astonishment to those anachronisms (still from the 19th century, when there was no railway line yet through the eastern Beskids, and Turka was approximately 50 kilometers away from the railway line) that were characteristic of our quicksilver-like[1] town, which incidentally was a regional administrative and business center for approximately 80 villages. It had a significant (for those years) wood industry (four sawmills, including a large sawmill with 12 gates and a large, steam driven factory with more than 500 Ukrainian, Polish and Jewish employees). It had a significant lumber industry and conducted significant export of lumber and planks.

However, those telegraphically calculated economic traits of the city were not the reason for our astonishment. The prime reason that the parable "heaven that is covered with rags" was a 180 degree full contradiction to us, the Jewish youth of Turka from those years was that the Jewish youth from out town – from all political leanings, from the Achva to the Communists – with their political and cultural activity, intelligence, progressiveness, with their commitment and interest in the national, socio–political and cultural problems of that stormy era, were not at all aloof from the youth of the larger Galician cities. It was the opposite. The number of progressive Jewish youth who broke away from the traditional way of life was significantly greater than in other cities and towns. Aside from this, the progress of our Jewish youth in the city had various traits that were very pleasant and positive in contrast to the snobbish attitudes of a series of cities and towns in Galicia.

[Page 409]

The number of our own, home–grown, "*shmendrick* assimilated"2 people (not counting those who have immigrated) in Turka was negligible. Speaking Yiddish was not a sign of backwardness, and speaking Polish during day to day activities, especially among the youth, was not a sign of progressiveness or haughtiness. Our students who used to come home from outside the country on occasion (V. From, Manes Bernas, Fani and Pepi Lerer, and others) used to speak Yiddish among themselves and with others, and would conduct discussions in Yiddish not only about politics, but also about ordinary scientific topics. The Shomrim of Turka were known within the Shomrim circles of Galicia as people with a good grasp of Hebrew and Yiddish language and literature. I recall that a member of the Peretz Farein (the Cultural Club named for Y. L. Peretz), who for a time functioned in another city in Galicia, returned to Turka and told the following: "They (i.e. a segment of the youth from that city) run about with their prayer books to worship, and speak Polish. We do not run to services, and speak Yiddish..."

Very characteristic of the mentality of the Jewish youth and influences upon the Jewish youth in Turka during the inter–war period is the fact that no religious or extreme right youth organizations existed at all in Turka during the 1930s. Young Mizrachi and Beitar (Brit Trumpeldor) were established just before the outbreak of the Second World War, and did not play a significant role. From among the populist parties, the Bund never played a role in our city. Even though it was a general phenomenon in the cities and towns of eastern Galicia, it had no relevance to our ideas.

[Page 410]

The "*fareinen*" [organizations] as the elder generation referred to the parties and organization throughout eastern Galicia and also in other cities, awakened and nurtured in their members an interest not only for national and socio–political problems, but also for elementary knowledge, literature, and art. This primarily touched Hashomer Hatzair (founder was Abba Chushai) and also Hechalutz (founder was Mendel Filinger of blessed memory), the rightist Poale Zion (founder was Shlomo Pelech of blessed memory), and the "Jugent" of the leftist Poale Zion (founders were Chaim Pelech, Uziel Tabel of blessed memory, and Yehoshua Artel of blessed memory), the Peretz Club during the 1920s through the offices of the "A.Y.A.P. (General Jewish Workers' Party) prior to its delegalization, and the Sports Club in the 1930s after the delegalization of the A.Y.A.P. Incidentally, the Sports Club had a very fine football team (the stars of the team were Yosha Bernanke, Ben–Zion Eisman, Kalman Meiner, and Mani Laufer of blessed memory), which used to beat other football teams in the city as well as in the "Sztszelec"3.

The founders of the Peretz Club were Zerach Shein (chairman of the committee until the delegalization), Shlomo (Ini) From (secretary until the end), Levi Hamerman (vice president), Eliahu Montel (chairman of the culture committee), Dr. Norbet April (honorary president), Pesi Szpigler and Leibush Mandel. The official founders of the A.Y.A.P. were David Bergsztejn and Wolf Hauer.

*

We can appropriately estimate the importance of the cultural enlightenment activity of the aforementioned organizations only if we take two things into account: a) the need, and 2) the results.

The working, proletariat, and poor youth of our city, who were already born before to the First World War and spent their childhood and school years during the difficult war years of 1914–1918 (on the so–called "*Flucht*"4) or the lean post–war years had completed two, three or four beginner's classes and were given over to at age 11, 12 or 13 to "ler" – to learn a trade and work from 10–12 hours a day, and often even more.

[Page 411]

In the parties, and in particular in the Peretz Club, whose membership consisted primarily of the aforementioned youth, the youth learned to appreciate literature and art, to differentiate between genuine, good literature and literary trash, between good artistic theater and trashy theater, between modern artistic theater and melodramatic, sentimentalist "*chinke pinke*"5 theater. Their primary love was their own Jewish culture. The leading members of the Peretz Club would often tell the members about all the new happenings in Jewish and world literature, about the famous theaters, theatrical doers and directors of that time (Habima, Vilner Troupe, Maurice Schwartz's artistic theater, Vikt, Max Reinhardt, Ervin Piscator, Michaels, Leon Schiller, etc.6) Alongside the educational activity in the cultural realm, the Peretz Club also conducted systematic socio–political educational activities.

It is characteristic and worthwhile to note that the drama circles that were active in our city during the 1920s and 1930s deviated from the traditional repertoires of the earlier drama circles (Gordon and Lateiner). In the 1920s, the Hashomer Hatzair drama club performed Hirschbein's "Joel" and "Green Fields"7. In the 1930s, the drama club of the Peretz Club, directed by Eliahu Montag, performed Sholom Aleicheim's "The Big Lottery," "The Golddiggers," and "People" [Menchen], and David Bergelson's "The Bread Man" ("The Deaf Man"). The directorship was considered to be at a fine level and some of the participants attained the level of amateur actors (Yeti Reifler of blessed memory and Hirschbein's "Green Fields," Yancha Weiss of blessed memory as the deaf man, Chaim Feiler of blessed memory as "Byk," Eliahu Montag as Yosele Babches in the "Bread Mill," and Bronia Kraus–Brandelstein as Fanichka in Shalom Aleichem's "Menchen".)

The results of the cultural educational activity undertaken by the organizations were astounding.

[Page 412]

Renowned and good Jewish theaters, theater troupes, actors, and directors who visited Turka performed in packed halls. This was not only for one evening, but often for two or three evenings in a row. The theatre troupe led by Prisament8 and Hart appeared in Turka, and performed about eight to ten performances in a two week period. I recall how on one occasion, the actor and manager Hart asked for the stage at the end of one performance, and introduced the following performance with the words, "Turka loves good and serious literature. Therefore, I will give you such literature. The coming performance is 'Three Gifts' by Y. L. Peretz."

During the first half of the 1930s, the Peretz Club organized three open literary judgments within a short time, on the topics of: 1) Georg Fink's "Mich Hungert" [I am Hungry] (Prosecutor – Zerach Shein; Defender – Eliahu Montag.) 2) Reimarque's "No News from the Western Front": (Prosecutor – Z. Schein; Chairman of the court – Yosha From). 3) Romain Rolland's "Jean–Christophe" (Prosecutor – Jan Jaworsky; Defender – Y. From; Chairman of the court – Z. Shein). All three literary judgments took place in a fully packed hall (The final judgment was in the Sokol Hall). Aside from the generally known constant discussion participants, many new faces participated as witnesses and discussion participants during the judgments.

*

In my sparse and short memoirs, I have only discussed a narrow segment of the Jewish youth in Turka during the 1920s and 1930s, and did not touch at all upon the problems of the Jewish youth (productivization, *hachsharah*, proletariatization, studying, *numerus clausus* quotas9, anti-Semitism, unemployment, emigration, etc.) that cannot be dealt with appropriately within the limited framework of a single article.

Translator's Footnotes:

89. Seemingly a reference to its speedy development at the time.
90. A colorful term, seemingly meaning those who are assimilated without any interest or concern for anything Jewish. It is not referring to the secularists, Communists and Bundists who retain a strong connection to Jewish culture if not religion.
91. I am not sure what this team means, but it seems to be the district of the region. This entire article has a large number of words that are likely local jargon.
92. Likely in "flight" or in exile from the town during the war.
93. In German, this term literally refers to hopscotch.
94. For examples, see http://en.wikipedia.org/wiki/Maurice_Schwartz http://en.wikipedia.org/wiki/Max_Reinhardt http://en.wikipedia.org/wiki/Erwin_Piscator
95. See http://en.wikipedia.org/wiki/Peretz_Hirschbein
96. See http://translate.google.ca/translate?hl=en&sl=pl&u=http://pl.wikipedia.org/wiki/Szlomo_Prisament&prev=/search%3Fq%3Dprisament%2Bwikipedia%26espv%3D210%26es_sm%3D93%26biw%3D866%26bih%3D614
97. See http://en.wikipedia.org/wiki/Numerus_clausus

[Page 413]

Additions

Yitzchak Zigelman. Editor of the Book

[Page 415]

{*Illustration of scroll introducing the memorial section of the book*: Turka on the Stryj. A Memorial Book to the community of Turka. A monument and memorial to the victims of the Holocaust. Signature at the bottom is M. Langenaur.}

[Page 416]

These are our brethren of the Sons of Israel, men, women and children from Turka and its surrounding villages, who were murdered, burned, or buried alive in sanctification of the Name and the nation – by the troops of the enemies and their assistants, in their city, in their wanderings, and in the concentration and death camps.

לזכר קדושי קהילת
טורקה
ענ"ס
שנהרגו נרצחו ונשרפו
על קדוש השם
בימי השואה
במלחמת העולם השניה
ת'נ'צ'ב'ה'

In Memory of the martyrs of Turka On the Stryj River Who were killed, murdered, and burnt In sanctification of the Divine Name During the Second World War May their souls be bound in the bonds of eternal life

{Translator's note: The style of this plaque indicates that it is from the Holocaust Cellar [Martef Hashoah] on Mount Zion.

The following section contains the photographs of pages 417-461.

The following entry, starting on page 417, was translated by Haim Sidor, who took the list of names, alphabetized it in English, and added valuable notes on family relationships and cross references into the book. His translation covers the list of names from page 417 until page 452. My [Jerrold Landau]'s translation will pick up from the Addendum of page 452. Haim Sidor's translation includes all but the first 3 items of the addendum, so I retranslated the entire addendum list on 452. Note that my rendering of the spelling of the names may differ from Haim Sidor's on occasion.

Page 419 Nachman Bernas – second from left

Page 420 Sender, Shula, Aharon Branenka

Page 421 top The family of David-Shia Binder

Page 421 bottom Dr. Tzvi (Heshiu) Buchman

Page 422 top The family of Yosef Meir Bank Yaakov and his wife Perl

Page 422 middle row, right to left Moshe and Yenta, Tzipora, Nechama

Page 422 bottom The family of Shalom Bruner

Page 428 The family of the dentist Avraham Weiss. His wife Sara. Children: Yitzchak, Yehuda, Henryk, Basia.

Page 430 The family of Shlomo Zehman

Page 432 The family of Yitzchak Lerer

Page 433 The family of Yosef Langenaur

Page 435 Ester May {Accompanied by a poem in writing (some of the letters are hard to make up, so the translation may not be fully literal):

Your memory is conjured up with the picture and the year
A group of friends at the top of a hill...
You included among them
And from this day, the brigade has already passed you
Then a thought comes to your mind
Your lips whisper and utter the words
How good and how wonderful!
For brothers to spend time together!...
For eternal memory, from your group Lehav.

Page 436 The family of Yitzchak-Aharon Nistel

Page 437 The family of Berl Naituch

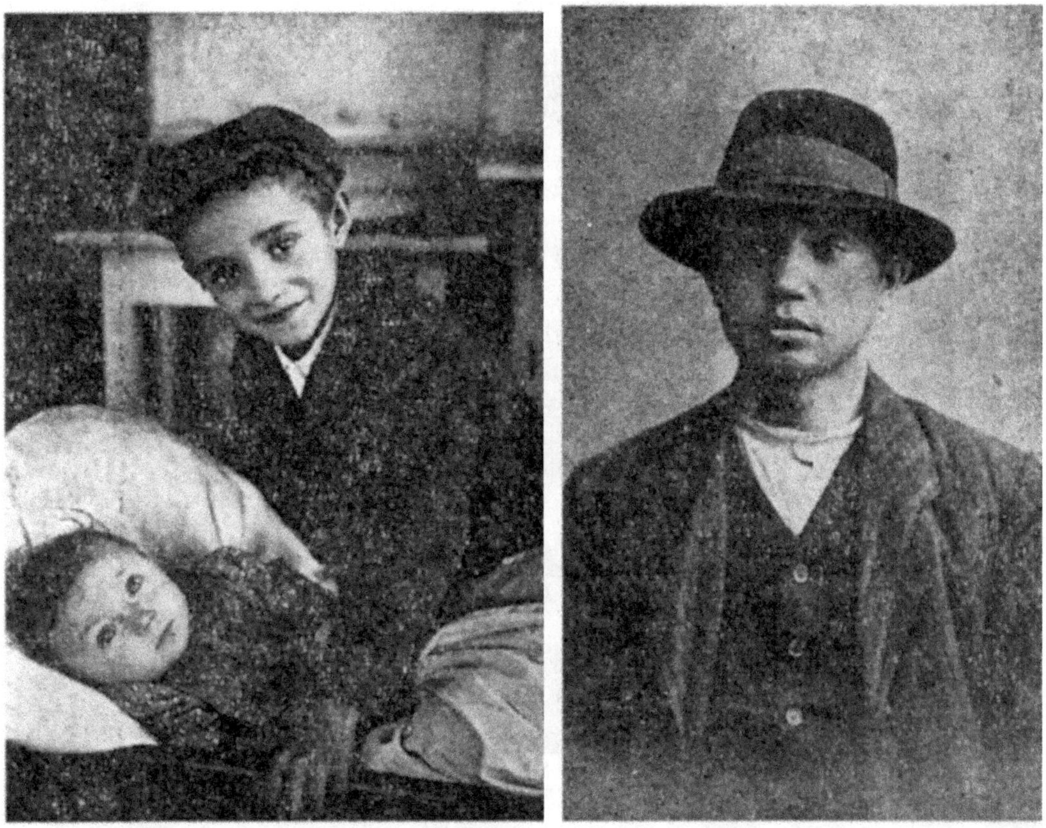

Page 438 The family of Yaakov Nagler

Page 439 Shlomo Pelech

Page 440 The family of Avraham Pelech

Page 442 The family of Ben-Zion Ferbel

Page 444 The family of Moshe-David Kesler

Page 447 Shlomo Rozen

Page 450 The family of Moshe Steininger

Page 451 right, and left (Yosef the son of Avraham Szprung; Avraham the son of Mendel Szprung

Page 454 Shmuel Gisinger and his wife

Page 461 Pinchas Neiman and Anita Neiman, partent of Aaron Sofer

[Page 417]

A Memorial to the Martyrs of the Holocaust

Translated by Haim Sidor

Dedication to my children:

Menachem David, Tzippora, Shabsi, Frimed and Pesha Baila May it be G-d's will that they never personally know the horror and tragedy of the Holocaust again. And all of us should live in PEACE...

Notes:

Family Name - as listed in the list
First Name - as listed - sometimes only the title Doctor was listed. Sometimes additional information was given such as "ben or bat" (son of or daughter of) or another name simply appeared in parenthesis and is listed here as it appears on the list (I presume it is the father's name but since it is not specified as such I did not take the chance and separately list it)
Spouse - in this column is either the spouses name OR the woman's maiden name (and sometimes a title Ha Rav / Ha Dayan/ Doctor). Spouses are double listed, once under the wife and once under the husband.
Family Code - c = child / cc = children (sometimes preceded by the number there of) / h = husband / wife / m or mom = mother / family = and the whole family / in some cases two names of the same sex were listed in one listing - they appear under both names listed.
Order Number - is the original order that the names were listed in.
Page Number - is the page on which the name is listed (page number from Original Yizkoe Book, not the page numbers of this Translation.

Family name	First name	Spouse	family code	order #	page
A					
Achtel	Laib		& wife	173	419
Ackerman	Avraham			100	418
Ackerman	Moshe Laib		& wife	98	418
Ackerman	Yisrael			99	418
Ackhoiz	(wife & 2 daughters)			172	419
Adelman	Avraham Moshe		wife & c	80	418
Adelman	Ben Tzion			77	418
Adelman	Eli			82	418
Adelman	Elisha			54	417
Adelman	Hanoch			76	418
Adelman	Hersh		wife & cc	75	417
Adelman	Hersh ben Moshe		wife & c	81	418
Adelman	Shifra Yehudit			79	418

Adelman	Tzivia			78	418
Adilheit	Shaul			32	417
Adilheit	Tova			33	417
Afril	Devorah	Filer		15	417
Afril	Hella			19	417
Afril	Leah			16	417
Afril	Naftali			14	417
Afril	Naftali	(Doctor)		18	417
Afril	Tziril			17	417
Afril	Yehoshua			20	417
Aidman	David			103	418
Aidman	Esther			102	418
Aidman	Fishel			107	418
Aidman	Leah			104	418
Aidman	Moshe Michal	Tova		166	419
Aidman	Nathan			105	418
Aidman	Sarah			168	419
Aidman	Sella			106	418
Aidman	Tova	Moshe Michal		167	419
Aigler	Hirsh ben Michal		& wife	149	418
Aigler	Hirsh ben Moshe		family	152	419
Aigler	Mailech			153	419
Aigler	Michal			148	418
Aigler	Moshe		family	151	419
Aigler	Motta		family	154	419
Aigler	Yosef		family	150	419
Akerman	Bluma		h & c	1869	452
Altman	Blima		h & 5cc	101	418
Altman	Shlomo Yitzhak		wife & 6cc	147	418
Angelmeir	Mondick			170	419
Angelmeir	Naftali		& wife	169	419
Angelmeir	Sella			171	419
Angelmeir	Yosha			118	418
Antner	(wife & cc)			28	417
Antner	Anshel			114	418
Antner	Avraham			113	418
Antner	Beril			143	418
Antner	Devorah			140	418
Antner	Elka			141	418
Antner	Haim Zvi			29	417
Antner	Hinda Feiga		& cc	110	418
Antner	Laib			27	417

Antner	Leah		& 2cc	30	417
Antner	Mintsha			142	418
Antner	Moshe			116	418
Antner	Moshe			144	418
Antner	Moshe			112	418
Antner	Tema	Binder	& c	117	418
Antner	Yosha			115	418
Antner	Yosha			111	418
Arbeit	Laizer		family	139	418
Arbeit	Leah			138	418
Arbeit	Shifra			137	418
Ardman	Esther			161	419
Ardman	Miriam	Mordecai		158	419
Ardman	Mordecai	Miriam		157	419
Ardman	Peretz			163	419
Ardman	Sarah			159	419
Ardman	Shmuel			162	419
Ardman	Zippora			160	419
Arlbaum	Teela			164	419
Arlbaum	Yosef			165	419
Artel	Aaron (Yaakov Shlomo)			51	417
Artel	Avish			92	418
Artel	Avraham			127	418
Artel	Bina			66	417
Artel	Bonia			53	417
Artel	Esther			49	417
Artel	Haim			45	417
Artel	Hannah	Broner		46	417
Artel	Hannah		& h	126	418
Artel	Hentchia			65	417
Artel	Hentchia			74	417
Artel	Hinda			125	418
Artel	Ita			35	417
Artel	Itia	Zil		48	417
Artel	Itia			69	417
Artel	Krania			124	418
Artel	Manny ben Yoshi			71	417
Artel	Martzia			73	417
Artel	Mindel			72	417
Artel	Mirel			34	417
Artel	Nachman			64	417
Artel	Pesil			68	417

Artel	Raizcha			52	417
Artel	Rotzchia	Zulinger		93	418
Artel	Shia Laib			123	418
Artel	Shimon			38	417
Artel	Susha			121	418
Artel	Tziril			122	418
Artel	Yehudah			50	417
Artel	Yehudit	Hitzer		39	417
Artel	Yenta			36	417
Artel	Yentzcha			63	417
Artel	Yosef			37	417
Artel	Yosha ben Manny			70	417
Artel	Zil	Itia		47	417
Ashklis	Shlomo			146	418
Ashklis	Sima		& cc	145	418
Avel	Itcha			119	418
Avig	Bella			59	417
Avig	Chaya			135	418
Avig	Chaya Sarah			130	418
Avig	Dora			136	418
Avig	Ethel			84	418
Avig	Ethel bat Yona		h & cc	94	418
Avig	Hirsh Laib			83	418
Avig	Leahchi			129	418
Avig	Mordecai			60	417
Avig	Mordecai David			128	418
Avig	Mottel		& cc	133	418
Avig	Rivka		h & cc	31	417
Avig	Shragai Feitel			131	418
Avig	Velvish			134	418
Avig	Yaakov			132	418
Avig	Yehudit			62	417
Avig	Yenta			61	417
Family name	**First name**	**Spouse**	**family code**	**order #**	**page**
B					
Bak	Chaya			288	423
Bak	David			289	423
Bak	Shlomo		wife & cc	336	424
Bak	Yehuda			290	423
Bank	Leah		h & cc	307	423
Bank	Moshe			310	423
Bank	Nechama		h & cc	308	423
Bank	Sarah		h & cc	305	423

Bank	Yaakov		wife & cc	306	423
Bank	Yenta			309	423
Baral	Chaya Sarah		& 6cc	275	423
Baral	Shlomo			274	423
Bart	Avraham			340	424
Bart	Laizer	Shifra		338	424
Bart	Miriam			341	424
Bart	Shifra	Laizer		339	424
Bart	Zippora			342	424
Baruch	(Doctor)		& wife	287	423
Baumgarten	Naftali		wife & cc	337	424
Beck	Bezalel			233	420
Beck	Rachel			235	420
Beck	Rivka			234	420
Beck	Yosef			232	420
Bentsher	Hannah		& h	219	420
Bentzcher	Rachel			246	421
Bentzcher	Yitzhak			247	421
Bentzer	Asher			253	423
Bentzer	Fraida			255	423
Bentzer	Liba			258	423
Bentzer	Miriam Ita			251	423
Bentzer	Mordecai		wife & cc	269	423
Bentzer	Moshe Avraham			254	423
Bentzer	Sarah Matel			257	423
Bentzer	Sender		& wife	1870	452
Bentzer	Shmuel			252	423
Bentzer	Tziril			248	423
Bentzer	Tzivia			256	423
Bentzer	Yehudit		h & cc	249	423
Bentzer	Yosef		& wife	270	423
Bentzer	Zalman			250	423
Berkowitz	Anshel			273	423
Berkowitz	Gittel		& 5cc	266	423
Berkowitz	Hannah			279	423
Berkowitz	Rachel			278	423
Berkowitz	Shia			265	423
Berman	Elimelech			241	421
Berman	Haim			242	421
Berman	Shmuel		wife & cc	347	424
Bernberg	Laib			318	423
Bernberg	Yaakov		& wife	320	423
Bernberg	Yehoshua			317	423

Bernberg	Yosef			319	423
Bernberg	Zigmund		& wife	316	423
Bernstein	(Doctor)		wife & cc	294	423
Bernstein	(wife & cc)	Kesirer		314	423
Binder	Aaron		wife & cc	301	423
Binder	Ben Tzion			313	423
Binder	Beril			297	423
Binder	Beril			329	424
Binder	Chava			296	423
Binder	David Shia			295	423
Binder	Elka			330	424
Binder	Esther			325	424
Binder	Krantzia		h & cc	302	423
Binder	Laib			221	420
Binder	Malka			327	424
Binder	Martzia		h	303	423
Binder	Meir Yehuda (BenZion)			271	423
Binder	Racha			304	423
Binder	Rachel	Fleshner		222	420
Binder	Rachel		& 7cc	281	423
Binder	Rachel			312	423
Binder	Raiza		& cc	298	423
Binder	Rivka			326	424
Binder	Roza		& cc	300	423
Binder	Shlomo			324	424
Binder	Shmuel			311	423
Binder	Yaakov		& wife	220	420
Binder	Yaakov			299	423
Binder	Yisrael Mendel			315	423
Binder	Yitzhak			280	423
Binder	Yosef			328	424
Binder	Yosef (Baruch Yekel)			243	421
Binder	Zissel			272	423
Birnberg	Shmuel			346	424
Birnberg	Tzipa	Yaakov		344	424
Birnberg	Yaakov	Tzipa		343	424
Birnberg	Yosef David			345	424
Blum	Getzel		family	322	423
Blum	Haim		family	323	424
Blum	Yankush			348	424
Blum	Yehoshua		family	335	424
Brandelstein	Bluma			214	420

Brandelstein	Faiga		h & cc	283	423
Brandelstein	Leah		h & cc	282	423
Brandelstein	Mordecai		wife & 7 cc	218	420
Brandelstein	Rivka			217	420
Brandelstein	Yaakov			216	420
Brandelstein	Zeinvel (Hirsh)			215	420
Branenka	Aaron			209	420
Branenka	Avraham			202	420
Branenka	Hannah			205	420
Branenka	Hirsh Melech			206	420
Branenka	Leah	Hertzig		207	420
Branenka	Leah		& c	212	420
Branenka	Mendel			201	420
Branenka	Moshe			208	420
Branenka	Pesha			213	420
Branenka	Sender			211	420
Branenka	Sheindel			210	420
Branenka	Shlomo			203	420
Branenka	Yechezkel			204	420
Branenka	Zippora			200	420
Brans	Chava			189	419
Brans	Chava		& 2cc	196	420
Brans	Efraim			259	423
Brans	Eliezar			198	420
Brans	Esther			182	419
Brans	Faiga			174	419
Brans	Fruma			187	419
Brans	Genia			193	419
Brans	Gittel			176	419
Brans	Hannah		& 2cc	199	420
Brans	Hentchia			191	419
Brans	Hirsh			186	419
Brans	Laib			179	419
Brans	Mendel			183	419
Brans	Monia			178	419
Brans	Moshe			175	419
Brans	Nachman (Zeinvel)			192	419
Brans	Perla			190	419
Brans	Rachel			181	419
Brans	Rivka			184	419
Brans	Sarah			194	420
Brans	Sheindel Esther			260	423
Brans	Yehoshua			180	419

Brans	Yisrael			188	419
Brans	Yosef			197	420
Brans	Zeinvel (Don)			195	420
Brans	Zeinvel (Leib)			177	419
Brans	Zeinvel (Yaakov)			185	419
Brant	Levy		wife & 4cc	321	423
Bravver	Leah		& h	277	423
Bravver	Melech			268	423
Bravver	Miriam		& h	276	423
Breitbert	Tziril			245	421
Breitbert	Veva			244	421
Broner	Chaya			286	423
Broner	Draizel			231	420
Broner	Elka (Frabel)			332	424
Broner	Esther			226	420
Broner	Esther (Shmuel)		& c	264	423
Broner	Ethel		& cc	334	424
Broner	Hanina (Mordecai)			263	423
Broner	Hannah			240	421
Broner	Henech		& mother	292	423
Broner	Kalman		& wife	267	423
Broner	Leah			237	420
Broner	Melech			291	423
Broner	Menachem		wife & cc	284	423
Broner	Michal			333	424
Broner	Moshe			285	423
Broner	Peril			262	423
Broner	Rivka			227	420
Broner	Shalom			236	420
Broner	Sheindel		h & daughter	293	423
Broner	Shlomo			228	420
Broner	Shlomo (Mordecai)			261	423
Broner	Yaakov Laib			331	424
Broner	Yisrael			229	420
Broner	Yisrael			239	420
Broner	Yitzhak (Izak)			238	420
Broner	Yona			230	420
Buchman	Hersh			224	420
Buchman	Sarah			225	420
Buchman	Shmuel			223	420
Family name	**First name**	**Spouse**	**family code**	**order #**	**page**
C					
Chachkas	Yosef		& wife	1368	443

Chail	Ita			770	431
Chail	Laizer		& wife	769	431
Chenals	Avraham			775	431
Chenals	Mendel			776	431
Chil	Aaron		& wife	774	431
Chil	Haim		& wife	773	431
Chil	Moshe			771	431
Chil	Simcha			772	431
Cordish	Dina		& cc	1469	445
Cordish	Moshe			1468	445
D					
Davider	Avraham			407	425
Davider	Henka	Broner		408	425
Davider	Rivka Ama			410	425
Davider	Zvi (Avraham)			409	425
Dim	Beinish			430	425
Dim	Elka	Zvi		431	425
Dim	Roiza			433	425
Dim	Zvi	Elka		432	425
Domonitz	Aidel			418	425
Domonitz	Ben Tzion			425	425
Domonitz	Chaya			427	425
Domonitz	Ethel			421	425
Domonitz	Faiga			417	425
Domonitz	Faiga			423	425
Domonitz	Fishel			420	425
Domonitz	Gittel			429	425
Domonitz	Haim			419	425
Domonitz	Henia			426	425
Domonitz	Leibish			415	425
Domonitz	Liba			416	425
Domonitz	Moshe Abba			422	425
Domonitz	Moshe Avraham	(HaShochet)	wife & cc	414	425
Domonitz	Rachel			428	425
Domonitz	Zvi Netta			424	425
Doner	Elimelech			404	425
Doner	Ita			406	425
Doner	Yitzhak			405	425
Doner	Yosef			402	425
Doner	Zippora			403	425
Dorlich	Aliz			441	425
Dorlich	Avraham			434	425

Dorlich	Moshe			437	425
Dorlich	Peril (Papa)			436	425
Dorlich	Rachel			438	425
Dorlich	Shalom			440	425
Dorlich	Tila			435	425
Dorlich	Yosel			439	425
Drucker	Mendel			411	425
Drucker	Shaul			413	425
Drucker	Zippora			412	425
Family name	**First name**	**Spouse**	**family code**	**order #**	**page**
E					
Eichenbaum	Faiga		& cc	120	418
Eichenbaum	Moshe		wife & cc	155	419
Eichenbaum	Yehoshua		wife & cc	156	419
Eichinger	Batsheva			96	418
Eichinger	Ben Tzion			97	418
Eichinger	Beril			85	418
Eichinger	Brana			91	418
Eichinger	Chava			23	417
Eichinger	Hersh ben Shmuel		wife & cc	108	418
Eichinger	Leah			22	417
Eichinger	Leah			87	418
Eichinger	Pesil			88	418
Eichinger	Rivka			89	418
Eichinger	Sarah			90	418
Eichinger	Shaul			26	417
Eichinger	Sheintzia			86	418
Eichinger	Shlomo			95	418
Eichinger	Yaakov			21	417
Eichinger	Yaakov ben Shmuel		wife & cc	109	418
Eichinger	Yisrael			24	417
Eichinger	Zippora			25	417
Eizman	Aaron			57	417
Eizman	Avraham			58	417
Eizman	Baruch			56	417
Eizman	Esther		& cc	43	417
Eizman	Henoch			42	417
Eizman	Hentchia			55	417
Eizman	Sheindel			41	417
Eizman	Tzivia			44	417
Eizman	Zvi			40	417
Erlich	Shlomo		& wife	67	417
Family name	**First name**	**Spouse**	**family code**	**order #**	**page**

F					
Feffer	Yaakov		& cc	1311	442
Ferbel	Avraham	Yavel Leah		1261	441
Ferbel	Ben Tzion			1258	441
Ferbel	Faiga		& Henia	1262	441
Ferbel	Henia		& Faiga	1263	441
Ferbel	Sarah			1259	441
Ferbel	Yavel Leah	Avraham		1260	441
Filer	(the son)		wife & cc	1318	442
Filer	Aaron (Bezalel)			1167	439
Filer	Avraham Meir			1154	439
Filer	Baruch		wife & cc	1294	442
Filer	Bezalel (Aaron)			1169	439
Filer	Bezalel (ben Shlomo)			1303	442
Filer	Esther			1172	439
Filer	Esther			1290	441
Filer	Godel (ben Bezalel)			1304	442
Filer	Golda			1246	441
Filer	Haim (ben Shlomo)			1302	442
Filer	Her (Shmuel Yaakov)			1291	441
Filer	Hindel		& 3cc	1292	442
Filer	Ita			1170	439
Filer	Matel			1155	439
Filer	Mordeccai			1288	441
Filer	Moshe		w & s (Bezalel)	1293	442
Filer	Perl			1157	439
Filer	Roza			1289	441
Filer	Roza		& 2cc	1296	442
Filer	Shaindel			1156	439
Filer	Shaindel			1168	439
Filer	Shalom			1317	442
Filer	Shifra		& h	1247	441
Filer	Shlomo (Bezalel)		wife & 2 daughters	1301	442
Filer	Shlomo (Izak)			1171	439
Filer	Wolf			1158	439
Filer	Yaakov			1295	442
Filer	Yosef			1271	441
Filinger	Alter			1334	443
Filinger	Beri			1332	443
Filinger	Faiga			1233	441
Filinger	Faiga			1319	442

Filinger	Fishel			1198	440
Filinger	Henia			1338	443
Filinger	Henik			1200	440
Filinger	Hersh			1234	441
Filinger	Hersh			1330	443
Filinger	Hirsh Wolf			1335	443
Filinger	Izak		& wife	1336	443
Filinger	Izak (Zvi)			1227	441
Filinger	Leah			1206	440
Filinger	Matel			1223	441
Filinger	Mendel			1232	441
Filinger	Mendel			1337	443
Filinger	Mendel ben Izak			1265	441
Filinger	Miriam		& 4cc	1331	443
Filinger	Moshe		wife & c	1242	441
Filinger	Moshe	(Doctor)	wife & cc	1264	441
Filinger	Naftali (Zvi)			1225	441
Filinger	Papka		& cc	1202	440
Filinger	Perl		h & cc	1320	442
Filinger	Pesha			1241	441
Filinger	Regina Meks		& 3 cc	1205	440
Filinger	Rivka			1203	440
Filinger	Rozka			1323	442
Filinger	Shlomo			1322	442
Filinger	Stefa		& cc	1199	440
Filinger	Tova		h & c	1224	441
Filinger	Yacht		& c	1204	440
Filinger	Yentzia		& wife	1235	441
Filinger	Yisrael		& his brother	1236	441
Filinger	Yisrael (Zvi)			1226	441
Filinger	Yitzhak			1201	440
Filinger	Zeinvell			1333	443
Filinger	Zippora			1197	440
Filinger	Zissel		h & cc	1321	442
Filinger	Zvi			1222	441
Fleder	Efraim		& wife	1299	442
Fleder	Moshe Shalom			1300	442
Fleishman	Arieh			1150	439
Fleishman	David			1151	439
Fleishman	Kaila	Kirshner	& c	1153	439
Fleishman	Moshe			1152	439
Fleishman	Shifra			1286	441
Fleishman	Zeev			1149	439

Fleishman	Zeinvell			1287	441
Fleshner	Baruch Meir		wife & cc	1195	440
Fleshner	Faiga		h & c	1196	440
Fleshner	Sarah Baila			1193	440
Fleshner	Shimon			1192	440
Fleshner	Yaakov		wife & c	1194	440
Fogel	Laib		& wife	1314	442
Fogel	Rivka		& her sister	1316	442
Fogel	Shimon		wife & cc	1312	442
Fogel	Yehuda		wife & cc	1315	442
Fogel	Zalman			1313	442
Fraiberg	Aidel			1161	439
Fraiberg	Benyamin			1166	439
Fraiberg	Haim			1165	439
Fraiberg	Haim Leibish			1163	439
Fraiberg	Machtza			1162	439
Fraiberg	Nachum			1164	439
Fraiberg	Sender			1159	439
Fraiberg	Shaintzia			1160	439
Frankel	Baila			1249	441
Frankel	Eli			1250	441
Frankel	Hersh			1248	441
Frankel	Rachel			1251	441
Frankel	Yisrael Laib		wife & c	1252	441
Frankel	Zeev		wife & c	1253	441
Freund	Lunka		& cc	1325	442
Freund	Rachel			1324	442
Freundlich	(Doctor)		wife & cc	1267	441
Fridfertig	Chaya		& c	1256	441
Fridfertig	Hersh		& 2cc	1257	441
Fridfertig	Tova			1254	441
Fridfertig	Wolf			1255	441
Frieberg	Bezalel			1297	442
Frieberg	Aharon (Avraham)			1281	441
Frieberg	Arna (Avraham)			1280	441
Frieberg	Avraham (Shmulik)			1278	441
Frieberg	Chaya (Avraham)			1282	441
Frieberg	David Yitzhak			1272	441
Frieberg	Gittle (David Yitzhak)			1275	441
Frieberg	Nesha (David Yitzhak)			1276	441
Frieberg	Penina			1279	441

Frieberg	Rivka			1273	441
Frieberg	Sheindel (David Yitzhak)			1274	441
Frieberg	Yenta (David Yitzhak)			1277	441
Frieberger	Laib		wife & cc	1209	440
Frieberger	Miriam			1208	440
Frieberger	Shia		& wife	1266	441
Frieberger	Yosef			1207	440
Friedman	Chaya			1329	443
Friedman	Elka (Rand)			1327	443
Friedman	Laib			1326	442
Friedman	Malka			1328	443
Frum	Hersh			1283	441
Frum	Sarah			1284	441
Frum	Yosef			1285	441
Fuchs	Devorah	Shtaiger		1244	441
Fuchs	Elka			1349	443
Fuchs	Faiga			1351	443
Fuchs	Hinda			1350	443
Fuchs	Meir		& wife	1875	452
Fuchs	Susha		& h	1245	441
Fuchs	Yehoshua			1243	441
Fuchs	Yosef			1348	443
Fuchs	Zelig			1352	443

G - L

Family name	**First name**	**Spouse**	**family code**	**order #**	**page**
G					
Gaier	Anshel			349	424
Gaier	Chaya	Brans		350	424
Gelb	Avraham			392	424
Gelb	Leibish			388	424
Gelb	Meir			391	424
Gelb	Mindel			389	424
Gelb	Wolf			390	424
Gelb	Yisrael			393	424
Gelb	Yitzhak			394	424
Gerstel	Avraham Laib			360	424
Gerstel	Charna			359	424
Gerstel	Faiga			363	424

Gerstel	Haim Leibish ben Yehoshua			371	424
Gerstel	Malka			362	424
Gerstel	Ratcha bat Haim Leibish			372	424
Gerstel	Rivka			361	424
Gisinger	Avraham			355	424
Gisinger	Ben Tzion			353	424
Gisinger	Beril	Rachel	& cc	397	424
Gisinger	Giza			357	424
Gisinger	Golda (Montag)		& cc	354	424
Gisinger	Mordecai Levy		family	358	424
Gisinger	Rachel	Beril	& cc	398	424
Gisinger	Raizel			352	424
Gisinger	Sarah		family	396	424
Gisinger	Yosef Levy		family	356	424
Glaich	Ethel		& 2cc	400	424
Glaich	Yoel			399	424
Glass	Hannah Leah			386	424
Glass	Malka		& cc	387	424
Glass	Yosef			385	424
Glick	Helena			351	424
Glick	Yaakov Yitzhak			395	424
Goldreich	Sender		& wife	401	425
Gotleib	Monish		wife & cc	366	424
Gotleib	Pinchas		& cc	364	424
Gotleib	Yokel			365	424
Gratner	Chaya			379	424
Gratner	Haim			377	424
Gratner	Haim			378	424
Gratner	Henia			380	424
Gratner	Peril			375	424
Gratner	Raizel			374	424
Gratner	Rivka			376	424
Gratner	Yonah			373	424
Gross	Avraham			367	424
Gross	Batsheva			384	424
Gross	Gitzia			382	424
Gross	Haim			381	424
Gross	Leah			369	424
Gross	Rivka			370	424
Gross	Sheindel			368	424
Gross	Yisrael			383	424

Gutman	Hersh		family	1889	452
Gutman	Yosef		wife & cc	1890	452

Family name	**First name**	**Spouse**	**family code**	**order #**	**page**
H					
Haber	Bano			571	427
Haber	Laib			542	426
Haber	Sarah		& c	543	426
Haberman	Benyamin		wife & 3cc	469	425
Haberman	Chaya Sarah			468	425
Haberman	Daniel Haim			460	425
Haberman	Devorah			472	425
Haberman	Hannah			464	425
Haberman	Hertzel			512	426
Haberman	Herzel		& 2cc	461	425
Haberman	Izik		& 8cc	467	425
Haberman	Mendel			471	425
Haberman	Miriam	Binder	& 3cc	462	425
Haberman	Moshe Zvi		wife & cc	463	425
Haberman	Rivka	Kirshner		459	425
Haberman	Sarah		& 10cc	466	425
Haberman	Tova			514	426
Haberman	Yosef			513	426
Haberman	Zeev			465	425
Haberman	Zissel			470	425
Hagler	Elka	Weiss		505	426
Hagler	Faitel			506	426
Hagler	Roza			507	426
Halprin	Eliyahu			546	426
Halprin	Elka			547	426
Halprin	Feibish			549	426
Halprin	Raizel			550	427
Halprin	Sheindel	Mainer	& cc	548	426
Hammerman	Berish		wife & c	1891	452
Hannes	Hersh Bar		wife & 2cc	442	425
Hannes	Ita			446	425
Hannes	Lippa		& c	444	425
Hannes	Shmuel			443	425
Hannes	Yaakov			447	425
Hannes	Zeinvell			445	425
Hans	Asher		& c	482	426
Hans	Baila			481	426
Hans	Lippa			478	426

Hans	Yeti			480	426
Hans	Zeinvell			479	426
Haor	Leah			452	425
Haor	Malka			451	425
Haor	Miriam			454	425
Haor	Yehuda		wife & cc	453	425
Hartmeir	Faiga			474	426
Hartmeir	Gittel		& h	476	426
Hartmeir	Leah			475	426
Hartmeir	Mattis			473	426
Hartmeir	Raizel			477	426
Havar	Elimelech			450	425
Hegler	Moshe			504	426
Heller	Shlomo		wife & cc	1893	452
Hertzig	Baruch			520	426
Hertzig	David			492	426
Hertzig	Eti		& 6cc	484	426
Hertzig	Fraida			485	426
Hertzig	Henia			494	426
Hertzig	Hirsh (ben Michal)			483	426
Hertzig	Sarah			521	426
Hertzig	Tova		& h	486	426
Hertzig	Yehezkel			495	426
Hertzig	Yehudit	Paist		487	426
Hertzig	Yitzhak		wife & cc	519	426
Hertzig	Zippora			493	426
Hertzlich	Ben Tzion		wife & cc & mom & sisters	1872	452
Hertzlich	Dina		& h	496	426
Hertzlich	Moshe		& wife	1871	452
Hertzlich	Moshe ben Leibish			1873	452
Hiltzer	Fishel			527	426
Hiltzer	Hersh	Pela		525	426
Hiltzer	Menachem Mendel			522	426
Hiltzer	Moshe			524	426
Hiltzer	Pela	Hersh		526	426
Hiltzer	Rivka			523	426
Hiltzer	Tzippa			528	426
Hirsh	Avraham			556	427
Hirsh	Chaya			532	426
Hirsh	Devorah			535	426
Hirsh	Fraida			562	427
Hirsh	Gittel			566	427

Hirsh	Glickel	Haim		560	427
Hirsh	Haim			449	425
Hirsh	Haim	Glickel		559	427
Hirsh	Izak			563	427
Hirsh	Leah			537	426
Hirsh	Liptzia			558	427
Hirsh	Mendel			534	426
Hirsh	Mendel ben Shimon			536	426
Hirsh	Miriam			539	426
Hirsh	Moshe			533	426
Hirsh	Moshe			561	427
Hirsh	Pinia	Artel		448	425
Hirsh	Rachel			540	426
Hirsh	Rachtzia			565	427
Hirsh	Sarah			538	426
Hirsh	Shaintzia			557	427
Hirsh	Shimon			531	426
Hirsh	Shimon		wife & daughters	1874	452
Hirsh	Yisrael			541	426
Hirsh	Yisrael			567	427
Hirsh	Yosef			564	427
Hirshhorn	Avraham			554	427
Hirshhorn	Ben Tzion	Hannah		551	427
Hirshhorn	Hannah	Ben Tzion		552	427
Hirshhorn	Leah			553	427
Hirshhorn	Wolf			555	427
Hirt	Devorah			458	425
Hirt	Fishel			455	425
Hirt	Hinda			456	425
Hirt	Hinda		& 2cc	545	426
Hirt	Ita			457	425
Hirt	Leah bat Moshe			572	427
Hirt	Manish			544	426
Hirt	Naftali ben Moshe			573	427
Holtzman	Devorah		& c	518	426
Holtzman	Hersh			517	426
Holtzman	Miriam		h & cc	516	426
Holtzman	Sarah Baila		& h	515	426
Hoptman	Arieh		& wife	510	426
Hoptman	Bratsha			529	426
Hoptman	Eda Matel			488	426

Hoptman	Esther			489	426
Hoptman	Esther		& cc	530	426
Hoptman	Haim			490	426
Hoptman	Hannah			497	426
Hoptman	Maniya			501	426
Hoptman	Mendel		wife & cc	509	426
Hoptman	Raizel			511	426
Hoptman	Sarah			502	426
Hoptman	Shmuel			508	426
Hoptman	Yaakov			500	426
Hoptman	Yeshiyahu			499	426
Hoptman	Yitzhak (Izak)			498	426
Hoptman	Yosef			491	426
Hoptman	Yosef			503	426
Hort	Hinda			569	427
Hort	Ita			570	427
Hort	Moshe Fishel			568	427

Family name	**First name**	**Spouse**	**family code**	**order #**	**page**
I					
Interator	(Baal Ha Tartak)		family	1896	452
K					
Karafiol	Esther			1515	446
Karafiol	Freida			1517	446
Karafiol	Laizer			1514	446
Karafiol	Naftali			1516	446
Katz	(wife & child)			821	431
Katz	Aiska			820	431
Katz	Akiva			816	431
Katz	Haim			814	431
Katz	Kalman			812	431
Katz	Naftali			818	431
Katz	Shlomo			819	431
Katz	Shmuel			815	431
Katz	Shosha			813	431
Katz	Shosha			817	431
Keller	Avish			1492	445
Keller	Dora			1402	444
Keller	Gerta			1497	445

Keller	Klara			1493	445
Keller	Malka			1398	443
Keller	Mendel			1397	443
Keller	Miriam			1400	444
Keller	Miriam			1495	445
Keller	Shifra			1401	444
Keller	Susha			1399	443
Keller	Tuvia			1403	444
Keller	Yisrael			1417	444
Keller	Yisrael			1496	445
Keller	Yona			1418	444
Keller	Yosef			1419	444
Keller	Zeev			1416	444
Keller	Zippora	Zeifert		1494	445
Kenernstein	Bella			1461	445
Kenernstein	Beril			1457	445
Kenernstein	Esther			1459	445
Kenernstein	Izak			1463	445
Kenernstein	Leah	Nistel		1456	445
Kenernstein	Lippa			1462	445
Kenernstein	Pesil			1458	445
Kenernstein	Yehoshua			1464	445
Kenernstein	Yenta			1460	445
Kenerstein	Meir		& wife	1532	446
Kessler	Esther			1421	444
Kessler	Faiga		& h	1404	444
Kessler	Haim			1423	444
Kessler	Pesil			1420	444
Kessler	Pintzia			1422	444
Kirshner	Aharon (Moshe)			1426	444
Kirshner	Amalia			1386	443
Kirshner	Arieh			1371	443
Kirshner	Avraham (Benyamin Leib)			1395	443
Kirshner	Benyamin (Moshe)			1425	444
Kirshner	BenZion ben David			1504	445
Kirshner	Beril (Benyamin Leib)			1394	443
Kirshner	Beril (S. Hirsh)			1369	443
Kirshner	Bina			1376	443
Kirshner	Charna (Moshe)			1424	444
Kirshner	Chaya			1379	443
Kirshner	David ben Shmuel			1500	445

	Hirsh				
Kirshner	Feitel			1374	443
Kirshner	Feitel			1383	443
Kirshner	Golda			1377	443
Kirshner	Golda		& cc	1396	443
Kirshner	Hannah		& 3cc	1388	443
Kirshner	Hannah	Klaist	& cc	1393	443
Kirshner	Hannah	Pelech	& cc	1513	446
Kirshner	Hannah ben David			1507	445
Kirshner	Hersh			1375	443
Kirshner	Hirsh (and Zeinvell)			1384	443
Kirshner	Izak ben David			1503	445
Kirshner	Laib			1378	443
Kirshner	Leah ben David			1508	445
Kirshner	Menachem ben David			1502	445
Kirshner	Mendel (Izak Aaron)			1387	443
Kirshner	Moshe (Benyamin Leib)			1392	443
Kirshner	Pelech	Hannah	& cc	1512	446
Kirshner	Rachel			1381	443
Kirshner	Raizel ben David			1509	445
Kirshner	Rivka		& c	1390	443
Kirshner	Sarah			1373	443
Kirshner	Sarah	Vizinger	& 2cc	1391	443
Kirshner	Shimon			1382	443
Kirshner	Shlomo (Izak Aaron)			1389	443
Kirshner	Shmuel ben David			1506	445
Kirshner	Tova			1380	443
Kirshner	Yenta			1372	443
Kirshner	Yisrael ben David			1505	445
Kirshner	Yitzhak			1370	443
Kirshner	Yitzhak Aaron (Benyamin Leib)			1385	443
Kirshner	Zippora			1501	445
Klein	BatSheva			1451	445
Klein	Bella			1491	445
Klein	Benyamin			1487	445
Klein	David			1543	446
Klein	David			1489	445
Klein	Fishel	Yenta		1540	446
Klein	Haim			1454	445

Klein	Haim Hirsh			1547	446
Klein	Miriam			1414	444
Klein	Moshe Aharon			1453	445
Klein	Raizel			1450	445
Klein	Raizel			1488	445
Klein	Sarah			1544	446
Klein	Shpintza			1542	446
Klein	Yaakov Hirsh		wife & cc	1548	446
Klein	Yehuda			1545	446
Klein	Yenta	Fishel		1541	446
Klein	Yisrael			1452	445
Klein	Yitzhak			1415	444
Klein	Yosef			1490	445
Klein	Zvi			1546	446
Kleist	Aaron			1445	445
Kleist	Atia		& c	1510	445
Kleist	Avraham			1446	445
Kleist	Avraham		wife & c	1466	445
Kleist	Ben Tzion			1527	446
Kleist	Beril		wife & c	1467	445
Kleist	Esther			1447	445
Kleist	Faiga			1449	445
Kleist	Gittel			1523	446
Kleist	Hannah		family	1880	452
Kleist	Meir		wife & cc & sisters	1879	452
Kleist	Melech		wife & c	1465	445
Kleist	Moshe Leib			1522	446
Kleist	Sarah			1448	445
Kleist	Shalom		& wife	1878	452
Kleist	Shlomo			1526	446
Kleist	Sima			1444	445
Kleist	Yisrael			1525	446
Kleist	Yosef			1524	446
Klugman	Avraham			1443	445
Klugman	Ita Pesha			1433	444
Klugman	Lippa			1437	444
Klugman	Malka			1440	445
Klugman	Moidel		wife & cc	1438	445
Klugman	Moshe			1439	445
Klugman	Natan			1432	444
Klugman	Rivka			1434	444
Klugman	Sarah			1442	445

Klugman	Yenta			1441	445
Klugman	Yitzhak			1436	444
Klugman	Yosef			1435	444
Konig	David			1408	444
Konig	Henia			1405	444
Konig	Rachel	Gerstel		1407	444
Konig	Shalom			1406	444
Konka	Bunim			1550	446
Konka	Esther	Weiss		1551	446
Konka	Wolf		wife & cc	1552	446
Konka	Yaakov Hirsh		& wife	1549	446
Kopel	Peretz		family	1888	452
Kopel	Yosef		& wife	1886	452
Kopel	Zarah			1887	452
Kozenmacher	Moshe Avraham		wife & cc	1498	445
Kozenmacher	Yosef		wife & cc	1499	445
Kramer	Efraim			1877	452
Kramer	Shmuel		wife & cc	1455	445
Kraus	Asher			1472	445
Kraus	Asher (Shmuel Leib)			1427	444
Kraus	Avraham			1470	445
Kraus	Avraham (Asher)			1428	444
Kraus	David			1536	446
Kraus	Esther			1480	445
Kraus	Faiga			1471	445
Kraus	Gittel			1474	445
Kraus	Haim Hirsh			1521	446
Kraus	Hannah			1483	445
Kraus	Hersh			1481	445
Kraus	Leah			1482	445
Kraus	Leah			1539	446
Kraus	Manya			1535	446
Kraus	Margola			1431	444
Kraus	Mela			1479	445
Kraus	Miriam		h & 2cc	1518	446
Kraus	Moshe			1484	445
Kraus	Naftali			1533	446
Kraus	Notta Ber			1519	446
Kraus	Pesil		& c	1534	446
Kraus	Pinchas			1473	445
Kraus	Rivka	Rozen		1430	444
Kraus	Roni			1520	446

Kraus	Shmuel Leib			1429	444
Kraus	Shmuel Leib ben Yitzhak			1478	445
Kraus	Uziel			1538	446
Kraus	Yitzhak			1475	445
Kraus	Yitzhak ben Shmuel Leib			1476	445
Kraus	Yocheved			1537	446
Kraus	Yosef		wife & cc	1511	445
Kraus	Zlata			1477	445
Kravis	Elka			1413	444
Kravis	Hersh			1411	444
Kravis	Moshe			1410	444
Kravis	Vita			1412	444
Kravis	Yaakov			1409	444
Kreigel	Rachel	Maorer		1486	445
Kreigel	Yankel			1485	445
Kupperberg	Elka			1529	446
Kupperberg	Faiga			1530	446
Kupperberg	Leah			1528	446
Kupperberg	Sheintzia			1531	446

Family name	**First name**	**Spouse**	**family code**	**order #**	**page**
L					
Landau	Devorah			893	433
Landau	Elka			894	433
Laufer	Hannah			887	433
Laufer	Malka			885	433
Laufer	Minna			888	433
Laufer	Pepi			886	433
Laufer	Yosef			884	433
Lecker	Leah			841	432
Lehrer	Basia			824	431
Lehrer	Chaya			826	431
Lehrer	Devorah			825	431
Lehrer	Esther			863	432
Lehrer	Hinda	Weiss		823	431
Lehrer	Leah			865	433
Lehrer	Milly			864	433
Lehrer	Pepi			848	432
Lehrer	Rachel			861	432
Lehrer	Raizel			847	432
Lehrer	Shmuel			827	431

Lehrer	Yaakov			822	431
Lehrer	Yehoshua			828	432
Lehrer	Yosef			862	432
Lehrer	Zisel	Velks		829	432
Leiber	Moshe		& wife	840	432
Leiber	Shmuel		wife & 4cc	839	432
Lib	Leib			836	432
Liberman	Rachel		& 2cc	838	432
Liberman	Zalman			837	432
Liberman	Zalman		wife & cc	866	433
Lichtman	Ita	Menashe		890	433
Lichtman	Menashe	Ita		889	433
Lichtman	Pepi			891	433
Lichtman	Zippora			892	433
Ling	(female)	Hirsh		860	432
Ling	Akiva			857	432
Ling	Brana		& cc	853	432
Ling	Chava			856	432
Ling	Faiza Vilda			859	432
Ling	Hannah		& h	851	432
Ling	Hersh ben Yosef			854	432
Ling	Laib			849	432
Ling	Sarah			850	432
Ling	Sarah		& cc	858	432
Ling	Shloma		wife & 5cc	843	432
Ling	Shmuel			855	432
Ling	Shprinza Baila		& cc	842	432
Ling	Yosef			852	432
Link	David ben Noah			882	433
Link	Golda			883	433
Loifer	Ben Tzion			874	433
Loifer	Chaya			877	433
Loifer	David			876	433
Loifer	Laizer			873	433
Loifer	Mendel			875	433
Loifer	Toiva			872	433
Loifer	Yosef			871	433
Longenavar	Avraham		& wife	844	432
Longenavar	David			846	432
Longenavar	Menachem			845	432
Longenavar	Yosef ben Yisrael			868	433
Longenavar	Zippora			870	433
Longenor	Henia			869	433

Longenor	Krania			878	433
Longenor	Rozia			879	433
Longenor	Shlomo			881	433
Longenor	Yehoshua			880	433
Longenor	Yisrael			867	433
Lorberbaum	Avraham			831	432
Lorberbaum	Brish			832	432
Lorberbaum	Hersh			833	432
Lorberbaum	Ita			835	432
Lorberbaum	Rivka			830	432
Lorberbaum	Yisrael			834	432

Family name	**First name**	**Spouse**	**family code**	**order #**	**page**
M					
Mainbach	Benyamin		wife & c	922	434
Mainbach	Devorah		& cc	985	435
Mainbach	Haim			923	434
Mainbach	Moshe			986	435
Mainbach	Sheindel	Zaifert		919	434
Mainbach	Sheindel		& 6cc	965	434
Mainbach	Yehuda			964	434
Mainbach	Yona Mendel		& wife	921	434
Maizels	Yehoshua		wife & cc	992	435
Maor	Fradel			910	434
Mattis	Elka			926	434
Mattis	Leibish		wife & c	925	434
Mattis	Raizel			927	434
Mattis	Rivka			928	434
Mattis	Yisrael		wife & cc	966	434
Mavis	Chaya			916	434
Mavis	Mattis			915	434
Mavis	Yaakov			917	434
Mavrer	Avraham			958	434
Mavrer	Chavtza			957	434
Mavrer	Haim			955	434
Mavrer	Izak			952	434
Mavrer	Laib			959	434
Mavrer	Moshe			962	434
Mavrer	Rivka			956	434
Mavrer	Roza			960	434
Mavrer	Shprinza	Rabinowitz		954	434
Mavrer	Yankel ben Laib			961	434

Mavrer	Yehuda			953	434
May	Baruch (Bobtzi)			980	435
May	Elka			978	435
May	Esther			979	435
Meir	Ben Tzion		wife & cc	995	435
Meir	Esther Navcha			900	433
Meir	Haim Laib			918	434
Meir	Hersh			996	435
Meir	Leah		& c	977	435
Meir	Liba			997	435
Meir	Michal			976	434
Meir	Miriam			998	435
Meir	Rachel			999	435
Meir	Raizel			901	433
Meir	Rivka			914	434
Meir	Sender			902	434
Meir	Shifra		& c	920	434
Meir	Shlomo			913	434
Mendel	Alter			989	435
Mendel	Dina			991	435
Mendel	Hannah			990	435
Mendel	Menachem			984	435
Mendel	Moshe			987	435
Mendel	Pinchas			983	435
Mendel	Rachel			982	435
Mendel	Shalom			981	435
Mendel	Yehoshua			988	435
Menster	Chava			993	435
Menster	Eliezar			907	434
Menster	Leibish		wife & c	909	434
Menster	Moshe			994	435
Menster	Rivka			908	434
Metzger	Chaya Leah			912	434
Metzger	Moshe			911	434
Miner	Avish		& wife	939	434
Miner	Devorah			943	434
Miner	Elka			949	434
Miner	Esther	Brans	& 3 daughters	938	434
Miner	Esther			947	434
Miner	Haim Shlomo ben Meir			944	434
Miner	Izak			940	434
Miner	Izak			948	434

Miner	Krantzia		& cc	941	434
Miner	Laizer			937	434
Miner	Leah	Lehrer	son Haim Shlomo	936	434
Miner	Meir ben Eli Ber			942	434
Miner	Melech		wife & c	934	434
Miner	Moshe		& wife	933	434
Miner	Racha			950	434
Miner	Racha bat Eli Ber		& cc	951	434
Miner	Rivka			945	434
Miner	Shimon			935	434
Miner	Yehoshua Nachman		wife & cc	932	434
Miner	Yehuda ben Eli Ber			946	434
Mishel	(HaRav) Eliezer			1000	435
Mishel	Moshe			1002	435
Mishel	Yitzhak Hersh			1001	435
Montag	Avraham Isser		wife & cc	963	434
Montag	Bartzia ben Shlomo			967	434
Montag	Esther			974	434
Montag	Esther Liba			931	434
Montag	Hannah			929	434
Montag	Hannah bat Yechezkel			975	434
Montag	Heniek			973	434
Montag	Lippa ben Moshe Aaron		wife & 2cc	969	434
Montag	Maniya			971	434
Montag	Mendel			970	434
Montag	Rachel			930	434
Montag	Rivka			906	434
Montag	Soivel			904	434
Montag	Tema			968	434
Montag	Wolf			903	434
Montag	Yitzhak			972	434
Montag	Zadok			905	434
Moritz	Chaya			898	433
Moritz	Freida			899	433
Moritz	Sarah			897	433
Moritz	Yaakov Yosef			896	433
Moskowitz	Matel		h & cc	895	433
Moskowitz	Perl			924	434

Family name	First name	Spouse	family code	order #	page
N					
Nagler	Ben Tzion			1099	438
Nagler	Bluma			1107	438
Nagler	Devorah			1101	438
Nagler	Faiga	Yaakov		1098	438
Nagler	Feivel		wife & cc	1108	438
Nagler	Hersh		& wife	1105	438
Nagler	Hersh		wife & cc	1123	439
Nagler	Hersh Melech		wife & cc	1124	439
Nagler	Laib			1032	436
Nagler	Laib		wife & cc	1102	438
Nagler	Meir	Racha	& cc	1121	438
Nagler	Miriam			1109	438
Nagler	Moshe Wolf			1106	438
Nagler	Racha	Meir	& cc	1122	439
Nagler	Rachel			1082	437
Nagler	Rivka			1100	438
Nagler	Shlomo		wife & 2cc	1081	437
Nagler	Tuvia			1110	438
Nagler	Yaakov	Faiga		1097	438
Nagler	Yehiel			1103	438
Nagler	Zippora			1104	438
Naituch	Beril			1083	437
Naituch	Blima		h & cc	1091	438
Naituch	Fanny	Izak		1088	438
Naituch	Hannah	Moshe		1086	438
Naituch	Izak	Fanny		1087	438
Naituch	Krantzia			1090	438
Naituch	Martzia		h & cc	1089	438
Naituch	Martzia	& son Yisrael Leib	d - Chava	1096	438
Naituch	Moshe	Hannah		1085	438
Naituch	Moshe		wife & cc	1095	438
Naituch	Pesha	Yaakov		1094	438
Naituch	Yaakov	Pesha		1093	438
Naituch	Zalman Hersh		wife & cc	1084	438
Naituch	Zil Leib		wife & cc	1092	438
Nistel	Avraham			1061	437
Nistel	Avraham	Sarah		1117	438
Nistel	Avraham			1041	436
Nistel	Avraham (Moshe)			1025	436
Nistel	Baila			1017	436

Nistel	Baila bat Avraham			1052	436
Nistel	Baruch			1075	437
Nistel	Ben Tzion			1111	438
Nistel	Beril		wife & c	1022	436
Nistel	Beril		wife & c	1043	436
Nistel	Beril		wife & c	1057	437
Nistel	Beril ben Meir			1068	437
Nistel	Bezalel			1071	437
Nistel	Brana			1073	437
Nistel	Chava			1072	437
Nistel	Chaya			1079	437
Nistel	Chaya Sara (Meir)			1008	435
Nistel	David			1031	436
Nistel	Devorah		h & c	1062	437
Nistel	Devorah (Moshe)			1026	436
Nistel	Dov (Beril)			1120	438
Nistel	Fishel			1112	438
Nistel	Gedalia			1036	436
Nistel	Gedalia			1045	436
Nistel	Gittel			1021	436
Nistel	Gittel bat Yitzhak Aharon			1056	437
Nistel	Gittla			1074	437
Nistel	Haim Isser		wife & cc	1023	436
Nistel	Haim Isser		wife & cc	1058	437
Nistel	Hannah			1069	437
Nistel	Hannah Devorah			1029	436
Nistel	Hentza (Meir)			1011	435
Nistel	Ita			1066	437
Nistel	Leah			1007	435
Nistel	Leah			1027	436
Nistel	Leah	Sheinfeld		1115	438
Nistel	Leah bat Shlomo			1063	437
Nistel	Malka			1020	436
Nistel	Malka bat Yitzhak Ahron			1055	437
Nistel	Meir		wife & cc	1116	438
Nistel	Meir (Y. Aharon)			1006	435
Nistel	Mendel			1042	436
Nistel	Mendel		& 2cc	1044	436
Nistel	Mendel			1070	437
Nistel	Mina			1015	436
Nistel	Mina			1050	436
Nistel	Mordecai (Moshe)			1024	436
Nistel	Mordecai ben Moshe			1060	437

Nistel	Moshe			1040	436
Nistel	Moshe (Ben Meir)		wife & cc	1037	436
Nistel	Moshe ben Meir			1076	437
Nistel	Moshe Mordecai			1059	437
Nistel	Moshe Yaakov			1028	436
Nistel	Moshe Yitzhak		family	1113	438
Nistel	Pesil			1078	437
Nistel	Rachel			1114	438
Nistel	Raizel			1067	437
Nistel	Raizel			1034	436
Nistel	Raizel (Meir)			1009	435
Nistel	Rivka			1077	437
Nistel	Rivka			1019	436
Nistel	Rivka bat Mordecai			1054	437
Nistel	Sarah			1016	436
Nistel	Sarah	Avraham		1118	438
Nistel	Sarah bat Zelig			1051	436
Nistel	Sheindel (Meir)			1010	435
Nistel	Shlomo			1080	437
Nistel	Shlomo (Yitzhak Aharon)			1033	436
Nistel	Shmuel			1014	436
Nistel	Shmuel ben Yaakov			1049	436
Nistel	Tzippa			1065	437
Nistel	Yaakov (Mordecai)			1012	435
Nistel	Yaakov ben Mordecai			1047	436
Nistel	Yisrael			1013	435
Nistel	Yisrael			1039	436
Nistel	Yisrael			1064	437
Nistel	Yisrael (ben Moshe)			1046	436
Nistel	Yisrael ben Yaakov			1048	436
Nistel	Yitzhak Aaron			1018	436
Nistel	Yitzhak Aharon ben Mordecai			1053	436
Nistel	Yitzhak Aharon ben Shlomo			1035	436
Nistel	Yosef			1030	436
Nistel	Zippora			1038	436
Nistel	Zvi			1119	438
Noiman	Meir		wife & cc	1004	435
Noiman	Moshe		wife & cc	1003	435
Noiman	Yaakov		& wife	1005	435

Family name	**First name**	**Spouse**	**family code**	**order #**	**page**
O					

Offerman	Genia			4	417
Offerman	Laib			12	417
Offerman	Leah			2	417
Offerman	Mattis			8	417
Offerman	Moshe Avraham			6	417
Offerman	Pesha			9	417
Offerman	Riva			10	417
Offerman	Sheindel		& 3cc	13	417
Offerman	Shmuel			7	417
Offerman	Tziril			11	417
Offerman	Yisrael			5	417
Offerman	Yitzhak			1	417
Offerman	Yosef			3	417
P					
Parnes	Moidel			1215	441
Parnes	Odel			1216	441
Parnes	Zippora			1214	440
Paste	Aharon		& wife	1229	441
Paste	Avraham			1228	441
Paste	Chaya Sarah			1239	441
Paste	Elka			1238	441
Paste	Esther			1240	441
Paste	Fishel			1237	441
Paste	Hannah	Vaicher		1231	441
Paste	Laib			1230	441
Pel	Golda			1211	440
Pel	Gosta			1213	440
Pel	Sarah			1210	440
Pel	Zofia			1212	440
Pelech	Avraham (Haim)			1185	440
Pelech	Chaya			1180	440
Pelech	Chaya	Wolf		1184	440
Pelech	David			1176	440
Pelech	Liba			1175	439
Pelech	Matel	Bart		1177	440
Pelech	Mintzia		h & cc	1181	440
Pelech	Shaindel			1179	440
Pelech	Shlomo			1173	439
Pelech	Tziril	Hans		1174	439
Pelech	Yenta			1178	440
Pelech	Yisrael			1183	440
Pelech	Yonah			1182	440
Pensner	Laitzia			1346	443

Pensner	Shmuel			1347	443
Pet	Eliezar			1220	441
Pet	Hannah			1218	441
Pet	Moshe			1221	441
Pet	Rivka			1219	441
Pet	Zvi			1217	441
Petrinick	Hinda Faiga		& 2cc	1876	452
Petrinik	Aharon		wife & c	1298	442
Petrinik	Aidel		& cc	1310	442
Petrinik	Esther		& cc	1269	441
Petrinik	Fraida		family	1345	443
Petrinik	Getzel	Rachel		1339	443
Petrinik	Hersh		& cc	1270	441
Petrinik	Kalman Leib			1309	442
Petrinik	Leib Ber			1306	442
Petrinik	Leibish			1341	443
Petrinik	Mendel			1342	443
Petrinik	Moshe		wife & cc	1308	442
Petrinik	Naftali			1268	441
Petrinik	Rachel	Getzel		1340	443
Petrinik	Toiba			1344	443
Petrinik	Yehudit			1307	442
Petrinik	Yenta			1343	443
Pickholtz	Chava	Frum		1191	440
Pickholtz	Haim			1186	440
Pickholtz	Leibish			1188	440
Pickholtz	Mordeccai			1190	440
Pickholtz	Pinchas			1189	440
Pickholtz	Shmuel			1187	440
Presser	Mordeccai		wife & 8cc	1305	442

Family name	**First name**	**Spouse**	**family code**	**order #**	**page**
R					
Raiz	Mendel		& his brother	1612	447
Raiz	Tova			1611	447
Rand	David			1562	446
Rand	Malka			1563	446
Rand	Sarah		h & cc	1566	446
Rand	Sheindel			1564	446
Rand	Shmue;			1568	446
Rand	Yaakov		& wife	1565	446
Rand	Yisrael		& wife	1567	446
Ratel	Ben Tzion		family	1642	447

Ratel	Eli		family	1641	447
Ravech	Gittel			1553	446
Ravech	Max			1554	446
Reich	Nisan		wife & cc	1674	448
Reis	Aharon (Moshe)			1581	446
Reis	Benyamin			1574	446
Reis	Chaya			1590	447
Reis	Esther			1607	447
Reis	Feivel			1579	446
Reis	Haim Mendel		wife & cc	1615	447
Reis	Henia			1605	447
Reis	Lippa			1578	446
Reis	Miriam Devorah	Bentzer		1575	446
Reis	Natan			1577	446
Reis	Sarah			1606	447
Reis	Shendel Blima			1580	446
Reis	Sofia			1591	447
Reis	Yehuda			1576	446
Reis	Yosef Hirsh			1604	447
Reiter	Anshel		family	1885	452
Reiter	Avraham			1679	448
Reiter	Avraham			1688	448
Reiter	Chaya	Fleishman		1556	446
Reiter	Devorah			1686	448
Reiter	Haim			1687	448
Reiter	Haim Wolf			1555	446
Reiter	Hannah	Michal		1683	448
Reiter	Laizer			1680	448
Reiter	Malka		& 2cc	1597	447
Reiter	Meir			1596	447
Reiter	Menachem			1678	448
Reiter	Michal	Hannah		1682	448
Reiter	Moshe			1681	448
Reiter	Rachel			1690	448
Reiter	Raizel			1689	448
Reiter	Ronia			1685	448
Reiter	Tila			1684	448
Reiter	Yekutiel		& wife	1884	452
Rettel	Bina			1559	446
Rettel	Chaya			1558	446
Rettel	Devorah			1560	446
Rettel	Eli			1557	446
Rettel	Leah		& 3cc	1573	446

Rettel	Sima			1561	446
Richter	Chantza	Zolinger		1610	447
Richter	Elisha			1609	447
Richter	Moshe		family	1677	448
Richter	Shlomo		family	1673	448
Richter	Yisrael		& wife	1675	448
Richter	Zissel		family	1676	448
Rintal	(Doctor)		wife & 3daughters	1595	447
Rokach	Shalom	(Ha Rav)	wife & cc	1899	452
Rotbaum	Zippora			1608	447
Rotenberg	Avraham	(Doctor)		1623	447
Rotenberg	Chaya			1594	447
Rotenberg	David			1632	447
Rotenberg	Rivka			1630	447
Rotenberg	Sarah			1629	447
Rotenberg	Shlomo			1634	447
Rotenberg	Shmuel		wife & c	1593	447
Rotenberg	Tonia			1631	447
Rotenberg	Yaakov			1633	447
Rotenberg	Yitzhak		wife & cc	1592	447
Rotfeld	Malka Leah			1570	446
Rotfeld	Rivka			1572	446
Rotfeld	Shimon			1571	446
Rotfeld	Yosef			1569	446
Rotman	Chaya			1663	448
Rotman	Chuli		& c	1672	448
Rotman	Dina			1667	448
Rotman	Faiga			1639	447
Rotman	Gittel		& 4cc	1640	447
Rotman	Gittel			1666	448
Rotman	Laib			1665	448
Rotman	Moshe			1662	448
Rotman	Perl			1599	447
Rotman	Rivka			1603	447
Rotman	Shlomo			1598	447
Rotman	Shlomo Laizer			1638	447
Rotman	Shmuel Sender		wife & c	1600	447
Rotman	Tzivia			1601	447
Rotman	Yehuda			1602	447
Rotman	Yehudit		family	1881	452
Rotman	Yitzhak Izak			1664	448
Rozen	Avraham			1584	446

Rozen	Baruch Aaron			1582	446
Rozen	Eliezar			1637	447
Rozen	Elka bat Eliezar			1648	448
Rozen	Elka bat Moshe			1645	448
Rozen	Elka bat Shmuel			1654	448
Rozen	Ethel			1585	446
Rozen	Faiga			1583	446
Rozen	Gittel bat Shmuel			1655	448
Rozen	Golda			1669	448
Rozen	Hannah			1652	448
Rozen	Hannah			1658	448
Rozen	Hirsh Ber		& wife	1635	447
Rozen	Ita			1668	448
Rozen	Laib			1589	447
Rozen	Moidel ben Mendel			1657	448
Rozen	Moshe			1670	448
Rozen	Moshe			1636	447
Rozen	Moshe ben Mendel		& cc	1628	447
Rozen	Moshe ben Mendel			1661	448
Rozen	Moshe ben Moidel			1659	448
Rozen	Rozia bat Yehiel			1649	448
Rozen	Sarah			1586	447
Rozen	Sarah bat Hirsh			1644	448
Rozen	Sarah bat Shmuel			1653	448
Rozen	Sarah Eta bat Mendel			1660	448
Rozen	Shlomo ben Yosef			1643	448
Rozen	Shmuel ben Hirsh Leib			1651	448
Rozen	Shoshana			1646	448
Rozen	Wolf			1671	448
Rozen	Wolf ben Eliezar			1647	448
Rozen	Yehoshua			1588	447
Rozen	Yekutiel			1587	447
Rozen	Yosef ben Eliezar			1650	448
Rozen	Yosef ben Shmuel			1656	448
Rozenberg	(Doctor)		wife & c	1616	447
Rozenberg	(Doctor)		& c (HGV')	1617	447
Rozenberg	Avraham		wife & c	1622	447
Rozenberg	BatSheva			1618	447
Rozenberg	Itsha		wife & cc	1613	447
Rozenberg	Kalman		wife & cc	1621	447
Rozenberg	Sender		wife & cc	1620	447
Rozenberg	Shia Hertz		wife & cc	1619	447
Rozenberg	Zalman			1614	447

Rozenhak	Yiddel	(Ha Dayan)	family	1897	452
Rozler	Avish		wife & cc	1883	452
Rozler	Avraham			1624	447
Rozler	Shlomo		wife & cc	1882	452
Rozler	Shmuel		wife & c	1625	447
Rozler	Yehezkel		wife & cc	1626	447
Rozler	Zalman Hirsh		wife & cc	1627	447

Family name	**First name**	**Spouse**	**family code**	**order #**	**page**
S					
Salis	Eli Wolf			1125	439
Salis	Rivka			1126	439
Salis	Zevulon			1127	439
Sandman	Aidel			1131	439
Sandman	Avraham			1146	439
Sandman	Ben Tzion			1142	439
Sandman	Ethel			1144	439
Sandman	Faiga			1132	439
Sandman	Faiga			1136	439
Sandman	Hersh			1148	439
Sandman	Lippa			1137	439
Sandman	Malka			1140	439
Sandman	Moshe			1130	439
Sandman	Moshe			1135	439
Sandman	Moshe Aharon			1138	439
Sandman	Pinchas			1145	439
Sandman	Rachel Leah			1134	439
Sandman	Sarah			1141	439
Sandman	Sarah Perl			1133	439
Sandman	Shaindel			1139	439
Sandman	Shlomo			1147	439
Sandman	Wolf		& wife	1129	439
Sandman	Yehudit			1143	439
Sandman	Yitzhak			1128	439
Satin	David		family	1824	451
Satin	Yaakov Wolf		family	1825	451
Schecter	Dov		wife & c	1716	448
Schecter	Gittel			1715	448
Schecter	Leah			1717	448
Schecter	Leah (Shmuel)			1714	448
Schecter	Mendel			1718	448
Schecter	Yeshiyahu			1713	448
Schmidt	Aharon (Moshe)			1697	448

Schmidt	Bracha			1693	448
Schmidt	Eliezar			1694	448
Schmidt	Laib			1696	448
Schmidt	Pini			1699	448
Schmidt	Raizel			1698	448
Schmidt	Reuven			1695	448
Schmidt	Rivka			1700	448
Schmidt	Yitzhak Hirsh			1692	448
Schneider	Avraham			1769	449
Schneider	Baila			1763	449
Schneider	Benyamin		wife & 2cc	1739	449
Schneider	Chaya			1721	449
Schneider	Elka			1691	448
Schneider	Esther			1766	449
Schneider	Haim Baruch			1761	449
Schneider	Haim Shmuel		wife & 2cc	1740	449
Schneider	Hinda			1764	449
Schneider	Isser			1738	449
Schneider	Laizer			1767	449
Schneider	Lemel			1765	449
Schneider	Matel			1741	449
Schneider	Matel			1770	449
Schneider	Nachum Leib			1719	449
Schneider	Rivka			1762	449
Schneider	Sheindel			1720	449
Schneider	Wolf			1768	449
Schneider-Kirshner	Moshe		wife & c	1736	449
Schreiber	Aidel			1834	451
Schreiber	Avish			1839	451
Schreiber	Avish			1848	451
Schreiber	Avraham			1845	451
Schreiber	Avraham		& wife	1850	451
Schreiber	Avraham ben Yisrael Moshe			1833	451
Schreiber	Berish			1861	452
Schreiber	Bezalel		& wife	1860	452
Schreiber	Chaya			1837	451
Schreiber	David			1857	452
Schreiber	Getzel			1862	452
Schreiber	Haim Hirsh			1853	452
Schreiber	Hannah			1841	451
Schreiber	Hannah Chava			1842	451
Schreiber	Hirsh Leib		wife & cc	1849	451

Schreiber	Hirsh Leib ben Avish			1843	451
Schreiber	Malka	Laib		1852	452
Schreiber	Miriam			1846	451
Schreiber	Miriam		& c	1854	452
Schreiber	Racha			1838	451
Schreiber	Racha	Yehoshua Nachman		1856	452
Schreiber	Sarah	Shmuel		1859	452
Schreiber	Shlomo			1840	451
Schreiber	Shmuel			1836	451
Schreiber	Shmuel			1847	451
Schreiber	Shmuel	Sarah		1858	452
Schreiber	Yehoshua			1844	451
Schreiber	Yehoshua Nachman	Racha		1855	452
Schreiber	Zippora			1835	451
Schwartz	Baila	Filer		1758	449
Schwartz	Chaya	Frum		1819	451
Schwartz	Haim			1757	449
Schwartz	Haim			1818	451
Schwartz	Zvi			1820	451
Shain	Leah			1803	450
Shain	Mordecai (Motti)			1802	450
Shain	Shmuel Nachum		& wife	1801	450
Shecter	Ben Tzion		wife & cc	1827	451
Shecter	Wolf		& wife	1826	451
Shein	Eliezar		& 3 sisters	1737	449
Shein	Shimon		& his sister	1832	451
Shindler	Bella			1746	449
Shindler	Benyamin		wife & 6cc	1722	449
Shindler	Beril			1730	449
Shindler	Chantza			1747	449
Shindler	Chava			1729	449
Shindler	Faiga			1748	449
Shindler	Haim Izak		& wife	1724	449
Shindler	Hannah			1755	449
Shindler	Hannah Rachel			1726	449
Shindler	Laib			1728	449
Shindler	Lemel			1753	449
Shindler	Mendel		wife & cc	1735	449
Shindler	Moshe		wife & 3cc	1734	449
Shindler	Noah			1745	449
Shindler	Patchia		wife & cc	1732	449
Shindler	Pintzia			1751	449

Shindler	Raizel			1731	449
Shindler	Rivka			1752	449
Shindler	Shaul		wife & cc	1733	449
Shindler	Sheindel		& Gitla	1756	449
Shindler	Shlomo			1750	449
Shindler	Shlomo (Yosef)			1725	449
Shindler	Yehuda		& 2 brothers	1727	449
Shindler	Yeti			1749	449
Shindler	Yitzhak			1754	449
Shindler	Zissel			1723	449
Shirel	Pinchas			1701	448
Shirel	Shaindel	Broner		1702	448
Shirel	Yehudit			1703	448
Shirel	Zvi			1704	448
Shneider	Laib	Malka		1851	452
Shor	Leah			1772	449
Shor	Liba			1773	449
Shor	Yisrael			1771	449
Shprung	Avraham			1821	451
Shprung	Irma			1823	451
Shprung	Yosef			1822	451
Shter	Devorah			1866	452
Shter	Faiga		family	1868	452
Shter	Michal	Tova		1863	452
Shter	Moshe		wife & c	1867	452
Shter	Shmuel			1865	452
Shter	Tova	Michal		1864	452
Speigler	Aharon			1796	450
Speigler	Faiga			1797	450
Speigler	Moshe			1799	450
Speigler	Pesha		& c	1800	450
Speigler	Yehuda			1798	450
Speilman	Anda			1830	451
Speilman	Ben Tzion			1828	451
Speilman	Roza			1831	451
Speilman	Sarah		& son	1829	451
Stark	Avraham		wife & cc	1742	449
Stark	Fraida			1743	449
Stark	Hannah		h & c	1744	449
Steiger	Beltzia			1816	451
Steiger	Devorah			1817	451
Steiger	Moshe			1778	449
Steiger	Nechama		& c	1815	451

Steiger	Sarah			1780	449
Steiger	Yehoshua		& wife	1712	448
Steiger	Zlata			1779	449
Steiger	Zvi		wife & cc	1781	449
Steininger	Avraham			1790	449
Steininger	Avraham ben Michal			1794	450
Steininger	Henia			1789	449
Steininger	Hirsh Ber			1787	449
Steininger	Izak			1791	449
Steininger	Michal			1792	450
Steininger	Nachum			1785	449
Steininger	Perl			1786	449
Steininger	Rivka			1788	449
Steininger	Roma			1795	450
Steininger	Sarah			1793	450
Sterman	Eliezar		wife & c	1810	451
Sterman	Mendel		wife & cc	1808	451
Sterman	Natan Leib		& his sister	1809	451
Stern	Baruch			1805	450
Stern	Eliezar		wife & cc	1804	450
Stern	Monio			1807	451
Stern	Yosef		& wife	1806	451
Sternbach	Asher			1774	449
Sternbach	Avraham			1782	449
Sternbach	Eliezar			1709	448
Sternbach	Hannah	Richter		1776	449
Sternbach	Hannah Ita			1813	451
Sternbach	Laib			1710	448
Sternbach	Laib			1811	451
Sternbach	Leah			1707	448
Sternbach	Michal			1784	449
Sternbach	Moshe			1711	448
Sternbach	Rola			1706	448
Sternbach	Sheindel			1814	451
Sternbach	Shlomo			1708	448
Sternbach	Shosha			1705	448
Sternbach	Yehoshua			1783	449
Sternbach	Yisrael			1777	449
Sternbach	Zippora			1812	451
Sternbach	Zvi			1775	449
Storch	Fishel		wife & cc	1759	449
Storch	Shmuel ben Hirsh Leib		wife & cc	1760	449

Family name	First name	Spouse	family code	order #	page
T					
Teichman	Nachum Ber		wife & c	801	431
Teichman	Sheindel			803	431
Teichman	Shifra			804	431
Teichman	Shlomo			802	431
Teichman	Yeti			800	431
Traiber	Antshel			786	431
Traiber	Arieh			779	431
Traiber	Avraham			777	431
Traiber	Avraham (David)			787	431
Traiber	Chava			778	431
Traiber	David			783	431
Traiber	Eliezar		wife & 4cc	789	431
Traiber	Golda			806	431
Traiber	Haim Aaron		family	1894	452
Traiber	Hersh			807	431
Traiber	Hertzel		wife & 4cc	788	431
Traiber	Krantzia			784	431
Traiber	Meir Leibish			805	431
Traiber	Nachum			808	431
Traiber	Rivka			785	431
Traiber	Sheindel		& 3cc	791	431
Traiber	Shlomo		wife & cc	810	431
Traiber	Shlomo Laizer			809	431
Traiber	Yaakov Yosef			790	431
Traiber	Yehuda			780	431
Traichman	Hirsh			782	431
Traichman	Moshe Avraham (Hirsh)			781	431
Trum	Faiga			793	431
Trum	Golda			797	431
Trum	Hersh Laib			794	431
Trum	Lippa			792	431
Trum	Moshe			795	431
Trum	Tziril			798	431
Trum	Yehoshua			796	431
Trum	Zisel			799	431

Family name	First name	Spouse	family code	order #	page
V					
Vaicher	Anshel			690	429
Vaicher	David			679	429
Vaicher	Devorah			600	427
Vaicher	Devorah			651	429
Vaicher	Dov			599	427
Vaicher	Faiga		& cc	639	428
Vaicher	Fradel			597	427
Vaicher	Gela			598	427
Vaicher	Leibish			653	429
Vaicher	Leon			602	427
Vaicher	Liba			688	429
Vaicher	Moshe			628	428
Vaicher	Neta			687	429
Vaicher	Pesach			654	429
Vaicher	Rivka			601	427
Vaicher	Rivka			652	429
Vaicher	Sarah	Ardman		691	429
Vaicher	Shia Hertz			638	428
Vaicher	Shlomo			596	427
Vaicher	Susha Miriam		& 2cc	627	428
Vaicher	Wolf		& wife	689	429
Vaicher	Yaakov			681	429
Vaicher	Yosef Ber			650	429
Vaicher	Zisel	Broner		680	429
Vaptza	Melamed		family	1895	452
Varzager	Bashia		h & cc	607	427
Varzager	Elisha			609	427
Varzager	Faiga			608	427
Varzager	Haim		wife & cc	606	427
Varzager	Miriam Elka			610	427
Varzager	Mordecai			604	427
Varzager	Sarah			605	427
Vechtelheim	Atiya			611	427
Vechtelheim	Dina		h & cc	676	429
Vechtelheim	Eta			622	427
Vechtelheim	Gittel			625	427
Vechtelheim	Hannah		& h	626	427
Vechtelheim	Laib			612	427
Vechtelheim	Laib (Yisrael Ber)			621	427
Vechtelheim	Moshe			613	427
Vechtelheim	Rozka			624	427

Vechtelheim	Yisrael Ber			623	427
Vechtelheim	Yocheved			673	429
Vechtelheim	Yosef			672	429
Veteloffer	Hannah			591	427
Veteloffer	Zigmund			590	427
Vilf	Elka			586	427
Vilf	Genka			588	427
Vilf	Loshia			589	427
Vilf	Shaul			585	427
Vilf	Yehiel			587	427
Vilig	Bluma			675	429
Vilig	Mendel			674	429
Vind	Hannah			694	429
Vind	Hersh			695	429
Vind	Tema			692	429
Vind	Yehoshua			693	429
Vind	Yonatan			686	429
Vind	Yonatan		& wife	696	429
Vizner	Melech		& wife	630	428
Vizner	Miriam			632	428
Vizner	Moshe			631	428
Vizner	Shmuel		daughter & wife	633	428

Family name	First name	Spouse	family code	order #	page
W					
Weinberger	David		& wife	682	429
Weinberger	Hersh			683	429
Weinberger	Tovtza		& 2cc	684	429
Weiss	Aaron			614	427
Weiss	Avraham (Eliezar)			578	427
Weiss	Avraham ben Yermiyahu			670	429
Weiss	Basia			582	427
Weiss	Basia			718	430
Weiss	Ben Izak			716	429
Weiss	Ben Tzion			647	429
Weiss	Ben Tzion			720	430
Weiss	Bina			678	429
Weiss	Chika			685	429
Weiss	David			660	429
Weiss	David			697	429
Weiss	David (Izak)			574	427
Weiss	Devorah			575	427

Weiss	Dora			721	430
Weiss	Eli			618	427
Weiss	Eli		wife & cc	657	429
Weiss	Eliezar		wife & c	644	428
Weiss	Elka			577	427
Weiss	Elka			714	429
Weiss	Elta		& cc	671	429
Weiss	Ethel			616	427
Weiss	Fraida (Yithak)			584	427
Weiss	Gila	Branenka		641	428
Weiss	Golda			717	429
Weiss	Haim Wolf			656	429
Weiss	Hannah	Felech		615	427
Weiss	Henia			715	429
Weiss	Hersh		& wife	699	429
Weiss	Izak			677	429
Weiss	Izak			712	429
Weiss	Izak Ber			640	428
Weiss	Karsel			698	429
Weiss	Leah			642	428
Weiss	Leibela			648	429
Weiss	Lota (Yitzhak)			583	427
Weiss	Mina			576	427
Weiss	Mintza		& c	620	427
Weiss	Miriam Yesha bat Shlomo			711	429
Weiss	Monish ben Yaakov			662	429
Weiss	Moshe			619	427
Weiss	Noah		wife & cc	658	429
Weiss	Pesil			659	429
Weiss	Rachel			709	429
Weiss	Rivka			617	427
Weiss	Roza			661	429
Weiss	Sarah			579	427
Weiss	Sarah			713	429
Weiss	Tova			655	429
Weiss	Yaakov			710	429
Weiss	Yaakov			719	430
Weiss	Yankaleh			645	429
Weiss	Yehiel Moshe		& wife	643	428
Weiss	Yehuda			580	427
Weiss	Yehudit			649	429
Weiss	Yisrael		wife & cc	646	429
Weiss	Zvi			581	427

Weissberg	Brish			701	429
Weissberg	Chenka			703	429
Weissberg	Hinda			702	429
Weissblum	Aaron Wolf	(Ha Dayan)	family	1898	452
Weissman	Faitel			667	429
Weissman	Hannah			666	429
Weissman	Hirsh Laizer			663	429
Weissman	Julia			669	429
Weissman	Milly			665	429
Weissman	Rachel Leah			664	429
Weissman	Rozka			668	429
Wexelberg	Yehoshua		wife & cc	700	429
Whitehorn	Leah		& 6cc	603	427
Whitman	Chaya			593	427
Whitman	Devorah			595	427
Whitman	Gershon			592	427
Whitman	Racha			594	427
Wolf				706	429
Wolf	Ben Tzion			637	428
Wolf	Hersh		wife & cc	629	428
Wolf	Hersh Mendel			636	428
Wolf	Malka		& h	708	429
Wolf	Racha			705	429
Wolf	Raizel			635	428
Wolf	Shmuel Hirsh			704	429
Wolf	Sima		& h	707	429
Wolf	Zeinvell			634	428

Family name	**First name**	**Spouse**	**family code**	**order #**	**page**
Y					
Yaakov	Yona			811	431
Yeger	Shmuel		& wife	1892	452
Yulis	Yaakov	(Ha Rav)	wife & cc	1900	452
Z					
Zaifert	Aimka			768	431
Zaifert	Alter			728	430
Zaifert	Baruch Yaakov		wife & cc	754	430
Zaifert	Benyamin		& wife	767	431
Zaifert	David Yosef		wife & cc	727	430
Zaifert	Gittel		& 2cc	729	430
Zaifert	Hannah (Shalom)			735	430
Zaifert	Hannah bat Shlomo			746	430
Zaifert	Hannah Esther		h & c	749	430

Zaifert	Meirtzia			751	430
Zaifert	Moshe			726	430
Zaifert	Moshe Laib		& wife	748	430
Zaifert	Mottel			747	430
Zaifert	Pesil			722	430
Zaifert	Rachel			725	430
Zaifert	Shalom			724	430
Zaifert	Yehuda			750	430
Zaifert	Yitzhak			723	430
Zantag	Melech		family	759	431
Zavarbron	Naftali			752	430
Zavarbron	Rachel		& c	753	430
Zehman	Avraham		wife & 2cc	742	430
Zehman	Don	Zisel		765	431
Zehman	Faiga	Yosef		764	431
Zehman	Krantzia	Shlomo		761	431
Zehman	Melech		& wife	762	431
Zehman	Shlomo	Krantzia		760	431
Zehman	Yosef	Faiga		763	431
Zehman	Zisel	Don		766	431
Zidverts	Avraham			736	430
Zidverts	Moshe			737	430
Zinger	Avraham			731	430
Zinger	Brana	Pelech		744	430
Zinger	Elka		& c	730	430
Zinger	Faiga			733	430
Zinger	Lippa			758	431
Zinger	Malka Ita			739	430
Zinger	Miriam	Kassel		732	430
Zinger	Mordecai			734	430
Zinger	Mordecai Wolf		& wife	756	431
Zinger	Moshe Avraham			755	430
Zinger	Raizel			745	430
Zinger	Riva			740	430
Zinger	Shmuel			741	430
Zinger	Yaakov			743	430
Zinger	Yisrael			738	430
Zinger	Zil			757	431
Zobel	Faiga			1361	443
Zobel	Fraida			1355	443
Zobel	Gittel		& 6cc	1366	443
Zobel	Kalman			1360	443
Zobel	Laizer Zvi			1365	443

Zobel	Leibish			1353	443
Zobel	Nachman		wife & 6cc	1364	443
Zobel	Yenta	Lehrer		1354	443
Zobel	Yenta			1363	443
Zobel	Yosha			1362	443
Zobel	Zil		wife & 2cc	1367	443
Zolinger	Devorah	Laks		1359	443
Zolinger	Pesil			1357	443
Zolinger	Yaakov			1358	443
Zolinger	Zalman Nachum			1356	443

Addendum [to the list of names that start on page 417]

{Translator's notes: all but the first 3 of these addendum entries are already included in the Haim Sidor's alphabetized list}

Ackerman Bluma, her husband and child
Ashklis Yisrael and his family
Ardman Yehoshua, his wife and children
Bencer Sender and his wife
Herclich Moshe and his wife
Herclich Ben-Zion, his wife and children, mother and sisters
Herclich Moshe the son of Leibish
Hirsh Shimon, his wife and daughters
Fuchs Meir and his wife
Petrinik Hinda Feiga and two children
Kremer Efraim
Kleist Shalom and his wife
Kleist Meir, his wife, children and sisters
Kleist Chana and her family
Rotman Yehudit and her family
Rozler Shlomo, his wife and children
Reiter Yekutiel and his wife
Reiter Anshel and his family
Kopel Yosef and his wife
Kopel Zerach
Kopel Peretz and his family
Gutman Hirsch and his family
Gutman Yosef, his wife and children
Hamerman Berish, his wife and child
Jener Shmuel and his wife
Heller Shlomo, his wife and children
Treiber Chaim Aharon and his family
Wapcha the teacher and his family
Intrator, the owner of the sawmill, and his family
Rozenhak Yidel (the rabbinical judge) and his family
Weisblum Aharon Wolf (the rabbinical judge) and his family
Rabbi Rokach Shalom, and his wife and children
Rabbi Yulis Yaakov, his wife and children

[Page 453]

In the Villages of the Area of Turka

{Translator's note: for the most part, the spelling of village names used was taken from the Communities tool of JewishGen: http://www.jewishgen.org/Communities/LocTown.asp Not every village could be definitively identified, although most could.}

Isaya (Isai)

Avraham Szindler
Michel Szindler and his daughter
Yosef Szindler and family
Yitzchak Szindler and family
Chaim Zandman and family
Avraham Ewyg and family

Ilnyk

David Yona Gleicher and family
Anshel Weiss and family
Feiga Kirszner
Yosef Garber and family
Herszberg and family
Avraham Szpilman and family
Yitzchak Szwarc and family
Yitzchak Rozen and family
Leib Sobel and family
Avraham Moshe Chanas and family
Yosef Chanas and family
Berish Fisz and family
Akiva Wolf and family
Alter Szpilman and family
Anshel Szwarc and family
Mendel Luterman and family
Berish Kac and family
Yitzchak Wolf Szwarc and family
Izik Weiss and family
Ben-Zion Berg and family
Recha Fuchs
Yitzchak Mendel Chanas and family
Abish Rozenberg and family
Yosef Aharon Fuchs and family
Levi Fuchs and family

Shimon Szindler and family
Mazosz Fuchs and family
David Zinger and family
Hirsch Nachman and family
Meir Nachman
Chaya Sandler and family
Aharon Sandler and family
Blimcha Sandler and family
Nachum Sandler and family
Yitzchak Izik Fuchs
Miriam Fuchs
Sender Fuchs
Yaakov Fuchs
Fruma Fuchs
Chana Fuchs
Tzvi Fuchs
Yisrael Rozenberg
Hirsch Ber and family
Yehuda Gajer and family
Yosef Aharon Fuchs and family
Lipa Rozenberg and family
Yaakov Szindler and family
Yisrael Mates
Rachel Mates
Laya Mates
Chuna Rozenberg

Borinya

Getzel Gisinger

[Page 454]

Yeti Gisinger
Shmuel Gisinger

Shmuel Gisinger and his wife}

Moshe Gisinger
Bela Gisinger
Yehuda Gisinger
Machla Gisinger
Recha Gisinger
Sender Gisinger
Eli Gisinger
Miriam Gisinger
Regina Tafer
Feibish Tafer
Mondik Tafer
Mina Tafer
Esther Tafer
Moshe Tafer
Moshe Rozen
Chana Rozen
Model Rozen
Noach Rozen
Levish Reifler
Mondek Reifler
Golda Reifler
Rivka Hager

Ackerman brothers
Chanales and his family
Ben-Zion Liberman
Miriam Liberman
Yisrael Liberman
Avraham Liberman
Esther Liberman
Feiga Liberman
Blima Liberman
Salomon Zalman Liberman
Aharon Liberman
Yehuda Liberman
Eliezer Liberman
Hirsch Liberman
Rivcha Liberman
Dina Liberman
Hirsch Motel Klopot-Hager and family
Yaakov Sztark and family
Yisrael Brener
Shlomo Leizer Brener
Hirsch Brener
Yisrael Cafon and family
Avraham Sztulbach

Bitlya

Gitel Sztar and her children
Abish Artel and family
Michael Sztar and family
Getzel Sztar and family
Chaim Sztar and family
Yaakov Hirsch Sztar and family

[Page 455]

Berish Sztar and family
Moshe Sztar and family
Shifra Sztar and family
Zyel Sztar and family
Moshe Storch and family
Meir Storch and family
Gitel Storch and her son Moshe Aharon
Michael Storch and family
Michael Kreber and family
Sara Rozenberg and her children
Yaakov Zeev Szwarc and family
Zelig Szwarc and family
Yosef Ber Kirszner and family
Mendel Nagler and family
Berish Bruner and family
Yehuda Gajer and family
Mendel Nistel and family
Hirsch Nistel and family
Berish Langenaur and family
Getzel Langenaur and family
Moshe Aharon Langenaur and family
Shmuel Yosef Langenaur and family

Berzuch

Liba Wolf
Sara Wolf and her children
Shimon Wolf, his family and sisters

Benjowa

Yaakov Apelderfer and family
Sara Liew and family
Shimon Szrajber and family
Yeshayahu Sobel and family
Mordechai Szternbach and family
Pesel Szternbach and family
Rachel Szternbach and family
Gitel Szternbach and family
Wolf Szternbach and family Leib Tuchman and family
Shlomo Tuchman and family
Moshe Tuchman and family
Sara Tuchman and family
Natan Neuman and family

Shlomo Kupferberg and family
Glajcher and family
Miriam Kuperberg
Elka Kuperberg
Sheindel Kuperberg
Feiga Kuperberg
Yisrael Kuperberg
Berish Apelderfer and family
Mordechai Apelderfer and family
Meir Apelderfer and family
Malka Apelderfer and family
Pepi Liber
Sara Liber
Chaya Liber and her daughters

Dobinac

Rivka Krupka and family
Wolf Krupka and family
Nachum Yitzchak Krupka and family
Necha Krupka and family
Avraham Meir Weltman and family
Wolf Nisztman and family
Yekutiel Gertler and family
Yitzchak Hagler and family
Gavriel Hagler
[Page 456]

Izik Hagler
Menashe Hagler
Naftali Bergman and family
Shlomo Bergman and family
Avraham Feler and family
Tovia Treiber and family
Gitel Blank and family
Eliezer Kac
Meir Kac
Gitel Rand and family
David Rand and family
Wolf Zinger and family
Nachum Katz
Rivka Katz and her daughter Chava
Gitel Zimmerman and family
Rachel Erlich and her children
David Sztempaf and family
Hinda Rand

Lipa Rand
Chaim Rand
Yisrael Rand
Shlomo Rand

Dnestrik

Avraham Meir and family
Shlomo Meir and family
Zanwil Wolf and family
Moshe Meir and family

Hanila

Yisrael Rozenberg
Beila Rozenberg
Miriam Rozenberg
Roza Rozenberg
Sima Rozenberg
Freda Rozenberg
Shoshana Rozenberg
Rivka Weiss
Yaakov Weiss
Serel Weiss
Dvora Meir
Yekutiel Meir
Shlomo Weiss
Dvora Weiss
Izik Weiss
Bina Weiss
Feiga Meir
Tzvi Meir
Chaya Meir
Freda Meir
Lemel Meir
Bluma Meir
Yosef Hager
Shlomo Hager
Shmuel Leib Hager
Hinda Hager
Frima Hager
Rivka Hager
Avraham Hager
Miriam Etl Hager
Keila Hager
Reizel Heiger

Volche

Avraham Klugman
Moshe Klugman and family

Husna-Viszna

Dov Benek Goldreich
David Goldreich
Baruch Hersch Goldreich and family
Moshe Weiss
Sara Ziman and family
Mates Matityahu and family
Meir Sternbach and family
[Page 457]

Michael Sternbach and family
Mordechai Sternbach and family
Fishel Ziman and family
Chaya Ziman and her son Yaakov
Feitel Fidler and family
Yehoshua Fidler and family
Gitel Fidler and family
Yaakov Hanes and family
Yitzchak Hanes and family
Yaakov Klein and family

Vysotzki Nyzhne

Leib Yosef Liberman
Hirsch Melech Liberman
Hani Liberman
Yitzchak Liberman
Malka Liberman
Shlomo Gisinger
Marchia Gisinger
Sara Chana Gisinger
David Tuchman
Donia Tuchman
David Yisrael Hager and family
David Zeinwil Montag and family
Shmuel Klein and family
Meir Klein and family
Yitzchak Klein and family

Shlomo Klein and family
Zeinwil Montag
Chana Montag
Leib Montag son of Zeinwil
Yisrael Montag
Yaakov Yehoshua Montag
Esther Majner
Freda Epzstejn
Rivka Tuchman
Rachel Montag son of Zeinwil
Moshe Montag
Leib Montag son of Yaakov
David Montag son of Yaakov
Rachel Montag daughter of Esther
Sheva Montag
Esther Montag
Dina Tuchman
Sheindel Tuchman
Eliahu Tuchman
Yehuda Majner
Yosef Tuchman
Mendel Tuchman
Yisrael Tuchman
Ezriel Tuchman
Dov Tuchman
David Chiel
Brana Chiel
Hersch Chiel
Yaakov Mendel Tuchman
Esther Tuchman
Mindel Tuchman
Shlomo Tuchman
Shabsel Tuchman

Vaskovich

Yisrael Dov Rozenberg
Golda Rozenberg and her daughter Chana
Dina Rozenberg and children
Esther Rozenberg and family

Volosyanka

David Hirsch and family

[Page 458]

Yehuda Teichman
Leib Teichman
Hendel Teichman
Yisrael Teichman
Naftali Teichman
Shlomo Fejler
Babatch Fejler
Esther Rivka Fejler
Malka Fejler
Avraham Fejler
Matityahu Fejler
Yitzchak Fejler
Yaakov Fejler
Sheindel Fejler
Moshe Fiszer
Leah Fiszer
Elimelech Fiszer
Yitzchak Fiszer
Eliahu Linek
Elimelech Tuchman
Elka Tuchman
Moshe Tuchman
Model Tuchman

Vysotzki Vyzhne

Walchi Goldreich and family
Levi Yisrael Goldreich and family
Shlomo Goldreich and family
Hisrael Hirt and family
Tzvi Zinger
Chaim Zinger
Tema Zinger
Reizel Zinger
Zalman Fuchs and family
Avraham Fuchs and family
Yaakov Leib Fuchs and family
Rivka Roth
Nesha Roth
Tzvi Roth
Moshe Roth
BenZion Roth
Binyamin Roth
Chava Roth

Freda Roth
Reizel Matel
Moshe Yosef Mates
BenZion Goldreich and family
Rachel Goldreich and family
Henchi Goldreich and family
Dov Reichman and family
Aryeh Reichman and family
Moshe Goldreich
Dov Goldreich
David Goldreich

Zawadka

Malka Epstein
Mordechai Frajdheim
Esther Lieba Frajdman
Sara Wolf (nee Frajdheim)
Yosef Shmuel Frajdheim
Leibish Frajdhaim
Meir-Dan Freidham
Matel Tzirel Frajdhaim
Yaakov Freidham
Melikl Linek (nee Frajdhaim)
Freida Mermelsztejn (nee Frajdhaim)
Nechi (nee Frajdhaim)
Rachel Weiss (nee Frajdhaim)
Henia (nee Frajdhaim)
Reuven Fisz
[Page 459]

Shmuel Fisz
Berish Fisz
Meir Fisz
Fishel Fisz
Shlomo Fisz
Yaakov Fisz
Chanoch Fisz
David Fisz
Dvora Fisz
Breindel Fisz
Yaakov Fiszer and family

Zadilesk

Dov Nistel
Leah Nistel
Henchi Nistel
Eliahu Betzalel Nistel
Gitel Nistel
Asher Lemel Nistel
Beila Nistel
Shmuel Nistel
Chana Nistel
Henchi Nistel
David Zeev Nistel
Binyamin Nistel
Feiga Malka Nistel
Yitzchak Aharon Nistel
Aharon Nistel and family
BenZion Nistel and family
Moshe Yosef the *shochet* Nistel and family
Tzvi Nistel and family
Mendel Nistel and family
Chaim Nistel and family
Yisrael Nistel and family
Sara Nistel
Rivka Nistel
Tova Nistel
Freda Nistel
Chaya Nistel
Zissel Nistel
David Zeev Zelig
Yehoshua Zelig
Baruch Zelig
Chana Zelig
Liba Zelig
Chaya Zelig
Reb Avrham the *shochet* Halpern and family
Yaakov Rozenberg and family
Zalman Tzvi Berg and family
Aryeh Sobel and family
Yisrael Gisinger
Shlomo Linek and family
Moshe Gisnberg and family
Avraham Dov Haberman and family
Tzvi Szternbach and family
Avraham Gisinger and family

Zukhotin

Yechiel Wolf and family
Izik Wininer and family and mother
Yisrael Lif and family

Zarich

Shlomo Szindler
Sheindel Szindler
Dina Szindler
Avraham Szindler
Sara Szindler
Henchi Szindler
Yona Szindler
Beila Szindler
[Page 460]

Noach Szindler
Yehuda Szindler
Zisel Szindler
Mani Szindler
Chana Szindler
Chana Szindler {Translator's note: there were two separate entries for this name}
Yitzchak Szindler
Reizel Szindler
Yisrael Gzimaluf
Breina Gzimaluf
Zisha Kastner
Marchi Kastner
Henich Kastner
Yehuda Kastner
Yona Berish Kastner
Rachel Kastner
Yisrael Hager
Zamel Hager
Rachel Hager
Tila Hager
Ita Hager
Esther Hager
Meir Klein
Elki Klein
Malia Klein
Avraham Klein
Noach Klein

Turiuchka

Tzirel Sztern
Yuta Frajdman
Lipsha Glajcher
Yitzchak Glajcher
Zeev Glajcher the son of Yitzchak
Yechezkel Glajcher
Tzvi Glajcher
Malka Glajcher
Rivka Glajcher
Reizel Glajcher the daughter of Yitzchak
Getzel Langenaur
Miriam Langenaur
Neshi Langenaur
Rivka Hirsz
Chola Glajcher
Chim Glajcher
Zeev Glajcher the son of Aharon
Reb Yehoshua Sztern
Baruch Sztern
Eidel Sztern
Shraga Tzvi Fisz
Tzvi Weiss
BenZion Wiczner
Aharon Wiczner
Avraham Glajcher
Nota Glajcher
Chana Rachel Glajcher
Shimon Glajcher
Freda Pesil Glajcher
Miriam Glajcher
Reizel Glajcher the daughter of Avraham
Henchi Glajcher
Heni Firszt
Mordechai Firszt
Minchi Firszt
Breini Weiss
Chaya Weiss
Dvora Hager
Feiga Brudner
Yitzchak Tzvi Brudner
Tzvia Brudner
Freida Brudner
Tzvi Yehuda Ewig
Etil Ewig
Kac and his family

[Page 461]

Tarnowa-Nizhna

Menashe Jager and family
Binyamin Brajer and family
Yaakov Lerer and family
Moshe Brajer and family
Mordechai Brajer and family
Shlomo Brajer and family
Pinchas Najman and family
Meir Fuchs and family
Chaim Gross and family
Shlomo From and family
Szpic and family
Zimmerman and family
Ester Malka Gertler and family
Yaakov Bernas and family
Chava Pikholc
Aryeh (Leibele) Szrajber
David Szrajber
Feiga Szrajber
Chava Szrajber
Yehoshua Szrajber
Malka Szrajber
Gitel Szrajber
Pinchas Neuman
Yenta Neuman (nee Szefer)
Eti Neuman
Chaim Neuman
Yosef Neuman
Sara Kesler
Gedalia Kesler
Malka Kesler
Eliahu Kesler
Berish Kesler

Jasionka

Yehoshua Ardman

In memory of my dear parents who perished in the Rovno Ghetto, Elul 5702 / 1942. Pinchas Najman, Yenta Najman – parents of Aharon Szefer.}

[Page 462]

Motel Ardman
Avraham Ardman
Aryeh Ardman
Yaakov Ardman
Yaakov Ardman son of Yehoshua
Ilka Goldreich
Sender Goldreich
Yitzchak Goldreich
Sara Bakenrot
Tzvi Bakenrot
Avraham Bakenrot
Tzipora Gross
Chaim Gross
Henrisha Gross
Margala Langenaur
Shmuel Langenaur
Sara Langenaur
Mordechai Ardman
Miriam Ardman
Sara Ardman
Tzipora Ardman
Esther Ardman

Shmuel Ardman
Yaakov Ardman son of Mordechai
Leibish Filinger
Meir Dovcza
Reizel Dovcza

Jasina

Yankel Artel
Hirsch-Ber Szindler
Moshe Szindler
Yeti Szindler
Yenti Szindler
Fetel Hirsch Szindler
Yehuda Szindler
Fishel Szindler
Sara Szindler
Etel Szindler
Shlomo Szindler
Avraham Szindler
Reiza Szindler
Rechi Szindler
Shmelki Szindler
Sara Szindler
Moshe Szindler
Leah Szindler
Etya Sztemerman
Yona Sztemerman
Chaim Leib Sztemerman
Gitel Sztemerman
Efraim Gisinger
Shmuel Sztemerman
Fetel Hirsch Sztemerman
Shaya (Yeshayahu) Szindler
Tzipora Szindler
Shprintza Szindler
Yaakov Szindler
Moshe Avraham Szindler
Hoda Szindler
Sheindel Szindler
Golda Szindler
Daniel SzindlerYehuda Szindler
Minchia Szindler
Sara Szindler
Hirsch Szindler
Yaakov Szindler

Rachel Szincler
Hirsch Szindler
Minche Szindler
Gitel Szindler
Yisrael Szindler
Roiza Szindler
Yisrael Szindler
[Page 463]

Zeinwil Szindler
Malka Szindler
Tzipra Szindler
Yitzchak Szindler
Avraham Haber
Feiga Haber
Sara Haber
Avraham Szindler
Brana Szindler
Avraham BenZion Szindler
Hena Szindler
Chava Szindler
Tabel (Yona) Szindler
Yosef BenZion Szindler
Chana Szindler
Meir Szindler
Sara Szindler
Naftali Szindler
Rivka Szindler
Yehuda Szindler
Tzipi Szindler
Yehoshua (Shea) Klein
Bela Klein
Moshe Fisz
Roiza Fisz

Jawora

Moshe-Wolf Nagler
Blima Nagler
Marta Nagler
Tova Nagler
Yaakov Lerer
Avraham Sztamerman
Karsel Sztamerman

Jablonow

Tzvi Dov Szindler and family
Moshe Szindler the son of Binyamin Yehuda and family
Shlomo Szindler the son of Binyamin Yehuda and family
Avraham Szindler the son of Leib and family
Moshe Szindler the son of Avraham and family
Yaakov Artel and family
Yehoshua Klein and family
Meir Szindler and family
BenZion Szindler and family
Shmuel Szindler and family
Avraham Szindler the son of Yisrael
Yitzchak Szindler and family
Yehuda the son of Yisrael Szindler and family
Yaakov Szindler and family
Shlomo the son of Aharon Szindler and family
Yisrael the son of Aharon Szindler Moisuczek and family
Shlomo Szindler Moisuczek and family
Yona Szindler and family
Yehuda the son of Yosef Szindler and family
Mindel Szindler and family
Zisel Szindler and family
Yuta Szindler and family
Sara Szindler and family
Meir Klein and family
Uziel Hager and family
Henia Szindler-Keler
[Page 464]

Zalman Klein and children
Shmuel Klein and family
Shlomo Klein and family
Yitzchak Klein and family
Mendel Yaakov Szwarc and family
Eliahu Sztamerman and family

Lomna

Avraham Hirt
Uziel his son-in-law
Moidel Zadman
Leib Awigder
Kalman his son-in-law
Shimon Weber, the *shochet*
Eizig Hamerman
Avraham Hirt the teacher

Avraham Maskrodna
Leib Hirt
Avraham Wenig
Yehoshua Moshe Hirt
Yehuda Hirsch Hirt
Naftali Hirt
Mendel Hirt
Yosef Moshe Szenberg
Shimale his son-in-law
Zalman Liebhart
Meir Liebhart
Moti Sztark
Yechiel Sztark
Leib Sztark
Yosef Kesler
Baruch Hirt
Moshe Hirt
Wolf Szechter
Avraham Eizig Szechter
Shamai Engelmajr
Akiva Ling
Szeindik family
Moshe Merzel
Reb Akiva Engelmajr
Chaim Aharon Engelmajr
Hirsch Melech his son-in-law
Yitzchak Sztark
Meir Waldman
Shika Waldman
Iser the shoemaker
Yaakov Leib Sztark
Aryeh the printer
Icha Engelmajr
Mordechai Engelmajr
Reizel Arbeit
Yehoshua Feld
Yudel Kampf
Yaakov Zeiner
Zusha Engelmajr
Henia Frej
Moti Engelmajr
Wolf Ling
Naftali Lieber
Yisrael Widman
Heshi Kesler
Yoshi Wechter
Yechezkel Sztark

Yaakov Leib Sztark
Shika Sztark
Shia Balinger
Ziel Rozenberg
Moshe Chalwikes
Yosha Wechter
Alter Henig
Chaya Fener
Yosef Meilech Zinger
[Page 465]

Hirsch Hirt
Yehoshua Hirt
Chaim Aharon Segal
Yitzchak Wechter
Hirsch Leib Lopuszanka
Shmuel Leib the grinder
Rabbi Mordechai Engelmajr
Tzvi Dov Rozen

Libokhora

Tzvi Rozenberg and family
Yaakov Rozenberg and family
Feiga Rozenberg and family
Yosef Kirszner and family
BenZion Szwarc and family
Lemel Artel and family
Chanoch Rozenberg and family
Rachel Rozenberg and family
Shlomo Rozenberg and family

Lokets

Berel Beret
Moshe Leib Brajer

Melnicha

Yitzchak Eizman
Tzipora Eizman
Avraham Artel
Pesia Artel
Roma Artel
Yosef Prycz

Rivka Prycz
Rachel Prycz
Moshe Mordechai Prycz
Eizik Prycz
Miriam Prycz
Pesia Rozen
Shmuel Rozen
Rachel Rozen
Malka Rozen
Moshe Rozen
Kalman Rozen
Moshe Yosef Szrajber
Chaya Sara Szrajber
Rivka Szrajber
Nechama Szrajber
Dvora Szrajber
Pesia Szrajber
Rachel Szrajber
Sara Szrajber
Moshe Mordechai Szrajber
Shmuel Szrajber
Dina Reizel
Yocheved Klein
Brachel Reizel
Reuven Klein
Rivka Artel
Yokel Artel
Chaim Artel
Esther Artel
Shlomo Kraus and family

Moldavsko

Yisrael Sztamerman
Idel Hirsch Sztamerman
Shmuel Sztamerman
Yete Sztamerman

Sochi-Potok

Berish Lerer and family
Karsel Lerer and family
[Page 466]

Sokoliki

Yaakov Chanas and family
Kuperberg family
Moshe Dinstag family
Baruch Dinstag family

Prislip

Moshe Bernas and family

Krivka

Avraham Chaim Heisler and family
Aharon Heisler and family
Uziel Heisler
Moshe Yosef Heisler the son of Menachem and family
Michael Heisler the son of Menachem and family
Perel Heisler and family
Mindel Heisler and family
Moshe Yosef Heisler the son of Yisrael and family
Avraham Heisler
Dvora Heisler
Michael Heisler the son of Shlomo
Moshe Heisler and family
Rachel Heisler and family
Avraham Szwarc HaKohen and family
Michael Zeman and family
Shlomo and family
Henes and family

Komarnik

Chaim Hirsch Fejler
Malka Fejler
Bilhah Fejler and family

Rozluch

Shlomo Lerer and family
Feiga Lerer and family
Bitzi Lerer and family
Naftali Lerer and family
Socha Lerer and family
Leah Lerer and family
Kalman Lerer and family
Margalia Lerer and family

Tzipora Feld and family
Ita Feld and family
Yechezkel Szmidt and family
Edelsztejn and family
Naftali Hejmer and family
Zalman Hirt and family
Yenta Hirt and family
Pesel Hirt and family
Zelda Hirt and family
Perel Hirt and family
Yona Hirt and family
Nachum Szulberg and family
Moshe Szulberg and family
Moshe Szulberg and family
Wolkan and family
Yitzchak Wolkan and family
Eliezer Zelig and family
Eizik Zelig and family
Yaakov Zelig and family
Shmuel Zelig and family
Wolf Zelig and family
David Zelig and family
[Page 467]

Yitzchak Parnas and family
Menchel Parnas and family
Reizel Parnas and family
Hirsch Haberman and family
Moshe Antner and family
Necha Antner and family
Leizer Antner and family
Reizel Leb and family

Rosokhach

Meir Zeiler and family

Sianki

Mendel Eiz
Tova Eiz and family
Lipa Linek
Tzipora Linek and family
Feiga Teichman
Hirsch Teichman and family
Shlomo Teichman and family

Avraham Moshe Teichman and family
Shlomo Kraus and family
Yehoshua Kraus and family
Leib Kirszner
Asher Kirszner
Machla Kirszner
Baruch Kraus and family
Zeev Kraus
Shlomo Kraus and family
Yoel Kraus
Shprintza Kraus
Hinda Kolb and her children
Rivka Kraus
Miriam Kraus
Shoshana Kraus
Feitel Wolf and family
[Page 468]

These are the names of the villages for which we did not receive lists, and of which we do not know the fate of their Jews:

Terszow
Lavrov
Lenina Velkaya
Lenina Mala
Potok
Busovisko
Tikha
Gleboka
Luzhki Gorno
Ploskia
Mizhenets
Vidava
Tysovitsa
Stshalki
Bistri
Graziowa
Nodzilna
Holobidka
Lopushanka
Makhnovtse
Gwozdziec
Lipwe
Dnestrik
Tozshe
Rypyany
Chaszczow
Smerochka
Zhukotin
Vapmarka
Dydeva
Shumyach
Shandrovech
Golovska
Yablonka
Losinets
Mokhnati
Radych
Swica
Bukovets
Bakhnovate
Rykuv
Butelka
Dolzhki
Myta
Krasne
Matkov
Ivashkevitz

Avraham Moshe Teichman and family
Shlomo Kraus and family
Yehoshua Kraus and family
Leib Kirszner
Asher Kirszner
Machla Kirszner
Baruch Kraus and family
Zeev Kraus
Shlomo Kraus and family
Yoel Kraus
Shprintza Kraus
Hinda Kolb and her children
Rivka Kraus
Miriam Kraus
Shoshana Kraus
Feitel Wolf and family
[Page 468]

These are the names of the villages for which we did not receive lists, and of which we do not know the fate of their Jews:

Terszow	Rypyany
Lavrov	Chaszczow
Lenina Velkaya	Smerochka
Lenina Mala	Zhukotin
Potok	Vapmarka
Busovisko	Dydeva
Tikha	Shumyach
Gleboka	Shandrovech
Luzhki Gorno	Golovska
Ploskia	Yablonka
Mizhenets	Losinets
Vidava	Mokhnati
Tysovitsa	Radych
Stshalki	Swica
Bistri	Bukovets
Graziowa	Bakhnovate
Nodzilna	Rykuv
Holobidka	Butelka
Lopushanka	Dolzhki
Makhnovtse	Myta
Gwozdziec	Krasne
Lipwe	Matkov
Dnestrik	Ivashkevitz
Tozshe	

The list of martyrs of Turka was compiled by Chaim Pelech, Moshe From and Moshe Kirszner. The list of martyrs of the villages in the area of Turka was compiled by Yechiel Hirt and Aharon Szefer (Neuman).

Due to obvious difficulties in compiling such a list, it is likely that there are omissions and errors. There were villages from which not one Jew survived...

If such errors exist – we apologize to all who are affected by this.

INDEX

A

B

J

K

L

M

N

O

P

R

S

T

V

W

Y

Z

www.ingramcontent.com/pod-product-compliance
Lightning Source LLC
Chambersburg PA
CBHW082006150426
42814CB00005BA/245
* 9 7 8 1 9 3 9 5 6 1 2 6 8 *